LAW APPLICABLE TO ARMED CONFLICT

Which law applies to armed conflict? This book investigates the applicability of international humanitarian law and international human rights law to armed conflict situations. The issue is examined by three scholars whose professional, theoretical and methodological backgrounds and outlooks differ greatly. These multiple perspectives expose the political factors and intellectual styles that influence scholarly approaches and legal answers, and the unique trialogical format encourages its participants to decentre their perspectives. By focusing on the authors' divergence and disagreement, a richer understanding of the law applicable to armed conflict is achieved. The book, first, provides a detailed study of the law applicable to armed conflict situations. Secondly, it explores the regimes' interrelation and the legal techniques for their coordination and prevention of potential norm conflicts. Thirdly, the book moves beyond the positive analysis of the law and probes the normative principles that guide the interpretation, application and development of law.

Ziv Bohrer is Senior Lecturer at the Faculty of Law, Bar-Ilan University. His main areas of research are in international criminal law and international humanitarian law. His chapter in this book was a winner of Israel's Junior Law Faculty Workshop Competition. Bohrer has previously held visiting positions at the University of Michigan (as a Fulbright Fellow), Hebrew University, University of Georgia and the University of Cambridge.

Janina Dill is Associate Professor of US Foreign Policy at Nuffield College, University of Oxford. Her previous publication, *Legitimate Targets? International Law, Social Construction and U.S. Bombing*, was included in the Cambridge Studies in International Relations series in 2015. The book was Runner-Up for the Birks Prize for Outstanding Legal Scholarship of the Society of Legal Scholars, and has received an Honourable Mention by the Theory Section of the International Studies Association.

Helen Duffy holds the Gieskes Chair in International Humanitarian Law and Human Rights at the Grotius Centre, Leiden University, and is Honorary Professor of International Law at the University of Glasgow. She also runs 'Human Rights in Practice', a law practice providing legal advice, legal representation and support in strategic human rights litigation before international and regional courts and bodies. Her previous publications include The *'War on Terror' and the Framework of International law* (Cambridge, 2015) and *Strategic Human Rights Litigation* (2018).

MAX PLANCK TRIALOGUES ON THE LAW OF PEACE AND WAR

In a *Max Planck Trialogue*, three authors discuss one topic within the international law surrounding armed conflict. Each trio is composed so as to engage different modes of legal thinking, intellectual paradigms, regional backgrounds and professional specialisation. By bringing the pluralism of premises and methods to the fore, the *Trialogues* facilitate the emergence and global refinement of common legal understandings.

Series Editors

Professor Anne Peters
Max Planck Institute for Comparative Public Law and International Law

Dr Christian Marxsen
Max Planck Institute for Comparative Public Law and International Law

A list of books in the series can be found at the end of this volume.

Law Applicable to Armed Conflict

ZIV BOHRER

Bar-Ilan University, Israel

JANINA DILL

University of Oxford

HELEN DUFFY

Leiden University

CAMBRIDGE
UNIVERSITY PRESS

University Printing House, Cambridge CB2 8BS, United Kingdom

One Liberty Plaza, 20th Floor, New York, NY 10006, USA

477 Williamstown Road, Port Melbourne, VIC 3207, Australia

314–321, 3rd Floor, Plot 3, Splendor Forum, Jasola District Centre,
New Delhi – 110025, India

79 Anson Road, #06–04/06, Singapore 079906

Cambridge University Press is part of the University of Cambridge.

It furthers the University's mission by disseminating knowledge in the pursuit of
education, learning, and research at the highest international levels of excellence.

www.cambridge.org
Information on this title: www.cambridge.org/9781108481588
DOI: 10.1017/9781108674416

© Ziv Bohrer, Janina Dill and Helen Duffy 2020

First published 2020

Printed in the United Kingdom by TJ International Ltd. Padstow Cornwall

A catalogue record for this publication is available from the British Library.

ISBN 978-1-108-48158-8 Hardback
ISBN 978-1-108-72298-8 Paperback

Cambridge University Press has no responsibility for the persistence or accuracy of
URLs for external or third-party internet websites referred to in this publication
and does not guarantee that any content on such websites is, or will remain,
accurate or appropriate.

Contents

Introduction: International Law Governing Armed Conflict

Christian Marxsen and Anne Peters

Wars are emergency situations, but in contrast to the saying that necessity knows no law, they are not lawless situations at all. Quite to the contrary, an extensive body of international treaties and customary international law provides detailed regulations. However, which rules do and should apply to what kinds of situation is a hotly debated issue and the subject of this book. Different regulatory paradigms are competing for how wartime situations shall be regulated – with significant legal, practical and institutional implications.

This book approaches the legal issue in a Trialogue. The characteristic feature of a Trialogue is to approach questions of international law from three perspectives, which differ in terms of their regional background, technical method, professional specialisation and worldview of the co-authors. The three authors (who are embedded in their particular social and cultural context) approach the law from their particular perspective, which invariably influences what they identify as the relevant rules and how they interpret and apply those. The core method of the 'Max Planck Trialogues on the Law of Peace and War' is to positively acknowledge the diversity of perspectives and to make constructive use of them (multi-perspectivism). The direct meeting of divergent views should expose that and how the political as well as regional factors and accompanying intellectual styles influence the scholarly approach taken and the legal answers given. By inviting the participants of the Trialogues to a conversation and by explicitly focusing on their divergence and disagreement (or their complementarity and synergies), a decentring of perspectives might be facilitated. This should ultimately contribute to a richer understanding of the legal question.[1]

---

[1] See on the methodology of the Trialogues: Anne Peters, 'Trialogical International Law – Introduction to the Series', in Mary Ellen O'Connell, Christian Tams and Dire Tladi,

I. THE APPLICATION OF INTERNATIONAL
HUMANITARIAN LAW

The classical legal regime applied to wartime situations is international humanitarian law (IHL). IHL pursues a double function. It aims to 'license' State
action in armed conflicts, and it aims to regulate or restrain it.[2] Under the
licensing function, acts that would be illegal under peacetime law are legalised.
For example, combatants in international armed conflicts enjoy immunity for
their acts and are therefore exempt from criminal prosecution for the killing of
other combatants during armed conflict (as long as they have complied with
applicable rules of IHL concerning the means and methods of warfare).[3] On the
other hand, IHL has a regulating function: it outlaws certain methods of warfare
and obliges belligerent parties and fighters to observe certain principles, such as
the principle of distinction and proportionality.[4] In doing so, IHL aims to
reconcile two opposing objectives. On the one hand, it seeks to secure military
effectiveness by acknowledging a legal principle of military necessity.[5] However,
if this were the sole principle to govern armed conflict, belligerents would be
free to take any effective measure for winning a war – with disastrous normative
consequences. Accordingly, IHL limits belligerents' choices based on counter-
principles flowing from humanitarian considerations. The entire body of law
thereby takes a 'middle road' between these opposing principles.[6]

The concrete rules governing armed conflicts under IHL significantly
depend on the type of conflict at hand. International armed conflicts (IACs)
are densely regulated by a range of international treaties. While the Hague

---

Self-Defence against Non-State Actors – Max Planck Trialogues on the Law of Peace and War:
Vol. I (Cambridge University Press, 2019), xi–xxv.

[2] Jens David Ohlin, *The Assault on International Law* (Oxford University Press, 2015), 171;
Geoffrey S. Corn, 'Mixing Apples and Hand Grenades: The Logical Limit of Applying
Human Rights Norms to Armed Conflict', *Journal of International Humanitarian Legal
Studies* 1 (2010), 52–94 (56).

[3] See, for example, Art. 43(2) Protocol Additional to the Geneva Conventions of 12 August 1949,
and relating to the Protection of Victims of International Armed Conflicts, Geneva,
8 June 1977, 1125 UNTS 3 (hereinafter: API), which stipulates that 'Members of the armed
forces of a Party to a conflict . . . have the right to participate directly in hostilities.'

[4] The term 'fighters' is used here to designate combatants as well as members of non-State armed
groups.

[5] The principle of military necessity allows belligerents 'to apply any amount and kind of force to
compel the complete submission of the enemy with the least possible expenditure of time, life,
and money.' Nuremberg Military Tribunals, *The Hostage Case*, Opinion and Judgment of the
Military Tribunal V, 19 February 1948, *Trials of War Criminals before the Nuremberg Military
Tribunals* (Washington DC: US Government Printing Office, 1950), 1253.

[6] Yoram Dinstein, 'Military Necessity', in Rüdiger Wolfrum (ed.), *Max Planck Encyclopedia of
Public International Law* (online edn.), September 2015, para. 2.

Conventions I–XIV of 1907 contain detailed rules on the conduct of hostilities, the Geneva Conventions I–IV of 1949 and Additional Protocol I (API), set out rules relating to the protection of persons not participating in hostilities. The 1949 Geneva Conventions apply to all cases of declared war, armed conflict, and military occupation.[7] Moreover, IACs are also regulated by a significant number of rules of customary international law.

Non-international armed conflicts (NIACs), by contrast, are only sparsely regulated by treaty law. Common Article 3 of the 1949 Geneva Conventions contains some basic rules. A more detailed framework is provided by Additional Protocol II (APII).[8] A significant legal evolution has taken place in customary international law so that today a range of rules for IACs also applies to NIACs.[9] Nevertheless, the application of IHL to NIACs is fraught with more legal uncertainty, for example, with regard to the identification of parties. Furthermore, there is not one single legal regime of NIACs. APII applies only when certain conditions (degree of organisation, territorial nexus and the like) are met, whereas the threshold of application of Common Article 3 of the four Geneva Conventions is lower.[10]

Debates on IHL are overshadowed by the perception of a crisis that is fuelled by the difficulties (and partly unwillingness) to apply the existing rules to the current realities of armed conflict. First, many discussants highlight the important role of non-State actors in contemporary armed conflicts and contrast this to a more or less imaginary historical past of State armies fighting against State armies. However, in empirical terms it is not clear whether non-State actors are in fact

[7] See Common Art. 2 Convention (I) for the Amelioration of the Condition of the Wounded and Sick in Armed Forces in the Field, Geneva, 12 August 1949, 75 UNTS 31; Convention (II) for the Amelioration of the Wounded, Sick and Shipwrecked Members of Armed Forces at Sea, Geneva, 12 August 1949, 75 UNTS 85; Convention (III) relative to the Treatment of Prisoners of War, Geneva, 12 August 1949, 75 UNTS 135; Convention (IV) relative to the Protection of Civilian Persons in Time of War, Geneva, 12 August 1949, 75 UNTS 287.

[8] Protocol Additional to the Geneva Conventions of 12 August 1949, and relating to the protection of victims of non-international armed conflicts, Geneva, 8 June 1977, 1125 UNTS 609.

[9] See ICTY, *Prosecutor v. Duško Tadić*, Case No. IT-94-1, Decision on the defence motion for interlocutory appeal on jurisdiction, 2 October 1995, paras. 119–27. See on the customary rules paralleling the codified rules of API Jean-Marie Henckaerts and Louise Doswald-Beck (eds.), *Customary International Humanitarian Law*, vol. I (Cambridge University Press, 2004), xxix.

[10] Common Art. 3 of the 1949 Geneva Conventions applies to 'armed conflict not of an international character occurring in the territory of one of the High Contracting Parties', whereas Art. 1 APII requires an armed conflict 'which take[s] place in the territory of a High Contracting Party between its armed forces and dissident armed forces or other organized armed groups which, under responsible command, exercise such control over a part of its territory as to enable them to carry out sustained and concerted military operations and to implement this Protocol.'

more relevant today than in bygone armed conflicts. Ziv Bohrer offers a strong argument that actually not much has changed.[11] Still, it is widely believed that the rise of non-State actors challenges the established and elaborated IAC framework and thus renders more prominent the legal framework governing NIACs, which is at the same time blurrier due to the significance of customary international law for these conflicts.

The (perceived) rise of non-State actors has, secondly, posed problems for applying the established legal framework;[12] Ziv Bohrer speaks of a felt 'classification crisis'.[13] We witness widespread uncertainty about the applicable legal frameworks, especially where conflicts internationalise, i.e., where States intervene in NIACs.[14]

A related phenomenon is, thirdly, that the boundaries of armed conflict are perceived to be unclear. What are the limits of armed conflicts, especially in geographical and temporal terms?[15] The idea of a potentially global armed conflict against non-State actors such as terrorist groups – in itself problematic – has brought 'gray zone conflicts'[16] into the debate's focus in which the wartime/peacetime divide is apparently blurred.

This situation is, fourthly, worsened by the fact that the institutional framework of IHL remains weak. In fact, effective institutions securing better compliance with IHL are lacking,[17] and even though especially international criminal tribunals have contributed significantly to the clarification of IHL, no specific IHL-related judicial bodies exist.

Fifthly, IHL faces a normative challenge. Its licensing function under which States may liberate themselves from the constraints of peacetime law is regarded by many to be normatively unsatisfactory. The licensing of certain

---

[11]   Bohrer in this volume, 109 *et seq.*
[12]   See Duffy in this volume, 17–18.
[13]   Bohrer in this volume, 109.
[14]   See on the dispute and on the different legal positions Dapo Akande, 'Classification of Armed Conflicts: Relevant Legal Concepts', in Elizabeth Wilmshurst (ed.), *International Law and the Classification of Conflicts* (Oxford University Press, 2012), 32–79 (56–64); see generally Kubo Mačák, *Internationalized Armed Conflicts in International Law* (Oxford University Press, 2018).
[15]   See on this point especially Duffy in this volume, 22–54. See further Claus Kreß, 'Some Reflections on the International Legal Framework Governing Transnational Armed Conflicts', *Journal of Conflict and Security Law* 15 (2010), 245–74 (264–7).
[16]   Asbjørn Eide, Allan Rosas and Theodor Meron, 'Combating Lawlessness in Gray Zone Conflicts Through Minimum Humanitarian Standards', *American Journal of International Law* 89 (1995), 215–23 (215).
[17]   See on recent initiatives aiming to establish mechanisms that could enhance States' compliance with IHL Jelena Pejic, 'Strengthening Compliance with IHL: The ICRC–Swiss Initiative', *International Review of the Red Cross* 98 (2016), 315–30.

types of violence may be seen to conflict with the objective of effectively protecting the individual, which is increasingly considered to be the actual *telos* of international law.[18]

II. THE EMERGENCE AND INFLUENCE OF HUMAN RIGHTS

While IHL has always been driven by a tension between the principle of military necessity, on the one hand, and humanitarian considerations, on the other, the latter became more prominent after the Second World War. In the post-1949 period we witness what Theodor Meron has described as the 'humanization of humanitarian law'.[19] This 'great transformation'[20] is characterised by a growing emphasis put on the protection of individuals: the 1949 Geneva Conventions focus on protecting persons not participating in hostilities, and their Common Article 3 contains a 'mini-human-rights treaty'.[21] The 1977 Additional Protocols further instilled human rights ideals into IHL.[22] Moreover, human rights considerations have more concretely influenced the interpretation of the rules of IHL.[23] The International Criminal Tribunal for the former Yugoslavia (ICTY) has made 'recourse to instruments and practices developed in the field of human rights law',[24] and explained that '[w]ith regard to certain of its aspects, international humanitarian law can be said to have fused with human rights law'.[25] Along this line, the ICTY has, for

[18] See generally Anne Peters, *Beyond Human Rights – The Legal Status of the Individual in International Law* (Cambridge University Press, 2016).

[19] Theodor Meron, 'The Humanization of Humanitarian Law', *American Journal of International Law* 94 (2000), 239–78 (239).

[20] David Luban, 'Human Rights Thinking and the Laws of War', in Jens David Ohlin (ed.), *Theoretical Boundaries of Armed Conflict and Human Rights* (Cambridge University Press, 2016), 45–77 (60).

[21] *Ibid.*

[22] API did so, for example, by establishing a prohibition of reprisals against the civilian population (see Art. 51(6)). APII creates an extensive framework for the protection of victims of NIACs. See generally Gabriella Blum, 'The Fog of Victory', *European Journal of International Law* 24 (2013), 391–421 (404).

[23] For example, the definition of protected persons under Geneva Convention IV has changed. The clear wording of Art. 4 covers only persons who 'find themselves, in case of a conflict or occupation, in the hands of a Party to the conflict or Occupying Power of which they are not nationals'. Nevertheless, the ICTY found that also persons holding the nationality of the controlling party or of the occupying power may be protected under certain circumstances (ICTY, *Prosecutor v. Tadić*, Case No. IT-94-1-A, Judgment of 15 July 1999, para. 169).

[24] ICTY, *Prosecutor v. Kunarac et al.*, Case Nos IT-96-23-T and IT-96-23/1-T, Judgment of 22 February 2001, para. 467.

[25] *Ibid.*, para. 467, adding, of course, 'that notions developed in the field of human rights can be transposed in international humanitarian law only if they take into consideration the specificities of the latter body of law' (*ibid.*, para. 471).

example, relied on international human rights law (IHRL)[26] to define the concept of torture within IHL.[27] Thus, IHRL is partly drawn on as the normative background system providing interpretive guidance.[28] Helen Duffy, in this book, provides a detailed analysis of this process of interpretative adaptation.[29]

In addition to the more indirect effect of human rights law for the interpretation of IHL rules, the relevant actors have in the last decades begun to directly apply human rights law to armed conflict situations.[30] '[T]here has been', as Geoffrey S. Corn put it, 'a steady march of human rights application into an area formerly subject exclusively to the law of armed conflict.'[31]

Such direct application of human rights law hinges on two legal premises. First, in the majority of conflicts where one State operates outside its territory, a legal precondition for the application of human rights to these actions is that they can also apply outside the State's territory.[32] Although such extraterritorial applicability is today acknowledged as a matter of principle, details remain complicated.[33] Also, the human rights treaties' clauses on derogations on which States might rely in situations of armed conflict differ.[34] Therefore, the extent of obligations arising under those human rights treaties remains the subject of controversy.

---

[26] This abbreviation will be used throughout the book, although it is not common outside the specific debate on the application of human rights law in armed conflict.

[27] ICTY, *Prosecutor v. Furundžija*, Case No. IT-95-17/1, Judgment of 10 December 1998, para. 159.

[28] Brian Orend speaks of 'filling the Law-of-War gap with human rights values', Brian Orend, 'The Next Geneva Convention – Filling a Law-of-War Gap with Human Rights Values', in Jens David Ohlin (ed.), *Theoretical Boundaries of Armed Conflict and Human Rights* (Cambridge University Press, 2016), 363–97 (363).

[29] Duffy in this volume, 71 *et seq.*

[30] See for the view that IHRL and IHL were two completely distinct bodies of law and that thus human rights did not apply in armed conflict, Henri Meyrowitz, 'Le droit de la guerre et les droits de l'homme', *Revue du droit public et de la science politique en France et à l'étranger* 88 (1972), 1059–105 (1076–7); Keith Suter, 'An Enquiry into the Meaning of the Phrase of Human Rights in Armed Conflicts', *Revue de droit pénal militaire et de droit de la guerre* 15 (1976), 393–439 (421–2).

[31] Corn, 'Mixing Apples and Hand Grenades' 2010 (n. 2), 56.

[32] See the human rights treaties' differing clauses on their territorial scope: Art. 2(1) International Covenant on Civil and Political Rights, 19 December 1966, 999 UNTS 171; Art. 1 American Convention on Human Rights, 22 November 1969, 1144 UNTS 123; Art. 1 [European] Convention for the Protection of Human Rights and Fundamental Freedoms, 4 November 1950, 213 UNTS 222.

[33] See Duffy in this volume, 71–83. See further Marko Milanovic, *Extraterritorial Application of Human Rights Treaties: Law, Principles, and Policy* (Oxford University Press, 2011), 209–22; Karen da Costa, *The Extraterritorial Application of Selected Human Rights Treaties* (Leiden: Martinus Nijhoff, 2013), 301–3.

[34] See Art. 4 ICCPR; Art. 5(1) ECHR; Art. 27 ACHR.

The second premise is that human rights law applies at all to armed conflict situations. Such application has, since the 1960s, been advocated in and by the United Nations, in particular by the UN General Assembly, but the issue remained contentious for decades.[35] The way for the general acceptance of the application of IHRL to armed conflict situations was ultimately paved by the International Court of Justice. In its *Nuclear Weapons* Advisory Opinion, the Court found that the International Covenant on Civil and Political Rights (ICCPR) continues to apply during armed conflicts.[36] This was confirmed in the *Wall* Advisory Opinion and reaffirmed in the *Armed Activities* case.[37] Since then, the tide has shifted, and today the applicability of IHRL to armed conflict situations is, in principle, widely accepted. However, this consensus does not provide answers to the question of how IHL and IHRL law interact or which one prevails in cases of substantive divergence.[38]

III. A CLASH OF PARADIGMS?

Human rights have emerged as a competing, or at least as an additional, paradigm for regulating armed conflict-related situations. But although IHL as well as IHRL both aim to protect human beings, the typical scenarios for which both regimes were created are quite different. Human rights law has historically been designed as the general peacetime law. It therefore creates a 'law enforcement framework'[39] or 'law and order' paradigm.[40] IHL, by

---

[35] See the Final Act of the International Conference on Human Rights, Teheran, 22 April to 13 May 1968, UN Doc. A/Conf.32/41, 18; GA Res. 2444 (XXIII) of 19 December 1968; GA Res. 2675 (XXV) of 9 December 1970.

[36] ICJ, *Legality of the Threat or Use of Nuclear Weapons*, Advisory Opinion, ICJ Reports 1996, 226, 240 (para. 25). Marko Milanovic has traced the emergence of the *'lex specialis'* principle in regard to the relationship between IHL and IHRL and found that it was largely introduced by the ICJ and could only hardly be found before the ICJ issued its opinion, Marko Milanovic, 'The Lost Origins of Lex Specialis: Rethinking the Relationship between HR and IHL', in Jens David Ohlin (ed.), *Theoretical Boundaries of Armed Conflict and Human Rights* (Cambridge University Press, 2016), 78–118 (82–103).

[37] ICJ, *Legal Consequences of the Construction of a Wall in the Occupied Palestinian Territory*, Advisory Opinion, ICJ Reports 2004, 136, 178 (para. 106); ICJ, *Armed Activities on the Territory of the Congo* (Democratic Republic of the Congo v. Uganda), Judgment, ICJ Reports 2005, 168, 242–3 (para. 216).

[38] See Andrew Clapham, 'Human Rights in Armed Conflict: Metaphors, Maxims, and the Move to Interoperability', *Human Rights and International Legal Discourse* 12 (2018), 9–22 (19).

[39] See Kenneth Watkin, *Fighting at the Legal Boundaries: Controlling the Use of Force in Contemporary Conflict* (Oxford University Press, 2016), 449.

[40] See Yuval Shany, 'Human Rights and Humanitarian Law as Competing Legal Paradigms for Fighting Terror', in Orna Ben-Naftali (ed.), *International Humanitarian Law and International Human Rights Law* (Oxford University Press, 2011), 13–33 (14–24).

contrast, is meant to govern 'situations of massive violence employed by collectives, often under conditions of considerable uncertainty (i.e. "the fog of war") and resource constraints'.[41]

The distinct original fields and environments of application of the two bodies of law (IHL and IHRL) have led to quite different regulatory approaches.[42] IHL relies largely on a system of obligations, as Ziv Bohrer highlights.[43] Whether and to what extent IHL also creates individual rights is subject of controversy.[44] IHL establishes rules of conduct for fighters, and the entire body of law takes into account the situation of those who have to make decisions in wartime situations. IHRL, by contrast, establishes individual rights, requires a rigorous analysis of rights that might potentially be affected and, thus, overall pays more attention to those potentially affected by armed conflict, not to those fighting the conflict.

The pros and cons of each normative framework for armed conflicts have been discussed in international legal scholarship at length. IHL is generally seen to be more in line with the necessities of wartime situations. It reduces complexities (for example, by declaring all enemy fighters to be legitimate targets) and gives military commanders significant discretion. The main objection against IHL results from this body of law's readiness to sacrifice individual rights for the sake of military benefits.

It is therefore often asserted that IHRL might do the better job in protecting individuals in wartime situations. The focus of the body of IHRL on individuals at first sight supports such an assumption. However, it remains disputed whether and under what conditions such protection really works. Sceptics point out that there is a significant gap between 'the legal debate at the strategic level and the reality facing military commanders on the ground'.[45] This gap results from IHRL's tendency to individualise situations and to analyse individual rights violations. Such individualisation can be in conflict with the group-based violence in

---

[41] *Ibid.*, 28–9.

[42] Laura Olson, 'Practical Challenges of Implementing the Complementarity between International Humanitarian and Human Rights Law – Demonstrated by the Procedural Regulation of Internment in Non-International Armed Conflict', *Case Western Reserve Journal of International Law* 40 (2009), 437–61 (450).

[43] Bohrer in this volume, 175 *et seq.*

[44] Contrast, for example, Kate Parlett, *The Individual in the International Legal System* (Cambridge University Press, 2012), 225, stating that IHL 'remains consistent with the nineteenth-century framework of the international legal system, as a system which creates only interstate rights'; and Peters, *Beyond Human Rights* 2016 (n. 18), 194–201, who argues that IHL may create rights also for individuals.

[45] Watkin, *Fighting at the Legal Boundaries* 2016 (n. 39), 152.

armed conflict which makes it difficult to take into account individual actors and to engage in a comprehensive analysis of potentially affected rights.[46] Moreover, rights will often conflict and demand different courses of action that need to be reconciled. Where numerous individuals are involved as fighters and civilians, each situation would need to be assessed, and multiple rights – including those of the fighters that are contemplating action – have to be taken into account. In complex situations of armed conflict, this seems to create excessive demands for fighters and commanders in real-life situations. The challenge against IHRL in armed conflict is therefore that of a 'problematic normative overreaching'.[47] IHRL is regarded as too complex, ultimately allowing 'second-guessing of a soldier's decision to use force, thereby weakening the protection of combatant immunity'.[48] Overall, many regard IHRL to 'impose unrealistic obligations on states'.[49] A possible consequence is that, in the long run, States could be less inclined to apply the law.[50]

This Trialogue teases out highly nuanced assessments of the pros and cons of the application of IHRL to armed conflict situations. Helen Duffy explores how human rights law can and has been interpreted in conflict situations through decades of jurisprudence. Duffy argues that the co-application of IHL and IHRL is beneficial from a legal, policy, victim-oriented and institutional perspective. Janina Dill, by contrast, conceptualises why and when the application of IHRL results in the said normative overreach. Her key argument is that IHRL provides better protection in situations of lower intensity where such overreach can be avoided. However, where intensity increases (as conflicts become 'protracted'[51]) IHL becomes the better legal framework.[52] Ziv Bohrer's appraisal is more radical. He argues that the application of human rights to situations of armed conflict

---

[46]   *Ibid.*, 556.

[47]   Shany, 'Human Rights and Humanitarian Law as Competing Legal Paradigms' 2011 (n. 40), 29. Luban, 'Human Rights Thinking and the Laws of War' 2016 (n. 20), 67–70, speaks of 'overextending human rights thinking'.

[48]   Michelle A. Hansen, 'Preventing the Emasculation of Warfare: Halting the Expansion of Human Rights Law into Armed Conflict', *Military Law Review* 194 (2007), 1–65 (55).

[49]   Claire Landais and Léa Bass, 'Reconciling the Rules of International Humanitarian Law with the Rules of European Human Rights Law', *International Review of the Red Cross* 97 (2015), 1295–311 (1296).

[50]   Françoise Hampson, 'Direct Participation in Hostilities and the Interoperability of the Law of Armed Conflict and Human Rights Law', *International Law Studies* 87 (2011), 187–213 (192): 'If some rules are perceived to be unrealistic, this is likely to lessen respect for those rules that can be applied in practice.'

[51]   'Protracted' is not mainly a temporal extension but denotes a degree of intensity (ICTY, *Tadić*, Decision on jurisdiction (n. 9), para. 70).

[52]   See Dill in this volume, esp. 257–63.

generally diminishes individual protection, because the entire logic of a rights-based legal regime results in weakened safeguards for the individual if compared with the protection offered by the obligation-based system of IHL.

Broader concerns against the application of human rights to wartime situations relate to the potential effects for human rights law outside armed conflict. Concessions to the necessities of armed conflict situations under human rights law might, in the end, backfire.[53] They might undermine the protection afforded by human rights in peacetime because, as Heike Krieger stresses, the concessions might 'spread so that gradually the idea that the state might lawfully kill innocent civilians for security reasons becomes part of human rights law'.[54]

IV. THREE VOICES IN A TRIALOGUE

Despite extensive studies, the law applicable to armed conflict remains controversial and contestable on various levels. First, the possibility of applying IHRL in an armed conflict as a matter of principle has been acknowledged only recently. Arguably, this legal development is not yet firm and can therefore quickly become the subject of dispute again. This is all the more likely as the centrality of the human being and the concomitant 'humanisation' of IHL might be drawn into question in the course of renewed statism and a shift of values in the international legal order away from the Western tradition. Secondly, many concrete legal questions, for example how to operationalise the potential interplay of IHRL and IHL, are not yet resolved. The crux of diverging standards and resulting norm conflicts persist. Law-appliers need very concrete tools to resolve them in a fair and predicable way, and such tools are still in the making only. Finally, some popular narratives about the law applicable to armed conflict – such as depicting the rise of non-State actors as a recent phenomenon and new challenge – might fall apart when more thoroughly analysed. The debunking of the myth may have consequences for our assessment of what the law is and what it should be. Against this background, the book aims to identify the current state of the law and, at the same time, to challenge some prevailing positions. This book both traces the black-letter debates and focuses on the normative questions that are the driving force behind many of the debates, including the doctrinal ones.

---

[53] Jean-Marie Henckaerts and Ellen Nohle, 'Concurrent Application of International Humanitarian Law and International Human Rights Law Revisited', *Human Rights and International Legal Discourse* 12 (2018), 23–43 (35).

[54] Heike Krieger, 'A Conflict of Norms: The Relationship between Humanitarian Law and Human Rights Law in the ICRC Customary Law Study', *Journal of Conflict and Security Law* 11 (2006), 265–91 (291).

The Trialogue (re-)raises three main questions. First, it asks *where, when and to whom* IHL and IHRL as the relevant bodies of law apply in armed conflict situations. Secondly, it explores the *interrelation* of IHL and IHRL and the legal techniques for *coordinating* the two regimes and for preventing or at least mitigating potential norm conflicts. State practice and human rights litigation before international courts are confronted with these norm conflicts, and the emerging and still changing techniques of coordination and underlying principles need to be identified and conceptualised.

Thirdly, and most importantly, this Trialogue moves beyond the positive analysis of the law as it stands and probes the normative principles that guide, or should be guiding, the interpretation, application and development of law applicable to armed conflict. At this juncture, the Trialogue method is expected to furnish most added value. In view of the indeterminacy of the norms at hand and the fuzziness of their interplay, such normative orientation seems particularly important.[55] For this Trialogue's question of 'applicability' of norms not only the familiar ambiguity and vagueness of the language, but additionally the uncertainty about the principles and techniques of coordination in fact grant interpreters and law-appliers plenty of freedom to bring to bear their own normative convictions. As it is well known, these convictions are not external to applying the law, but provide the background, the *Vorverständnis*, against which the meaning of the norms is constructed and their interaction designed. Put differently (and this is a truism), normative choices are not alien to the process of applying the law, but rather form its constitutive part. Specifically with regard to the application of international law in armed conflict, Marko Milanovic has observed: 'One can solemnly intone that one is applying the law as it is, the *lex lata*, not as it should be, but the reality is that the law – particularly *this* kind of law – cannot be divorced from its political context and normative preferences.'[56] The Trialogue specifically seeks to engage in this normative discourse which is a steady undercurrent to the practical and theoretical debates on the law applicable to armed conflict, and it does so through its multi-perspectivism.

---

[55] Cf. for the problem of indeterminacy and legal interpretation Christian Marxsen and Anne Peters, 'Conclusion: Self-defence against Non-State Actors – The Way Ahead', in O'Connell, Tams and Tladi (n. 1), 258–81 (264–9).

[56] Marko Milanovic, 'Accounting for the Complexity of the Law Applicable to Modern Armed Conflicts', in Winston S. Williams and Christopher M. Ford (eds.), *Complex Battlespaces: The Law of Armed Conflict and the Dynamics of Modern Warfare* (Oxford University Press, 2019), 33–60 (38).

The perspectives of the three co-authors differ in terms of their regional background, technical method, professional specialisation and worldview. Helen Duffy was invited to the Trialogue as a distinguished expert both on human rights law and on IHL who is an academic and at the same time deeply rooted in practice. She is Professor of International Humanitarian Law and Human Rights at Leiden University (the Netherlands), and also runs 'Human Rights in Practice', an international legal practice that provides legal advice and representation in strategic human rights litigation before international, regional and domestic courts. In her chapter, Duffy introduces the complexities of the application of IHL and IHRL to armed conflict situations, hereby providing an answer to the first question posed above. While explaining the settled state of the law in relation to material, personal and temporal dimensions of the applicability of IHL and IHRL, Duffy also shows where the law is unclear and where legal developments are currently underway. Analysing international adjudication and practice, Duffy investigates how the tide has shifted from separating IHL and IHRL as two distinct regimes to their co-application in situations of armed conflict. Duffy's normative vision for the interrelation between IHL and IHRL is embodied in her framework of co-applicability. Within this framework, IHL and IHRL shall, as far as possible, be interpreted in a harmonious way. For cases in which applicable norms conflict in particular contexts, Duffy proposes specific mechanisms of co-application of both legal regimes.

The second Trialogue co-author is Ziv Bohrer, assistant professor at Bar-Ilan University (Israel). Bohrer is an expert on IHL. His past work includes both articles that research current IHL and papers that uncover IHL history. In his present contribution, he combines these two lines of research and employs a historical and critical approach to the question of which legal regimes do and should apply to armed conflict. He first addresses the above-mentioned classification crisis, that is, the apparent incapability of IHL to deal with new forms of conflict in which non-State actors play a significant role. Bohrer rejects the crisis narrative and shows that these developments are, in fact, not new. He traces the debates of IHL and shows that complaints about the blurring of the wartime/peacetime divide, the demise of classical inter-State conflicts which are fought out in battles, or the talk of unprecedented wars that cannot be addressed within the existing legal framework of IHL, have been present since the nineteenth century. According to Bohrer, the occasionally perceived inability of IHL to deal with the realities of contemporary conflict results inter alia from a misconception which he explains as 'temporocentrism', the attitude that exaggerates the relevance of most recent developments.[57] In contrast to such crisis narratives, Bohrer asserts that IHL is highly capable of dealing with current challenges. He points out that IHL comprises all legal tools to adapt to new developments and challenges. Bohrer suggests espousing an 'adaptation approach', acknowledging that IHL rules can be strengthened and complemented with the help of already existing principles of IHL.

Bohrer points out that the actual crises of the law governing armed conflict results from the 'jurisdictional struggle' between IHL and IHRL. He rejects the strategy, advocated, *inter alia*, by Helen Duffy, of co-applying IHL and IHRL. According to him, the 'righting of IHL' with its shift from an obligation-based to a rights-based system in the regulation of armed conflicts comes with significant dangers.[58] In contrast to such a 'righting' of IHL, Bohrer asks us to rely more on the internal logic of IHL and to use the adaptation approach in order to make IHL fit to face current challenges. This would avoid abandoning the inherent logic of IHL, especially its obligation-based character, which Bohrer finds to be the better system to guide military operations.

The third Trialogue co-author is Janina Dill. Dill is Associate Professor at the Department of Politics and International Relations at the University of Oxford (UK). Janina Dill was invited to the Trialogue for her background in political theory and expertise on the international regulation and normative dynamics of armed conflicts. Dill approaches the topic of legal regulation of armed conflict situations not as a question of black-letter law, but rather as a moral question. As a starting point, she argues that the law regulating armed conflict has two moral tasks. The first task is to guide soldiers 'towards the course of action that conforms to their moral obligations',[59] that is, it should guide soldiers to direct their fire 'only against individuals who have forfeited their individual moral right to life',[60] or against individuals whose harming can be justified as a lesser moral evil. The second task, according to Dill, does not relate to the moral obligations of the individual combatant or fighter, but asks for the moral desirability of the outcome of their conduct on the battle-field. Specifically, law should 'avoid and reduce as much as possible all morally unjustified infringements (i.e., violations) of individual rights in war'.[61] Dill shows that, because IHRL more closely reflects fundamental moral principles about the permissibility of individual rights infringements,

---

[57]   Bohrer in this volume, 134.
[58]   *Ibid.*, 173 *et seq.*
[59]   Dill in this volume, 198.
[60]   *Ibid.*, 199.
[61]   *Ibid.*

it provides 'the *prima facie* morally better law for governing hostilities'.[62] However, Dill identifies a turning point. Where armed conflicts become protracted,[63] epistemic barriers make it difficult to realise the standards provided for by IHRL, and volitional defects make it unlikely that soldiers will attempt to live up to these standards. While IHRL remains the better law for reminding soldiers of their moral obligations, it nevertheless leads to morally undesirable outcomes during protracted hostilities. Dill therefore argues that, from a moral point of view, IHRL should be the standard legal regime to guide armed conflict situations, but where such conflicts become 'protracted' (i.e., during all NIACs and during protracted IACs), IHL should displace IHRL and become the applicable legal framework.

In their interplay, overlap and partial disagreement, the three voices in this Trialogue not only provide a comprehensive account of the current state of the law, of its trajectory, and of hidden inconsistencies. Moreover, through a nuanced critique of the law and its underlying premises, the contributions invite us to an open engagement with the law's normative undercurrents that inform and influence positions taken on the substance of the law, but are nevertheless often neglected in the debate.

[62]   Dill in this volume, 200.
[63]   See for the term *supra*, n. 51.

1

Trials and Tribulations: Co-Applicability of IHL and Human Rights in an Age of Adjudication

Helen Duffy

I. INTRODUCTION

Writing back in the 1970s, Baxter noted that 'the first line of defence against international humanitarian law is to deny that it applies at all'.[1] Controversy around international humanitarian law (IHL) applicability has been a staple feature of international practice for decades: denials that armed conflicts exist lest 'terrorist' adversaries be legitimised; or exorbitant claims that they arise from intransigent problems of law enforcement such as drug-related violence or terrorism. Today, controversies concerning the applicability of IHL, and its significance, are ongoing, and increasingly inextricably bound up with the question of co-applicability with other areas of international law, in particular international human rights law (IHRL).

The implications of over- and under-inclusive approaches to IHL applicability depend to a large extent on the approach taken to co-applicable law. On the one hand, the denial of IHL applicability to evade the strictures of that body of law assumes a narrow view of IHL as the only relevant constraining law, the non-applicability of which leaves a legal vacuum to be exploited. On the other hand, overreaching approaches to IHL are in turn often predicated on assertions that if IHL does apply it displaces the normally applicable standards of IHRL. Conversely, denial of IHRL applicability has at times been supported by reference to applicable IHL, without grappling with the normative or procedural implications of this exclusive approach. Understanding applicable law inevitably involves viewing the law governing armed conflict in its broader framework, considering IHL and IHRL together and grappling with the thorny issue of how they interact in theory and, most importantly, in practice.

[1] Richard Baxter, 'Some Existing Problems of Humanitarian Law', *Military Law and Law of War Review* 14 (1975), 297–303 (298).

While disputes around the applicability of IHL, IHRL and the nature of their interrelationship are not new, the international landscape within which these issues are considered has been transformed in recent years. Several developments are worth highlighting at the outset, as they emerge recurrently throughout our enquiry into the law, and outstanding controversies, in relation to applicability and co-applicability. The first set relate to the factual and political context within which the discussion is set, and the second to the changing legal and institutional context in which questions of co-applicability arise in practice.

A. *Practice, Politics and Positioning of Parties*

Conflict recognition and classification have long been fraught political issues,[2] particularly in the context of non-international armed conflicts (NIACs), which form the majority of armed conflicts in the world today. Not uncommonly, States' positions bear limited relation to legal standards or facts on the ground. Yet as we will see, in practice the position of a State influences a great deal; not only its own approach to applicable law, but arguments advanced in litigation[3] and, rightly or wrongly, sometimes also the approach of courts to (co-)applicability.[4] The murky reality that States' positions are rarely transparent and frequently disputed, for a range of legal and political reasons, renders determinations as to applicable law more challenging. It also makes it all the more important, in line with the principle of legality and the proper functioning of IHL, that the existence of an armed conflict (and the applicability of IHL) are treated as legal questions capable of being objectively applied, not dependent on the position of one or more affected parties.[5]

---

[2] Bohrer in this volume, 109 *et seq*. See generally, Elizabeth Wilmshurst (ed.), *International Law and Classification of Conflicts* (Oxford University Press, 2012); Andrea Bianchi and Yasmin Naqvi, *International Humanitarian Law and Terrorism* (Oxford: Hart, 2011), ch. 1.

[3] Both States and applicants to rights litigation may deny the applicability of IHL for various reasons; Section III and Larissa van den Herik and Helen Duffy, 'Human Rights Bodies and International Humanitarian Law: Common but Differentiated Approaches', in Carla M. Buckley, Alice Donald and Philip Leach (eds.), *Towards Convergence in International Human Rights Law: Approaches of Regional and International Systems* (Leiden: Brill/ Nijhoff, 2016), 366–406; Françoise J. Hampson, 'The Relationship between International Humanitarian Law and Human Rights Law from the Perspective of a Human Rights Treaty Body', *International Review of the Red Cross* 90 (2008), 549–72 (549).

[4] E.g., ECtHR, *Hassan v. United Kingdom*, Grand Chamber Judgment of 16 September 2014, Application No. 29750/09, discussed in Section III.

[5] The test for the applicability of IHL is, and has to be, a legal one; see Section II, see also, e.g., ICTY, *Prosecutor v. Duško Tadić*, Case No. IT-94-1-T, Trial Chamber Judgment of 7 May 1997.

Notorious recent examples of extreme selectivity, or 'strategic'[6] approaches to the applicability of IHL, IHRL, or both, provide part of the backdrop to the normative discussion on co-applicability. Such an approach characterised much of the 'war on terror', wherein disputes about *applicability* of legal frameworks have featured centre stage,[7] inflating the perceived relevance of IHL and, indeed, interplay in the counter-terrorism context.[8] Many of the worst excesses of counter-terrorism practice (torture, arbitrary detention or burgeoning targeted killings) may reveal a broader legality issue – an unwillingness to be constrained by law – rather than genuine differences of view on applicability and co-applicability.[9] Nonetheless, it was through the blanket – and, as will be argued, erroneous – invocation of IHL as *'lex specialis'*, purportedly displacing human rights norms and the jurisdiction of human rights courts and bodies (without applying consistently norms of IHL either), that accountability for such practices before national courts and international human rights bodies has been avoided.[10] This gruelling tug of war between paradigms of recent decades underscores the importance of understanding and clarifying applicable law and ensuring effective oversight.

B. *The Complexity of Conflict*

Another crucial aspect of the factual landscape is the undeniable transnational, multi-actor complexity of many contemporary armed conflicts. However much we wish it were not so, in practice this can make it difficult

---

6 Yuvul Shany, 'Human Rights and Humanitarian Law as Competing Legal Paradigms for Fighting Terror', in Orna Ben-Naftali (ed.), *International Humanitarian Law and International Human Rights Law* (Oxford University Press, 2011), 13–33 (13). See also, Beth Van Schaak, 'The United States' Position on the Extraterritorial Application of Human Rights Obligations: Now is the Time for Change', *International Law Studies* 90 (2014).

7 Helen Duffy, *War on Terror and the Framework of International Law*, 2nd edn. (Cambridge University Press, 2015), chs. 6 and 7.

8 *Ibid.* Policies of targeted killings by, e.g., Russia, the United States and Israel are not limited to conflict situations, yet are justified by broad reference to IHL.

9 On drones reflecting disputes about whether international law applies at all rather than applicable law, see UNHRC, 'Report of the Special Rapporteur on Extrajudicial, Summary or Arbitrary Executions, Philip Alston', 28 May 2010, UN Doc. A/HRC/14/24/Add.6.

10 See, e.g., US submissions to the United Nations Human Rights Council (UNHRC) or Committee against Torture (CAT) arguing that its treaty obligations do not apply in armed conflict; e.g., US Department of State, 'Second, Third and Fourth Periodic Reports of the United States of America to the UN Committee on Human Rights Concerning the International Covenant on Civil and Political Rights', 21 October 2005, available at: www.state.gov/j/drl/rls/55504.htm, and 30 December 2011, available at: www.state.gov/j/drl/rls/179781.htm.

to distinguish between certain situations of violent unrest and organised crime and NIAC, or between international and non-international conflicts.[11]

The transnational nature of the violence, the multiplicity of States (some failed and failing) that may intervene,[12] and, in particular, the range, scale and capacity of non-State actors (NSAs) resorting to force,[13] from insurgent groups, terrorist networks or franchises to organised criminal entities, are part of this factual complexity.[14] For example, while dispute has often focused on the applicability of IHL to 'terrorist' entities,[15] comparable questions emerge increasingly in the light of the extreme violence and control by organised criminal groups in parts of Latin America,[16] raising the spectre of IHL as the legal framework of choice when law is at 'its wits' end' in the struggle against NSAs.[17] This new frontier in the battle over IHL applicability reminds us that, at a minimum, how we approach definitions of conflict and applicability in one situation, such as in relation to counter-terrorism, may have an impact in other emerging contexts. This again enhances the importance of clear and cautious approaches to what constitutes an 'armed conflict' to which IHL applies.

The second group of broad trends worthy of preliminary note relate to legal and institutional changes which impact inescapably on the context within which our discussion takes place.

---

[11] Development, Concepts and Doctrine Centre, 'Global Strategic Trends Out to 2040', MOD 02/10c30 (2010) and UK Strategic Defence and Security Review 2010, cited in Wilmshurst (ed.), *Classification of Conflicts* 2012 (n. 2), 1–8 (4).

[12] Robin Geiß, 'Armed Violence in Fragile States', *International Review of the Red Cross* 91 (2009), 127–42.

[13] Michael Ignatieff, *The Warrior's Honor: Ethnic War and the Modern Conscience* (New York: Henry Holt, 1997), referred to the decisive 'breaking of the monopoly of the means of violence'.

[14] See Section II.A.1.b.

[15] Section II.

[16] E.g., IACommHR, 'The Human Rights Situation in Mexico', 31 December 2015, OEA/Ser.L/V/II. Doc. 44/15, available at: www.oas.org/en/iachr/reports/pdfs/Mexico2016-en.pdf; Annyssa Bellal, 'The War Report: Armed Conflicts in 2017', *The Geneva Academy of International Humanitarian Law and Human Rights*, March 2018, 86, suggesting that Mexican cartels are parties to an armed conflict with the Mexican armed forces. Amy Carpenter, 'Civilian Protection in Mexico and Guatemala: Humanitarian Engagement with Druglords and Gangs', *Homeland Security Review* 6 (2012), 109–36.

[17] See Carrie Comer and Daniel Mburu, 'Humanitarian Law at Wits' End: Does the Violence Arising from the "War on Drugs" in Mexico Meet the International Criminal Court's Non-International Armed Conflict Threshold?', *Yearbook of International Humanitarian Law* 18 (2015), 67–89; Carina Bergal, 'The Mexican Drug War: The Case for a Non-International Armed Conflict Classification', *Fordham International Law Journal* 34 (2011), 1042–88; ICRC, 31st International Conference of the Red Cross and Red Crescent, 'International Humanitarian Law and the Challenges of Contemporary Armed Conflicts', 31IC/11/5.1.2, October 2011 (hereinafter the 'Challenges of Contemporary Armed Conflicts'), 11.

C. Co-applicability Confirmed

While at one time the applicability of IHRL in conflict situations in general was itself contentious, in recent decades there has been an overwhelming shift, such that the vast weight of international authority and opinion now confirms that IHRL continues to apply in times of armed conflict.[18] As such, the focus of the debate has shifted to *how* it co-applies alongside IHL, addressed at Sections III and IV. While, undoubtedly, some dispute on the relevance and applicability of human rights in armed conflict remains,[19] as reflected in the sections that follow and in the approach of other chapters to this volume, it is suggested that much of this reflects differing views on the pros and cons of how the law has developed, its historical or moral force, rather than on where the law stands today.[20]

A further normative shift – less emphatic but nonetheless perceptible – may also be underway in terms of how the relationship between IHL and IHRL is conceptualised. As explored in Section IV, simplistic approaches to co-applicability, such as seeing one body of law as a *'lex specialis'* to displace another, are ceding to a more nuanced approach to ongoing, weighted co-applicability.

Numerous commentators also point to 'narrowing gaps' between relevant areas of applicable law. There has certainly long been recognition of substantial overlap between IHL and IHRL in terms of objectives, principles and areas of substantive coherence.[21] This is most obvious in respect of humane treatment or fair trial, for example, but as explored in Section V there may be further movement on less obvious issues such as detention, the right to life or duty to investigate. Caution is also due not to overstate the convergence. It is in part the real substantive differences that remain – as regards starting points, processes and in some cases outcomes – that make it so important to ascertain applicable law. So far as the areas of law develop through practice over time, gaps may narrow, and the normative significance of debates on applicability may diminish to an extent.[22]

---

[18]   Section II on, e.g., the position of States, ICJ, ICRC, and Section III on the voluminous body of practice of IHRL courts and tribunals.

[19]   Section II on, e.g., US and Israeli positions.

[20]   Section II.A; Ziv Bohrer in this volume, Chapter 2, and Janina Dill in this volume, Chapter 3, lend historical and moral perspectives on co-applicability.

[21]   See, e.g., Cordula Droege, 'The Interplay between International Humanitarian Law and International Human Rights Law in Situations of Armed Conflicts', *Israel Law Review* 40 (2007), 310–55 (310).

[22]   The law on NIAC and IAC moving closer is reflected in ICRC, Jean-Marie Henckaerts and Louise Doswald-Beck (eds.), *Customary International Humanitarian Law* (Cambridge University Press, 2005) (hereinafter the *ICRC Customary Study*).

Likewise, within IHL, while a gap remains between the detailed body of IHL treaty standards governing international armed conflict (IAC) and the quite limited treaty law directed to NIAC,[23] the divide has also substantially narrowed. In large part this development was also influenced by the work of tribunals, and the development of customary international law in NIAC.[24]

D. *Applicability in an Age of Adjudication*

A final transformative shift in the international institutional landscape relates to the emergence of an 'era of international adjudication'.[25] Various levels of international adjudication are relevant here, and have played decisive roles in determining issues of applicable law. First, the international criminal tribunals, beginning with the pioneering International Criminal Tribunal for the former Yugoslavia (ICTY), that breathed life into skeletal provisions of IHL. As this chapter discusses, the ad hoc tribunals and the International Criminal Court (ICC) have provided authoritative interpretations on the scope of application of IHL as well as its content,[26] and arguably en route have strengthened its enforcement.[27] The International Court of Justice (ICJ) in

---

[23] Common Art. 3 of Convention (I) for the Amelioration of the Condition of the Wounded and Sick in Armed Forces in the Field, Geneva, 12 August 1949, 75 UNTS 31 (hereinafter: GCI), Convention (II) for the Amelioration of the Condition of Wounded, Sick and Shipwrecked Members of Armed Forces at Sea, Geneva, 12 August 1969, 75 UNTS 85 (hereinafter: GCII), Convention (III) relative to the Treatment of Prisoners of War, Geneva, 12 August 1949, 75 UNTS 135 (hereinafter: GCIII), Convention (IV) relative to the Protection of Civilian Persons in Time of War, Geneva, 12 August 1949, 75 UNTS 287 (hereinafter: GCIV) and Protocol Additional to the Geneva Conventions of 12 August 1949, and Relating to the Protection of Victims of Non-International Armed Conflicts (Protocol II), Geneva, 8 June 1977, 1125 UNTS 609 (hereinafter: APII), (where the legal threshold is met) govern NIACs, contrasting with the body of Hague and Geneva law applicable in IACs. Many early IHL treaties were born in a period when international law was essentially an inter-State affair, though post WWII and recent treaties (e.g. Rome Statute of the International Criminal Court, 17 July 1998, 2187 UNTS 3 (hereinafter: ICC Statute) retain the distinction.

[24] E.g., the ICRC *Customary Study* 2005 (n. 22) identifies 148 customary rules applicable in NIACs. The influence of adjudication, especially the work of tribunals and human rights bodies, is clear.

[25] Helen Duffy, *Strategic Human Rights Litigation* (Oxford: Hart, 2018), ch. 2, citing Christopher Greenwood's speech at Leiden University (2015).

[26] E.g., ICC, *Prosecutor v. Bosco Ntaganda*, Case No. ICC-01/04-02/06 OA5, Appeals Chamber Decision of 15 June 2017, defining child soldiers on the same side as protected persons under IHL.

[27] Although the tribunals developed ICL, focused only on those aspects of IHL giving rise to criminal responsibility and not the fuller preventive purpose of IHL, their influence on IHL is indisputable.

turn had a crucial role in determining the applicability of IHRL in conflict, and the principle of co-applicability.

More recent, and certainly more voluminous, is the burgeoning resort to human rights courts and tribunals, including to address violations in armed conflict. Within this practice we see an incremental but decisive shift in the level and nature of engagement, by a multiplicity of IHRL mechanisms, with IHL. Whether one lauds or laments this development (on which my co-contributors and I may take different views), the fact is that it is increasingly through the development of jurisprudence that questions of the scope of application of IHRL, and interplay with IHL, will be addressed, and given content.[28] As explored in Section IV, this engagement with IHL has certainly been uneven and sometimes faltering. But it holds promise for both the relevance and operability of IHRL in conflict situations, and for the prospect of judicial oversight and remedies for victims that have long been elusive.[29] This is particularly so given the stark contrast between the expanding architecture of human rights litigation and the continuing lack of an international IHL complaints mechanism.[30]

In short, we come to the issue of applicability necessarily informed by the political and historical context, and mindful of the normative, institutional and practical significance of the theoretical discussion.[31]

This chapter's primary goal is to explore where law and practice stand on the applicability of IHL, IHRL and their co-applicability, while acknowledging complexities and areas of uncertainty. Although significant doctrinal discussion has been dedicated to the theoretical issues of co-applicability, these are

---

[28] As we will see, skeletal treaties often do not, on their face, provide answers on many key questions, enhancing the normative influence of the judicial process.

[29] This is particularly so where national remedies are blocked in security-charged situations, e.g., through non-justiciability, state secrecy or immunities; see, e.g., Sharon Weill, *The Role of National Courts in Applying International Humanitarian Law* (Oxford University Press, 2014); Helen Duffy, 'Accountability for Counter-terrorism: Challenges and Potential in the Role of the Courts', in Fergal F. Davis and Fiona de Londras (eds.), *Critical Debates on Counter Terrorism Judicial Review* (Cambridge University Press, 2016), 324–64.

[30] The IHL supervisory systems that comprise the Protecting Power mechanism, the enquiry procedure and the International Fact-Finding Commission envisaged in Art. 90 of Protocol Additional to the Geneva Conventions of 12 August 1949, and relating to the Protection of Victims of International Armed Conflicts (Protocol I), Geneva, 12 December 1977, 1125 UNTS 3 (hereinafter: API) are under-utilised. The confidential supervisory role of the ICRC is crucial but is not a complaints procedure.

[31] See Section II.A.1.b; Terry D. Gill, 'Classifying the Conflict in Syria', *International Law Studies Series. US Naval War College* 92 (2016), 353–80 (378); see, e.g., Duffy, *War on Terror* 2015 (n. 7), ch. 7B.

not the object of this chapter.[32] Instead, it seeks to bring a practical perspective to the legal issues – considering how questions of applicability and interplay arise, and are determined, in practice, and exposing some of the array of relevant contextual, legal, political and institutional factors that may have a bearing on co-applicability.

Section II seeks to set out the basic legal framework governing applicability (*ratione materiae, personae, loci* and *temporis*) of IHL, and more briefly IHRL, revealing convergence and divergence, evolution and complexities in each. Section III explores the increasingly significant approach of human rights courts and bodies to IHL and co-applicability with IHRL. Section IV suggests a law and practice-based framework for understanding the interplay between these branches of law. Section V looks at what this framework of co-applicability means in practice, through the prism of particular issues, namely, review of the lawfulness of detention, targeted killings, cyber operations and investigations.

II. APPLICABILITY OF IHL AND IHRL, AND OUTSTANDING CONTROVERSIES

A. *Applicability* Ratione Materiae

1. The Material Applicability of IHL in Conflict

A) THE SINE QUA NON: EXISTENCE OF AND NEXUS TO AN INTERNATIONAL OR NON-INTERNATIONAL ARMED CONFLICT The scope of IHL is limited *ratione materiae* to situations of armed conflict. It provides a body of rules specifically directed at limiting the effects of war, by protecting persons who are not or are no longer participating in the hostilities and regulating means and methods of warfare. The elemental question upon which IHL applicability depends is then what constitutes an 'armed conflict'. The connected question is which type of conflict and which body of IHL applies. Despite the developments in

---

[32] See, e.g., Droege, 'Interplay between IHL and IHRL' 2007 (n. 21), 310; Gerald Draper, 'Humanitarian Law and Human Rights', *Acta Juridica* (1979), 193–206 (193); Dietrich Schindler, 'Human Rights and Humanitarian Law: Interrelationship of the Laws', *American University Law Review* 31 (1982), 935–43; Noam Lubell, 'Parallel Application of International Humanitarian Law and International Human Rights Law: An Examination of the Debate', *Israel Law Review* 40 (2007), 648–60; Nancie Prud'homme, '*Lex Specialis*: Oversimplifying a More Complex and Multifaceted Relationship?', *Israel Law Review* 40 (2007), 356–95 (385); Marko Milanovic, 'The Lost Origins of *Lex Specialis*: Rethinking the Relationship between HR and IHL', in Jens David Ohlin (ed.), *Theoretical Boundaries of Armed Conflict and Human Rights* (New York: Oxford University Press, 2016), 78–118.

the 'typology' or nature of conflicts around the globe,[33] and some convincing questioning of such distinctions,[34] it appears to hold true as a matter of law today that there are two types of armed conflict, IAC and NIAC, with significance for applicable IHL.[35]

IHL is applicable to conduct with a *nexus* to or which is 'associated' with the armed conflict, not to any and all conduct that takes place in the broad *context* of the conflict.[36] In any event, the determination as to whether particular conduct is carried out as part of an armed conflict is a prerequisite to IHL applicability, before any question of co-applicability arises. It may be questioned how clearly defined and understood, for the purposes of IHL applicability, this nexus criterion is. What is clear is that the nexus requirement does not derive from the nature of the actors involved; militaries around the world often engage in activities abroad that do not form part of any armed conflict, while other actors exercise their authority in diverse ways within armed conflict.[37]

The test for the applicability of IHL is a legal one, depending on whether the facts meet the definition of 'armed conflict' in international law. It is perhaps remarkable, given the normative significance of the existence of 'armed conflict' and the exceptional framework it triggers, that the term was not defined in IHL (or human rights) treaties.

In the absence of a treaty definition, international courts have stepped into the breach. While the ICJ and human rights bodies have provided relatively slight guidance on this point,[38] it has been through the first level of

---

[33] Sylvain Vité, 'Typology of Armed Conflicts in International Humanitarian Law: Legal Concepts and Actual Situations', *International Review of the Red Cross* 91 (2009), 69–94 (89); Marko Milanovic and Vidan Hadzi-Vidanovic, 'A Taxonomy of Armed Conflict', in Nigel D. White and Christian Henderson (eds.), *Research Handbook on International Conflict and Security Law* (Cheltenham: Edward Elgar, 2012), 256–314 (257 *et seq.*).

[34] E.g., James Stewart, 'Towards a Single Definition of Armed Conflict in International Humanitarian Law: A Critique of Internationalized Armed Conflict', *International Review of the Red Cross* 85 (2003), 313–50.

[35] E.g., Wilmshurst, *Classification of Conflicts* 2012 (n. 2), chs. 1, 2–8; ICRC, *Convention (I) for the Amelioration of the Condition of the Wounded and Sick in Armed Forces in the Field. Geneva, 12 August 1949*, Commentary (online edn.), 2016, Art. 3, para. 472.

[36] The nexus requirement is explored in most detail in relation to 'war crimes'; ICC, *Elements of Crimes* (The Hague: International Criminal Court, 2011); e.g., Knut Dörmann, 'Preparatory Commission for the International Criminal Court: the Elements of War Crimes', *International Review of the Red Cross* 83 (2001), 461–87.

[37] *Ibid.*; Darragh Murray, Elizabeth Wilmshurst and Francoise Hampson *et al.*, *Practitioners' Guide to Human Rights Law in Armed Conflict* (Oxford University Press, 2016) (hereinafter: *Practitioners' Guide*).

[38] As noted in Section III, they have been reluctant to address the existence of conflict 'applicability' question.

international adjudication referred to above[39] – by international criminal courts and tribunals – that the basic elements of a broadly accepted definition of armed conflict have been identified. The ICTY in the *Tadić* case, since widely replicated, including by the International Criminal Tribunal for Rwanda (ICTR), the ICC, the Special Court for Sierra Leone and others, provides a broadly accepted starting point:

> [A]n armed conflict exists whenever there is a resort to armed force between States or protracted armed violence between governmental authorities and organized armed groups or between such groups within a State.[40]

Whether an armed conflict exists is then an essentially factual assessment. It is independent of the position of the parties or their acknowledgement that they are in a state of war.[41] In practice, as already noted, the position of parties to the conflict may well be significant,[42] but legally we will see that the existence of a conflict, and its international or non-international nature, reduces to a determination of the use and nature of the force and of those employing it.

B) CLASSIFICATION AND APPLICABILITY: INTERNATIONAL ARMED CONFLICT
Classification of the conflict, according to the differing thresholds and criteria, is crucial; just in legal terms it influences applicable treaty law, to an extent relevant IHL standards,[43] and potentially co-applicability with IHRL.[44] Once again, the answers to the classification questions are not, however, transparent from the treaties themselves. Beyond, for example, Common Article 2 (CA2) of the Geneva Conventions making clear that it applies to conflicts 'between two or more of the High Contracting Parties', IHL treaties do not define IACs. Once again, in significant measure it has been international criminal tribunals, supported by the work of the International Committee of the Red Cross (ICRC), that have provided guidance as to the basic criteria for IAC.

---

[39] Section I.
[40] See, ICTY, *Tadić*, Trial Chamber Judgment (n. 5), para. 561. See also ICC, *Prosecutor v. Thomas Lubanga Dyilo*, Case No. ICC-01/04-01/06, Judgment of 14 March 2012, para. 539 (hereinafter: ICC, *Lubanga*, Judgment).
[41] Common Art. 2 (CA2) to the Geneva Conventions.
[42] Section IV on interplay, where the classification is one factor of influence. Political significance is noted below.
[43] Narrowing gaps, including the role of ICRC *Customary Study* 2005 (n. 22), is noted in Section I.
[44] See Section IV, on multiple factors relevant to determining the priority to be afforded to which area of law, (only) one of which may be the nature of the conflict.

i) Any Use of Force or a Minimum Threshold? The ICRC's CA2 Commentary notes that 'any difference arising between two States and leading to the intervention of armed forces is an armed conflict'.[45] This view, reflected in, for example, ICTY jurisprudence and by many if not most commentators, is that an IAC arises when there is recourse to any armed force between two or more States.[46] This is a low threshold, wherein factors such as duration and intensity (central to NIACs) are generally not considered relevant.

Some commentators have begun to question whether practice indicates at least some kind of 'intensity' requirement for any kind of armed conflict, IAC or NIAC.[47] On the one hand, there is support for the proposition that, in practice, States operate as if there were an intensity threshold; minor incidents at inter-State borders or brief interventions on another State's territory against specific terrorist targets without apparent territorial State consent have not generally led to assertions by affected States that an IAC has arisen as a result.[48] Silence on the existence of a conflict may, of course, be explained by other reasons, including political factors or the opaque nature of State consent.[49] But reluctance to invoke the armed conflict paradigm may also reflect the degree of force used. It has also been suggested that this reflects the traditional idea of war as excluding minor armed incidents.[50]

The predominant view of current law appears to be that there is no intensity threshold requirement for IAC, unlike for NIAC considered

---

[45] Jean S. Pictet (ed.), *Commentary on the Geneva Conventions of 12 August 1949*, vol. 1 (Geneva: International Committee of the Red Cross, 1952), 32.

[46] IHL in IAC also applies to total or partial military occupation, even if met with no armed resistance, and wars of self-determination against colonial domination.

[47] See, e.g., Jann Kleffner, 'Scope of Application of International Humanitarian Law', in Dieter Fleck (ed.), *The Handbook of International Humanitarian Law*, 3rd edn. (Oxford University Press, 2013), 43–78; Robert Kolb, *Advanced Introduction to International Humanitarian Law* (Cheltenham: Edward Elgar, 2014), 22; Use of Force Committee, 'Final Report on the Meaning of Armed Conflict', in Christine Chinkin, Sarah Nouwen and Christopher Ward (eds.), *International Law Association: Report of The Seventy-Fourth Conference* (2010), 676–721 (692–708).

[48] Bianchi and Naqvi, *International Humanitarian Law and Terrorism* 2011 (n. 2).

[49] See, e.g., Duffy, *War on Terror* 2015 (n. 7), lethal attacks in Yemen or Pakistan in chs. 5 and 6 or the Bin Laden operation in ch. 9. See also, Bianchi and Naqvi, *International Humanitarian Law and Terrorism* 2011 (n. 2), 76–7.

[50] See Dapo Akande, 'Classification of Armed Conflicts: Relevant Legal Concepts', in Wilmshurst (ed.), *Classification of Conflicts* 2012 (n. 2), ch. 3, 32–79; and Steven Haines, 'The Nature of War and the Character of Contemporary Armed Conflict', in Wilmshurst (ed.), *Classification of Conflicts* 2012 (n. 2), ch. 2, 9–31; Yoram Dinstein, *Non-International Armed Conflict in International Law* (Cambridge University Press, 2014), 11–13.

below.[51] There is, however, at least scope for differences of view as to whether a certain minimal threshold of force separates random acts of violence from IAC, as it does for NIAC, and as to the direction that legal development may take in the future. The debate on the law may also reflect divergent views on the policy and normative implications; whether an inclusive view ensures that IHL operates as a constraining legal framework, or lowers standards of protection otherwise provided by IHRL, as well as the broader potential repercussions of classification as an IAC for escalation of conflicts.[52]

ii) States Using Force Transnationally: IAC or NIAC? Other issues of dispute in relation to the classification of IACs go to the heart of what renders a conflict 'international': is it the nature of the parties or a feature of geography? It appears to be increasingly accepted that territorial limits are not as key as they were once thought to be, for IACs or for NIACs. As noted below, NIACs may and often do extend beyond frontiers without ceasing to be NIACs, while as the ICTY definition set out above shows, the key determinant with regard to IAC is whether there are State forces on either side. This is reflected plainly in the ICC's *Lubanga* judgment that 'in the absence of two States opposing each other, there is no international armed conflict'.[53] Numerous areas of uncertainty and controversy nonetheless remain.

Internationalising NIACS? : Where a State intervenes directly or indirectly in a pre-existing NIAC abroad, the question arises as to whether the conflict is necessarily rendered 'international'?[54] Where a State intervenes on the side of a non-State party, and exercises 'overall control'[55] over it, such that there are then States engaged in the conflict on each side, the conflict would be

---

[51]   E.g., Jean S. Pictet (ed.), *Commentary on the Geneva Conventions of 12 August 1949*, vol. 3 (Geneva: International Committee of the Red Cross, 1960), 22 *et seq.*; ICTY, *Prosecutor v. Duško Tadić*, Case No. IT-94-1-A, Appeal Chamber Judgment of 15 July 1999, para. 70 (hereinafter: ICTY, *Tadić*, Appeal Chamber Judgment); and Gabriella Venturini, 'The Temporal Scope of Application of the Conventions', in Andrew Clapham, Paola Gaeta and Marco Sassòli (eds.), *The 1949 Geneva Conventions: a Commentary* (Oxford University Press, 2015), 52–66 (51 *et seq.*, 55).

[52]   See, Pictet, *The Geneva Convention (I) Commentary* 1952 (n. 45), Art. 2; Jelena Pejic, 'The Protective Scope of Common Art. 3: More than Meets the Eye', *International Review of the Red Cross* 93 (2011), 189–225, on policy reasons for rejecting a threshold for IACs; ICRC, 32nd International Conference of the Red Cross and Red Crescent, International Humanitarian Law and the Challenges of Contemporary Armed Conflicts, Report, 8–10 December 2015, Report, Geneva, October 2015, 32IC/15/11, 8; Kleffner, 'Scope of Application of International Humanitarian Law' 2013 (n. 47), 45. Note *infra* concerns regarding the implications of classification of the Syria conflict.

[53]   ICC, *Lubanga*, Judgment (n. 40), para. 541.

[54]   See, ICTY, *Tadić*, Appeal Chamber Judgment (n. 51), paras. 137–40.

[55]   *Ibid.*, para. 120.

internationalised.[56] Where a State intervenes on another State's territory on the side of the State, however, the resulting conflict involves States – including a foreign State – on one side and a non-State actor(s) on another. Experts differ as to the classification of such a conflict,[57] though the emphasis on the nature of the parties as a key consideration may suggest that the conflict remains a NIAC as far as it remains 'asymmetric', with State and non-State parties on each side.[58]

iii) Intervention Directed against NSAs Without State Consent?: An associated question of great recent import is whether an IAC automatically arises when a State intervenes against an armed group on another State's territory, without the territorial State's consent.[59] Academics and commentators differ on whether it matters whether the military action is *directed* solely against the armed group, as opposed to against the State's institutions as such. On one view, any use of force on another State's territory in the absence of that State's consent will constitute an IAC.[60] On another, if military action is directed solely against an armed group and the force employed is not *between* States, the conflict remains a NIAC.[61]

---

[56] ICC, *Lubanga*, Judgment (n. 40), para. 541; Tristian Ferraro, 'The ICRC's Legal Position on the Notion of Armed Conflict Involving Foreign Intervention and on Determining the IHL Applicable to this Type of Conflict', *International Review of the Red Cross* 97 (2015), 1227–52 (1231, 1250).

[57] Differing views are reflected in, e.g., Wilmshurst, *Classification of Conflicts* 2012 (n. 2); see also, Dill in this volume, Chapter 3; George Aldrich, 'The Laws of War on Land', *American Journal of International Law* 94 (2000), 42–63 (62).

[58] ICC, *Prosecutor v. Jean-Pierre Bemba Gombo*, Case No. ICC-01/05-01/08, Confirmation of Charges Decision of 15 June 2009, para. 246 – the presence of limited foreign troops 'not directed against the State of the CAR and its authorities' did not change the NIAC; ICC, *Lubanga*, Judgment (n. 40), para. 541; see also, Sandesh Sivakumaran, *The Law of Non-International Armed Conflict* (Oxford University Press, 2012), 224.

[59] Gill, 'Classifying the Conflict in Syria' 2016 (n. 31), 353, 371, provides examples. In addition to Syria, 'drone strikes by the United States against various jihadist armed groups in Pakistan and Yemen, the intervention of Turkey against PKK positions in northern Iraq, cross-border action by the armed forces of Kenya into Somalia in pursuit of Al-Shabaab fighters, and Colombian incursions into Ecuador against FARC rebels. In none of these did any of the States concerned ever consider themselves in a situation of armed conflict with each other.'

[60] Akande, 'Classification of Armed Conflicts: Relevant Legal Concepts' 2012 (n. 50), 73. See also, Marco Sassòli, 'Transnational Armed Groups and International Humanitarian Law', *HPCR Occasional Paper Series* (2006), 4–5; Dieter Fleck, 'The Law of Non-International Armed Conflicts', in Dieter Fleck (ed.), *The Handbook of International Humanitarian Law*, 3rd edn. (Oxford University Press, 2013), 581–609 (584–5).

[61] Gill, 'Classifying the Conflict in Syria' 2016 (n. 31); ICC, *Bemba*, Confirmation Decision (n. 58), para. 246.

Here, as elsewhere, much depends on the 'factual realities' on the ground as regards who and what is *targeted* and *affected* by the intervention, whatever its underlying purpose. No ready boundaries can be drawn between the territorial State and its population, public property and infrastructure, themselves constituent elements of the State, quite apart from the fact that the State is more likely to become embroiled in the conflict where force is used on its territory. It has therefore been suggested that '[f]or these reasons and others, it better corresponds to the factual reality to conclude that an international armed conflict arises between the territorial State and the intervening State when force is used on the former's territory without its consent.'[62] A pragmatic approach, and State practice cited above, would favour careful evaluation of particular facts, including first and foremost the nature of the parties fighting one another, the targets of the intervention and its impact, rather than blanket conclusions.[63]

The complexity of conflict classification is heightened by the fact that, in practice, the question may not be whether there is *an* armed conflict and which type, but which legal regimes apply to the complex cluster of conflicts, involving myriad parties and participants, that may arise in any one situation. There are several historical examples of this,[64] though the conflict in Syria following the interventions by coalition forces against ISIS from 2014 takes the complexities of conflict classification to a new level.

iv) Syria: Epitomising Classification Conundra The Syrian conflict, which began as an uprising and escalated into a complex mosaic of overlapping armed conflicts, epitomises the classification challenges. We have identified the nature of the parties to the conflict as a central question for classification purposes, but even brief consideration of the array of actors participating in hostilities in Syria shows that this provides no easy answers.

First, there is an armed conflict between armed groups participating in the Syrian conflict, of which there are said to be hundreds, and the Syrian State. However repressive, and despite withdrawal of recognition by some States and the EU, Assad's government continues to represent Syria (it is not a failed State, for example)[65] and to constitute a State party to the conflict fighting

---

[62] ICRC, *The Geneva Convention (I) Commentary* 2016 (n. 35), Art. 2, para. 262.

[63] On caution in State practice labelling a conflict 'international' and discussion of Syria, see, Gill, 'Classifying the Conflict in Syria' 2016 (n. 31).

[64] See Gill, 'Classifying the Conflict in Syria' 2016 (n. 31), 353; Louise Arimatsu and Mohbuba Choudhury, 'The Legal Classification of the Armed Conflicts in Syria, Yemen and Libya', *International Law PP 2014/01* (London: Chatham House, 2014).

[65] Gill, 'Classifying the Conflict in Syria' 2016 (n. 31), 353.

against non-State armed groups. The State fights with foreign support –
militias provided with Iranian assistance, foreign fighters from Lebanon,
Iraq and Afghanistan, and Iranian and Russian military force. However, as
far as all this external intervention is on the side of the State, this would not
seem to affect the non-international nature of the conflict between the State's
forces and organised armed groups (OAGs).

Within this conflict, questions also arise as to the OAGs (which are diverse
in nature, organisation and *modi operandi*) of relevance to whether they – and
which of them – constitute parties to the conflict. Some fractioning and
breakaway groups, with shifting allegiances and relationships to one another,
is common in a NIAC, but for groups to be considered together to constitute
a party to a conflict there may need to be some level of cohesiveness, beyond
a shared enemy and overlapping goals. As such, it has been suggested that
there are most likely several non-State armed parties to the Syrian conflict(s),[66]
further problematising the scene.

A second armed conflict arose when Coalition States commenced aerial
operations against ISIS-held positions and forces in Syria in August 2014. The
United States led the coalition, consisting of a group of some ten Western and
regional States, most of which were also engaged in conducting operations
against ISIS in Iraq. Unlike in Iraq, the Syrian government has not consented
to the Coalition's operations, which it has characterised as violations of its
territorial sovereignty, raising the question of the relevance of consent in conflict
classification.[67] In turn, Coalition airstrikes have not targeted Syrian government forces, installations or territory held by government forces, but have
generally been directed against ISIS forces or resources they control, such as
oil installations.[68] Leaving aside controversial attacks against other non-State
groups, the conflict might then be said to be *directed* against ISIS, a NSA.

On one view of this situation, 'the US is at war with Syria'.[69] An
IAC between Syria and Coalition States arose from the use of force

---

[66] E.g., the Syrian National Coalition, the collective of non-State groups comprising allegedly
      Al-Qaeda linked groups (e.g., Al-Nusra Front) and ISIS; Gill, 'Classifying the Conflict in
      Syria' 2016 (n. 31).
[67] Nor did the Syrian government always actively oppose airstrikes, raising common questions
      around how to identify 'consent' or lack thereof.
[68] While there have been allegations by Syria of attacks on pro-government forces, the Coalition
      has reasserted that its conflict is with ISIS, see, 'Syria and Russia Condemn US-led Attack on
      pro-Assad Forces', BBC, 19 May 2017, available at: www.bbc.com/news/world-middle-east-
      39972271.
[69] Adil A. Haque, 'The United States is at War with Syria (according to the ICRC's New Geneva
      Conventions Commentary)', *EJIL:Talk!*, 8 April 2016, available at: www.ejiltalk.org/the-united-
      States-is-at-war-with-syria-according-to-the-icrcs-new-geneva-convention-commentary.

without State consent, whatever the States in question might say about it.[70] This view is apparently supported by the ICRC's position that if the territorial State does *not* consent to the use of force – even force directed exclusively at an organised armed group – then an IAC arises (albeit potentially alongside a NIAC with the armed groups).[71] Consequently, according to the ICRC's approach, the United States is both in a NIAC with ISIS *and* in an IAC with Syria, for example, and both branches of IHL govern different aspects of US military operations in Syria.[72] A murky factual and normative reality unfolds in which questions arise as to which operations, and the conduct of which actors, are governed by which body of law.[73]

Finally, for the sake of completeness it should be noted that there is most likely a third conflict involving the organised Kurdish forces which control territory in northern Syria (as there is between the Iraqi government and Kurdish forces in the Kurdish autonomous region of northern Iraq). A significant number of States have supported the Syrian or Iraqi govern-ments, and the United States has coordinated with the Kurdish groups to assist them in retaking control of key towns from ISIS. Turkey is in turn in conflict with these Kurdish militias, on the basis of alleged links to the PKK engaged in a separate conflict in southeast Turkey; questions arise as to whether this is a spill-over of that conflict or another separate conflict, raising several addi-tional issues regarding identification of parties and applicable law.[74]

The Syria conflict is emblematic of the complexity of modern conflicts and controversies around classification. While the ICRC's views on IHL applicability are extremely authoritative, its view that Coalition forces are engaged in an IAC in Syria is not uncontroversial.[75] A persuasive case is made that the asymmetric nature of the parties engaged in conflict means

---

[70] E.g., Brian Egan, 'International Law, Legal Diplomacy and the Counter-ISIL Campaign', Speech at the American Society of International Law, 1 April 2016, available at: www .justsecurity.org/wp-content/uploads/2016/04/Egan-ASIL-speech.pdf: 'Because we are engaged in an armed conflict against a non-State actor, our war against ISIL is a non-international armed conflict, or NIAC.'

[71] See, ICRC, *The Geneva Convention (I) Commentary* 2016 (n. 35), Art. 2, para. 261.

[72] Haque, 'The United States is at War with Syria (according to the ICRC's New Geneva Convention Commentary)' 2016 (n. 69).

[73] Different obligations may also arise as between the various States involved.

[74] There does not seem to be any serious suggestion the United States controls those troops, or that it is in conflict with Turkey, but the number of actors engaged renders the application of the law more complex.

[75] Gill, 'Classifying the Conflict in Syria' 2016 (n. 31).

that it remains non-international in nature despite the role of Coalition forces.[76]

Although the questions are, of course, legally distinct, the debate also reveals how controversy may again reflect, and be influenced by, the perceived impact of classification in practice. For example, it has been suggested that considering Coalition forces to be engaged in an IAC with Syria and a NIAC with ISIS, means civilians enjoy the extensive or at least explicit protections afforded by the law covering IACs,[77] without providing enhanced protection to ISIS fighters.[78] These distinctions and asserted implications are, however, far from straightforward. While a NIAC carries less specific IHL protections for detainees – as there is no prisoner of war (POW) status with additional rights and no specific provisions governing procedural guarantees – this does not equate with a legal gap as far as there are customary rules of IHL as well as applicable IHRL.[79] IHL rules on distinction and protection of civilians – and loss of protection for those participating in conflict – apply for both types of conflict and most of the serious allegations in the Syrian conflict would amount to violations, and war crimes, for either.[80] But there are a few exceptions (such as disproportionate attacks or starvation of the civilian population which arguably arise only in respect of IACs), which may in turn arguably have a potential impact on accountability potential.[81] The perceived implications may, however, be more political than normative or institutional. As one commentator has noted:

> Anyone who thinks that the coalition States presently engaged in an armed conflict with ISIS are also at war with Syria, Iran and Russia, should think again and do a serious reality check. This is not simply a question of academic purity

---

[76] *Ibid.*; *Practitioners' Guide* 2016 (n. 37).

[77] E.g., GCIV contains a range of protections for civilians in IAC that 'find themselves ... in the hands of a Party to the Conflict or Occupying power of which they are not nationals' (Art. 4), including protection of the right to religious and family rights (Arts. 27, 38(3)), freedom of movement (Arts. 35, 38(4)), the right to work (Art. 39), the right to humanitarian protection (Arts. 23, 38, 59). API also provides procedural and fair trial protections in this context (e.g., Art. 75 API).

[78] *Ibid.*

[79] See e.g., Section V on rules governing detentions; unlike for IAC, in NIAC, IHL may not provide a clear legal framework and IHRL has a stronger influence, providing basic non-derogable safeguards. There is no POW status during a NIAC.

[80] Allegations regarding, e.g., systematic targeting of civilians, denial of humanitarian assistance, among others, are covered by custom for either conflict, and prohibited in, e.g., Art. 6 ICC Statute.

[81] This is true at least as regards criminalisation under Art. 7 ICC Statute, though even in the unlikely event of ICC prosecution, these crimes overlap with and may well be prosecuted as other crimes.

in applying IHL, but one which has potentially far-reaching consequences. The adage of 'be careful what you wish for' is apropos in this context.[82]

Whatever view one takes of the Syrian conflict, it forces us to acknowledge the complexity surrounding classification of armed conflicts and applicable IHL today, and grapple with its implications. It may indeed highlight the inadequacy of the bifurcated classification of conflicts and of IHL, lending support to proponents of a unified approach down the line. What is clear for now is that classification and applicable IHL depend on a sometimes highly complex factual assessment of the nature of the parties and their relationships – involving multiple States in diverse roles, and myriad armed groups – and to an extent the force employed, with the result that within any one broad armed conflict scenario, there may be IAC, NIAC or multiple variants of each.

c) MATERIAL APPLICABILITY: NON-INTERNATIONAL ARMED CONFLICTS The classification of NIAC under IHL is generally considered more complex than that of IACs.[83] IHL treaty law provides little guidance, providing only negative definitions by exclusion. Armed conflict does *not* cover 'internal disturbances and tensions [or] isolated and sporadic acts of violence'.[84] Common Article 3 negatively refers to conflicts '*not* of an international character'. Additional Protocol 2 to the Geneva Conventions does contain certain additional thresholds for the applicability of that protocol (including control of territory), but it is well established that this does not purport to be a threshold for NIAC, only for that particular protocol to apply. Thus, while APII conflicts are one type of NIAC, they do not qualify – or provide guidance on – the definition and scope of NIACs.[85]

In this context, the ICTY as the first modern international tribunal charged with giving effect to IHL through the prosecution of war crimes, stepped into the breach. It set down twofold criteria for a NIAC: the use of force of some intensity or duration and the nature and organisation of the non-State parties.

i) Intensity NIAC clearly involves armed force that meets a threshold beyond the tensions and 'sporadic' acts of violence that are explicitly excluded. There is some difference of approach as to how best to characterise this intensity threshold however. The ICTY,[86] and the ICC Statute

---

82 Gill, 'Classifying the Conflict in Syria' 2016 (n. 31).
83 32nd International Conference of the ICRC 2015 (n. 52), 8.
84 Article 1(2) API.
85 Article 1(1) APII.
86 See the definition first advanced in ICTY, *Tadić*, Trial Chamber Judgment (n. 5).

and jurisprudence,[87] have both referred to 'protracted' violence. They do so somewhat differently, with *Tadić* suggesting protracted violence as an element of the definition, whereas the ICC more recently affirming that the groups involved need to have the *ability* to plan and carry out operations 'for a prolonged period of time'[88] (overlapping with the second criterion below on the nature and capacity of the groups).

Later judgments of the ICTY, such as the *Haradinaj* judgment, placed the emphasis on the *intensity* rather than the duration of violence.[89] This approach is arguably consistent with the general exclusion historically of many situations of long-running NSA violence from the definition of conflict[90] (though, as noted, politics and the positions of the States may be the more influential factor).[91] Conversely, where intense armed hostilities broke out between Israel and Hezbollah in Lebanon in July 2006, or attacks on ISIS in 2014, the debate was immediately on the *nature* of the conflict(s), supporting the view that duration is not a prerequisite. One question to arise is whether, in practice, the cross-border nature of the use of force has prompted a more flexible approach to intensity and any duration requirement.[92]

In any event, the basic rule for NIACs as a matter of law is that the force in question must be of a certain intensity; it will generally also be prolonged, to be sufficiently sustained to surpass the excluded sporadic violence, but this will not always be the case. The law does not attempt to identify precisely the sort of factual scenarios in which the intensity threshold is met, which will always be a question of applying the broad twofold legal framework to the particular facts.

The ICTY has identified certain intensity 'indicators' which assist in this assessment. They include the number of confrontations, types of weaponry used, and the extent of injuries and destruction.[93] The motivation or purpose

---

[87] Article 8 refers to 'protracted armed conflict between government and armed groups or between such groups' for war crimes, though this may be a threshold for ICC purposes, not for NIACs as such. See also, Akande, 'Classification of Armed Conflicts: Relevant Legal Concepts' 2012 (n. 50), 56; ICC, *Lubanga*, Judgment (n. 40).

[88] ICC, *Prosecutor v. Thomas Lubanga Dyilo*, Case No. ICC-01/04-01/06, Decision on the Confirmation of Charges of 28 January 2007, para. 234.

[89] ICTY, *Prosecutor v. Ramush Haradinaj*, Case No. IT-04-84-T, Trial Chamber Judgment of 3 April 2008 (hereinafter: ICTY, *Haradinaj*, Trial Chamber Judgment), paras. 49, 60.

[90] It may be argued that ETA or the IRA were not widely regarded as engaged in armed conflict, perhaps influenced by intensity considerations at any one time, among others.

[91] Duffy, *War on Terror* 2015 (n. 7), ch. 6.

[92] Of course, if the cross border force gave rise to an IAC, the threshold would not apply, though one question is whether cross-border NIACs may justify a similar approach.

[93] ICTY, *Haradinaj*, Trial Chamber Judgment (n. 89).

of the violence does not emerge from jurisprudence, or elsewhere, as a relevant part of the test.[94] Factually, it may be that what most flagrantly distinguishes armed conflict from the intense violence associated with 'organised crime' in Latin America, for example, is its very different ideological or political purpose, though the purpose of the violence, the actors' objectives or perhaps even legitimacy have no obvious relevance under existing law. At present these groups' *raison d'être* would appear principally to have a bearing on whether they meet the second criterion, relating to the nature of parties to the conflict.

ii) Nature of the Parties A key question of contemporary significance relates to when an armed non-State entity may constitute a party to an armed conflict. IHL requires that non-State (sometimes called 'insurgent') groups must be capable of identification as a party and have attained a certain degree of internal organisation for IHL to operate effectively. What this means has been clarified and expanded upon by the first level of adjudication, the work of international criminal tribunals.

The ICTY again led the way (and others followed) in identifying several 'indicators' or 'non-exhaustive criteria' to establish whether the organisational requirement is fulfilled.[95] These include the existence of a command structure and disciplinary rules and systems within the group; potentially (but not necessarily) the existence of an operational headquarters; the ability to procure arms and to plan and carry out controlled military operations; the extent, the seriousness and intensity of the group's military operations; and their ability to coordinate and negotiate settlement of the conflict. Control of territory is not a requirement to constitute a party to a NIAC (only a jurisdictional threshold for Additional Protocol II as noted above), but it may provide a strong indicator that the non-State entity has the requisite military organisation and *modus operandi*. Finally, while compliance with IHL is not itself a criterion, the group must be *capable* of observing and ensuring respect from their ranks with the rules of IHL, on which the framework of IHL rules and principles of distinction and responsibility rest. Domestic courts have also grappled with the criteria, and as one recent UK Supreme Court judgment put it, in somewhat different terms: 'in short, the test is whether the operations conducted by NSAs are characteristic of those conducted by the armed forces of the State, as

---

[94] See, e.g., preamble of API – application without distinction based on 'causes', and the key legal criteria for armed conflict set out in this section.

[95] See the ICTY in several cases, including the *Haradinaj*, Trial Chamber Judgment (n. 89), followed by the ICC in *Lubanga* case (n. 40).

opposed to its police force'.[96] Whatever its precise contours, the test requires close consideration of the particular group's structure, operations and capability.

iii) Transnational Terrorism as NIAC? The qualification of a NIAC and, in particular, the requirements for constituting a party, set out above, lie at the heart of controversies surrounding the use of force by and against 'terrorist' organisations and networks.[97] The question of whether terrorist groups can be parties to a conflict is not a question that can be answered in the abstract but depends on whether, in particular contexts, the criteria for NIAC are met.

The question emerged most dramatically post-9/11, where a chasm of significant practical import separated the US view on global armed conflict with 'Al-Qaeda and associated groups', and a sceptical majority. Since 9/11, successive US administrations have argued, in varying forms of words, that there was (is) an armed conflict of global reach with Al-Qaeda and 'associated' forces, and more recently with a broader network of violent extremist groups.[98] The position of the Bush administration originally suggested that this conflict was akin to an international conflict, albeit a 'new kind of war' that did not fit into any of the IHL categories, which ran alongside the conflicts in Afghanistan and Iraq.[99] The Obama administration abandoned the 'war on terror' epithet,[100] but (as seen in the government's position in litigation brought by war on terror victims, for example) the assertion of an armed conflict with Al-Qaeda and associated forces remained intact.[101] The groups purportedly embroiled in the conflict have expanded to include disparate groups.[102] This conflict, once considered

---

[96] UKSC, *Abd Ali Hameed Al-Waheed (Appellant) v. Ministry of Defence (Respondent)* and *Serdar Mohammed (Respondent) v. Ministry of Defence* (Appellant), Judgment of 17 January 2017, [2017] UKSC 2, para. 11.

[97] Duffy, *War on Terror* 2015 (n. 7), ch. 6B.

[98] Bush and Obama administrations, *ibid.*

[99] Duffy, *War on Terror* 2015 (n. 7), ch. 6.

[100] Al Kamen, 'The End of the Global War on Terror', *The Washington Post*, 24 March 2009, available at: http://voices.washingtonpost.com/44/2009/03/23/the_end_of_the_global_war_on_t.html, on how the 'Global War on Terror' was changed to 'Overseas Contingency Operation'.

[101] E.g., Barack Obama, 'Remarks by the President on National Security', The White House Office of the Press Secretary, 21 May 2009, available at: https://obamawhitehouse.archives.gov/the-press-office/remarks-president-national-security-5-21-09. For others, and broad continuity in the Obama presidency's approach to litigation, see Duffy, *War on Terror* 2015 (n. 7), ch. 6B.1. Obama outlined the position in several speeches in 2009, 2013 and 2016.

[102] Al-Shabaab is described as an Al-Qaeda affiliate, and ISIS as ideologically similar but operationally distant from Al-Qaeda, having significant territorial control at its height, and its use of Hezbollah's model of service provision to the civilian population: Press Briefing by Press Secretary Josh Earnest, The White House, 7 March 2016, available at: www.whitehouse.gov/

international,[103] came to be seen by the administration as non-international in
nature.[104]

Few would doubt that an entity, such as ISIS at the height of its control
in Syria or Iraq – militarily organised, extremely violent, controlling
territory, exerting strict control over persons and territory, and dispensing
brutal discipline – would meet the criteria of a party to an armed conflict.
Whether there is global conflict with ISIS, Al-Shabaab and others, embracing distinct groups and the apparently quite separate conflicts in Syria,
Iraq and Somalia supposedly alongside a broader conflict, is a different
matter – giving rise to the same basis for scepticism as earlier incarnations
of the war on terror.[105] Whether the cluster of supposed affiliates,[106] many
of which are quite separate and distinct, some of which have split from
and been in conflict with one another at certain junctures,[107] can be said
to cohere into one party to this conflict is more doubtful still. There is
scant support for a 'network of networks',[108] 'a series of loosely connected
operational and support cells',[109] or even 'a far-reaching network of

the-press-office/2016/03/07/press-briefing-press-secretary-josh-earnest-372016; Charlie Savage,
Eric Schmitt and Mark Mazzetti, 'Obama Expands War With Al Qaeda to Include Shabab
in Somalia', *New York Times*, 27 November 2016, available at: www.nytimes.com/2016/11/27/us/
politics/obama-expands-war-with-al-qaeda-to-include-shabab-in-somalia.html.

[103] See, e.g., Jelena Pejic, '"Unlawful/Enemy Combatants": Interpretations and Consequences',
in Michael Schmitt and Jelena Pejic (eds.), *International Law and Armed Conflict: Exploring
the Faultlines* (Leiden: Koninklijke Brill, 2007), 335–55 (341).

[104] See, e.g. Speech of 1 April 2016 by Brian Egan, US State Department Legal Advisor,
'International Law, Legal Diplomacy, and the Counter-ISIL Campaign: Some
Observations', *International Law Studies* 92 (2016), 235–48 (242). Support was found
in the decision of the US Supreme Court in *Hamdan v. Rumsfeld*, 29 June 2006, 548
US 557, 630, which found that CA3 would apply irrespective of the nature of the
conflict, but is cited as finding that the global conflict with Al-Qaeda and others was a
NIAC.

[105] There is little doubt the conflict in Iraq is a NIAC given State consent to the Coalition's
intervention, while controversy surrounds the status of the Syrian intervention (see Section II.
A.1.b).

[106] Peter Margulies and Matthew Sinot, 'Crossing Borders to Target Al-Qaeda and Its Affiliates:
Defining Networks as Organized Armed Groups in Non-International Armed Conflicts',
Yearbook of International Humanitarian Law 16 (2013), 319–45.

[107] UNHRC, 'Report of the Independent International Commission of Inquiry on the Syrian
Arab Republic', 13 August 2015, UN Doc. A/HRC/30/48, 3–6. See also, 'Syria al-Qaeda Group
Gives Rival Jihadists Ultimatum', BBC, 8 February 2017, available at: www.bbc.com/news/
world-middle-east-26338341.

[108] Noam Lubell, 'The War(?) against Al-Qaeda', Wilmshurst (ed.), *Classification of Conflicts*
2012 (n. 2), 421–54 (424).

[109] See SC, Letter dated 19 September 2002 from the Chairman of the Security Council
Committee established pursuant to Resolution 1267 of 1999 concerning Afghanistan

violence and hatred"[110] meeting the requirements of a structured organisation, under military command and control, as envisaged by IHL.[111]

Most other States,[112] the ICRC, other inter-governmental organisations and authoritative commentators have overwhelmingly rejected the notion of a potentially global armed conflict with Al-Qaeda and associated groups.[113] Recent attacks in Europe saw the re-emergence of global war rhetoric–terror attacks as *'actes de guerre'* for example – underscoring the importance of clarity as to whether (and, if so, in what circumstances) there is, or can be, a conflict with terrorist networks such as Al-Qaeda, ISIS or others.[114] Looked at more closely, however, these explicitly did not amount to a US-style assertion of a wide-reaching NIAC on terrorist groups.[115]

Overreaching assertions of a global war on terrorist groups must be distinguished from the fact that some groups (rightly or wrongly) labelled 'terrorist' may constitute parties to particular, defined armed conflicts, as they have throughout history and across the globe.[116] Whether the legal criteria are met needs to be assessed in particular contexts and over time.[117]

addressed to the President of the Security Council, 20 September 2002, UN Doc. S/2002/1050. See also, UK cases, 'Special Immigration Appeals Commission (SIAC), "Generic Determination"', 29 October 2003, cases SC/1/2002; SC/6/2002; SC/7/2002; SC/9/2002; SC/10/2002, para. 130.

[110] Barack Obama, Inaugural Address, 21 January 2009, available at: https://obamawhitehouse .archives.gov/blog/2009/01/21/president-barack-obamas-inaugural-address: 'Our nation is at war, against a far-reaching network of violence and hatred.'

[111] See, e.g., Gill, 'Classifying the Conflict in Syria' 2016 (n. 31), on the nature of parties in Syria, and similar analysis re Al-Qaeda in 2008 in Marja Lehto, 'War on Terror – Armed Conflict with Al Qaeda?', *Nordic Journal of International Law* 78 (2009), 499–511 (508).

[112] Attacks in London, Madrid, Denmark, Belgium and elsewhere did not provoke claims from affected States that an armed conflict had arisen, and indeed those governments distanced themselves from the war paradigm. Examples of State practice and Statements at Duffy, *War on Terror* 2015 (n. 7), ch. 6B.1.

[113] See, e.g., ICRC, 28th International Conference of the Red Cross and Red Crescent, International Humanitarian Law and the Challenges of Contemporary Armed Conflicts, 2–6 December 2003, Report, December 2003, 03/IC/09: 'the ICRC does not share the view that a global war is being waged and it takes a case-by-case approach to the legal qualification of situations of violence'.

[114] President Hollande referred to the Paris attacks (2015) as an 'act of war' ('Hollande Calls Paris Attacks an "Act of War"', *Al Jazeera*, 14 November 2015, available at: www.aljazeera.com/news/ 2015/11/hollande-paris-france-attacks-concern-stadium-isil-151114103631610.html), but distanced himself subsequently. See Anthony Dworkin, 'France Maps Out its War against Islamic State', European Council on Foreign Relations, 19 November 2015, available at: www.ecfr .eu/article/commentary_france_maps_out_its_war_against_the_islamic_state5021.

[115] Hollande Statement, and Dworkin, *ibid.*

[116] See, Duffy, *War on Terror* 2015 (n. 7), ch. 6.

[117] Claus Kreβ, 'Some Reflections on the International Legal Framework Governing Transnational Armed Conflicts', *Journal of Conflict & Security Law* 15 (2010), 245–74 (261);

Relevant questions of fact include whether particular groups have sufficient organisation, structure, membership and capability to enforce IHL,[118] but also critically the relationship between diverse groups deemed to constitute the party to the conflict, and whether they have sufficient cohesion (while certainly absolute unity is not required[119]). Identifying the alleged 'party', and those 'directly participating' on its behalf, is impossible if comprised of disparate regional, national, local or individual manifestations of a broadly similar ideology, rather than a structured organisation. The stated positions – whether by the authors of attacks or by States seeking to invoke IHL rules on targeting – do not change the answers to these factual questions. The logic, structure and effective operation of IHL depend precisely on the ability to identify and distinguish the opposing party, with critical implications for targeting and humanitarian protection.[120]

d) APPLICATION *RATIONE MATERIAE*: BELLIGERENT OCCUPATION Finally, the material applicability of IHL (specifically the 1949 Geneva Conventions and API) to situations of occupation is, as a matter of theory at least, relatively straightforward, as reflected in the treaties themselves.[121] The definitional deficit is again apparent as far as there is no definition of occupation in the Geneva Conventions, although Article 42 of the 1907 Hague Regulations, which refers to 'territory actually placed under the control of the hostile army', is broadly considered to reflect customary international law.[122] Common Article 2 makes clear that a situation of occupation can exist even where the occupying forces met with no armed resistance. IHL is therefore potentially applicable to all situations in which territory is taken over by armed forces which replace the authority of the

---

the Director of the FBI referred to the al-Qaeda 'franchise model' – Robert Mueller, Director FBI, 'From 9/11 to 7/7: Global Terrorism Today and the Challenges of Tomorrow', Chatham House, 7 April 2008, available at: www.chathamhouse.org/sites/default/files/public/Meetings/Meeting%20Transcripts/070408mueller.pdf.

[118]   ICTY, *Haradinaj*, Trial Chamber Judgment (n. 89), paras. 49, 60; ICTY, *Prosecutor v. Boškoski*, Case No. IT-04-82-T, Trial Chamber Judgment of 10 July 2008, paras. 194–205, and generally, Marko Sassòli and Laura Olson, 'The Relationship between International Humanitarian and Human Rights Law where it Matters: Admissible Killing and Internment of Fighters in Non-international Armed Conflicts', *International Review of the Red Cross* 90 (2008), 599–627.

[119]   See Gill, 'Classifying the Conflict in Syria' 2016 (n. 31).

[120]   See ICRC, 'Challenges of Contemporary Armed Conflicts' 2011 (n. 17), 19.

[121]   See Common Art. 2 Geneva Conventions and Art. 1(3) API.

[122]   ICJ, *Legal Consequences of the Construction of a Wall in the Occupied Palestinian Territory*, Advisory Opinion of 9 July 2004, ICJ Reports 2004, 136, paras. 78, 89; ICJ, *Armed Activities on the Territory of the Congo* (Democratic Republic of the Congo v. Uganda), Judgment of 19 December 2005, ICJ Reports 2005, 168, para. 172.

ousted sovereign, giving rise to obvious and broad overlap with IHRL, to which we now turn.[123] As this section has shown, the law on the material applicability of IHL has developed and been clarified in recent years – largely through international adjudication. However, there are unquestionably areas of complexity and controversy as to IHL applicability, just as there are in relation to the overlapping human rights framework.

2. Applicability *Ratione Materiae* of International Human Rights Law

Whereas IHL is applicable exceptionally in times of conflict, the starting point for an assessment of the applicability of IHRL is universality. It is in the essence of IHRL that it applies, in principle, at all times and to all people by virtue of their humanity.

As noted above, while at one time the applicability of IHRL in conflict situations in general was seriously questioned, international authority and opinion now overwhelmingly confirms that IHRL continues to apply in times of armed conflict.[124] The proposition enjoys extensive acceptance by States.[125] It has been affirmed by the ICJ on several occasions.[126] As discussed below in Section III, it is further supported by the increasingly consistent view of other international and regional courts, treaty bodies and special procedures, as well as the ICRC,[127] regional political bodies,[128] the United Nations Security Council and General Assembly, among others.[129]

There are, of course, also those who disagree. State practice from the United States and Israel specifically has drawn most attention for the refusal to accept IHRL applicability in particular situations of armed conflict (and in relation to extraterritoriality explored under *ratione loci* below).[130] The nature of their positions, and responses to them, are seen, for example, in deliberations before

---

[123] See Kleffner, 'Scope of Application of International Humanitarian Law' 2013 (n. 47), 205. Section IV on co-applicability.

[124] States, ICJ, ICRC, human rights courts and bodies and UN bodies, referred to in this section.

[125] E.g., Hampson, 'The Relationship between International Humanitarian Law and Human Rights Law from the Perspective of a Human Rights Treaty Body' 2008 (n. 3), 549–50.

[126] First confirmed by the ICJ in *Legality of the Threat or Use of Nuclear Weapons*, Advisory Opinion of 8 July 1996, ICJ Reports 1996, 226, para. 25; ICJ, *Legality of the Consequences of the Construction of a Wall* (n. 122), paras. 105–6; ICJ, *Armed Activities* (n. 122), para. 216.

[127] *ICRC Customary Study* 2005 (n. 22).

[128] See, e.g., Peace and Security Council of the African Union, Statement on Libya, Communiqué of 23 February 2011, PSC/PR/COMM(CCLXI).

[129] See, e.g., SC Res. 1019 of 9 November 1995 and GA Res. 50/193 of 22 December 1995 (Former Yugoslavia); SC Res. 1653 of 27 January 2006 (Great Lakes); GA Res. 46/135 of 19 December 1991 (Kuwait under Iraqi occupation), among others.

[130] See, e.g., Concluding observations of the Committee against Torture (CAT) on the periodic reports of the United States regretting 'the State party's opinion that the Convention is not applicable in times and in the context of armed conflict' (18 May 2006, CAT/C/USA/CO/2, at

human rights bodies.[131] The fact the US position shifted even slightly, to acknowledge continued application of IHRL in conflict situations in principle,[132] may itself be an indication of the extent of the shift internationally. In any event, in the light of the sea change on the international level, the key areas of legal dispute are now located in *how* the framework operates in theory and in practice in conflict situations, not *whether* it is applicable at all.

IHRL is clearly far broader in its scope than IHL. In stark contrast to the status determinations and principle of distinction at the core of IHL, IHRL is based on universality, and explicitly applies 'without distinction' based on nationality, residence, sex, origin, race, religion, language or other status. It consists of a system of international norms designed to secure a baseline of protection for all, reflecting the inherent value of all human persons. This fundamental purpose may, in turn, be reflected in the momentum towards an inclusive approach to IHRL applicability. This is seen not only in relation to applicability in armed conflict in general, but in relation to personal and geographic scope, as seen in relation to evolution of approaches to non-State actors, and extraterritorial application, as addressed below.

B. Applicability Ratione Personae: *Personal Applicability*

1. Personal Scope of Duty-bearers under IHL and IHRL

IHRL and IHL are, at least in part, directed at different actors, which has often been cited as a crucial area of divergence.[133] As branches of international law, both impose obligations on States. But IHL binds parties to armed conflict be they State or non-State 'organised armed groups'.[134] While perhaps less

---

para. 14). See also the fourth periodic report of the United States to the UNHRC (30 December 2011, CCPR/C/USA/4, at para. 507). UNHRC, Consideration of reports submitted by States parties under article 40 of the Covenant pursuant to the optional reporting procedure, Fourth periodic reports of States parties, Israel, 14 October 2013, UN Doc. CCPR/C/ISR/4, 12 December 2013, para. 47, recognising debates but asserting that the regimes apply in different circumstances.

[131] *Ibid.*

[132] UNHRC, Consideration of reports submitted by States parties under article 40 of the Covenant, Fourth periodic report, United States of America, 30 December 2011, UN Doc. CCPR/C/USA/4, 22 May 2012, para. 507, acknowledging that 'Determining the international law rule that applies to a particular action [in] armed conflict is a fact-specific determination.' The United States, however, resists applicability to relevant issues raised by the UNHRC, such as detentions, renditions and targeted killings.

[133] Sandesh Sivakumaran, 'Re-envisaging the International Law of Internal Armed Conflict', *European Journal of International Law* 22 (2011), 219–64 (240–2).

[134] For obligations on non-party State parties to the Geneva Conventions, see Art. 1.

straightforward to explain doctrinally, this has now long been accepted, a corollary of factual developments in the nature of conflict and its participants. By contrast, IHRL was traditionally seen to impose obligations on States, which were later accepted as extending to international organisations, and it still struggles to grapple with factual realities around NSA responsibility, arguably hampering its relevance in the modern world. The disparity between State and non-State parties to a conflict (both of whom would be bound by IHL and only the former also by IHRL) has been cited – in the author's view unconvincingly – also as an impediment to co-applicability, and the role of human rights courts, given supposedly 'lop-sided obligations'.[135] It is therefore particularly noteworthy that IHRL may in fact also be evolving in this regard, albeit falteringly, as seen by the growing body of international *practice* referring to the obligations of non-State armed groups under IHRL in certain circumstances.

It has been suggested by the CAT that when non-State armed groups exercise functions normally associated with a State, they 'may be equated to State officials for the purposes of certain human rights obligations'.[136] Likewise, in conflict situations where the NSA controls an area of a State's territory, such that the State can no longer exercise its protective function and there would otherwise be a 'vacuum of protection',[137] growing international practice – from the UN Human Rights Council (UNHRC), Commissions of Inquiry, UN Special Rapporteurs and others – refers to non-State groups' human rights obligations.[138] The Libya Commission reporting to the UNHRC described it as 'increasingly accepted that where non-State groups exercise de facto control over territory they must respect fundamental human rights of persons in that territory'.[139] The former UN Special Rapporteur on

---

[135] Jelena Pejic, 'Conflict Classification and the Law Applicable to Detention and the Use of Force', in Wilmshurst (ed.), *Classification of Conflicts* 2012 (n. 2), 80–116 (115). In the author's view this does not reflect the nature of States' IHRL obligations.

[136] CAT, *Sadiq Shek Elmi v. Australia*, Communication No. 120/1998, 25 May 1999, UN Doc. CAT/C/22/D/120/1998, para. 6.5.

[137] E.g., ECtHR, *Al-Skeini v. United Kingdom*, Grand Chamber Judgment of 7 July 2011, Application No. 55721/07 (ECtHR, *Al-Skeini v. United Kingdom*), para. 142, and principles of interpretation at Section IV. State responsibility may also, or alternatively, arise where NSAs control the area but States control the NSAs: see, e.g., *Ilaşcu and Others v. Moldova and Russia*, Grand Chamber Judgment of 8 July 2004, Application No. 48797/99; *Catan and Others v. Moldova and Russia*, Grand Chamber Judgment of 19 October 2012, Application Nos. 43370/04, 8252/05 and 18454/06.

[138] See, e.g., Andrew Clapham, 'Non State Actors', in Daniel Moeckli, Sangeeta Shah and Sandesh Sivakumaran (eds.), *International Human Rights Law*, 3rd edn. (Oxford University Press, 2018), 557–79.

[139] UNHRC, Report of the International Commission of Inquiry to investigate all alleged violations of international human rights law in the Libyan Arab Jamahiriya, 1 June 2011, UN Doc. A/HRC/17/44, para. 72.

Terrorism and Human Rights reached similar conclusions in relation to
ISIS.[140] Peace accords or truth commissions provide further recognition of
'gross violations of human rights and international humanitarian law by all
warring factions',[141] implying that IHRL applied to all sides in the first place.[142]

Recognising, at least implicitly, that such groups do not ratify and are not
strictly bound by IHRL treaties, reference is often made to customary international law as binding, in principle on States and NSAs alike. The Syrian
Commission, which found anti-government armed groups could be 'assessed
against customary international law principles', is one example.[143]

A pinch of legal salt may sometimes be needed in assessing the significance
of broad references to violence by 'rebels, terrorist groups and other organised
transnational criminal networks' as human rights violations as such.[144] But
such references, often in the context of an armed conflict, reflect a growing
tendency to see IHRL as somehow relevant alongside IHL to evaluating the
conduct of non-State armed groups.

It is also noteworthy that most of the shifts towards recognising NSA
responsibility (apart from corporate responsibility) arise in respect of
armed groups in armed conflict situations. The influence of IHL on the
development of IHRL appears to loom large. Not least, IHL speaks to IHRL
on the fact that, while there are huge challenges to enforcement (under
either area of law), NSA responsibility for human rights violations is hardly
implausible. As far as it may now be arguable that OAGs have obligations
under both bodies of law, it remains to be seen whether IHL will have
a normative influence on IHRL as regards a definition of such groups,[145] or

---

[140] UNHRC, Report of the Special Rapporteur on the promotion and protection of human rights
      and fundamental freedoms while countering terrorism, Ben Emmerson, 16 June 2015, UN
      Doc. A/HRC/29/51.
[141] Sierra Leone Truth and Reconciliation Commission, 'Witness to Truth', *Report* (Accra: GPL
      Press, 2004), vol. 1, ch. 2, para. 23. See also Guatemala Commission for Historical
      Clarification, 'Guatemala: Memory of Silence', Conclusions and Recommendations,
      Report, 1999, para. 21.
[142] Clapham, 'Non State Actors' 2018 (n. 138), 280.
[143] See others in Andrew Clapham, 'Introduction', in Andrew Clapham (ed.), *Human Rights
      and Non-State Actors* (Cheltenham: Elgar, 2013), xxii.
[144] UNHRC, Senegal (on behalf of the Group of African States): draft resolution, 20/ . . .
      Situation of human rights in the Republic of Mali, 3 July 2012, UN Doc. A/HRC/20/L.20,
      para. 2 on Mali. States undoubtedly have positive human rights obligations to prevent and
      respond, whether the NSA itself has legal responsibility.
[145] Marko Sassòli, 'The Role of Human Rights and International Humanitarian Law in New
      Types of Armed Conflicts', in Ben-Naftali (ed.), *International Humanitarian Law and
      International Human Rights Law* 2011 (n. 6), 34–94 (56).

whether a distinct approach will follow the different purpose and content of the areas of law.[146]

Convergence and progress in applicability *rationae personae* should not be overstated. States remain the focus of IHRL obligations. It is unclear to what extent international law has yet shifted, or if we are hearing a clarion call from diverse actors for progressive development to keep pace with reality. In addition, while issues of enforcement and mechanisms are, and should perhaps be kept, distinct from the existence of obligations, the whole architecture of the international legal system remains State-centric. We are a long way from individuals being able to enforce rights vis-à-vis non-State armed groups on the international level.[147] While there are indications of the role that national courts can and do play, such as the recent decision of the Swedish District Court that non-State armed groups had the capacity to ensure particular rights in certain situations,[148] in general this is rarely possible domestically either.[149] There is, however, growing engagement by international entities, NGOs and others with NSAs of various types, and trends towards recognition of some form of NSA responsibility.[150] While the gap remains, contemporary practice seems determined to bridge it.

2. Rights-bearers under IHL and IHRL?

Finally, although not strictly speaking a question *ratione personae*, the nature or scope of the beneficiaries of the relevant rules is worthy of brief comment. It is often noted that IHL was traditionally formulated in terms of rules of conduct for States and armed groups, not in terms of rights for individuals. This stands in obvious contrast to IHRL, which has at its core

---

[146] Note, e.g., the European Court of Justice in *Aboubacar Diakité v. Commissaire general aux réfugiés et aux apatrides*, Fourth Chamber Judgment of 30 January 2014, on a Preliminary Ruling, Case C-285/12, suggested armed conflict for refugee purposes is not the same as for IHL. Non-State actors are not now defined in IHRL.

[147] Section III. See, e.g., lack of a regional mechanism in Asia and much of the Middle East, and limited State acceptance of treaty bodies. See further, Duffy, *Strategic Human Rights Litigation* 2018 (n. 25), ch. 2.

[148] Jonathan Somer, 'Opening the Floodgates, Controlling the Flow: Swedish Court Rules on the Legal Capacity of Armed Groups to Establish Courts', *EJIL:Talk!*, 10 March 2017, available at: www.ejiltalk.org/opening-the-floodgates-controlling-the-flow-swedish-court-rules-on-the-legal-capacity-of-armed-groups-to-establish-courts.

[149] Helen Duffy, 'Non-State Actors in the Americas: Challenging International Law?' *Grotius Working Paper* (2018).

[150] See, e.g., the practice of 'deeds of commitment' on IHL and associated monitoring by NGO Geneva Call; major NGOs such as Human Rights Watch now routinely address non-State actor violations.

the conferral of rights, vis-à-vis the State, and which incontrovertibly enshrines both rights and obligations.

However, this distinction was never clear cut.[151] A number of rules of IHL are formulated in terms of rights,[152] while other provisions provide for the protection of civil and political rights as well as economic, social and cultural rights, whether or not framed as such.[153] More broadly, many (though certainly not all) IHL rules may be seen as seeking to give effect to the right of persons to protection, albeit taking into account military necessity and the peculiarities of armed conflicts. There may then be primary rights under IHL, independent of the separate question of whether they are enforceable by the individual against the State in respect of violations, where multiple challenges arise.[154] In this respect it is worth recalling, however, the UN Principles on the Right to a Remedy which may contribute to the narrowing gap by confirming victims' rights to a remedy in relation to violations of either area of law.[155]

C. *Applicability* Ratione Loci: *the Question of Geographic Scope*

Another area of difference, overlap and a degree of complexity is the geographic scope of applicability of IHL and IHRL. This is an issue of considerable controversy in respect of each body of law.

---

[151]   See generally, Peters, *Beyond Human Rights* 2016 (n. 18), ch. 7.

[152]   See, Liesbeth Zegveld, 'Remedies for Victims of Violations of International Humanitarian Law', *International Review of the Red Cross* 85 (2003), 497–527 (497); Vito Todeschini, 'Emerging Voices: The Right to a Remedy in Armed Conflict – International Humanitarian Law, Human Rights Law and the Principle of Systemic Integration', *Opinio Juris*, 5 August 2015, available at: opiniojuris.org/2015/08/05/emerging-voices-the-right-to-a-remedy-in-armed-conflict-international-humanitarian-law-human-rights-law-and-the-principle-of-systemic-integration.

[153]   Examples of such 'rights' include the rights of persons whose liberty is restricted, of families to know the fate of their relatives, to compensation, of POWs to be repatriated after the conflict, while others framed differently may include, e.g., the right to life of enemies placed hors de combat, to judicial guarantees of the wounded and the sick to be protected, collected and cared for, to health and food, and group rights, e.g., the right to a healthy environment.

[154]   Peters, *Beyond Human Rights* 2016 (n. 18), ch. 7.2, on 'secondary rights of individuals' in armed conflict *de lege lata*, referring to courts in several States having recognised at times primary 'rights', but rejected claims by individuals as the right of claim was held to correspond to the State of nationality.

[155]   UN Basic Principles and Guidelines on the Right to a Remedy and Reparation for Victims of Gross Violations of International Human Rights Law and Serious Violations of International Humanitarian Law, GA Res. 60/147 of 16 December 2005, UN Doc. A/RES/60/147, 21 March 2005 (hereinafter the UN Basic Principles).

1. The Geographic Scope of Applicability of IHL

Treaty law is silent as to the precise geographical scope of IHL. Both Common Article 3 and Additional Protocol II may on their face suggest a broad applicability throughout the entire territory of the State where the conflict is occurring. International criminal adjudication has once again weighed in and ventured something like a definition of scope, albeit in a way that leaves some questions unanswered.[156]

A) THROUGHOUT THE TERRITORIES? According to the ICTY Appeals Chamber, 'international humanitarian law continues to apply in the whole territory of the warring States or, in the case of internal conflicts, the whole territory under the control of a party, whether or not actual combat takes place there',[157] However traditional assumptions that IHL applies throughout the territories of parties to a conflict and not beyond them, are increasingly questioned as both over-expansive and under-inclusive.

It has been noted, for example, that: 'the existence of a NIAC in a limited portion of a State's overall territory cannot serve as the legal basis for the unqualified application of IHL to any and all situations of civil unrest and violence within that State'.[158] In support of this view, the ICRC conference drafting process to Additional Protocol II records that government experts 'considered it inconceivable that, in the case of a disturbance in one specific part of a territory (in a town, for instance) the whole territory of the State should be subjected to the application of the Protocol'.[159]

There is, therefore, a need for a somewhat fluid, and context-specific, approach to applicability, reflecting real-life conflict scenarios. IHL is not applicable *in abstracto*, but to particular conduct with a nexus to the armed conflict. This is a question of fact, in the determination of which geographic parameters may be one factor among others. Much may also depend on the rule in question: it is inherent in the different rules that some, such as on conduct of hostilities, will apply only where there is fighting, while others, say

---

[156] Noam Lubell and Nathan Derejko, 'A Global Battlefield? Drones and the Geographical Scope of Armed Conflict', *Journal of International Criminal Justice* 11 (2013), 65–88.

[157] ICTY, *Tadić*, Appeal Chamber Judgment (n. 51), para. 70. For NIACs, see ICTR, *Prosecutor v. Jean-Paul Akayesu*, Case No. ICTR-96-4-T, Trial Chamber Judgment of 2 September 1998, para. 635; Kleffner, 'Scope of Application of International Humanitarian Law' 2013 (n. 47), 59.

[158] Lubell and Derejko, 'A Global Battlefield? Drones and the Geographical Scope of Armed Conflict' 2013 (n. 156).

[159] ICRC, Conference of Government Experts on the Reaffirmation and Development of International Humanitarian Law Applicable in Armed Conflicts, Report on the Work of the Conference, Second Session, 3 May–3 June 1972, vol. I, July 1972, 68, para. 2.59. in *ibid*.

on detention, need to apply wherever the detention takes place.[160] Arguably, it follows then that IHL applicability analysis requires careful consideration, rule by rule and context by context.[161]

B) BEYOND THE TERRITORIES OF STATE PARTIES, OR BEYOND TERRITORY?
Likewise, while traditionally IHL was not considered to extend to the territory of States not party to the conflict,[162] the *Tadić* and *Lubanga* judgments, among others, recognise that armed conflicts can (and often do) cross borders into the territories of States not party to the conflict.[163] As the ICTY noted, NIACs generally arise 'within a State', but do not necessarily unfold entirely within one State's geographic borders.[164] The Rwanda Statute implicitly acknowledged the same by reference to the cross-border history of that conflict.[165] The ICRC, and abundant commentary, likewise reflects that a NIAC may 'spill over' or even be 'cross-border' without necessarily altering the non-international nature of the conflict.[166]

   Whether the territorial dimension can be dispensed with entirely, however, is another question. Whether or not there is a rigid 'legal geography of war',[167] the US government's assertion of a conflict with no territorial nexus or limits, providing a basis to invoke 'law of war' rules on targeting and detention anywhere in the world,[168] has been described as 'perhaps the most

---

[160] Lubell and Derejko, *ibid.*, discussing the difference between conduct of hostilities versus rules on prisoners of war; see also ICTY, *Tadić*, Appeal Chamber Judgment (n. 51), para. 68.

[161] See Section IV suggesting this is the governing principle for determining co-applicability.

[162] Christopher Greenwood, 'Scope of Application of IHL', in Dieter Fleck (ed.), *The Handbook of International Humanitarian Law*, 2nd edn. (Oxford University Press, 2008), 45–78 (51).

[163] See Bianchi and Naqvi, *International Humanitarian Law and Terrorism* 2011 (n. 2), 30.

[164] ICTY, *Tadić*, Appeal Chamber Judgment (n. 51), para. 70.

[165] Article 7 Statute for the International Criminal Tribunal for Rwanda, SC Res. 955 of 8 November 1994, 33 ILM 1598 (1994) (hereinafter: ICTR Statute), refers to *the territory of Rwanda and neighbouring States.*

[166] See Pejic, 'The Protective Scope of Common Article 3: More than Meets the Eye' 2011 (n. 52), 195; see, e.g., Nico Schrijver and Larissa van den Herik, 'Leiden Policy Recommendations on Counterterrorism and International Law', *Grotius Centre for International Legal Studies* (2010), para. 63; Cf. Dapo Akande, 'Are Extraterritorial Armed Conflicts with Non-State Groups International or Non-International?' *EJIL:Talk!*, 18 October 2011, available at: www.ejiltalk.org/are-extraterritorial-armed-conflicts-with-non-state-groups-international-or-non-international.

[167] Kenneth Anderson, 'Targeted Killing and Drone Warfare: How We Came to Debate Whether there is a Legal Geography of War', *Hoover Institution 'Future Challenges' essay series* (online edn. 2011), 3–15.

[168] Duffy, *War on Terror* 2015 (n. 7), ch. 6.1, e.g., Jeh Johnson's Speech (2012) on 'National Security Law, Lawyers and Lawyering in the Obama Administration' on the US right to use force 'without a geographic limitation', see Jeh C. Johnson, 'National Security Law, Lawyers, and Lawyering in the Obama Administration, Dean's Lecture at Yale Law School,

controversial aspect' of the US position.[169] The notion of a limitless global conflict jars with the inherently limited, definable and exceptional nature of armed conflict (and applicable IHL as an exceptional regime).

Concerns are, as ever, not purely legal. They relate in part to the 'international chaos' that would ensue if other States took the same view,[170] and the potential for escalation of conflicts contrary to the UN Charter.[171] Counter-terror legislation in the Russian Federation, authorising the lethal use of force to eliminate the terrorist threat wherever it arises around the globe,[172] and corresponding assassination practices, exposed, *inter alia*, through litigation,[173] is a reminder of the dangers.

While proponents of the 'global' armed conflict suggest that it is necessary to ensure that individuals forming part of an armed conflict, but operating outside of the zone of conflict, cannot escape the consequences of applicable IHL,[174] others argue there must be some territorial 'hook' within which to assess whether the criteria for armed conflict are met.[175] There seems little doubt though that where a conflict does exist, it may yet expand, exceptionally, across borders.[176]

February 22, 2012', *Yale Law & Polity Review* 31 (2012), 141–50. US District Court, District of Columbia, *Al-Aulaqi v. Obama*, Opposition to Plaintiff's Motion for Preliminary Injunction and Memorandum in Support of Defendant's Motion to Dismiss, 7 December 2010, 727 F. Supp. 2d 1 (D.D.C. 2010) (No. 10 Civ. 1469), 1.

[169] Ashley Deeks, 'Pakistan's Sovereignty and the Killing of Osama bin Laden', *ASIL Insights* 15 (2011), 2; Kenneth Anderson, 'Rise of the Drones: Unmanned Systems and the Future of War', Written Testimony to the US House of Representatives Subcommittee on National Security and Foreign Affairs, 23 March 2010, 5, para. 11, available at: www.fas.org/irp/congress/2010_hr/032310anderson.pdf.

[170] Scott Horton, 'Rules for Drone Wars: Six Questions for Philip Alston', *Harper's Magazine*, 9 June 2010, available at: https://harpers.org/blog/2010/06/rules-for-drone-wars-six-questions-for-philip-alston.

[171] Articles 1 and 2(4) UN Charter.

[172] See generally, Seth Bridge, 'Russia's New Counteracting Terrorism Law: the Legal Implications of Pursuing Terrorists beyond the Borders of the Russian Federation', *Columbia Journal of East European Law* 3 (2009).

[173] See, e.g., 2012 Qatari court conviction of two Russian intelligence agents for the assassination of the former Chechen separatist leader Zelimkhan Yandarbiyev outside a mosque in Doha. Steven Lee Myers, 'Qatar Court Convicts 2 Russians in Top Chechen's Death', *New York Times*, 1 July 2004, available at: www.nytimes.com/2004/07/01/world/qatar-court-convicts-2-russians-in-top-chechen-s-death.html.

[174] See, e.g., Michael Lewis, 'The Boundaries of the Battlefield', *Opinio Juris*, 15 May 2011, available at: http://opiniojuris.org/2011/05/15/the-boundaries-of-the-battlefield, para. 5, noting that individuals should not be 'immune from targeting based purely on geography'.

[175] See, *ibid.*: Pejic, 'The Protective Scope of Common Article 3: More than Meets the Eye' 2011 (n. 52), 17, suggests there must be a 'hook' to a national ; ICRC, 'Challenges of Contemporary Armed Conflicts' 2011 (n. 17), 10.

[176] See, e.g., Pejic, 'Conflict Classification and the Law Applicable to Detention and the Use of Force' 2012 (n. 135).

It is suggested that the key applicability questions continue to relate to the *ratione materiae* questions criteria above – intensity and the nature of the parties – to which geographic locus may be relevant. For example, it may naturally be more difficult to determine whether lethal use of force remote from hostilities was in reality 'associated' with the conflict, whether a potential target was 'directly participating' in hostilities, whether the geographically dispersed persons form an identifiable, cohesive OAG that meets the criteria of a party to a conflict.

Moreover, where IHL is applicable in principle, geographic locus – in particular distance from the 'battlefield' – is likely to influence the *interpretation* of IHL and/or IHRL.[177] Geography may also be relevant to, but will not determine, the interrelationship with IHRL. Where IHL *is* applicable, it must be interpreted and applied alongside IHRL, but the priority afforded to co-applicable norms will depend on a range of factors; distance from hostilities may lead to affording greater weight to IHRL, or to interpreting the requirements of either body differently in light of a contextual analysis, as explored in Sections IV and V.[178]

In conclusion, geography is less determinative of the applicability of IHL and the nature of the conflict than was once the case, and a more flexible approach to territorial limits reflects law keeping pace with practice. The territorial scope of that conflict is not determinative of the *nature* of the conflict either but, rather, as the ICC noted, that depends primarily on the parties. It may be, however, that at a minimum for IHL to apply, there must be *some* nexus to a particular territory – a locus of an armed conflict – where the legal criteria for armed conflict are met. Geographic factors may provide *indicators* that the criteria for IHL applicability are met, or lacking, and influence the contextual interpretation and application of IHL, and its interrelationship with IHRL.

2. IHRL *Rationae Loci*: Extraterritorial Applicability of IHRL

IHRL is applicable throughout States' own territories and wherever they exercise 'jurisdiction' abroad.[179] A State owes human rights obligations

---

[177] Section IV.4. Nils Melzer, 'Interpretive Guidance on the Notion of Direct Participation of Hostilities under International Humanitarian Law', ICRC (2009) and capture v. kill at Section V.

[178] See *Practitioners' Guide* 2016 (n. 37), which suggests this may be so both for targeting issues and for detention, discussed in Section V.

[179] Article 2(1) International Covenant on Civil and Political Rights, 16 December 1966, 999 UNTS 171 (hereinafter the ICCPR), refers to the State party's obligations to 'respect and ensure to all individuals within its territory and subject to its jurisdiction the rights recognized

throughout its sovereign territories, even if armed groups seize control and impede their ability to protect rights in practice.[180] Beyond its borders, one of the key issues is whether the individuals come within the 'jurisdiction' of the State, such that IHRL is applicable. As States' spheres of operation and influence grow in a globalised world, a rigid approach to territorial human rights obligations (just like to IHL) has become untenable, and law has developed, sometimes awkwardly, to keep pace.

The precise language delineating the scope of human rights obligations varies between treaties. The ICCPR imposes obligations towards persons 'within [the State party's] territory and subject to its jurisdiction', which has been interpreted as a disjunctive test,[181] while some regional treaties refer to obligations towards persons within the State's 'jurisdiction' and do not mention 'territory' at all.[182] Yet for both, jurisprudence and authoritative guidance from human rights bodies makes clear that States have obligations towards persons within its borders and, exceptionally, beyond them – where the State exercises 'jurisdiction' – sometimes referred to as 'authority', 'power' or 'effective control' – abroad.[183]

As to when such control arises, the law has for the most part evolved case by case, therefore in a somewhat piecemeal way. Whether this is the optimal approach to legal development can easily be questioned, particularly in the light of the confusing and at times contradictory way some of the jurisprudence has unfolded.[184]

---

in the present convention'. Art. 1 Convention for the Protection of Human Rights and Fundamental Freedoms, 4 November 1950, 213 UNTS 221 (hereinafter the ECHR), and American Convention on Human Rights 'Pact of San José, Costa Rica', 22 November 1969, 1144 UNTS 123 (hereinafter the ACHR).

[180] The State may not be responsible for *violations*, if it has done everything within its power to regain control, but the obligations remain 'applicable': see, e.g., ECtHR, *Catan v. Moldova and Russia* (n. 137). The author was one of the representatives of the applicants.

[181] E.g., see Theodor Meron, *Human Rights in Internal Strife: Their Protection* (Cambridge: Grotius, 1987), 40.

[182] Article 1 ECHR refers to 'secur[ing]' to everyone within their jurisdiction' the rights protected therein; likewise Art. 1 ACHR, while the African Charter makes no reference to jurisdiction or territory.

[183] ECtHR, *Al-Skeini v. United Kingdom* (n. 137).

[184] The ECtHR case law has 'not spoken with one voice', as stated by Judge Bonello, Concurring Opinion, *Al-Skeini v. United Kingdom* (n. 137), para. 6. Several cases involved territorial control – e.g., Turkish control of Northern Cyprus (*Loizidou v. Turkey*, Court (Chamber) Judgment of 18 December 1996, Application No. 15318/89) – or failed due to lack of it (*Banković and Others v. Belgium and 16 other Contracting States*, Admissibility Decision of 19 December 1999, Application No. 52207/99, concerning the bombardment of Belgrade by NATO forces). Territorial control is now clearly only one basis of jurisdiction, alongside state agent authority (*Al-Skeini v. United Kingdom* (n. 137)).

However, over time greater consistency has emerged between courts and bodies. While there remain grey areas, IHRL treaty obligations now clearly apply abroad in certain circumstances. The first is where the State exercises effective control of territory abroad,[185] such as directly through military occupation or indirectly through control of a 'subordinate administration'.[186] In this situation the 'full range' of positive and negative obligations arises.[187] Secondly, extraterritorial jurisdiction arises where the State acts outside its own territory through the conduct of its agents abroad ('State agent authority' jurisdiction). IHRL then applies in respect of that particular conduct.

This has long been accepted by most international and regional bodies from the earliest cases where the Human Rights Committee described it as 'unconscionable' to 'interpret the responsibility under the . . . Covenant as to permit a State party to perpetrate violations of the Covenant on the territory of another State, which violations it could not perpetrate on its own territory'.[188]

Many courts and bodies, including the ICJ, have now found IHRL to be applicable extraterritorially in conflict situations.[189] The test as set down by the Human Rights Committee, in General Comment No. 31, is whether the person is 'within the *power or effective control* of that State Party, even if not situated within the territory of the State Party'.[190] More expansively, the recent General Comment No. 36 on the right to life includes those whose right to life is 'impacted' in a 'direct and reasonably foreseeable manner' by the State's extraterritorial conduct.[191] The Inter-American system has clarified that 'given

---

[185] *Ibid.*

[186] E.g., ECtHR, *Cyprus v. Turkey*, Grand Chamber Judgment of 12 May 2014, Application No. 25781/94; for control through occupation, see, e.g., ACHPR, *DRC v. Burundi, Rwanda, and Uganda*, Merits Decision of 29 May 2003, Communication No. 227/99, and control through subordinate administrations, see, e.g., ECtHR, *Catan v. Moldova and Russia* (n. 137).

[187] ECtHR, *Al-Skeini v. United Kingdom* (n. 137), para. 138, on 'the controlling State' having responsibility 'to secure, within the area under its control, the entire range of substantive rights set out in the Convention'. Positive duties to prevent and respond sit alongside positive occupiers' obligations under IHL in occupation.

[188] UNHRC, *Lopez Burgos v. Uruguay*, Merits Decision of 29 July 1979, Communication No. 52/1979, para. 12.

[189] ICJ, *Legality of the Consequences of the Construction of a Wall* (n. 122), paras. 111, 109. The ICJ relied on reports and cases from the UN Human Rights Committee in finding that 'while the jurisdiction of States is primarily territorial, it may sometimes be exercised outside the national territory'.

[190] UNHRC, General Comment No. 31, *Nature of the General Legal Obligation on States Parties to the Covenant*, 26 May 2004, UN Doc. CCPR/C/21/Rev.1/Add.13.

[191] UNHRC, General Comment No. 36, Art. 6 (Right to life), 20 October 2018, UN Doc. CCPR/C/GC/36, para. 63, includes persons located outside any territory effectively controlled by the State, whose right to life is nonetheless impacted by its military or other activities in a 'direct and reasonably foreseeable manner'.

that individual rights inhere simply by virtue of a person's humanity', where an individual is 'subject to the *control* of another State', obligations still apply.[192] More recent formulations by the Inter-American Court have again been somewhat more expansive, referring to the 'causal effects' of States' conduct.[193] The African Commission on Human and Peoples' Rights (ACHPR) in turn had no trouble determining State responsibility in the face of allegations of massive violations by agents of Burundi, Rwanda and Uganda in neighbouring DRC.[194]

The geographic scope issue proved more controversial in the ECHR context, where jurisprudence has developed in a more erratic fashion. Early decisions of the European Commission and the European Court of Human Rights (ECtHR) found States' obligations to apply to 'all persons under their actual responsibility, whether that authority is exercised within their own territory or abroad'.[195] In *Banković v. Belgium*, however, the Court adopted an apparently more restrictive approach, finding that the aerial bombardment by NATO troops of the TV station in Belgrade fell outside the human rights jurisdiction of the States on the basis of their lack of *control of the territory* on which the alleged violations took place.[196] In justifying its reasoning, the *Banković* judgment asserted that the Convention was intended to apply within the *'espace juridique'* of the ECHR, of which the former Yugoslavia was not then part,[197] igniting a ream of debate on the relevance of the geographic scope of the convention as a whole and the implications for double standards in rights protection.

However, in June 2011 in the *Al-Skeini v. UK* judgment concerning the UK's obligations in Iraq, the Court distanced itself from the *Banković* approach.[198]

---

[192] Examples including Guantánamo and Grenada; e.g., IACHR, *Coard et al. v. United States*, Judgment of 29 September 1999, Case No. 10.951, para. 37.

[193] IACtHR, 'Environment and Human Rights', Advisory Opinion of 15 November 2017, OC-23/17, referring to the 'authority' or 'control' over a person, including through cross-border *effects*, where there is a 'causal relationship' between the polluting activities in the state's territory and the cross-border impact on rights. UNHRC, General Comment No. 31 (2004) (n. 190).

[194] ACHPR, *DRC v. Burundi et al.* (n. 186). See also the broad formulation in ACommHPR General Comment No. 3 (2015).

[195] See, e.g., ECtHR, *Cyprus v. Turkey* (n. 186), 282; *Issa and Others v. Turkey*, Admissibility Decision of 20 May 2000, Application No. 31821/96, concerning Iraqi shepherds killed by Turkish forces during a military operation in Iraq; *Ilaşcu v. Moldova and Russia* (n. 137) and *Öcalan v. Turkey*, Admissibility Decision of 14 December 2000, Application No. 46221/99; *Catan v. Moldova and Russia* (n. 137).

[196] ECtHR, *Banković v. Belgium* (n. 184), para. 70.

[197] *Banković, ibid.*, para. 80.

[198] ECtHR, *Al-Skeini v. United Kingdom* (n. 137). See also ECtHR, *Jaloud v. the Netherlands*, Grand Chamber Judgment of 20 November 2014, Application No. 47708/08, or the ECtHR, *Hassan v. United Kingdom* (n. 4).

The Court took a purposive interpretation,[199] clarifying that the Convention applies extraterritorially where a State either controls territory abroad *or* exercises 'physical power and control over the person in question'.[200] The *Al-Skeini* judgment and others since bring ECtHR jurisprudence broadly into line with the long-established jurisprudence of other courts and human rights treaty bodies. There are now many examples of human rights courts and bodies, international and regional, recognising that when a State exercises, variously, its 'power', 'authority' or 'control' over areas and individuals, it assumes the obligations to respect the human rights of persons affected.

A notable amount of such cases involve extraterritorial action by States in armed conflict or occupation scenarios. This includes the Human Rights Committee finding Israel responsible for violations in occupied territory,[201] or questioning the United States on violations in Afghanistan, Iraq and beyond in the purported 'war on terror'.[202] The ECtHR found Turkey responsible for violations by its military in Cyprus,[203] Russia in the Transnistrian region of Moldova and Chechnya,[204] Armenia for violations in Nagorno-Karabakh,[205] the United Kingdom and the Netherlands in Iraq.[206] The Inter-American Commission on Human Rights (IACHR) acknowledged that the human rights obligations of the United States continued to apply during the US invasion of Grenada[207] and in respect of the detainees in Guantánamo Bay,[208] while the ACHPR addressed violations by Burundi, Rwanda and

---

[199] *Ibid.*, para. 110.

[200] E.g., ECtHR, *Al-Skeini v. United Kingdom* (n. 137), para. 136. It also applies, e.g., on ships controlled by a State or which fly its flag, see, e.g., ECtHR, *Hirsi Jamaa v. Italy*, Grand Chamber Judgment of 23 February 2012, Application No. 27765/09.

[201] UNHRC, Concluding Observations, Israel, 18 August 1998, UN Doc. CCPR/C/79/Add.93; UNHRC, Concluding Observations, Israel, 21 August 2003, UN Doc. CCPR/CO/78/ISR.

[202] Note the United States contests the extraterritorial scope of the convention, though it has softened its position slightly in recent years. See US 4th periodic to the UNHRC and the UNHRC response (n. 132).

[203] ECtHR, *Loizidou v. Turkey* (n. 184). See also, *Cyprus v. Turkey* (n. 186).

[204] ECtHR, *Ilaşcu v. Moldova and Russia* (n. 137) and *Catan v. Moldova and Russia* (n. 137).

[205] ECtHR, *Chiragov and Others v. Armenia*, Grand Chamber Judgment of 16 June 2015, Application No. 13216/05.

[206] ECtHR, *Al-Skeini v. United Kingdom* (n. 137); *Jaloud v. the Netherlands* (n. 198); *Hassan v. United Kingdom* (n. 4).

[207] See IACHR, *Coard v. United States* (n. 192). The IACHR referred to similar previous cases involving the assassination of a Chilean diplomat in the United States and attacks by Surinamese officials in the Netherlands. See, e.g., IACHR, Report on the Situation of Human Rights in Chile, 9 September 1985, OEA/Ser.L/V/II.66, Doc. 17 (referring to Letelier assassination in Washington, DC); also IACHR, Second Report on the Situation of Human Rights in Suriname, 2 October 1985, OEA/Ser.L/V/II.66, Doc. 21, rev. 1.

[208] IACHR, *Precautionary Measures in Guantanamo Bay, Cuba*, 13 March 2002, citing *Coard v. United States* (n. 192).

Uganda during the conflict with DRC.[209] The applicability of IHRL in time of peace or armed conflict and, in most scenarios, whether the State operates inside or outside its own borders, is therefore now well established (though the nature of the obligations arising, and whether there are violations, will of course depend on many factors, including to an extent the degree of control exercised).

The geography of IHRL applicability, like that of war, has therefore expanded in line with the scope of States' activity. Through various processes, including human rights litigation, opposition to extraterritoriality has been voiced, policies challenged, the relevance of IHRL extraterritorially reasserted, and standards around applicability gradually clarified.[210]

D. *Applicability* Ratione Temporis

IHL generally applies until the definitive cessation of the conflict – therefore, as long as the requirements for the existence of an armed conflict set out above are met and specific rules govern occupation. IHRL applies, by contrast, at all times.[211] For reasons of space, this chapter does not deal in detail with temporal applicability, but notes that this too has been controversial, and subject to development, in recent years.

Particularly in the light of alleged armed conflicts with ill-defined parties and ideological associates, concerns arise as to 'war without end'. The implications for the extended or permanent applicability of the exceptional legal framework of IHL are serious.[212] A different manifestation of an expansive approach to temporal scope was revealed in recent national litigation in the interlocutory appeal in the *Al-Nashiri* case before the District of Columbia Circuit Court.[213] US prosecutors argued that the starting point of the conflict with Al-Qaeda could be extended back in time, so as to cover the alleged

---

[209] ACHPR, *DRC v. Burundi et al.* (n. 186).

[210] See the series of Iraq cases before the ECtHR raising both issues given extraterritorial operations in armed conflicts, e.g., *Al-Skeini v. United Kingdom* (n. 137), *Jaloud v. the Netherlands* (n. 198), *Hassan v. United Kingdom* (n. 4).

[211] Questions on the temporal limits of IHRL also arise, e.g., when obligations were assumed by the relevant State, and whether they are continuing, e.g., are also common disputes in litigation: see, e.g., ECtHR, *Palić v. Bosnia and Herzegovina*, Judgment of 15 February 2011, Application No. 4704/04; *Broniowski v. Poland*, Grand Chamber Judgment of 22 June 2004, Application No. 31443/96; *Janowiec and Others v. Russia*, Judgment of 16 April 2012, Application Nos. 55508/07 and 29520/09.

[212] See Duffy, *War on Terror* 2015 (n. 7), ch. 6B.

[213] United States Court of Appeals for the District of Columbia Circuit, *In Re Abd Al-Rahim Hussein Muhammed Al-Nashiri, Petitioner*, On Petition for Writ of Mandamus and Appeal from the United States District Court for the District of Columbia, Case No. 15-1023, 30 August 2016.

bombing of a French civilian ship off the coast of Yemen in October 2000, before the alleged armed conflict between Al-Qaeda and the United States said to have been triggered by the 9/11 attacks.

The scope of war, and IHL, has thus expanded not only *out* to cover broad terrorist entities and threats, with potentially limitless temporal scope for the future, but *back* in time to cover 'strategies of war' that Al-Qaeda would have been developing at the time.[214] The assessment after the fact, at trial, that the 'conflict' in fact started earlier than had previously been asserted compounds concerns as to the supposed elasticity of IHL.

III. CO-APPLICABILITY AND HUMAN RIGHTS LITIGATION

The significant overlap in the scope of applicability of IHL and IHRL set out in the previous section makes consideration of how norms co-apply a matter of practical necessity. This section focuses on how international adjudication – specifically this time human rights litigation – has evolved to grapple with co-applicability. Its purpose is to map the development of this voluminous emerging body of jurisprudence with a view to understanding the implications for applicability and co-applicability in law and practice in the future. Practice suggests various *factors* that have influenced evolving judicial and quasi-judicial approaches – from the changing nature of the particular treaties to which they give effect, their jurisdiction and mandate, to the positions of the parties to litigation – and how these too may be evolving.

A. *Context: Increased Engagement across Diverse Treaties and Treaty-body Functions*

Unlike the ICJ with its general competence in respect of international law, human rights courts and bodies derive their existence and purpose from particular treaties, and their approach is influenced by their own jurisdictional limits. They are, *generally* speaking, mandated to focus on the interpretation and application of the particular human rights treaty from which their competence derives.[215] As will be seen below, for the most part, this restricts human rights bodies to the application of IHRL, albeit interpreting it in the light of other areas of law such as IHL.

---

[214] *Ibid.*, 49: the government claimed hostilities could be established by looking to Al-Qaeda's strategy to wage war against the United States, publicly declared in 1996 and in preparation before 9/11.

[215] This is true of, e.g., the Inter-American bodies, the UNHRC or the ECHR, but not the African Commission and Court which have broader competence over 'any . . . relevant human rights treaty' binding on the State.

Most 'general' human rights treaties do not mention IHL.[216] There are glances across in some treaties, such as the ECHR and ACHR, which allow for derogation 'in times of war' or other emergency, thereby implicitly acknowledging the continued applicability of IHRL in such situations (and arguably reflecting assumptions that invoking IHL would coincide with derogation).[217] But for the most part, the increased engagement with IHL has been through the interpretation of human rights provisions in conflict situations.[218]

It is worthy of brief note, however, that human rights treaties themselves may be changing, reflecting the widespread recognition of co-application. A number of more recent treaties refer specifically to IHL, some stipulating obligations for States to respect IHL or acknowledging the interrelatedness of the two fields of law;[219] this brings IHL squarely within the mandate of the relevant court or body. A clear example is Article 38 of the Convention on the Rights of the Child (CRC)[220] embodying the general undertaking to respect and ensure respect for IHL relevant to the child. As such, it is a tailored incorporation into a human rights treaty of Common Article 1 of the 1949 Geneva Conventions. Subsequent instruments, such as the Optional Protocol on the Involvement of Children in Armed Conflict, enshrine more specific obligations to protect children from participation in, and from the effects of, armed conflict.[221] The Convention on the Rights of Persons with Disabilities (CRPD)[222] tailors obligations of protection in respect of persons with disabilities in armed conflict, while the International Convention for the Protection of All Persons from Enforced

---

[216] General treaties include the ICCPR, the International Covenant on Economic, Social and Cultural Rights, 16 December 1966, 993 UNTS 3 (ICESCR), the EHCR, the ACHR, and the African Charter on Human and Peoples' Rights, 27 June 1981, 1520 UNTS 217 (ACHPR).

[217] See ECtHR, *Hassan v. United Kingdom*, below, and dissent by Spano J *et al.* generally on the ECHR derogation, P. Kempees, *Thoughts on Article 15 of the European Convention on Human Rights* (Osterwijk: Wolf Legal, 2017).

[218] Section IV on the principles of interpretation that make this possible and shape their approach.

[219] See Walter Kälin, 'Universal Human Rights Bodies and International Humanitarian Law', in Robert Kolb and Gloria Gaggioli (eds.), *Research Handbook on Human Rights and Humanitarian Law* (Cheltenham: Elgar, 2013) 441–65 (446–7).

[220] Convention on the Rights of the Child, 20 November 1989, 1577 UNTS 3 (hereinafter the CRC); Hans-Joachim Heintze, 'Children Need more Protection under International Humanitarian Law: Recent Developments Concerning Article 38 of the UN Child Convention as a Challenge to the Red Cross and Red Crescent Movement', *Humanitäres Völkerrecht* 8 (1995), 200–3.

[221] Optional Protocol to the Convention on the Rights of the Child on the Involvement of Children in Armed Conflict, 25 May 2000, 2173 UNTS 222.

[222] Article 11 Convention on the Rights of Persons with Disabilities, 13 December 2006, 2515 UNTS 3, requiring States to take all necessary measures to ensure the protection and safety of persons with disabilities in situations of armed conflict in accordance with IHL.

Disappearance (ICPPED) prohibits *refoulement* to a State in face of a risk of serious violations of IHL.[223] As this trend towards more explicit engagement is likely to continue in new treaties, it will naturally influence the nature and degree of engagement of the relevant body charged with monitoring, interpreting and adjudicating on the law in the future.

As explored in more detail elsewhere,[224] it is also worthy of preliminary note that adjudication – although the focus here – is only one of various ways in which human rights courts and bodies engage with co-applicability. The ten UN treaty bodies, for example, have multifaceted identities and functions, in the context of each of which they have engaged, increasingly, with IHL.[225]

The particular functions may in turn influence their approach to IHL. For example, it was in the standard-setting role that the UN Human Rights Committee handed down General Comment No. 31, offering a relatively clear, if broadly framed, pronouncement on the interrelationship of IHRL in armed conflict as 'complementary, not mutually exclusive'.[226] Consistent with the role of General Comments, the framework stopped short of clarifying more complex issues of co-applicability that arise in practice in particular situations. In their 'promotional role' several international[227] and regional[228] systems have, however, called on States to take a range of actions, including generally respecting IHL,[229] ratifying certain IHL conventions,[230] ensuring criminal accountability, establishing

---

[223] Article 16 International Convention for the Protection of All Persons from Enforced Disappearance, 20 December 2006, 2176 UNTS 3. Art. 43 also states that the Convention is without prejudice to the provisions of IHL, including the Geneva Conventions.

[224] van den Herik and Duffy, 'Human Rights Bodies and International Humanitarian Law' 2016 (n. 3).

[225] Human Rights Committee (UNHRC), Committee on Economic, Social and Cultural Rights (CESCR), Committee on the Elimination of Racial Discrimination (CERD), Committee on the Elimination of Discrimination Against Women (CEDAW), Committee Against Torture (CAT), Committee on the Rights of the Child (CRC), Committee on the Rights of Persons with Disabilities (CRPD), Committee on Migrant Workers (CMW), Committee on Enforced Disappearances (CED), Subcommittee on Prevention of Torture and other Cruel, Inhuman or Degrading Treatment or Punishment (SPT).

[226] UNHRC, General Comment No. 31 (n. 190), e.g., para. 11. See also ACommHPR General Comment No. 3 on the right to life (n. 194). Others have made cursory reference to IHL, e.g., UNHRC General Comment No. 36 (n. 191); CESCR, General Comment No. 15, The Right to Water, 20 January 2003, UN Doc. E/C.12/2002/11, para. 22.

[227] The CRC has on several occasions called on States parties to take into account IHL.

[228] As early as the 1970s the IACHR's reports reference IHL: e.g., IACHR, Report on the Situation of Human Rights in Nicaragua, 17 November 1978, OEA/Ser.L/V/II.45, doc. 16 rev. 1, chapter 2.

[229] E.g., CRC, General Comment No. 6, Treatment of Unaccompanied and Separated Children Outside their Country of Origin, 1 September 2005, UN Doc. CRC/GC/2005/6, para. 26.

[230] CRC, General Comment No. 5, General measures on the implementation of the Convention on the Rights of the Child, 27 November 2003, UN Doc. CRC/GC/2003/5, para. 17; CRC, General Comment No. 6 (n. 229), para. 15.

relevant tribunals to prosecute IHL breaches,[231] cooperating with IHL treaty regimes, such as on land mines,[232] and ensuring adequate education on IHL standards.[233]

The State reporting system involves a somewhat more diplomatic process of dialogue and engagement with States. This may explain an often correspondingly cautious approach in general, and in relation to IHL in particular, reflecting the political sensitivities that surround questions of applicability for States. IHL has, however, also grown in significance in Concluding Observations in recent years. For the most part, the emphasis has been on confirming the relevant body's (contested) competence to monitor human rights situations during armed conflict, and references to IHL have most often been generic.[234] Occasionally, they have involved a more substantive consideration of IHL, such as in relation to a range of civil, political, economic, social and cultural rights in Israel,[235] and US responsibility in Afghanistan.[236] A rare focus on the overreaching approach to *applicability* of IHL is seen in the UNHRC Concluding Observations on the US use of drones.[237]

In the *recommendations* to States, committees have on several occasions been fairly specific in calling on States to investigate serious violations of

---

[231] CERD, General Recommendation XVIII on the Establishment of an International Tribunal to Prosecute Crimes Against Humanity, 18 March 1994, UN Doc. CERD/C/365, Annex I.

[232] CRC, General Comment No. 9, The Rights of Children with Disabilities, 27 February 2007, UN Doc. CRC/C/GC/9, para. 23.

[233] CRC, General Comment No. 1, The Aims of Education, 17 April 2001, UN Doc. CRC/GC/2001/1, para. 16.

[234] E.g., CESCR, Concluding Observations, 9 December 2010, UN Doc. E/C.12/LKA/CO/2-4, para. 28; CESCR, Concluding Observations, 20 November 2009, UN Doc. E/C.12/COD/CO/4, para. 25; CESCR, Concluding Observations, Israel, UN Doc. E/C.12/1/Add.90, 23 May 2003, para. 31.

[235] CAT, Concluding Observations, Israel, 14 May 2009, UN Doc. CAT/C/ISR/CO/4, para. 29 on Gaza; CESCR, Concluding Observations, Israel, UN Doc. E/C.12/1/Add.90, 26 June 2003, UN Doc. E/C.12/1/Add.90, paras. 15, 31; CESCR, Concluding Observations, Israel, 16 December 2011, UN Doc. E/C.12/ISR/CO/3, para. 8; UNHRC, Concluding Observations, Israel, 21 August 2003, UN Doc. CCPR/CO/78/ISR, para. 11; CAT, Concluding Observations, Israel, 23 June 2009, UN Doc. CAT/C/ISR/CO/4, para. 11. These observations neither endorse the *lex specialis* rule, nor grappled with how interplay might work in practice.

[236] CRC, Concluding Observations, United States, 28 January 2013, UN Doc. CRC/C/OPAC/USA/CO/2, para. 7.

[237] UNHRC, Concluding Observations, United States, 23 April 2014, UN Doc. CCPR/C/USA/CO/4, para. 9, questioning the 'very broad approach to the definition and geographical scope of an armed conflict, including the end of hostilities ... unclear interpretation of what constitutes an "imminent threat" and who is a combatant or civilian ... the unclear position on the nexus that should exist between any particular use of lethal force and any specific theatre of hostilities, as well as the precautionary measures taken to avoid civilian casualties in practice'.

IHL by States and NSAs,[238] to reconsider the applicability of statutory limitations in reparation proceedings for war crimes,[239] to refrain from offering amnesty for such violations,[240] to cooperate with international criminal tribunals,[241] and to ensure redress and reparations, for example.[242] A definite evolution is discernible towards greater engagement with IHL across the multiple functions of human rights bodies. It remains to be seen whether, as engagement becomes the norm and confidence rises, they will grapple more fully with issues of applicability and the somewhat generic, broad-brush approach to IHL will become more substantive.

The judicial or quasi-judicial nature of the bodies and of the adjudicative process, which is the focus here, distinguishes it from these other functions and processes highlighted above, and arguably influences the approach to IHL.

The judicial process ultimately involves adjudicating concrete factual situations and real-life contexts that lie behind particular cases, albeit in a way that should be mindful of the law-making role of human rights jurisprudence. It is through cases that *abstracto* declarations on interplay are necessarily taken a step further, applied and given content. In a context in which courts must reach a decision in favour of one or the other party to the case, they cannot entirely avoid controversial engagements that might alienate States if they are to discharge their mandate. Ultimately, the judicial or quasi-judicial nature of these proceedings may call for a more decisive, clear and precise approach to technical articulations on matters of substantive law and interplay than other functions.[243] Judicial practice and its approach to applicable law may, however, also be influenced by an array of other considerations, including notably the particular facts from which legal standards emerge, and the positions and arguments advanced by parties to the litigation, in particular State parties.

---

[238]   E.g., CRC, Concluding Observations, Russia, 31 January 2014, UN Doc. CRC/C/OPAC/ RUS/CO/1, para. 16; UNHRC, Concluding Observations, Colombia, 4 August 2010, UN Doc. CCPR/C/COL/CO/6, para. 9.

[239]   UNHRC, Concluding Observations, Serbia, 20 May 2011, UN Doc. CPR/C/SRB/CO/2, para. 10.

[240]   UNHRC, Concluding Observations, Colombia, 26 May 2004, UN Doc. CCPR/CO/80/ COL, para. 8.

[241]   *Ibid.*, para. 13.

[242]   The UNHRC indicated that Russia should ensure that victims of serious human rights violations *and* IHL are provided with an effective remedy, including the right to compensation and reparations: see UNHRC, Concluding Observations, Russia, 24 November 2009, UN Doc. CCPR/C/RUS/CO/6, para. 13.

[243]   van den Herik and Duffy, 'Human Rights Bodies and International Humanitarian Law' 2016 (n. 3).

B. Evolving Approaches to Co-applicability in Human Rights Adjudication

Human rights litigation of violations in armed conflict today is a particularly dynamic and evolving area of practice. Myriad international and regional bodies now exist to hear such complaints, and the case-load of each is voluminous and growing. As set out below, across the globe these regional and international courts and bodies are increasingly engaged with IHL through the adjudication of human rights obligations in armed conflict situations.

1. Push and Shove within the Pioneering Inter-American System

The Inter-American system for the protection of human rights was the first of the regional systems to engage openly with IHL. The Inter-American Commission on Human Rights got off to a bold but faltering start in the *Abella* case,[244] in which it directly and explicitly 'applied' IHL. The case concerned an attack by a group of individuals on military barracks in Buenos Aires in 1989, in the context of what was described as a 'military uprising'. The Commission reasoned that it was addressing a 'combat situation'[245] which 'none of the human rights instruments was designed to regulate',[246] and that it therefore simply *could* not apply Article 4 on the right to life without regard to IHL (the only alternative being to decline to adjudicate).[247] The attack took place five years after the transition from dictatorship to democracy and outwith what, on any view, might constitute an armed conflict.

The case is often cited as a key example of recognition of the relevance of IHL by human rights bodies.[248] The overreach on material applicability is, however, perhaps the most stunning feature of the decision, and oddly neglected in commentary.[249]

The case has even been cited in support of a particular understanding of the legal tests for applicability, namely, that the Commission considered that an armed conflict may be short in duration (relevant to material applicability).[250] But there is reason to doubt that the IHL applicability criteria (whether the

---

[244] IACtHR, *Abella v. Argentina*, Judgment of 18 November 1997, Case No. 11.137, para. 1.

[245] *Ibid.*

[246] *Ibid.*, para. 158.

[247] *Ibid.*, para. 161.

[248] For a different critique, see Liesbeth Zegveld, 'The Inter-American Commission on Human Rights and International Humanitarian Law: a Comment on the Tablada Case', *International Review of the Red Cross* 38 (1998), 505–11.

[249] The *Practitioners' Guide* 2016 (n. 37) cites it as an example of the 'hostilities' framework being applied, rendering IHL the primary framework without considering if IHL was applicable.

[250] Sassòli, 'The Role of Human Rights and International Humanitarian Law in New Types of Armed Conflicts' 2011 (n. 145).

group was sufficiently organised and the intensity threshold met) was given much attention at all. Also doubtful is the Commission's assessment – which may have coloured its approach – that IHL would provide 'greater protection for victims' in the particular case.[251] This first case should perhaps serve as a cautionary tale, underscoring the importance of the crucial preliminary step of ascertaining IHL applicability, for which resort to violence and the challenges it poses are clearly insufficient.

While later cases from the region indicate a more cautious approach to co-applicability (by the Commission and Court), *Abella* does not stand alone in its reluctance to confront the IHL applicability question. In most cases from this region, the relative absence of controversy regarding the existence of long-running NIACs in Colombia or Guatemala, for example, and the nexus between the events and the conflict may partly account for the Commission and Court not considering it necessary to make determinations as to the conflict.

There has, however, been more controversy as to the precise role that IHL should play before the Commission and Court. When the question of how to engage with IHL came before the Inter-American Court (IACtHR), first in the *Las Palmeras v. Colombia* case of 2001, the Court made clear that it considered the Commission to have overreached jurisdictionally in applying IHL directly in *Abella*. It noted that the Court's role and mandate is:

> to say whether or not that norm or that fact is compatible with the American Convention. The latter has only given the Court competence to determine whether the acts or the norms of the States are compatible with the Convention itself, and not with the 1949 Geneva Conventions.[252]

The Court and the Commission have, however, consistently continued to assert the co-application of the two branches of law, albeit with the emphasis on the relevance of IHL to the interpretation of the Convention.[253] Accordingly, in *Coard et al. v. United States* in the context of the US invasion of Grenada, the Commission found that IHL provided 'authoritative guidance' and 'specific standards' relevant to the Convention.[254] Occasionally, as in cases involving the conflict in El Salvador, it has described IHL as an authoritative interpretative tool, but has gone on to 'note . . . grave infractions

---

[251] IACommHR, *Abella v. Argentina* (n. 244), paras. 158–9.
[252] IACtHR, *Las Palmeras v. Colombia*, Judgment of 6 December 2001, IACtHR Series C, No. 90, para. 22.
[253] E.g., *ibid.*, para. 121; IACHR, *Serrano Cruz Sisters v. El Salvador*, Admissibility Report of 23 February 2001, Case No. 12.132; IACtHR, *Mapiripán Massacre v. Colombia*, Judgment of 15 September 2005, IACtHR Series C, No. 134, para. 115.
[254] IACHR, *Coard v. United States* (n. 192), para. 42.

of IHL' and violations of the convention 'in conjunction with' IHL, en route.[255] On several occasions, including in granting precautionary measures in relation to Guantánamo, the Commission noted that the rules of IHL and IHRL 'may be distinct' and that it may be 'necessary to deduce the applicable standard by reference to IHL as the applicable *lex specialis*'.[256] Subsequently, in numerous cases against Colombia, the Commission emphasised more broadly that the two bodies of law 'complement each other or become integrated to specify their scope or content'.[257]

The IACtHR for its part has underscored the importance of seeing the two bodies of law as co-applicable and that 'the relevant provisions of the Geneva Conventions may be taken into consideration as elements for the interpretation of the American Convention'.[258] In *Santa Domingo v. Colombia* it explicitly rejected the idea of 'a ranking between normative systems', but supported the need to have regard to more specific norms in defining obligations under the Convention in particular contexts.[259] Rather than endorsing a simplistic approach to '*lex specialis*' as providing the sole relevant legal basis, in *Serrano Cruz v. El Salvador*, it emphasised that even 'the specificity of the provisions of IHL ... do not prevent the convergence and application of the provisions of [IHRL]'.[260]

A few clusters of cases provide insights into the Court's approach to co-applicability and factors that may influence it. In the *Bámaca Velásquez v. Guatemala* case, for example, concerning the capture, disappearance and

---

[255] See IACtHR, *Monsignor Oscar Amulfo Romero y Galdámez v. El Salvador*, Case No. 11.481, para. 66 ('*not[ing]* that the assassination of Monsignor Romero constitutes a grave infraction of the basic principles of international humanitarian law ...', and para. 76 ('El Salvador has violated [the American Convention] in conjunction with the principles of Common Article 3'); see also IACtHR, *Extrajudicial Executions and Forced Disappearances v. Peru*, Judgment of 11 October 2001, Case No. 10.247 *et al.*

[256] IACHR, *Precautionary Measures in Guantanamo Bay* (n. 208). See also *Coard v. US* (n. 192). A similarly broad approach to *lex specialis* was evident in its 2002 Report on Terrorism and Human Rights, OEA/Ser.L./V/II.116, doc. 5 rev. 1, corr. (2002). However, it refers to IHL as '*lex specialis*' in interpreting and applying human rights protections in situations of armed conflict' (para. 2).

[257] IACHR, *Mapiripán Massacre v. Colombia* (n. 253). See also, e.g., IACtHR, *Avilán v. Colombia*, Judgment of 30 September 1997, Case No. 11.142, paras. 131–42, 159–60, 166–78, 198–203; IACHR, Third Report on the Human Rights Situation in Colombia, Chapter IV, Violence and Violations of International Human Rights Law and International Humanitarian Law, February 1999 OEA/Ser.L/V/II.102, Doc. 9 rev. 1, 26; IACtHR, *Prada González y Bolaño Castro v. Colombia*, Judgment of 25 September 1998, Case No. 11.710, Report No. 63/01, 2000, 781.

[258] IACtHR, *Bámaca-Velásquez v. Guatemala*, Judgment of 25 November 2000, IACtHR Series C, No. 70, para. 209.

[259] IACtHR, *Santa Domingo v. Colombia*, 30 November 2012, IACtHR Series C, No. 259.

[260] IACHR, *Serrano Cruz v. El Salvador* (n. 253), para. 112.

death of a former guerrilla commander, the Court had detailed regard to IHL standards.[261] Notably, it did so in considering his right to life, but remained with an IHRL approach to issues related to his detention and torture. The Court was not explicit or clear as to why, though the dearth of detailed IHL on detention in NIAC, or the remote locus of his detention from any situation of active hostilities, may have had a bearing on the Court's emphasis on each area of law.[262] It is also noteworthy that in this case, as in most other cases in which IHL had been invoked, the impact of IHL on the outcome of the case is unclear. As the Court indicated, in the particular case the conduct in question would constitute violations of IHRL *or* IHL (IHL providing no justification for killing a rebel commander no longer participating in the conflict, for torture or for arbitrary detention without any legal process).[263] In addition, the nature of the conflict, and the position of the parties, may also have played a role. In the *Bámaca* case, the State did not dispute the relevance of IHL as a tool of interpretation, but nor was it central to either party's case.[264] Nor in turn was there any doubt about the armed conflict (the longest running NIAC in the region, lasting some 36 years) or the deceased's connection to it. It may be said then it was relatively easy for the Court to grapple with IHL here; its competence to do so was not under attack and it did not bring the Court into any political fray.

The context has been markedly different in other more recent cases. In a series of cases, the Colombian State has put the relevance of IHL centre stage by arguing that, as the matter is governed by IHL, the Inter-American supervisory bodies lack competence *ratione materiae*.[265] In relation to the right to life in *Colombia v. Ecuador*,[266] or *Santa Domingo v. Colombia*[267] or hostage-taking in *Rodriguez Vera (The Disappeared from the Palace of Justice)*

---

[261]   IACtHR, *Bámaca-Velásquez v. Guatemala* (n. 258), para. 121.

[262]   See the approach suggested in *Practitioners' Guide* 2016 (n. 37) to the effect that the more remote from hostilities, the more the framework of IHRL takes priority and can fully address the situation at hand.

[263]   IACHR, *Bámaca v. Guatemala* (n. 258), para. 145. The Court implicitly found that there were no rules of IHL that created any conflict with those of IHRL in this case.

[264]   *Ibid.*, para. 208.

[265]   *Ibid.* See below on similar arguments advanced by the State in IACtHR, *Carlos Augusto Rodríguez Vera and Others v. Colombia* ('*Palace of Justice*'), Judgment of 14 November 2014, Case No. 10.738. The case concerned, *inter alia*, hostage-taking and disappearances. The author was *amicus curiae*.

[266]   IACHR, *Franklin Guillermo Aisalla Molina Ecuador – Colombia*, Inter-State Petition on Admissibility of 21 October 2010, Report No. 112/10, para. 115.

[267]   Cluster munitions were used against villagers, allegedly targeting FARC operatives hiding in woods nearby.

v. Colombia,[268] it has sought to rely on IHL *as 'the special, main and exclusive law'*,[269] to render violations beyond the purview of the Court.[270] The Court has consistently given such arguments relatively short shrift in reaffirming the role of IHL in the interpretation of the convention, not its displacement.[271]

The latest stage in the Court's jurisprudential journey is the *Cruz Sanchez v. Peru* case, which has taken the Court's approach to IHL a step further.[272] It builds on its 'interpretative' approach but, unlike its predecessor cases, reaches conclusions on the right to life which are directly defined by reference to IHL, and more permissive as a result. The lethal use of force against members of organised armed groups while they were 'directly participating in the armed conflict' were not considered violations of the convention as they were permitted under IHL; by contrast, killings (where evidence indicated the individual was hors de combat) were arbitrary deprivations of life under the convention.

A couple of features of this latest judgment are worthy of note. First, and most obvious, is the court's willingness to reach conclusions based essentially on IHL standards, even when it had a direct impact on the decision, *and* the outcome was not more favourable to the victims. Secondly, it continued to have regard to IHRL alongside IHL throughout its assessment. Thirdly, in its regard to both areas of co-applicable law, the Court emphasised the need to look carefully at the particular facts and 'take into account all the circumstances and the context of the facts'.[273] These included the existence of the NIAC, the fact that the deceased were members of armed groups, and the objective and *modus operandi* of the operation – a difficult rescue operation, planned and executed with the goal of liberating hostages and capturing the individuals in question. The Court thus draws in considerations from IHRL alongside IHL standards, in the light of the particular circumstances and context of each of the deaths.[274]

The Inter-American system has remained true to its pioneering role in recognising the importance of, and not recoiling from, IHL. The Court and the Commission's approach to recognising IHL as co-applicable law, and using

---

[268] *Ibid.*

[269] *Ibid.*, para. 38. On lack of clarity in its position, see Judgment, e.g., footnote 37.

[270] *Ibid.*

[271] *Ibid.*, IACtHR, *Palace of Justice* (n. 265), paras. 116–26.

[272] IACtHR, *Cruz Sanchez v. Peru*, Judgment of 17 April 2015, IACtHR Series C, No. 292 (in Spanish; translations are the author's).

[273] *Ibid.*, para. 266.

[274] The lethal force used against most of the guerrillas was lawful but not against those effectively captured before being killed.

it to interpret and give full effect to the Convention in the particular context, is now the prevalent approach to co-applicability by human rights bodies.

2. The Limited but Significant Case Law of the African Commission and Court

The African system is the youngest of the three regional siblings and the volume of its decisions limited in comparison with the others. Although it has engaged through its standard-setting function, it is perhaps surprising that in a continent plagued by conflict the issue has not (yet) arisen with greater frequency in human rights litigation.[275]

In general, the African Commission on Human Rights and Peoples' Rights has tended to emphasise that due to the lack of any mechanism for derogation from the Charter, the Charter obligations continue to apply 'even in civil war'.[276] In the inter-State *DRC v. Burundi, Rwanda and Uganda* case, concerning violations by armed forces of the respondent States during occupation of the DRC, the Commission embraced IHL more fully as 'part of the general principles of law recognised by African States' which the Commission could take 'into consideration in the determination of this case'.[277] The Commission was willing to go further than most in finding violations by reference to specific provisions of the Geneva Conventions and Additional Protocols, referring to IHL and IHRL depending in which area of law provided more specific norms.[278] It might be relevant that the application of IHL did not, on the facts, alter the human rights standards or offer less protection, but it gave rise to additional violations of provisions of IHL.

Also deserving of brief note is the fact that the African Court of Justice and Human Rights' nascent practice signals one rare type of human rights litigation in armed conflict not seen elsewhere, namely, the resort to precautionary or interim measures to prevent imminent conflict-related violations. In one of

---

[275] Duffy, *Strategic Human Rights Litigation* 2018 (n. 25), ch. 2. ACommHPR General Comment No. 3 (n. 194).

[276] ACHPR, Commission Nationale des Droits de l'Homme et de Libertés/Chad, 11 October 1995, Communication No. 74/92, para. 21.

[277] ACHPR, *DRC v. Burundi et al.* (n. 186). See Arts. 60 and 61 of the African Charter on Human and Peoples Rights, 27 June 1981, 1520 UNTS 217, which provide a basis for this outward-looking approach to other norms.

[278] The Commission found violations during occupation inconsistent with the Geneva Convention IV (n. 23) and API (n. 30), e.g., that 'the indiscriminate dumping of and or mass burial of victims were contrary to Article 34 of Additional Protocol I', as well as the Charter and Convention on the Elimination of All Forms of Discrimination against Women (CEDAW), 18 December 1979, 1249 UNTS 13.

its first decisions, the Court adopted an Order for Provisional Measures against Libya, explicitly noting the situation of 'ongoing conflict' and that the Peace and Security Council of the African Union had referred to 'violations of human rights and international humanitarian law ...'[279] The case suggests the Court will not be blind to IHL, though its role in deliberations remains unclear.[280]

The African Court remains in its infancy, and limited possibilities of access to the Court mean it is too early to assess its approach or impact on co-applicability in the future. Its treaty framework and the factual realities of conflicts within its jurisdiction suggest that it is certainly one to watch.

3. Out of the Closet? The Evolving Approach of the European Court

The ECtHR's approach to IHL stands somewhat apart from that of other bodies. It has perhaps had most occasion to consider IHL, given the volume of cases concerning situations of (arguable or established) armed conflict from southeast Turkey to Chechnya, Transnistria, Ukraine, Crimea, South Ossetia, Abkhazia, Nagorno-Karabakh, northern Cyprus, Iraq and beyond.[281] Unlike its Inter-American sister, the cases have frequently emerged from contexts where the existence of conflict was itself a matter of dispute. Perhaps for this reason, among others, a striking feature of much of its practice has been its extreme reluctance to recognise the existence of armed conflict and to engage with questions of IHL applicability.[282] However, over time its position has shifted substantially.[283]

For a long time, the Court's approach was not to engage directly with the existence of 'conflicts' but to take a threefold approach. First, it emphasised that derogation is the appropriate legal vehicle to adjust standards where exigencies so required, as reflected in the explicit reference in Article 15 to war as a permissible basis for derogation. It found in several cases that where the respondent States have not derogated (and they rarely do), the 'normal

---

[279] ACtHPR, *ACHPR v. Libya*, Order for Provisional Measures, 25 March 2011, Application No. 004/2011, paras. 13, 21.

[280] *Ibid.*, para. 25.

[281] Many cases concerned Northern Ireland where on one view there was a conflict though it was never recognised as such; see Steven Haines, 'Northern Ireland 1968–1998', in Wilmshurst (ed.), *Classification of Conflicts* 2012 (n. 2), 117–45 (117–24). Other relevant IACs arose in the former Yugoslavia, Russia/Georgia, Ukraine and Iraq.

[282] On some occasions, although the existence of armed conflict has been recognised, still no reference to IHL has been made. E.g., ECtHR, *Ilaşcu v. Moldova and Russia* (n. 137), para. 42.

[283] This is not linear and as noted below the Court's approach has depended on many factors.

legal background' continues to apply.[284] Secondly, despite this formal position, in line with its consistent emphasis on rendering rights 'practical and
effective' not 'theoretical and illusory',[285] the Court has often noted the need to
have close regard to the facts and context including the realities of clashes or
conflict.[286] Thus, thirdly, as part of this approach, even where the Court has
generally made little explicit reference to IHL, it has had close regard to
principles of IHL in reaching its conclusions in appropriate cases.[287]

The extent to which the Court has done so, and invoked even IHL-related
language and concepts, has been context-dependent. In respect of the use of
force against individuals or small groups of alleged terrorists, even within the
broad context of conflicts, the Court has broadly maintained a law enforcement approach (with just occasional glances to IHL). It has required, for
example, that the State plan and carry out operations to avoid the use of
force, minimise threats to life, referring to the use of weapons that minimise
human suffering and the importance of warnings.[288]

But as far as it has considered higher intensity armed confrontations, while
not being explicit on IHL, it has reached conclusions more directly reflective
of IHL principles. Examples emerge from several cases in southeast Turkey
and Chechnya. For example, in *Ergi v. Turkey* and *Özkan v. Turkey*, the Court
required 'feasible precautions in the choice of means and methods of
a security operation mounted against an opposing group with a view to
avoiding and, in any event, to minimising, incidental loss of *civilian* life'.[289]
In *Benzer and Others v. Turkey*, the judgment rebukes the failure to secure
humanitarian aid in the wake of aerial bombardment.[290] In *Isayeva Yusupova*

---

[284]   See, e.g., ECtHR, *Isayeva, Yusupova and Bazayeva v. Russia*, Judgment of 24 February 2005,
        Application No. 57950/00, para. 191. Derogation would affect derogable rights, notably liberty,
        under Art. 5, which contains enumerated grounds for detention and safeguards which diverge
        from IHL. In conflicts overseas, some question whether a State *can* derogate: Marko Milanovic,
        'Extraterritorial Derogations from Human Rights Treaties in Armed Conflict', in Nehal Bhuta
        (ed.), *The Frontiers of Human Rights* (Oxford University Press, 2016), 55–88.

[285]   ECtHR, *Airey v. Ireland*, Judgment of 9 October 1979, Application No. 6289/73, para. 24.

[286]   See, e.g., ECtHR, *Palić v. Bosnia and Herzegovina* (n. 211), as one example; see Section IV on
        principles of interpretation.

[287]   See, e.g., pioneering study in William Abresch, 'A Human Rights Law of Internal Armed
        Conflict: the European Court of Human Rights in Chechnya', *European Journal of
        International Law* 16 (2005), 741–67.

[288]   See, e.g., ECtHR, *McCann v. United Kingdom*, Grand Chamber Judgment of
        27 September 1995, Application No. 18984/91; *Gül v. Turkey*, Judgment of 13 December 2000,
        Application No. 22676/93; *Hamiyet Kaplan v. Turkey*, Judgment of 13 September 2005,
        Application No. 36749/97.

[289]   ECtHR, *Ergi v. Turkey*, Judgment of 28 July 1998, Application No. 23818/94, para. 79; *Ahmet
        Özkan and Others v. Turkey*, Judgment of 6 April 2004, Application No. 21689/93, para. 297.

[290]   ECtHR, *Benzer and Others v. Turkey*, Judgment of 12 November 2013, Application No.
        23502/06.

and Bazayeva v. Russia, it found a violation in the light of the failure to assess and prevent 'possible harm to civilians who might have been present . . . in the vicinity of what the military could have perceived as legitimate targets'.[291] The Court's reference to 'civilians' and 'legitimate targets' is a plain, if not explicit, reference to IHL. Whether we should understand the decision as the co-applicability of norms is unclear due to the Court's failure to explain its approach or acknowledge the relationship between IHRL and IHL.

Particular uncertainty arises from *Finogenov v. Russia* (a hostage-taking case), where the Court relies predominantly on Convention standards, but employs language from IHL, albeit with confusing logic that may not correspond to either body of law. It appears to have found no violation of the right to life of the hostages and hostage-takers through the use of poisoned gas on the curious basis that the use of gas, even if dangerous or potentially lethal, was not an 'indiscriminate attack' as the hostages had a high chance of survival.[292] (Those chances were diminished by a botched subsequent rescue operation in relation to which the Court did find a violation.[293]) While the language is resonant of IHL, the standards are not, and as was typical the Court did not explain.[294]

In more recent cases, however, the Court's opaque, if not myopic, approach has ceded to overt recognition of the relationship between the Convention and IHL. There are many plausible explanations for this, from the growing tide of international legal thinking on interplay, to the Court's own emphasis on the importance of a coherent approach to the Convention consistent with other areas of international law, among others.[295] However, it is suggested that the shift (also, or perhaps principally) relates to the different armed conflicts from which cases have arisen and the different positions of the States concerned vis-à-vis the existence of an armed conflict and the applicability of IHL. The Turkish or Chechen cases, similar to Northern Ireland-related cases before them, often concerned violations where controversy surrounded the existence of an armed conflict. Therefore, IHL was not invoked by the State (and often for different reasons, not by the applicants either).[296] In those contexts, the Court could only address the factually and legally complex issue of interplay if it had first made, on

---

[291]   ECtHR, *Isayeva v. Russia* (n. 284), para. 175.
[292]   ECtHR, *Finogenov and Others v. Russia*, Judgment of 20 December 2011, Application Nos. 18299/03 and 27311/03, paras. 231–2.
[293]   *Ibid.*, paras. 263–6.
[294]   ICRC *Customary Study* 2005 (n. 22), Customary Rule 11.
[295]   See Section III.
[296]   There was, e.g., no reference to IHL in pleadings concerning the killing of the former Chechen leader in *Maskhadova v. Russia*, Judgment of 6 June 2013, Application No. 18071/ 05. The author was one of the representatives of the applicants.

its own motion, politically controversial assessments concerning the existence of armed conflict. The Court was reluctant to do so.

By contrast, situations that were, incontrovertibly, armed conflicts at the relevant time have recently made their way to the Court, perhaps influencing the more overt approach to IHL. While a series of cases concerning NATO action in the former Yugoslavia were deemed inadmissible,[297] a minor step forward was taken when the Court explicitly addressed IHL in cases concerning the consistency with principles of legality and non-retroactivity of prosecuting individuals for war crimes during the Second World War.[298] Much more significant, however, is the series of cases concerning the conduct of British troops in Iraq, which gave rise to the most notable shift in the Court's practice.

In some cases, such as *Al-Skeini v. UK*, the significance of engaging IHL did not appear to go beyond citing it in some detail in the record of 'applicable law' at the outset of the judgment, without relying on it in its deliberations or resolution of the case. This inclusion may reflect the fact that applicants and third parties cited IHL,[299] while the omission from the Court's reasoning may reflect the fact that the State did not invoke IHL.[300] The oversight of IHL was particularly controversial in *Al-Jedda v. UK*, which had at its heart an issue on which IHRL and IHL drive in competing directions, namely, the lawfulness of internment and applicable procedural safeguards.[301] While citing IHL as 'relevant international law materials', it was criticised by some for not questioning whether another legal regime – namely IHL – co-applied and provided an alternative legal basis for detention and, arguably, different procedural rules.[302] But then, nor had the parties asked it to.[303]

A decisively different and more robust approach to IHL is seen in *Hassan v. United Kingdom* decided on 16 September 2014. While the judgment is rightly open to criticism on other grounds,[304] the focus here is on the Court's

---

[297] ECtHR, *Banković v. Belgium* (n. 184).

[298] These cases looked to IHL only as regards how national courts applied international law.

[299] *Al-Skeini v. United Kingdom* (n. 137). The author represented one of the *amicus* interveners concerning occupiers' obligations and extraterritoriality.

[300] See, ECtHR, *Hassan v. United Kingdom* (n. 4).

[301] ECtHR, *Al-Jedda v. United Kingdom*, Judgment of 7 July 2011, Application No. 27021/08, 29.

[302] See Jelena Pejic, 'The European Court of Human Rights' Al-Jedda Judgment: the Oversight of International Humanitarian Law', *International Review of the Red Cross* 93 (2011), 837–51.

[303] The government chose not to argue IHL but the alternative purported justification of Security Council authorisation of detentions, which the Court rejected.

[304] And the applicant, his brother, unsuccessfully alleged violation of the right to life. The Court adopted an unduly flexible approach to the right of life where the detainee died in suspicious circumstances apparently shortly after his release. Although Ziv Bohrer suggests IHL would have been more protective, arguably so is IHRL.

approach to IHL in relation to the lawfulness of the detention of the applicant's brother at UK detention facilities in the context of the international
armed conflict in Iraq. The question arose whether IHL might provide
a lawful basis for detention and govern the relevant procedural safeguards.

The Court clarified that it 'must endeavour to interpret and apply the
Convention in a manner consistent with the framework of international law
delineated by the International Court of Justice'. The State had not derogated,
which, as explained above, it should have done in order to invoke IHL in the
way anticipated in the Convention.[305] Despite this, the Court found it could
not ignore the existence of the conflict. For the first time, its decision was
based explicitly on IHL.

Considering the permissible grounds of detention under IHL applicable in
IACs, which included imperative reasons of security, it found the deceased's
detention had a lawful basis. This is particularly noteworthy in relation to the
ECHR, which (unlike the ICCPR, for example, with its broad prohibition on
'arbitrary' detention[306]) provides explicit and exhaustive grounds of permissible detention which notably do not including security detention. Likewise, it
found the safeguards of access to a 'competent body' applicable in IAC
sufficient where it is not 'practicable' to afford the right to 'judicial review'
normally applicable under the Convention.[307] The Court suggested it was
'interpreting' IHL and the Convention consistently, despite the facial clash
between the two.[308]

A few points are noteworthy as regards the Court's approach to co-
applicability and its significance. First, the judgment makes clear that the
Convention is not displaced by these rules of IHL, but co-applies; the proposition that the Convention was essentially inapplicable in IAC, which was
'instead' governed by IHL, was rejected.[309] Secondly, each area of law
informed the interpretation of the other – in interpreting the relevant rules
of IHL, namely, the review by a competent body with 'sufficient guarantees of
impartiality and fair procedure', the Court returned to Convention
standards.[310] The ongoing interplay of the two sets of norms is therefore
evident, in stark contrast to a simplistic displacement approach.

---

[305] Article 15. See the dissent on this suggesting the *only* proper way to alter Art. 5 obligations is
derogation.

[306] The ICCPR prohibits 'arbitrary deprivation of liberty' and 'arbitrary deprivation of life'
which, as the ICJ has noted, implies situations where detention or killing are not governed
by IHL; *Legality of the Threat or Use of Nuclear Weapons* (n. 126), para. 25.

[307] *Ibid.*, para. 106.

[308] ECtHR, *Hassan v. United Kingdom* (n. 4), paras. 105–7.

[309] ECtHR, *Hassan v. United Kingdom* (n. 4), paras. 7, 86–8.

[310] *Ibid.*, para. 106.

Where the Court saw a clear conflict, however, it followed IHL. This might be seen as a *lex specialis* approach, but it is interesting that the Court does not use that language, and indeed suggests it may not be the most helpful frame of reference. This may have been influenced by third-party interveners' invitation to refrain from becoming embroiled in analysis of '*lex specialis*'. Instead, the Court adopted an (admittedly at times strained) 'interpretative' approach, within which it was necessary to 'accommodate so far as possible' IHL.[311]

The extent of controversy around the judgment is evident from commentary, but opposition is given its most powerful voice in a strident dissenting judgment of four judges.[312] Contending that the majority judgment's interpretative approach seeks to 'reconcile the irreconcilable', the dissent argues that the judgment in fact provides for the *effective* displacement of Article 5 protections in armed conflict.[313] It also asserts that the judgment risks rendering redundant the Convention's derogation provisions, noting compellingly that derogation could and should have been invoked by the government.[314]

Despite the controversies, the *Hassan* case is a significant shift for the European Court in giving effect to applicable law in armed conflict. It accepted the principle of co-application and where possible harmonious interpretation of the Convention and IHL, alongside willingness to grapple explicitly with IHL even when it has a decisive impact on the outcome in the concrete case. It promotes ongoing regard to both areas of law to limit departures from normally applicable law to those strictly justified by more specific rules of IHL.

The Court itself makes clear that its willingness to co-apply IHL in this way will arise only in limited circumstances, and its rationale in so doing raises questions for the future. First, it seeks to limit the scope and impact of this shift by noting that it applies only to IAC, and explicitly not to occupation or NIAC.[315] The sharp distinction the Court adopted between IAC and NIAC is open to question, however, particularly in the light of the narrowing of the gap between the bodies of law. As a matter of practice, the Court's distinction

---

[311]   *Ibid.*, para. 104.
[312]   Partly Dissenting Opinion of Judge Spano, joined by Judges Nicolaou, Bianku and Kalaydjieva, paras. 2–9, 18–19. See also, e.g., Lawrence Hill-Cawthorne, 'The Grand Chamber Judgment in Hassan v UK', *EJIL:Talk!*, 16 September 2014, available at: www .ejiltalk.org/the-grand-chamber-judgment-in-hassan-v-uk. Silvia Borelli, 'Jaloud v. The Netherlands and Hassan v. United Kingdom: Time for a Principled Approach in the Application of the ECHR to Military Action Abroad', *Questions of International Law* 16 (2015), 25–43.
[313]   *Ibid.*, Partly Dissenting Opinion.
[314]   *Ibid.*, Partly Dissenting Opinion, paras. 7–9.
[315]   *Ibid.*, Majority Judgment, para. 104.

may mean that it will need to look in some detail at the difficult question of classification of conflicts in the future.

Secondly, the Court confirmed the impact of the arguments of the parties, in particular the position of States. It noted that this was the first case in which a respondent State had 'requested the Court to disapply its obligations under Article 5 or in some other way to interpret them ... in the light of [IHL]',[316] and went on to state:

> the provisions of Article 5 will be interpreted and applied in the light of the relevant provisions of international humanitarian law only where this is specifically pleaded by the respondent State. It is not for the Court to assume that a State intends to modify the commitments which it has undertaken by ratifying the Convention in the absence of a clear indication to that effect.[317]

This qualification also raises a number of questions, including whether and why the Court should not have regard to applicable law *proprio motu*, or where the other party (the applicants) or third-party interveners so request. The desire to hold States to their IHRL obligations unless they specifically invoke IHL is understandable, but it may also reflect erroneous assumptions (in stark contrast to the *Abella* decision where this survey started) that IHRL *always* provides the higher standards of protection.

A final question arguably of broader significance relates to the potential impact of the Court's approach on States' positions and practice in respect of IHL. It remains to be seen if the Court's emphasis might influence government positions in pleadings before the Court, and trigger greater transparency around applicability of IHL and classification of conflicts, with potentially significant implications.

IV. CO-APPLICABILITY AND INTERPLAY: HARMONIOUS INTERPRETATION, *LEX SPECIALIS* AND BEYOND

This section will highlight some of the major features of the way in which, in this author's view, co-applicability of IHL and IHRL should be understood. Several approaches emerge from and are consistent with the growing body of practice discussed in Section III.

The starting point for co-applicable norms, of particular significance in the co-applicability of IHL and IHRL, is harmonious interpretation (Section A,

---

[316] It noted that 'in *Al-Jedda* ... [the] Government did not contend that Article 5 was modified or displaced by the powers of detention provided for by the Third and Fourth Geneva Conventions'.

[317] ECtHR, *Hassan v. United Kingdom* (n. 4), para. 107.

below). In practice, however, questions may and often do arise as to the *prioritisation* of norms, notably in face of conflict, and how the determination as to priority can be made. This may in certain circumstances be through the vehicle of the *'lex specialis'* construct (Section B, below) or, increasingly, through an apparently more nuanced approach to co-applicability of primary and secondary norms (Section C, below). Finally, understanding co-applicability requires an appreciation of the principles of interpretation of international law and in particular human rights law (Section D, below), indicating that IHRL must be interpreted purposively, flexibly, contextually and effectively, in armed conflict situations as elsewhere.

A. *Harmonious Interpretation*

The starting point for an assessment of the relationship between IHL and IHRL is what has been called the theory of complementarity, which emphasises the scope for harmonious interpretation of the two bodies of law.[318] As one proponent of the view states: '[c]omplementarity means that human rights law and humanitarian law do not contradict each other but, being based on the same principles and values can influence and reinforce each other mutually'.[319]

An emphasis on harmonious interpretation appears throughout the jurisprudence of human rights courts referred to in the previous section.[320] It is supported by the fact that, as the International Law Commission has stated, '[i]n international law, there is a strong presumption against normative conflict'.[321] This drives those applying the law to seek an interpretation whereby all applicable norms can be co-applied and understood not in conflict but in harmony. In some areas this is relatively straightforward; in the many areas of IHL and IHRL where there is normative similarity, each can inform the substantially similar provisions of the other. This harmonious approach features

---

[318] Droege, 'Interplay between IHL and IHRL' 2007 (n. 21), 337.

[319] *Ibid.*

[320] E.g., IHL 'nourishing' the interpretation of the ACHR in *Sanchez v. Peru; DRC v. Burundi, Rwanda and Uganda* (n. 186); or, controversially, the *Hassan* case, which was framed similarly as consistent interpretation, reflecting general reluctance to acknowledge normative conflict.

[321] ILC, '*Fragmentation of International Law: Difficulties Arising from the Diversification and Expansion of International Law*', Report of the Study Group of the ILC, finalised by Martti Koskenniemi, 13 April 2006, UN Doc. A/CN.4/L.682 (hereafter: 'ILC Report 2006'), para. 37. The report talks of interpretation as being about 'avoiding or mitigating conflict'.

strongly not only in the practice of human rights courts, but also in international criminal adjudication, or indeed the ICRC study on customary IHL.[322]

IHRL will more often provide the meat on the comparable, but skeletal, framework of IHL provisions; examples may include the meaning of humane treatment, fair trial standards affording 'essential judicial guarantees', the definition of slavery,[323] protection of family life[324] or health.[325] However, this will not always be so, and IHL will occasionally be more specific on some aspects, such as the right of family reunification or humanitarian assistance, for example.[326]

If we accept harmonious interpretation as a starting point, we also need to acknowledge where it ends, notably where norms conflict. As the ILC report notes, there is a 'definite limit to harmonisation'.[327] However, it also notes that harmonious interpretation should not be seen as automatically being ruled out by the existence of differing or potentially conflicting norms, if they may be reconcilable after a certain 'adjustment', without distorting the nature and purpose of the norms:

> Of course in such case, it is still possible to reach the conclusion that although the two norms seemed to point in diverging directions, after some adjustment, it is still possible to apply or understand them in such way that no overlap or conflict will remain ... [This may be] through an attempt to reach a resolution that integrates the conflicting obligations in some optimal way in the general context of international law.[328]

As one commentator put it, while this approach 'may resolve apparent conflicts; it cannot resolve genuine conflicts'.[329] One question is, of course, what constitutes a 'conflict', which may embrace a direct conflict of obligations, where the two bodies pull States in conflicting directions, or a conflict of norms of a permissive nature, or indeed, perhaps, as regards the norms' purposes or objectives. The ILC report on fragmentation states that where:

---

[322] As the standards explored in Section II make clear, the criminal tribunals frequently interpreted IHL/ICL by reference to human rights standards, and the ICRC Customary law study refers also to human rights practice.

[323] *ICRC Customary Study* 2005 (n. 22), Customary Rule 94, 329–30.

[324] *Ibid.*, Customary Rule 105, 379–83.

[325] See, e.g., Lindsay Moir, *The Law of Internal Armed Conflict* (Cambridge University Press, 2009), 200, referring to APII the duty not to subject to treatment not specified by the State of health.

[326] *Ibid.*, ch. 5. Moir recognises that on some issues IHL in IAC will be more specific, such as human experimentation. See further Section V examples.

[327] ILC Report 2006 (n. 321), para. 42.

[328] ILC Report 2006 (n. 321), para. 43.

[329] Christopher Borgen, 'Resolving Treaty Conflicts', *George Washington International Law Review* 37 (2005), 573–648 (605–6).

the question of conflict arises regarding the fulfilment of the objectives (instead of the obligations) of the different instruments, little may be done to integrate the two and avoid conflict. In relation to certain issues even in face of conflict the question may well need to be addressed by way of contextual analysis of underlying purposes and principles.[330]

It is often noted that IHL and IHRL pursue similar but not identical purposes, and reflect overlapping but distinct principles (the principle of humanity and the principle of distinction being the most obvious examples of each). One question in deciding whether particular norms are reconcilable is therefore whether the norms in question in fact pursue different purposes or reflect different principles, as opposed to pursuing them in different ways depending on what may be assumed to be prevailing contextual realities.[331]

B. Lex specialis! *The Harry Potter Approach?*

As has been noted in the WTO context, 'the *lex specialis* principle is assumed to apply if "harmonious interpretation" turns out to be impossible, that is, to overrule a general standard by a conflicting special one'.[332] There is a difference of view as to whether *lex specialis* applies only where norms conflict, as opposed to also where one set of norms is more detailed and specific than the other, though it is in the face of irreconcilable conflicts that many see the importance of *lex specialis* coming to the fore.[333]

It was international adjudication – this time before the ICJ in several advisory opinions – that provided the oft-cited starting point for most discussions of co-applicability and the *lex specialis* principle. In the *Nuclear Weapons* Advisory Opinion, the Court endorsed the notion specifically in relation to the right to life in the context of armed hostilities,[334] finding in pertinent part that:

> [i]n principle, the right not arbitrarily to be deprived of one's life applies also in hostilities. The test of what is an arbitrary deprivation of life, however, then falls to be *determined by the applicable lex specialis*, namely, the law

---

[330] ILC Report 2006 (n. 321), para. 33. See also treatment of conflict as arising from 'preventing the fulfilment of the other obligation or undermining its object and purpose', para. 130.

[331] See *infra*, Section IV.E on the separate question of prioritisation, and whether a clear and specific norm can or should defer to a principle or purpose. See also Duffy, *War on Terror* 2015 (n. 7).

[332] ILC Report 2006 (n. 321), paras. 88–9; see also, ILC Articles on the Responsibility of States for Internationally Wrongful Acts, GAOR, 56th Sess., Suppl. 10, Art. 55(4).

[333] See, e.g., ILC Report 2006 (n. 321); Expert Meeting on the Right to Life in Armed Conflict and Situations of Occupation, Geneva, 1–2 September 2005, University Centre for International Humanitarian Law, available at: www.adh-geneve.ch/pdfs/3rapport_droit_vie .pdf (hereinafter: the Expert Meeting 2005), 19.

[334] ICJ, *Legality of the Threat or Use of Nuclear Weapons* (n. 126).

applicable in armed conflict which is designed to regulate the conduct of hostilities. Thus whether a particular loss of life, through the use of a certain weapon in warfare, is to be considered an arbitrary deprivation of life . . . *can only be decided by reference to the law applicable in armed conflict and not deduced from the terms of the Covenant itself.*[335]

While affirming the continued application of IHRL in armed conflict, the ICJ therefore found that it must be applied by reference to IHL as the 'directly relevant applicable law'.[336] Eight years later, the Court came to consider a broader range of human rights treaty obligations arising in occupation (to which IHL applicable in IAC applied), and referred to *lex specialis* in a somewhat more nuanced (if not entirely illuminating) way. In its *Wall* Advisory Opinion it recognised the need to consider norm by norm which area of law governed, as 'some rights [were] exclusively matters of international humanitarian law; others may be exclusively matters of human rights law; yet others may be matters of both these branches'.[337]

The following year, in the *Armed Activities* case – the first contentious case to address the issue – the ICJ notably dropped the language of *lex specialis* altogether, stating simply that 'both branches of international law, namely international human rights law and international humanitarian law, would have to be taken into consideration'.[338] This suggested a more fluid interrelationship than the ICJ's earlier formulation of *lex specialis* (and certainly some approaches in State practice) might be understood to indicate, clarifying the concurrent and symbiotic role for both areas of applicable law.

The ICJ's formulation of the relationship as *lex specialis* has been and remains influential, and it undoubtedly remains a relevant, and probably still the dominant, approach. There are, however, also indications of trends away from reliance on *lex specialis* not only by the ICJ but also by other courts and bodies.[339]

---

[335] *Ibid.*, para. 25 (emphasis added).

[336] *Ibid.*, para. 35.

[337] ICJ, *Legality of the Consequences of the Construction of a Wall* (n. 122), para. 106.

[338] ICJ, *Armed Activities* (n. 122), para. 216, on alleged violations by the Ugandan military and agents during hostilities in the DRC.

[339] Remarks by Judge Sicilianos of the ECtHR at Leiden University, January 2017, suggesting the ICJ omission was deliberate. See also, Marko Milanovic, 'Norm Conflict, International Humanitarian Law, and Human Rights Law', in Ben-Naftali (ed.), *International Humanitarian Law and International Human Rights Law* 2011 (n. 6), 95–125. Droege, 'Interplay between IHL and IHRL' 2007 (n. 21), 338. Note that UNHRC, General Comment No. 31 (n. 190), outlining the applicability of IHRL in

This judicial shift may in part be explained by the different facts and processes before courts and bodies at any one time.[340] But it may also reflect a sensitivity to growing criticism of *lex specialis*, including among academics.[341] Critically, it may also be influenced by the overreaching reliance on IHL as a regime-wide *lex specialis* to negate the applicability of IHRL and 'strategically' avoid oversight[342] – by the United States on Guantánamo, rendition black sites, Iraq or Afghanistan, or by Colombia to avoid IACtHR jurisdiction – which has been robustly rejected, including by the relevant supervisory courts and bodies.[343]

Such overreaching approaches have caricatured, and exposed, some dubious assumptions concerning *lex specialis*. One is that it can operate on a regime-wide basis, rather than involving a determination as to which rule applies more specifically to the situation at hand on a norm-by-norm and situation-by-situation basis.[344] Despite its attractive simplicity, IHL cannot be seen as monolithically constituting *lex specialis*, just as normative conflict can arise only on the level of *particular norms* not of legal regimes as a whole. The prioritisation of norms cannot, moreover, be considered in abstract as it depends necessarily on context. As one commentator noted: '*lex specialis* is in some sense a contextual principle. It is difficult to use when determining conflicts between two normative orders *in abstracto*, and is, instead, more suited to the determination of relations between two norms in a concrete case.'[345] Another erroneous assumption is that IHL as opposed to IHRL always

---

armed conflict, was issued just a few months after the *Wall* Opinion, and notably did not utilise *lex specialis* terminology.

[340] E.g., for the ICJ, the shift from right to life in hostilities (*Nuclear Weapons*), to broader rights issues. For human rights bodies, see Section II.B on how the facts and functions influence the approach.

[341] Describing rejection of *lex specialis* as one of the few points of agreement between academics, see Paul Eden and Matthew Happold, 'Symposium: the Relationship between International Humanitarian Law and International Human Rights Law', *Journal of Conflict and Security Law* 14 (2009), 441–7. See also the *Practitioners' Guide* 2016 (n. 37); Milanovic, 'Norm Conflict' 2011 (n. 339); Hampson, 'The Relationship between International Humanitarian Law and Human Rights Law from the Perspective of a Human Rights Treaty Body' 2008 (n. 3), among others.

[342] See Section I.

[343] Section II and III.B, respectively.

[344] Others arguing in favour of a case-specific approach, and noting that on occasion human rights rules may constitute *lex specialis*, include Noam Lubell, 'Challenges in Applying Human Rights Law to Armed Conflict', *International Review of the Red Cross* 87 (2005), 737–54 (751). Some are concerned as to the practicality of a case-by-case approach: Hampson, 'The Relationship between International Humanitarian Law and Human Rights Law from the Perspective of a Human Rights Treaty Body' 2008 (n. 3), 562.

[345] Anja Lindroos, 'Addressing Norm Conflicts in a Fragmented Legal System: the Doctrine of Lex Specialis', *Nordic Journal of International Law* 74 (2005), 27–66.

provides the detailed and specific 'special rule' in times of armed conflict.[346] A third is that *lex specialis* operates to displace or trump the other law, which therefore becomes irrelevant.

Understood in this way, arguably the problems relate less to inherent difficulties with the concept of *lex specialis* than with its application in practice, to justify the displacement of one regime by another. But confusing and overreaching approaches to the concept may well have had the unintended consequence of contributing to a discernible movement away from framing the debate on interplay in terms of the *lex specialis* language.

C. Weighted Co-applicability and Prioritisation

An alternative approach to co-applicability draws on the strengths of *lex specialis* properly understood, while avoiding the pitfalls. Contextual co-applicability considers the particular context and identifies whether there are relevant co-applicable norms to be applied. Where necessary as norms conflict, greater weight is afforded to norms that are more specifically and appropriately directed to the particular context.

One example of such an approach, without reference to the *lex specialis* doctrine, is found in the *Practitioners' Guide to Human Rights in Armed Conflict*.[347] It emphasises an approach that begins with the factual circumstances on the ground. Leaving aside, of course, conduct with no nexus to the conflict (governed by IHRL as IHL does not apply), it considers first whether the conduct falls within what it calls an 'armed hostilities' or a 'security operations' framework.[348] The former will be 'primarily' governed by IHL, and the latter primarily by IHRL. Within a conflict either IHL or IHRL may provide the 'starting point' or the 'initial reference point with regard to the regulation of a particular situation'.[349] In general, the closer to active hostilities, the greater weight afforded to IHL and the further from them, the greater emphasis given to IHRL.

One strength of this approach, perhaps somewhat superficially, is that it avoids the use of a Latin term that sounds like a Harry Potter spell and creates an illusion of a magic solution. It is undeniable that some of the criticism concerning the lack of clarity around *lex specialis* arguably applies with just as

---

[346] Despite assumptions, IHL is not necessarily more specific in its content than IHRL, see, e.g., the rules on review of detention or remedy in Section V.

[347] *Practitioners' Guide* 2016 (n. 37).

[348] Arguably, these labels bring their own definitional problems, and these categories may not be necessary.

[349] *Practitioners' Guide* 2016 (n. 37), paras. 4.02–4.24.

much force to the 'law enforcement' and 'hostilities' paradigms and the associated weighted, context-dependent scale.

More importantly, it focuses on the need for a context-driven evaluation of facts, not assumptions, as to which rules more specifically address particular situations. This approach reminds us of the vast array of conduct within conflict that goes beyond active hostilities, to which the 'security framework' is more specifically and appropriately directed. It may also avoid controversies that have beset *lex specialis*,[350] including as regards whether it should be seen as a rule for conflict avoidance or conflict resolution, by placing less emphasis on normative conflict[351] or hierarchy of norms. Critically, it makes clear that there is no place for the regime-wide displacement approach to *lex specialis* noted in practice.[352] In contrast to the (misleading) presentation of *lex specialis* as an invitation to States to ignore their human rights obligations in armed conflict, prioritisation emphasises the continuing relevance of applicable norms.

D. *Interpretative Approaches to IHRL of Relevance to Co-applicability*

Finally, it is also relevant to bear in mind the influence of approaches to (and principles of) interpretation of applicable law. General principles of interpretation in Article 31(3)(c) of the Vienna Convention on the Law of Treaties (VCLT) call for interpretation in line with the ordinary meaning, purpose and context of a treaty, alongside other 'relevant rules of international law applicable in the relations between the parties'.[353] This reflects the increased focus on seeing international law as a 'system' that is coherent and not fragmented.[354]

In addition, specific interpretative approaches developed by human rights courts and bodies inform our interpretation of IHRL treaties.[355] Key

---

[350]   Cordula Droege, 'Elective Affinities? Human Rights Law and Humanitarian Law', *International Review of the Red Cross* 90 (2008), 501–48; Jean d'Aspremont, 'Articulating International Human Rights and International Humanitarian Law: Conciliatory Interpretation under the Guise of Conflict of Norms-Resolution', in Malgosia Fitzmaurice-Lachs and Panos Merkouris (eds.), *The Interpretation and Application of the European Convention on Human Rights: Legal and Practical Implications* (Leiden: Martinus Nijhoff, 2013), 3–31.

[351]   Martti Koskenniemi, '*Study on the Function and Scope of the Lex Specialis Rule and the Question of "Self-Contained Regimes"*', ILC (LVI)/SG/FIL/CRD.1 (2004) and Add.1, at 4. The *Practitioners' Guide* 2016 (n. 37), by contrast is not framed in terms of conflict resolution.

[352]   Explicitly rejected in the *Practitioners' Guide* 2016 (n. 37), para. 4.03.

[353]   Article 31(3)(c) Vienna Convention on the Law of Treaties, 23 May 1969, 1155 UNTS 331. E.g., ECtHR, *Al-Adsani v. United Kingdom*, Grand Chamber Judgment of 21 November 2001, Application No. 35763/97, paras. 54, 55.

[354]   ILC Report 2006 (n. 321), paras. 37–43.

[355]   On human rights interpretative principles generally, see IACHR, *Murillo v. Costa Rica*, Judgment of 28 November 2012, Case No. 12.361.

principles – of contextual interpretation, of 'effectiveness' and of interpretation in the light of the particular (protective) purpose of human rights treaties[356] – all seek to ensure that rights are interpreted so as to be 'practical and effective not theoretical and illusory'.[357] They have been relied upon to avoid 'vacuums of protection', but also to ensure that treaties do not pose an impossibly onerous burden on States. Evolutive interpretation ensures that human rights treaties are 'living instruments' that evolve over time in line with the changing realities they are bound to address.[358] Finally, as already suggested above, there is growing recognition of the need for an outward looking 'holistic' interpretation of human rights provisions as part of a broader body of international law,[359] and in the light of the practice of other courts and bodies.[360] Openness to IHL specifically is therefore simply part of a broader phenomenon of holistic interpretation of relevant international law.

The various principles of interpretation of IHRL seek to ensure its relevance, flexibility and effectiveness. They ensure that IHRL is not applied in an abstract way, but in context, in the light of unfolding realities, in a manner capable of effective application and in the light of other applicable norms. Such an approach to the interpretation of each body of applicable law can contribute to ensuring sensitivity to challenging contexts and the need to develop in the light of one another. As we will see in relation to specific issues in Section V, this approach to interpretation is also contributing to a narrowing of the gaps between IHL and IHRL.

E. Conclusions on Contextual Co-Applicability: Norms and Context

The following section suggests certain core aspects of how co-applicability should be understood today. It reflects the practice in Section III, and draws on

---

[356] The Inter-American system also refers to the '*pro homine*' principle in that 'if in the same situation both the American Convention and another international treaty are applicable, the rule most favourable to the individual must prevail'; IACHR, 'Compulsory Membership in an Association Prescribed by Law for the Practice of Journalism', 13 November 1985, Advisory Opinion OC-5/85. Cf. IACtHR, *Cruz Sanchez v. Peru* (n. 272).

[357] ECtHR, *Marckx v. Belgium*, Judgment of 13 June 1979, Application No. 6833/74; IACtHR, *Barrios Altos v. Peru*, Judgment of 14 March 2001, IACHR Series C, No. 83.

[358] The content of human rights evolves over time; see, e.g., ECtHR, *Selmouni v. France*, Judgment of 28 July 1999, Application No. 25803/94; ECtHR, *Christine Goodwin v. United Kingdom*, Judgment of 11 July 2002, Application No. 28957/95; IACHR, *Murillo v. Costa Rica* (n. 356).

[359] See, e.g., *Al-Adsani v. United Kingdom* (n. 353); IACHR, *Murillo v. Costa Rica* (n. 355).

[360] Courts having regard to parallel approaches of other courts to similar issues is now commonplace. See generally, Duffy, *Strategic Human Rights Litigation* 2018 (n. 25), ch. 2 on 'transjudicial dialogue'.

the approaches to interpretation and interplay in Section IV. In essence, it requires an approach that carefully identifies all relevant applicable norms, interpreted and (co-)applied in context.

1. A Norm-(by-Norm) and Context-(by-Context) Analysis

The rejection of regime-wide *lex specialis* has already been underscored. Both a *lex specialis* analysis, properly understood, and the alternative 'weighted prioritisation' approach entail the careful evaluation of two factors – context and rules. The prioritisation of conflicting norms must be resolved norm by norm in the light of the particular situation and context.

These approaches combine two conceptually quite distinct considerations: one is based on contextual relevance or appropriateness, on the one hand, and the other on the clarity and precision of the norms, on the other. The first places the emphasis on the rules that are most closely directed to and better able to 'take account of particular circumstances', or 'regulate ... the matter more effectively'.[361] The second refers to the rules the content of which more 'concretely', 'definitely', 'directly' and 'with clarity' address the issue at hand.[362] While different approaches to interplay emphasise one or the other, both are required for an analysis of co-applicability. The *Practitioners' Guide* weighted co-applicability may start with considering the specific factual context and circumstances but, as practice attests, the exercise depends on their *being* identifiable co-applicable norms.[363] Likewise, *lex specialis* seeks the norms more *specifically* directed to the conduct and *context* in question.[364]

As the examples in Section V illustrate, it is impossible to determine co-applicability without regard to the identification of all applicable norms and a determination of how they can be interpreted and applied in particular contexts. Neither the careful identification of applicable norms, nor their interpretation in context can be neglected.

---

[361] ILC Report 2006 (n. 321), para. 60. Note also differences of view set out in Expert Meeting 2005 (n. 333), 19–20: some emphasised specific content and others context, i.e., which law was 'designed for the given situation'.

[362] ILC Report 2006, *ibid.*, notes that 'sensitivity to context, capacity to reflect State will, concreteness, clarity, definiteness' are all relevant to assessment of and operation of the *lex specialis* principle, stating that '[n]o general, context-independent answers can be given to such questions'.

[363] E.g., discussion of the *Hassan* approach arising in IAC not NIAC, and Section V.

[364] See NIAC, at Sections III.B and V.A. See also Art. 55 of the International Law Commission's (ILC) draft articles on State responsibility, setting out a minority view that the *lex specialis* norm will be the one with 'more specific content'.

2. Identifying the *Particular* Context within the Conflict

What is also clear and common to either approach is that the analysis has to be made on a situation-by-situation basis, taking into account the particular factual context. It is not so much the existence or not of an armed conflict that provides this context, but the particular *situations* arising within the broader armed conflict to which specific IHL norms may be more specifically addressed.

Some of the assumptions regarding IHL as generally providing the *lex specialis* are based on the attention dedicated to the right to life in active hostilities or security detentions in IAC, where IHL provides direction. But the assumptions are further strained in many other situations in which the military engages, most obviously in occupation, for example, where their functions, and the context which need not involve clashes at all, may be more akin to the sort of situation IHRL was directed towards. IHL standards may also be less appropriate, as human rights bodies have reflected, in scenarios where the State's role, and the level of control it exercises, may have more in common with law enforcement than conduct of hostilities. This has generally been true for some hostage-taking situations arising in the broader context of armed conflict, though the particular degree of control in the particular context will also be relevant.[365] It is clear that the analysis of co-applicable law depends on a broader range of contextual factors than simply the existence of armed conflict or indeed the nature of that conflict.

3. The Type of Conflict as (Only) a Factor?

It is suggested that the nature of the conflict, while relevant, is not a determining contextual factor as regards the prioritisation to be afforded to IHL or IHRL. In practice, it may be more often the case that in situations of occupation, or NIAC within the State's own territory, where the occupying State is responsible for ensuring the full range of civil, political, economic and social rights, for example, and has an active law enforcement role, that IHRL assumes particular relevance. IHL may indeed not be relevant at all to many incidents not linked to the conflict.

Moreover, particular questions arise as to the extent of IHL as *lex specialis* in NIACs where it may not be clear whether there *is* an applicable norm of IHL at all. A norm- and context-specific determination requires looking beyond the

---

[365] UNHRC, *Camargo v. Colombia*, 31 March 1982, Communication No. 45/1979; or ECtHR, *Finogenov v. Russia* (n. 292); but cf. the particular context drawing the Court to IHL in the IACHR, *Cruz Sanchez v. Peru* (n. 272).

nature of the conflict to the facts on the ground and the relevant law applicable to the particular situation.[366]

4. Identifying Specific Norms (and the Sound of Silence?)

Obvious challenges arise in relation to identifying applicable norms in NIAC situations, given the relative normative weakness for this type of conflict. This may be true of targeting,[367] and *a fortiori* detention in NIAC, where there may be no clear and explicit rules as highlighted in Section V. If there is no norm specifically directed to the situation, there is no *lex*, and presumably no *lex specialis*, and no norm to take priority over another.

Difficult questions may, however, arise as to the significance of treaty silence and the implications for co-application.[368] It might be argued that even in the absence of rules, one body of law may have underlying *principles* that govern a customary law, or inform treaty interpretation. Working out whether there is in fact law in relation to a particular situation under IHL, and under IHRL, is not always straightforward, but a crucial challenge to be met. Finally, either IHL or IHRL may be the primary, or more specific, norm in armed conflict situations.[369]

It has been noted that in international law 'nothing indicates which of two norms is the *lex specialis* or the *lex generalis*, particularly between human rights law and humanitarian law'.[370] As noted above, while IHL is often directed more specifically towards hostilities, IHRL may be more specifically directed to particular types of operation within the broader conflict. Each body of law may provide rules that are more specific, detailed and targeted to particular scenarios.[371]

5. Ongoing Relevance and Influence of Both Norms

A final observation relates to the consequences of one norm assuming priority for the other co-applicable norm. As noted above, one disadvantage of the *lex specialis*

---

[366]   Lubell, 'Parallel Application of International Humanitarian Law and International Human Rights Law: An Examination of the Debate' 2007 (n. 32), 748, speaks to the lack of clear rules on targeting 'participants' in NIAC.

[367]   *Ibid.*

[368]   See e.g., *Practitioners' Guide* 2016 (n. 37), para. 4.67, noting a 'gap may be a deliberate omission'.

[369]   Prud'homme, '*Lex Specialis*: Oversimplifying a More Complex and Multifaceted Relationship?' 2007 (n. 32), 385.

[370]   Droege, 'Interplay between IHL and IHRL' 2007 (n. 21), 338.

[371]   Consider, e.g., provision of humanitarian assistance, detention rights, repatriation or due process guarantees where each body may lend specific provisions of relevance.

language is that, on a narrow and rigid approach to what it means, it has appeared to provide the exclusive basis for determining the matter, with the other norm effectively displaced. On the stronger view, there remains an ongoing role for the other body of norms. It is suggested that while judicial practice drives in both directions, evolving practice supports the view that both bodies of law co-apply and interrelate on an ongoing basis. The dynamic interrelationship means that such norms may be further 'in the background', but potentially still relevant to the interpretation of the priority norms.[372] This ensures that the human rights norms are not set aside to a greater extent than justified, consistent with the principle of IHRL that permissible restrictions on rights should be no more than necessary.[373] It also meets the objectives of harmonious interpretation as far as possible, minimising and mitigating conflict on an ongoing basis, as set out at the start of this section.[374]

Both IHL and IHRL are applicable in armed conflict situations. Giving meaningful effect to co-applicability means considering applicable norms in the particular contexts; while norms from one or the other area of law may take precedence, both remain applicable and potentially relevant. In this framework, co-applicability provides a basis for a comprehensive and dynamic approach to the law governing armed conflict. It also poses undoubted – and unavoidable – challenges for those seeking to give effect to the law, not least for the courts and bodies before whom, increasingly, these matters fall to be determined.

V. EXAMPLES OF INTERPLAY AND OUTSTANDING QUESTIONS

This section examines what the different approaches to interplay mean in practice by highlighting State practice, adjudicative responses, and the issues, challenges and controversies arising in relation to particular contentious issues. In some areas it also demonstrates how IHL and IHRL may be moving closer together through legal and practical developments.

---

[372] See, e.g., Sassòli and Olson, 'The Relationship between International Humanitarian and Human Rights Law where it Matters' 2008 (n. 118); see also the *Hassan* case on procedural safeguards (n. 4).

[373] Section IV; specific IHL rules have led the Court's analysis, but IHRL has remained relevant to its interpretation, e.g., IACtHR, *Cruz Sanchez v. Peru* (n. 272); *Bámaca v. Guatemala* (n. 258); ECtHR, *Hassan v. United Kingdom* (n. 4).

[374] ILC Report 2006 (n. 321), para. 37; see also Sassòli and Olson, 'The Relationship between International Humanitarian and Human Rights Law where it Matters' 2008 (n. 118).

A. Detention (and Review of Lawfulness) in Non-International Armed Conflict?

Much controversy, and considerable litigation at the national and international levels, has been dedicated to challenging the lawful basis of detention and, in particular, the procedural safeguards to which 'security detainees' are entitled (and whether it includes judicial review).[375] As discussed in Section II, many detentions pursuant to the putative 'conflict with Al-Qaeda and others' were not related to a genuine armed conflict, and as such no issue of IHL should arise. Lawfulness and safeguards fall to be determined by reference to IHRL, which applies to those who are detained by – therefore under the control of – the State, where operating at home or abroad.[376] However, where detainees *have* been captured or detained in the context of IACs, and in particular NIACs,[377] multiple questions arise concerning the applicability and interplay of IHL and IHRL.[378]

Three litigation processes, before different fora, expose how IHL standards have been invoked by States in various contexts in support of the argument that IHRL procedural protections did not apply, giving rise to differing judicial responses.

A first set of cases emerges from US courts. While the US Supreme Court in the 2008 *Boumidiene* case famously found persons detained at Guantánamo Bay (pursuant to a NIAC) were entitled to *habeas corpus*,[379] the application of *habeas* to detainees held in Afghanistan has thus far been denied.[380] One of the grounds for this was that detention in a zone of 'active combat' rendered *habeas* review impracticable. In the *Maqaleh* litigation, petitions for *habeas* relief were brought by applicants who claimed to have been captured outside Afghanistan, far from combat zones, and transferred *into* the Baghram Air Base military prison in Afghanistan for imprisonment.[381] The Federal District

---

[375] The question of whether such detention is lawful at all is also controversial, but is arguably 'implicit' in IHL as a corollary of the right to use force. See, e.g., Sivakumaran, *The Law of Non-International Armed Conflict* 2012 (n. 58), 303.

[376] See Section II.C, geographic scope, citing, e.g., *Al-Skeini v. United Kingdom* (n. 137) or IACHR, *Precautionary Measures in Guantanamo Bay* (n. 208).

[377] As noted below, NIACs raise particular uncertainty given the lack of explicit IHL.

[378] The classification of some conflicts has changed mid-course; see, e.g., Afghanistan and Iraq, Duffy, *War on Terror* 2015 (n. 7), ch. 6.

[379] US Supreme Court, *Lakhdar Boumediene et al., Petitioners v. George W. Bush, President of the United States et al.* 553 US 723 (2008). See Duffy, *War on Terror* 2015 (n. 7), ch. 8.

[380] US Court of Appeals for the District of Columbia Circuit, *Al-Maqaleh et al. v. Gates et al.*, Case No. 09-5265, decided on 21 May 2010.

[381] US Court of Appeals for the District of Columbia Circuit, *Al-Maqaleh v. Gates* case, *ibid.*: the applicants alleged capture in Thailand, Pakistan and elsewhere outside Afghanistan, far from hostilities.

Court judge ruled that as these detainees were not *captured* in an area of war, they had the right to challenge their detention (although others that had been captured in Afghanistan and held there did not). However, the Federal Appeals Court for the District of Columbia overturned the decision. As the site of *detention* was in a 'theatre of active military combat',[382] and there were 'practical obstacles'[383] in overseas detention, the detainees had no constitutional right to challenge their detention in a US court.

The applicants sought review based on new evidence. This included evidence of the government's intent to evade the writ of *habeas* and hold them indefinitely by transferring them into Baghram. It also included evidence contesting that logistical difficulties at Baghram in fact rendered *habeas* review infeasible, and of the inadequacy of the alternative procedures advanced. Rejecting the applicants' claim, the Court reiterated that Baghram, unlike Guantánamo, lies in an 'active theater of war'.[384] It appeared to acknowledge that, with sufficient resources, *habeas* petitions may indeed be entertained at Baghram, but that it would not 'divert efforts and attention from the military offensive abroad to the legal defensive at home'.[385] The Supreme Court declined to exercise jurisdiction.[386]

The net effect – years after the 'historic victory' of the *Boumidiene* Supreme Court judgment finding Guantánamo detainees had the right to *habeas corpus* – is a judicially endorsed void to which detainees captured anywhere in the world could be deposited to avoid judicial oversight.[387] The first instance District Court decision also signalled the potential of the judicial role to look past the formal question of an armed conflict to the reality on the ground, the feasibility (or not) of *habeas* and the State's motivation, including implicitly whether the context of 'active hostilities' was being exploited to avoid judicial review. But as this was overturned, the case may suggest that even if individuals are transferred *into* a conflict zone, and even if *habeas* is

---

[382] *Ibid.*, 4.

[383] *Ibid.*, 22.

[384] US Court of Appeals for the District of Columbia, *Amanatullah v. Obama* and *Hamidullah v. Obama*, Case No. 12-5404, 24 December 2013, 31.

[385] *Ibid.*, 28. For all four judgments, see Rehan Abeyratne, 'Al Maqaleh and the Diminishing Reach of Habeas Corpus', *Nebraska Law Review* 96 (2016), 146–93.

[386] On 23 March 2015, the US Supreme Court granted *certiorari* and disposed of the *Al Maqaleh v. Hagel* case.

[387] Both the extraterritorial issue and armed conflict are at play. See the US Court of Appeals for the District of Columbia, *Al-Maqaleh* case, where the Court stated that 'the *Boumediene* analysis has no application beyond territories that are, like Guantánamo, outside the *de jure* sovereignty of the United States but are subject to its *de facto* sovereignty'.

still feasible, invoking the 'theatre of war' argument provides a pretext to deny rights protections.[388]

A second group of cases arose from detentions by the UK forces abroad.[389] As discussed previously (Section IV), in *Hassan v. UK* the ECtHR for the first time took a close, direct and open look at IHL, and found that where there were explicit IHL rules governing detention invoked expressly by the State, IHRL had to be 'interpreted' in line with IHL. The Court notably emphasised, however, that its approach would have been different in a NIAC.

Which takes us naturally to the cases in which this very issue of detention in NIAC came before the UK courts, culminating in the *Serdar Mohammed* case.[390] The English courts found that there was no lawful basis for the applicant's detention by UK forces in the NIAC in Afghanistan. Absent a clear rule of IHL authorising and regulating detention, IHRL governed, and, absent derogation, there was no lawful basis. On appeal, the Supreme Court found a different lawful basis for detention in Iraq (namely, that of the Security Council, so the lawfulness of detention under NIAC was rendered moot).[391] The approach of the courts in the *Serdar Mohammed* case is therefore more instructive for present purposes than its outcome.

The starting point in relation to the power to detain was a pragmatic contextual one. It was recognised, for example, that 'whether or not it represents a legal right, detention is inherent in virtually all military operations of a sufficient duration and intensity to qualify as armed conflicts, whether or not they are international', which had to 'have a bearing on the interpretation' of relevant law.[392] However, the Court of Appeal ultimately could not find sufficient consensus on the right to detain under customary IHL.[393] Although in this case the issue was rendered moot by the finding of an implied power to detain derived from Security Council resolutions, a shadow was cast over detention in NIAC for future clarification. But it is also important that,

---

[388] US Court of Appeals for the District of Columbia, *Al-Maqaleh v. Hagel* case, *Amanatullah v. Obama* case and *Hamidullah v. Obama* case (n. 384). The Appeals Court Decision, para. 25, suggested that its decision may have been different if the applicants had been transferred deliberately to preclude judicial oversight.

[389] From a long line of cases concerning detention by UK forces overseas, a few (ECtHR, *Hassan v. United Kingdom* (n. 4); UK Supreme Court, *Al-Waheed and Serdar Mohammed* case (n. 96); ECtHR, *Al-Jedda* and *Al-Skeini v. United Kingdom* (n. 137)) are discussed here.

[390] UK Court of Appeal, *Serdar Mohammed and Others v. Secretary of State for Defence*, 30 July 2015, [2015] EWCA Civ 843; *Al-Waheed and Serdar Mohammed* case (n. 96).

[391] UK Supreme Court, *Al-Waheed and Serdar Mohammed* case 2017 (n. 96).

[392] UK Court of Appeal, *Serdar Mohammed* case 2015 (n. 390); UK Court of Appeal (Civil Division), *Rahmatullah v. MoD*, Judgment of 30 July 2015, [2015] EWCA Civ 843, para. 15.

[393] *Ibid.*, para. 14.

although there was an alternative lawful basis for detention, the procedural safeguards under the ECHR continued to apply and had been violated.

The judgment (and several concurring and dissenting separate opinions) is an indication of the growing engagement of national courts with issues of interplay, cross-referring between IHRL, IHL and the law on peace and security. It also shows how, relying on the ECHR's *Hassan* approach, the Court sought ways to reach an 'accommodation' between relevant areas of co-applicable international law.[394] It would not, however, read into IHL powers and procedures that were not there in respect of NIACs, nor ultimately dispense with judicial guarantees for detainees.

The case also reveals shadows of what has been described as 'background political concerns that ... pervade the judicial approach in this case'.[395] Whether or not it did or should shape its approach or the outcome, Lord Wilson expressed his 'relief' to have avoided a conflict between security measures and human rights in a way that might have brought the convention 'into international disrepute'.[396]

The case reserves the question for the future; by which law, and which approach to interplay, should we consider the extent of detainee's entitlement to *habeas* review under international law? Is it IHRL with its clear right to judicially challenge lawfulness before an independent court, or IHL?

If the conflict were international, there would be explicit and clear rules of the Geneva Conventions III and IV – on review procedures for POWs and civilians detained for imperative reasons of security – as *Hassan* attests.[397] By providing for review by an 'appropriate court *or* administrative body', Geneva Convention IV accepts that judicial review is not always appropriate or possible, while implicitly reflecting its importance where the particular context means that it is. But for NIAC, there are no specific IHL treaty provisions on challenging lawfulness at all.

A separate question that must be asked is whether a new *customary* norm of IHL has arisen for NIAC, though the *Serdar* case may suggest otherwise. The prohibition on arbitrary detention in general has been described as customary law in either type of conflict, but it is noteworthy that the ICRC commentary

---

[394]   UK Supreme Court, *Al-Waheed and Serdar Mohammed* case 2017 (n. 96), para. 59, and critique in Fiona Ni Aolain, 'To Detain Lawfully or Not to Detain: Reflections on UK Supreme Court Decision in Serdar Mohammad', *Just Security*, 2 February 2017, available at: www.justsecurity.org/37013/detain-lawfully-detain-question-reflection-uk-supreme-court-decision-serdar-mohammed.

[395]   *Ibid.*

[396]   Lord Wilson in UK Supreme Court, *Al-Waheed and Serdar Mohammed* case 2017 (n. 96), para. 134.

[397]   See e.g., Art. 5 Geneva Convention III and Arts. 43 and 78 of Geneva Convention IV.

when focusing on NIACs looks to human rights law to flesh out the meaning of non-arbitrariness.[398] Practice will continue to develop in this field and the law may evolve with it. But until it does, and while neither treaty nor customary IHL makes any specific provision, there is no norm of IHL or issue of co-applicability, still less normative conflict.

One alternative approach that has been suggested is the application by 'analogy' of law applicable in IAC.[399] But there is reason to doubt that there is any principled legal basis for 'analogising' rules that apply in IAC in the context of NIAC to effectively displace binding rights and obligations under IHRL.[400] Moreover, if IHRL is applicable, then there is not a 'gap' to be filled that might justify such application by analogy. Furthermore, courts and tribunals will inevitably have to rule on these issues based on applicable law, not the application of principles by analogy.

However one conceptualises interplay, the identification of applicable law is an inescapable prerequisite to considering interplay in context. On this basis, if IHL does not govern procedural guarantees, the primary framework must be IHRL; this finds support in case law and in the *Practitioners' Guide* which concludes simply that 'internment review is regulated by human rights law'.[401] However, in practice, this proposition continues to meet real resistance. This is often based, it seems, on a sense that respect for IHRL is inappropriate or unrealistic – which is not an argument as to where the law stands but rather as to how one feels about it.

Difficulties in meeting international obligations, including under IHL or IHRL, cannot per se render them inapplicable.[402] Moreover, and in any event, on the facts it may be that persons captured in an 'area of combat' *can* in fact be detained elsewhere (as indeed is reflected in IHL obligations) and safeguards

---

[398]　*ICRC Customary Study* 2005 (n. 22), Customary Rule 99, 344. By contrast to IACs, for NIACs, it is IHRL that is cited. Sivakumaran, *The Law of Non-International Armed Conflict* 2012 (n. 58), 303, notes 'both State and non-State armed groups are obliged to review detention through independent and impartial mechanisms', citing a domestic example by the Pristina District Court which found unlawful detention by members of the KLA.

[399]　Sassòli and Olson, 'The Relationship between International Humanitarian and Human Rights Law where it Matters' 2008 (n. 118), 623.

[400]　See Kevin Jon Heller, 'The Use and Abuse of Analogy in IHL', in Jens David Ohlin (ed.), *Theoretical Boundaries of Armed Conflict & Human Rights* (Cambridge University Press, 2015), 232–85 (234), which argues that there is 'no basis in international law for taking rules of IHL that exist as a matter of convention and custom only in IAC and applying them in NIAC by analogy . . .' He notes US courts' reliance on analogy to ill effect and without explanation.

[401]　E.g., ECtHR, *Hassan v. United Kingdom* (n. 4), and *Mohammad* cases (nn. 96, 390). *Practitioners' Guide* 2016 (n. 37), paras. 8.50–8.59.

[402]　Rene Provost, *International Human Rights and Humanitarian Law* (Cambridge University Press, 2002), 315.

afforded.[403] Likewise, the IHRL framework for its part often *can* and does adequately accommodate security situations and the implications for the right to liberty in many ways, including through derogation,[404] and its inherent flexibility to adjust to contextual realities.[405] It is routine for human rights bodies to ask whether or not the overall effect of the 'totality' of proceedings, in all the circumstances, sufficiently protected rights and afforded a meaningful opportunity to challenge, for example.[406]

Judicial review of the lawfulness of detention is not a right that can be dispensed with, even in situations of emergency, and the importance of prompt review to safeguard against arbitrariness and abuse, including torture, is plain.[407] This is not to deny a degree of flexibility as regards the nature and timing of judicial review; the determination of what constitutes the requirement of being brought before a judge 'as soon as practicable' is an inherently contextual analysis.[408] It remains to be seen how human rights courts would respond to genuine battlefield detentions, where the State provided independent but non-judicial review immediately due to genuine lack of immediate access to regularly constituted courts, and judicial oversight as soon as possible. The contexts in which the issue has arisen in practice have generally been quite different.

While the focus of controversy is on procedural guarantees during NIACs, developments have implications for procedures applicable in IAC too. IHL provides the normative starting point for the analysis based on specific IHL provisions and procedures. However, in interpreting and giving effect to the IHL framework, the more developed standards of IHRL remain relevant. This was seen clearly from the *Hassan* judgment (and *Serdar Mohammed*) where the basic guarantees of procedural overview by a 'competent body' fell to be considered by reference to benchmarks provided in IHRL. In this process much depends upon context. As the *Practitioners' Guide* has suggested, where

---

[403] Both Geneva Conventions III and IV contain such provisions on obligations towards detainees.

[404] Duffy, *War on Terror* 2015 (n. 7), ch. 7. Derogation is subject to safeguards and the essence of the right cannot be set aside.

[405] Section IV.D.

[406] See, e.g., jurisprudence of the ECHR on fair trial, e.g., ECtHR, *Brogan and Others v. United Kingdom*, Judgment of 29 November 1988, Application Nos. 11209/84, 11234/84, 11266/84, 11386/85.

[407] IACtHR, 'Emergency Situations', 30 January 1987, Advisory Opinion OC-8/87, Ser. A, No. 9; ECtHR, *Brogan v. United Kingdom* (n. 406); UNHRC, General Comment No. 8, Art. 9 (Sixteenth session, 1982), Compilation of General Comments and General Recommendations Adopted by Human Rights Treaty Bodies, 29 July 1994, UN Doc. HRI/GEN/1/Rev.1, 8.

[408] E.g., ECtHR, *Khudyakova v. Russia*, Judgment of 8 January 2009, Application No. 13476/04.

individuals are detained far from hostilities, in situations where the State exercises a greater degree of control, greater weight is likely to be afforded to IHRL.[409] If so, even in IACs, where there are two sets of applicable norms under IHL and IHRL, where circumstances such as distance from hostilities make respect for the stricter guarantees of IHRL possible (including judicial review), at that point such review should be provided.[410]

A contrario, transfer *into* conflict situations by their captors, as in the *Baghram* cases referred to at the beginning of this section, cannot on any purposive, contextual or effective interpretation of law provide a basis to rely on the exigencies of the situation as a basis for denying such review. These cases are a reminder of the need for vigilance to ensure that illusory battlefield scenarios do not provide an opportunity to circumvent rights and avoid accountability.

B. *Lethal Force and 'Targeted Killings'*

The classic scenario in which 'the *lex specialis* of IHL' has long been invoked is in relation to the lethal targeting of combatants or persons taking a direct part in hostilities.[411] While not beyond dispute, IHL governs the targeting of individuals in IAC and NIAC.[412] The rules of IHRL and IHL are, moreover, plainly different on this issue, with the former prohibiting force that is 'more than absolutely necessary' and the latter providing more detailed rules of targeting based on the status of the individual.[413] The assumptions on which the rules are based are often cited as fundamentally different, notably the principle of distinction that underpins IHL and the universality of human rights protections. What then, if anything, is the continuing role of IHRL and interplay in the interpretation and application of the law on the lethal use of force in armed conflict?

The clearest manifestation of the tensions surrounding interplay in this area is the controversial question of whether, and if so when, there is an obligation to capture rather than kill combatants or persons who are otherwise legitimate

---

[409]   *Practitioners' Guide* 2016 (n. 37), para. 440.

[410]   See, e.g., ECtHR, *Hassan v. United Kingdom* (n. 4) paras. 106, 109, on the relevance of 'context'.

[411]   See ICJ, *Nuclear Weapons* (n. 126); David Kretzmer, 'Rethinking the Application of International Humanitarian Law in Non-International Armed Conflicts', *Israel Law Review* 42 (2009), 8–45.

[412]   Sivakumaran, *The Law of Non-International Armed Conflict* 2012 (n. 58), 336 and ch. 9, noting whether international law regulates use of force in NIAC has long been disputed.

[413]   As noted, under IHRL the use of force must be 'no more than absolutely necessary'.

objects of attack. Some interesting emerging approaches, from limited practice to date, are worthy of note.

An oft-cited national decision was the Israeli Supreme Court seminal
'targeted killings' judgment,[414] which found that while civilians lose their
immunity from attack for as long as they participate in hostilities,[415] where
their arrest was feasible in all the circumstances and posed no risk to the
opposing party, lethal force would be unlawful.[416] More recently, the ICRC
Guidance on Direct Participation in Hostilities adopted a broadly similar
approach.[417]

The Israeli Court and the ICRC Guidance began with identifying relevant
rules, while reflecting the importance of context to their interpretation and
application. Within the broad context of armed conflict, there are certain
factual scenarios closer to IHRL than to IHL; whether operations unfold in the
supermarket versus the battlefield may make a difference to lawful responses.
The Supreme Court adopts language drawn over from the human rights
world, and is often cited in support of mutual influence of IHRL and IHL.
It is open to question, however, to what extent these developments involve the
co-application of IHRL and IHL, or the progressive interpretation of IHL
itself – of military necessity and, in the ICRC commentary, of humanity.[418]

Similarly, as noted in Section IV, human rights courts and bodies have,
often implicitly, begun with IHRL; they have, however, interpreted it in the
light of IHL in the context of high-intensity hostilities.[419] Where capture
instead of killing was possible, and lethal force avoidable, this had to be
done 'before resorting to the use of deadly force, all measures to arrest
a person suspected of being in the process of committing acts of terror must
be exhausted'.[420] The issue has also been considered in a comparable, but
somewhat more abstract, way by the African Commission and the former

---

[414] Public Committee Against Torture in Supreme Court of Israel, *Israel v. Government of Israel*,
13 December 2006, Case No. HCJ 769/02.

[415] *ICRC Customary Study* 2005 (n. 22), Rule 6 applicable in IAC and NIAC; Melzer, 'Guidance
on Direct Participation in Hostilities' 2009 (n. 177).

[416] *Ibid.*

[417] Melzer, 'Guidance on Direct Participation in Hostilities' 2009 (n. 177), recognises this may
not work in a classic battlefield scenario involving high-intensity conflict.

[418] ICRC Guidance suggests that it would 'defy the basic notions of humanity' not to give an
opportunity to surrender where there is no necessity for the use of lethal force.

[419] Section IV; see also *Practitioners' Guide* 2016 (n. 37), para. 5.41.

[420] UNHRC, Concluding Observations, Israel 2003 (n. 235), para. 15; discussion in
Ryan Goodman, 'The Power to Kill or Capture Enemy Combatants', *European Journal of
International Law* 24 (2013), 819–53, and the reply by Michael N. Schmitt, 'Wound, Capture,
or Kill: a Reply to Ryan Goodman's "The Power to Kill or Capture Enemy Combatants"',
European Journal of International Law 24 (2013), 855–61; Ryan Goodman, 'The Power to Kill

Special Rapporteur on Extrajudicial Executions.[421] He emphasises the need for a context-specific analysis of what IHL itself permits and requires by reference, *inter alia*, to 'military necessity', and where IHL is not in fact clear, regard should be had to IHRL.

The *Practitioners' Guide* suggests factors relevant to the relative weight afforded to IHL and IHRL rules. Sustained fighting and lack of territorial control are likely to lead to the 'hostilities' framework taking priority,[422] whereas for operations against a political leader of an armed group located – and controlling hostilities – from abroad, it may be that the human rights framework in fact 'reflects the realities on the ground'.[423] An assessment of these realities has to be made on a case-by-case basis.[424]

Each of these approaches, notably the judgment of a domestic court applying IHL, the UNHRC Observations applying the ICCPR, and the Special Rapporteur's report, take different starting points and approaches. The starting point for analysis of lethal force in armed conflict for most would be the specific and more permissive rules of IHL, though for courts whose competence derives from IHRL, the starting point may be its constituent instrument. But in either case, the other applicable law and principles may also be taken into account in the particular context to determine whether the lethal use of force can be justified in the light of all prevailing circumstances.

The examples may suggest even in respect of targeting in armed conflict where IHL and IHRL appear starkly different, that the outcome of the application of IHL might not be dissimilar to an application of IHRL. This may reflect the evolution and 'humanisation' of IHL, influenced by the parallel development of IHRL, and the 'contextualisation' of IHRL in certain armed conflict situations. So far as this approach continues to evolve, gaps should narrow and the issue of normative conflict in this field should become less significant.

---

or Capture Enemy Combatants: A Rejoinder to Michael N. Schmitt', *European Journal of International Law* 24 (2013), 863–6.

[421] See Alston, 'Report of the Special Rapporteur on Extrajudicial, Summary or Arbitrary Executions' 2010 (n. 9), paras. 29–30. ACommHPR General Comment No. 3 on right to life, referring to IHL providing a lawful basis for lethal force when 'necessary from a military perspective' (n. 194, para. 32).

[422] *Practitioners' Guide* 2016 (n. 37), para. 5.20.

[423] Sivakumaran, *The Law of Non-International Armed Conflict* 2012 (n. 58), 371, though he notes this remains 'very much *lex ferenda*'.

[424] *Ibid.*, 372.

C. Cyberspace

The challenge for all law is to keep pace with reality. Part of the contemporary reality is that it is increasingly through cyberspace that attacks are launched, information obtained and rights restricted on a global scale. This raises a number of questions of applicability of both IHL and IHRL, and interplay, with potentially significant rule of law implications. Adjudication in this field is challenging and remains limited. The growth in practice and related concern surrounding 'cyber warfare' and excessive foreign surveillance suggest this is likely to change.

First, as regards IHL applicability, complex questions of applicability arise as to whether and when cyberattacks might themselves give rise to an armed conflict – when they amount to 'armed force between States', or when the intense or protracted 'violence' and 'organised' OAGs' requirements of NIACs might be met and, if so, what the geographic locus and scope of cyber armed conflict might be?

There is no intensity threshold for IACs, and the nature of the 'force' is not defined or qualified.[425] The fact that the law is not explicit on these emerging phenomena does not, of course, mean that existing rules cannot be applied. For example, cyber operations by one State on the territory of another that cause death, destruction or harm to property may quite readily be interpreted as giving rise to armed conflict and be governed by IHL. It would be debatable whether other cyberattacks, accessing information, damaging data or perhaps even exercising a degree of control over infrastructure, despite the profound impact on States and their citizens, would amount to use of 'force' between States under IHL. While it has been suggested that 'the law has no requirement for hostilities at all',[426] uncertainty as to where the line should be drawn for cyber operations by one State against another to trigger an armed conflict poses important challenges for the future.

For NIAC, the intensity threshold would plainly exclude random hackers. The rules governing the level of organisation of a group would render it doubtful whether even a sophisticated virtually organised group of hackers might themselves constitute a militarily organised armed group for the purposes of IHL applicability. At a certain point, the relevant intensity and organisational requirements may be met, but only by, for example, 'destructive

---

[425] Cf. the use of 'force' that might constitute an armed attack triggering the right to self-defence under the *ius ad bellum*, where a 'scale and effects' criterion is relevant: Haines, 'Northern Ireland 1968–1998' 2012 (n. 281), 461; Duffy, *War on Terror* 2015 (n. 7), ch. 5.

[426] Michael N. Schmitt, 'Classification in Future Conflict', in Wilmshurst (ed.), *Classification of Conflicts* 2012 (n. 2), 455–77, suggests detention may give rise to an IAC.

and sustained' cyberattacks by organised cyber groups.[427] Although the geography of conflict is less key to classification of conflicts than was once assumed, whether a conflict be waged 'virtually' such that the 'armed' group for the purposes of IHL might exist, organise and operate only in cyberspace, is also uncertain. What would the implications be for the ability to clearly define participants in the conflict, and potentially the over-inclusive resort to IHL? Particular challenges of proof as regards responsibility, organisation, nexus between individuals and the groups, and causation pose additional, albeit somewhat separate, challenges.[428]

Where each area of law *is* potentially applicable, the usual questions arise as to how they will co-apply. For the most part, with regard to cyberattacks within armed conflict, the relevant rules on targeting and legitimate military objects would apply.[429] But for cyber *surveillance or monitoring*, however, identifying applicable IHL is more challenging. The normative gap between IAC and NIACs once again rears its head. IHL in IAC has specific provision on seeking information on enemy forces and the State,[430] but NIAC has no such provision. Moreover, it has been suggested that, as IHL makes no provision on surveillance of civilians, for either type of conflict, foreign surveillance even during armed conflict would be covered by IHRL.[431] As usual, this would depend on an analysis of the factual operations and context, and applicable law.

Questions may also arise concerning the applicability of IHRL to extraterritorial cyber surveillance. As set out above, the exceptions to the 'primarily territorial' reach of human rights of treaties, carved out case by case, have tended to include detention, torture and, eventually, lethal use of force that brought persons under the 'physical power and control' of State agents. An issue thus far avoided by human rights courts[432] is whether for extraterritorial surveillance it will suffice that there is effective control over

---

[427] Schmitt, 'Classification', *ibid.*, 464 – only 'destructive' and 'sustained' cyberattacks by organised groups would meet NIAC criteria.

[428] *Ibid.*, 463.

[429] The type of attack, norms and context would indicate applicable IHL and relationship to IHRL. See, e.g., the *Practitioners' Guide* 2016 (n. 37), para. 15.12.

[430] Article 23, Hague Regulations Respecting the Laws and Customs of War on Land, Annex to the Convention (IV) Respecting the Laws and Customs of War on Land, The Hague, 18 October 1907, 187 CTS 227.

[431] *Practitioners' Guide* 2016 (n. 37), para. 5.18.

[432] The ECtHR avoided the issue in the recent *Big Brother Watch and Others v. United Kingdom*, Judgment of 13 September 2018, Application Nos. 58170/13, 62322/14 and 24960/15, probably as the United Kingdom did not contest jurisdiction.

the information, and the ensuing impact on privacy and potentially other associated rights?[433]

Where treaties are silent, and case law falters forward file by file, soft law standards can have a vital role in suggesting authoritative interpretations of the law. A prime example is the OHCHR report 'Privacy in a Digital Age'.[434] The report suggests that obligations under the ICCPR extend to foreign surveillance, by virtue of which persons are brought within the State's 'authority'.[435] The recent UNHRC General Comment No. 36 similarly suggests that the ICCPR is applicable to those directly and foreseeably 'impacted' by the State's conduct, which resonates in the surveillance context. By appealing to basic principles, purposive interpretation that avoids protection gaps and 'incentives' to evade obligations,[436] a progressive approach to the applicability of human rights law to surveillance abroad is advanced. Case law in support of that view is, as yet, more elusive.

This issue reminds us of the challenges to the applicability of both IHL and HRL that may arise in adjusting to the contemporary realities of cyberspace. It suggests how apparent gaps in the law, or areas of uncertainty, can gradually be influenced through soft law standards, which may, in the fullness of time, be consolidated through practice of courts and tribunals, State practice, and customary law as practice unfolds.

D. *Investigation and Accountability*

Over the past two decades, IHRL has experienced a tidal wave of development in respect of accountability norms. The result is a detailed body of law setting out the existence of obligations to investigate and prosecute serious violations

---

[433] Surveillance implicates many rights: e.g., privacy, freedom of expression, right to property and, depending on how used, a host of others, e.g., life or torture. Office of the United Nations High Commissioner for Human Rights (OHCHR), 'The Right to Privacy in the Digital Age', Report, 30 June 2014, UN Doc. A/HRC/27/37.

[434] *Ibid.*

[435] See *ibid.*, para. 32. Similar broad approaches are reflected in recent developments elsewhere. E.g., in the IACHR Advisory Opinion on Environment and Human Rights (State Obligations in Relation to the Environment in the Context of the Protection and Guarantee of the Rights to Life and to Personal Integrity – Interpretation and Scope of Articles 4(1) and 5(1) of the American Convention on Human Rights), OC-23/18, IACtHR (ser. A), No. 23 (15 November 2017) (in Spanish), para. 81; and UNHRC General Comment No. 36 on the Right to Life, CCPR/C/GC/36, 30 October 2018, para. 36: 'This includes persons located outside any territory effectively controlled by the State, whose right to life is nonetheless impacted by its military or other activities in a direct and reasonably foreseeable manner.'

[436] *Ibid.*, para. 33.

of human rights, and providing detail as to the content of these norms.[437] These duties are non-derogable in situations of emergency, and continue to apply in situations of armed conflict.[438]

IHL has, of course, not developed in the same way, due not least to the relative dearth of supervisory mechanisms and jurisprudential development. In some ways under IHL the existence of a duty to investigate violations is more controversial, though most scholars agree that such a duty exists.[439] On the other hand, unlike most human rights treaties which contain no explicit obligations in this respect,[440] the four Geneva Conventions actually specify the obligation to seek out and bring to justice those responsible for grave breaches.[441] Other provisions reflect specific obligations to investigate deaths of POWs or civilian detainees.[442] While these specific obligations relate to IACs, in relation to both IAC and NIAC it has been suggested that a parallel obligation under customary law may also have emerged.[443]

Both areas of law are therefore said to 'establish a general obligation to investigate suspected violations of the law under their respective legal frameworks', including through criminal investigations.[444] These obligations

---

[437] Investigation should be prompt, thorough, effective and independent, and provide the basis for individual accountability for serious violations. See, e.g., ECtHR, *Abu Zubaydah v. Lithuania*, Judgment of 31 May 2018, Application No. 46454/11; *Jaloud v. the Netherlands* (n. 198); *Cobzaru v. Romania*, Judgment of 26 July 2007, Application No. 48254/99, para. 68; IACtHR, *Velásquez Rodríguez v. Honduras*, Judgment of 29 July 1988, IACtHR Series C, No. 4; *Barrios Altos v. Peru* (n. 357).

[438] See ECtHR, *Al-Skeini v. United Kingdom* (n. 137), paras. 162, 164, referring to a long line of cases that arose in the context of 'difficult security conditions, including in a context of armed conflict'.

[439] Amichai Cohen and Yuval Shany, 'Beyond the Grave Breaches Regime: the Duty to Investigate Alleged Violations of International Law Governing Armed Conflicts', *Yearbook of International Humanitarian Law* 14 (2011), 37–84; Michelle Lesh and Alon Margalit, 'A Critical Discussion of the Second Turkel Report and How It Engages with the Duty to Investigate Under International Law', *Yearbook of International Humanitarian Law* 16 (2013), ch. 6, 119–45 and ch. 7, 155–86; Michael Schmitt, 'Investigating Violations of International Law in Armed Conflict', *Harvard National Security Journal* 2 (2011), 31–84.

[440] Some IHRL treaties do specify the duty, e.g., CAT, UNPED, but general treaties, e.g., ICCPR, ECHR, ACHR, ACHPR, do not.

[441] Articles 49, 50, 129 and 146 of the four Geneva Conventions and Art. 85, API.

[442] Articles 121 and 131 GCIV.

[443] Claus Kreß, 'Universal Jurisdiction over International Crimes and the Institut de Droit international', *Journal of International Criminal Justice* 4 (2006), 561–85.

[444] *Practitioners' Guide* 2016 (n. 37), paras. 17.03, 17.05; for IHL the duty arises for grave breaches or war crimes.

overlap with the 'right of families to know the fate of their relatives', and with reparation rights, reflected in both.[445]

While the obligation to investigate is reflected in IHL, its scope and content is less clear. There has been some discussion, for example, as to whether only grave breaches are subject to a duty to investigate,[446] or a broader duty to investigate all IHL violations based on the duty to 'suppress',[447] and what are the prerequisites or benchmarks of investigation?

The starting point for co-applicability on this issue, unlike perhaps life or liberty, is then that both IHL and IHRL reflect the same principles and enshrine comparable if distinct rules – albeit ones that do not provide the same level of detail as to the content of the norm. This is therefore an area ripe for harmonious interpretation, whereby IHRL can help to clarify the precise nature of States' obligations to, for example, carry out a prompt, thorough, effective and independent investigation into alleged serious violations of IHL.[448] Perceived tensions with, for example, IHL obligations on commanders to report violations and thus to investigate (which would not meet the independence criteria), may be reconciled as far as this IHL duty sits alongside, not in place of and not to the detriment of, that under IHRL.[449]

Practice suggests considerable areas of mutual influence. Some decisions of human rights bodies have gone as far as to lend weight to the existence of such a duty under IHL itself. In *The Massacres of El Mozote and Nearby Places v. El Salvador*, the IACtHR upheld the obligation under IHL 'to investigate and prosecute war crimes',[450] while in *Gelman v. Uruguay*, amnesties for war crimes or crimes against humanity were deemed inconsistent with this IHL obligation, by reference to the ICRC Customary IHL study.[451] Similarly, the ECtHR Grand Chamber in *Marguš v. Croatia* (citing these Inter-American

---

[445] ICRC *Customary Study* 2005 (n. 22), Customary Rule 150. UN Basic Principles on Reparation (2005) applies to violations of IHL and IHRL, and provides another example of the role the UN can play in the cross-fertilisation between the two areas of law.

[446] Schmitt, 'Investigating Violations of International Law in Armed Conflict' 2011 (n. 439).

[447] Cohen and Shany, 'Beyond the Grave Breaches Regime: the Duty to Investigate Alleged Violations of International Law Governing Armed Conflicts' 2011 (n. 439). OHCHR, 'International Legal Protection of Human Rights in Armed Conflict', 2011, UN Doc. HR/PUB/11/01, 81.

[448] Of these, the greatest resistance attends the duty of independent investigation, which is not a (common) feature of military investigations to date.

[449] E.g., ICRC *Customary Study* 2005 (n. 22), Customary Rule 153.

[450] IACtHR, *The Massacres of El Mozote and Nearby Places v. El Salvador*, Judgment of 25 October 2012, IACtHR Series C, No. 252, para. 286.

[451] IACtHR, *Gelman v. Uruguay*, Judgment of 24 February 2011, IACtHR Series C, No. 221, para. 210; ICRC *Customary Study* 2005 (n. 22), 692.

cases) referred to the duty to *prosecute*, albeit en route to the application of the ECHR.[452] The brief reference by the ECtHR Grand Chamber in *Al-Skeini v. UK* may lend some further weight to this view. The courts tend not to grapple in detail with this obligation, reflecting in part the general reluctance to engage with IHL in detail as outlined in Section IV and the broad consistency with relevant IHRL.

Conversely, IHL has influenced IHRL on issues such as the right to truth.[453] More broadly, the existence of a conflict and the applicability of IHL may have an influence on human rights standards in other ways. First in the circumstances that trigger the duty to investigate, not every loss of life in the context of hostilities requires investigation, for example, only those that create reasonable suspicion of a violation of IHL.[454] IHRL then provides benchmarks for effective investigation.[455] However, as human rights courts have made clear, in turn the practical realities of armed conflict must be taken into account, including obstacles or concrete constraints that may affect the speed or nature of the investigation.[456] This is seen concretely in the *Al-Skeini* and *Jaloud* judgments, which explicitly reflect such challenges and the need for some adjustment in the way the duty to investigate is discharged.[457]

The implication in this situation of co-applicability, and inherent flexibility, is well encapsulated in the Report of the United Nations Special Rapporteur on Extrajudicial, Summary or Arbitrary Executions:

> Armed conflict and occupation do not discharge the State's duty to investigate and prosecute human rights abuses … It is undeniable that during armed conflicts circumstances will sometimes impede investigation. Such circumstances will never discharge the obligation to investigate – this would eviscerate the non-derogable character of the right to life – but they may affect the modalities or particulars of the investigation. In addition to being fully responsible for the conduct of their agents, in relation to the acts of private actors States are also held to a standard of due diligence in armed conflicts as well as peace. On a case-by-case basis a State might utilize less effective measures of investigation in response to concrete constraints. For example,

---

[452] ECtHR, *Marguš v. Croatia*, Grand Chamber Judgment of 27 May 2014, Application No. 4455/10, para. 132; see also brief reference in ECtHR, *Al-Skeini v. United Kingdom* (n. 137).

[453] Droege, 'Interplay Between IHRL and IHL' 2007 (n. 21).

[454] Sivakumaran, *The Law of Non-International Armed Conflict* 2012 (n. 58), 373; this would lead to the obligation 'collapsing under its own weight'. *Practitioners' Guide* 2016 (n. 37), paras. 17.17, 17.21: incidents of 'possible war crimes' must be investigated also for individual criminal responsibility.

[455] *Practitioners' Guide* 2016 (n. 37), para. 17.22.

[456] ECtHR, *Al-Skeini v. United Kingdom* (n. 137), paras. 164–7.

[457] *Ibid.*, paras. 171–7; ECtHR, *Jaloud v. the Netherlands* (n. 198), paras. 157–228.

when hostile forces control the scene of a shooting, conducting an autopsy may prove impossible. Regardless of the circumstances, however, investigations must always be conducted as effectively as possible and never be reduced to mere formality . . .[458]

Co-applicability of IHL and IHRL obligations in this respect is of real practical import. There are many examples of States seeking to avoid carrying out independent investigations, or oversight of investigations, by arguing the applicability of IHL in displacement of IHRL duties. Where this amounts to the misuse of IHL to avoid accountability it is a perversion of that body of law's basic principles. Effective investigation and, where appropriate, individual accountability, are legal imperatives and not only policy options, but it is only through mechanisms available to individuals, not only to States, that the law can be given effect. Investigation is also a crucial vehicle to learn lessons from the past and contribute to non-repetition and greater respect for both areas of law, and the rule of law more broadly, in the future.

VI. CONCLUSION: LEANING IN

If the first line of defence against IHL has been to deny that it applies at all,[459] a further line of defence against accountability under IHL has been to deny the applicability of IHRL. Through its simplistic promotion as an alternative body of law displacing IHRL, IHL has been manipulated to circumvent rights protections and the oversight of international courts and bodies.

There is, however, no longer any reasonable doubt that, as a matter of law, IHRL applies in armed conflict, and that it does so alongside and in dynamic relationship with IHL. Both areas of law have developed considerably in relevant ways in the past 20 years. Both have evolved in their approaches to the scope of applicability *ratione materiae, personae* and *loci* in line with unfolding contextual realities.[460] In relation to both there remain areas where the law may be uncertain, or in flux, as it constantly struggles to keep pace with reality in the face of ever more complex and contested conflict scenarios, multiple actors, new methods and means of warfare, and the growing array of activity (within and beyond conflicts) in which States and the military engage around the world.

---

[458] UNHRC, 'Extrajudicial, Summary or Arbitrary Executions', Philip Alston, Report, 8 March 2006, UN Doc. E/CN.4/2006/53, para. 36.

[459] Section I.

[460] Section II.

Many factors and processes have contributed to the evolution to date, and will be decisive to further development. One of them is undoubtedly the dawn of an era of international adjudication. The international criminal tribunals made a crucial contribution on the scope of applicability of IHL through their evolving jurisprudence. The ICJ had a role in putting beyond dispute the applicability of IHRL in armed conflict, and the need to grapple with inter-relationship. In turn, a proliferation of human rights adjudication now commonly addresses the nature and scope of States' human rights obligations abroad, including in armed conflicts, international and non-international, and interplay with IHL. The need to interpret human rights law contextually, in a way that renders it practical and effective, and holistically, as part of broader body international law, including IHL, are now recognised across human rights systems. This complements the role national courts increasingly play in the interpretation and application of international law. The future undoubtedly holds an increased volume of conflict-related adjudication before a growing architecture of courts and tribunals.

The contemporary landscape is therefore one that, normatively, institutionally and factually, reveals a certain, inescapable level of complexity. Borrowing a psychological term, it may be time to 'lean in' to this complexity, ignoring neither the challenges nor the opportunities that the evolving landscape represents. One thing on which my co-authors to this volume and I appear to agree is in relation to this complexity, which (as their chapters support) is not unique to, or necessarily a result of, the co-applicability of IHL and IHRL. It is inherent in the effective, contextual and holistic interpretation of each area of applicable law as well as their co-application.

Co-applicability of IHRL and IHL matters. It ensures that human rights can be protected to the greatest extent possible in armed conflict situations where they are most vulnerable, but in a manner that is capable of responding to the realities of conflict scenarios. It ensures avenues for redress internationally for victims through applicable IHRL, at least in respect of State responsibility, currently lacking internationally under IHL; as noted above and emphasised in Chapter 2, IHL may at times be as or more protective than IHRL, but the procedural disparity is inescapable.[461] Co-applicability means that international remedies complement and catalyse individual accountability for crimes derived from serious violations of

---

[461] Ziv Bohrer claims IHL would have been more protective than the ECHR as applied in ECtHR, *Hassan v. United Kingdom* (n. 4). This may be so, or the ECHR may not have been rigorously applied by the Court on that aspect of the case. Either way, the fact is a case based on IHL would never have been heard internationally.

both IHL and IHRL. It provides the potential to clarify the law in armed conflict as it arises in the context of real concrete situations and cases.

There is, however, also considerable wariness in relation to this unfolding landscape and its implications, which deserves reflection. Undoubtedly, challenges of a legal, political or practical nature (relating to capacity, fact-finding, training and resources, for example) face human rights courts and tribunals as they seek to give effect to co-applicability in practice. Some of the challenges – of interplay of legal regimes – are not new or unique to the IHL/IHRL relationship.[462] But with co-applicability of IHRL and IHL now a recognised legal fact, there is no choice but to grapple with what interplay means in practice.

There has been a sea change towards a more explicit and robust engagement with IHL by human rights courts and bodies; this trend will inevitably continue, and as it does, engagement should become more confident, informed and consistent. The fact is that, while the practice of human rights courts and bodies explored in this chapter has evolved greatly, it remains a young field. Too much practice to date has been opaque and faltering. In particular, it is imperative that human rights bodies address and determine the preliminary question of *applicability* of IHL. Among the most problematic features of past practice has been the reluctance to engage in any analysis of this fundamental question upon which (co-)applicable law depends. However politically sensitive the issue, dodging the question of whether there is a conflict at all, or taking it for granted based on what States say or fail to say, is untenable. The result has at times been overreaching application of IHL to violent exchanges not part of a conflict, and at others underreaching failure to have due regard to IHL in the determination of issues properly regulated by it in conflict situations.

Myriad factors have been identified that influence the approach of human rights bodies; some of these may be inevitable and appropriate, and others arguably more problematic. For example, human rights courts and bodies are naturally constrained by their own jurisdictional limitations, which they should not (and for co-applicability *need* not) exceed. This may change as the competence of some bodies expands obligations more broadly, or becomes more explicit in terms of IHL.[463] Recent practice across systems reflects a generally

---

462 E.g., issues such as immunities and sanctions; see, e.g., ECtHR, *Al-Adsani v. United Kingdom* (n. 353) and Section IV on holistic interpretation.

463 See Section IV, noting some treaties cover IHL and IHRL (CRC), some bodies have jurisdiction over violations under relevant treaties (e.g., African Commission/Court), some bodies expanded their own original jurisdiction (ECOWAS), while others (ECtHR, UNHRC, IACHR) are limited to adjudicating rights under particular treaties.

cautious awareness of these limits, such that courts and bodies now rarely 'apply' or find violations of IHL but interpret and apply IHRL in the light of it.

Likewise, beyond any jurisdictional strictures, the purpose and mandate of human rights courts and bodies, and the nature of proceedings, necessarily influences their approach to some extent at least. While theoretical discussions on approaches to interplay abound, it is worth reflecting on the extent to which, in practice, approaches to applicability depend on who asks, and who answers, the questions, and why.

The fact is that human rights bodies will naturally view the issue first through the prism of their own constituent instruments. The human rights starting point of the analysis of human rights courts may in turn lead them, generally, to take a strict approach to departure from normally applicable human rights standards (at least as far as IHL is seen to lessen protections as will often, but not always, be the case.). As IHRL is the generally applicable law, this starting point, and a rigorous approach to the circumstances in which IHL standard alters the outcome of the case, and ensuring it is no more than is justified under the co-applicable area of law, should not be problematic. What does matter is that there is a robust and nuanced approach to identifying and assessing applicable law, IHL and IHRL, and a willingness to grapple with sometimes difficult questions of what co-applicability means in relation to particular norms and contexts (see further below).

We have also seen how the pleadings of parties and politics play a role. Further careful consideration is due as to whether the positions of States should (as has been suggested by the ECtHR[464]) be determinative of the relevance of IHL standards. The politicisation and selectivity of conflict classification underscore the importance of the role of oversight bodies in these essential legal determinations. More broadly, while judicial 'relief' at avoiding politically sensitive issues of IHL may be understandable, the need to ensure it is not determinative goes without saying.[465]

Despite various formulations, and room for controversy, some things do now seem clearer as regards co-applicability, and need to be embraced by all those seeking to give effect to the law, including adjudicators.

Determining applicable law in an armed conflict depends not only on the existence or not of armed conflict, or its nature, but also on the identification of particular norms, their content and objectives, as they apply to a particular factual scenario within the conflict. As this chapter has shown, assumptions

---

[464] Section III, ECtHR, *Hassan v. United Kingdom* (n. 4).

[465] Section V, referring to judicial comments in the UK Court of Appeal, *Serdar Mohammed* case 2015 (n. 390).

about applicable law – which area provides norms more specifically targeted towards particular military activity, or which are more detailed or more protective – are best avoided.

Close attention to both identifying particular applicable norms and to context are essential. In particular (but not only), in NIAC there may be no clear norms of IHL in relation to a particular issue at all. There is then no co-applicable law (and obviously no normative conflict), and the applicable norms of IHRL govern. They will, of course, still need to be interpreted in a context-sensitive manner, perhaps informed by reference to the principles of IHL, to ensure that the legal framework does not impose impossible burdens on States, but this is distinct from co-applicability.

Where there *are* relevant norms from each area, hasty and simplistic conclusions on IHL as *lex specialis* must be resisted. The starting point is harmonious interpretation, for which we have seen ample scope and examples where co-applicable norms each inform the interpretation of the other. The limits of harmonious interpretation are also undeniable, where normative conflict cannot be ignored or interpreted away.

The relationship between these norms and context then becomes key in determining whether on the particular facts one or the other norm is more specifically directed to the situation. There is no simple formula, but a considerable body of practice explored in this chapter suggests factors that may determine the weight of norms from one area or the other. One is whether the context is one of 'active hostilities', in particular high-intensity conflict, as opposed to the many scenarios within conflict more akin to 'law enforcement' or other exercise of State power where human rights law is the more relevant norm. The level of *control* exercised by the State in the particular situation is another factor that, within conflict and in the event of conflicting norms, has provided a basis to afford greater prominence to IHRL standards.[466] Thus, in certain circumstances, even in relation to issues where the areas of law are seen to be irreconcilable – the right to life or detention – the control may be such that capturing rather than use of lethal force, or affording higher standards of judicial review than those required by IHL, may be possible in all the circumstances. Put differently, there may be no 'necessity' to depart from the generally applicable standards of human rights law in the particular context.

The case, norm and context-specific analysis that the law requires, explored in this chapter, means that simple solutions are, unfortunately, likely to prove elusive. As human rights courts turn to IHL, they should recognise that many of the perceived problems with co-application to date relate to the way

---

[466] Section III cases.

interrelationship has been simplistically framed and erroneously approached to justify the wholesale displacement of IHRL. While grappling more confidently and explicitly with IHL, they need to acknowledge that armed conflict and IHL applicability is no magic wand that automatically transforms the factual context or States' obligations. The danger of judicial endorsement of unduly narrow and rigid approaches to *lex specialis* to exclude human rights law are given graphic illustration in the chapter, such as in reliance on 'armed conflict' in Afghanistan to justify the creation of (another) black hole for detainees to be transferred to avoid judicial protection.

The challenges that arise have implications that go far beyond adjudicators. It is essential that all those giving effect to and affected by the law can foresee and conform their behaviour to it. The law needs to serve and protect potential victims but also members of armed forces on the ground, for whom there are implications for added vulnerability and criminal sanction if the requirements of the law are not met. Sufficiently accessible, clear and coherent parameters to applicable law are necessary for legal security and predictability, providing protection against arbitrariness; in other words they are inherent in the principle of legality.

At the same time, it has been noted that the law is not always straightforward, and the quest for predetermined solutions to all scenarios has been described as legal folly.[467] Indeed, normative and contextual complexity and the real challenges posed in armed conflict are not, as some might suggest, a feature of the applicability of IHRL or interplay. As we have seen repeatedly, the applicability of IHL itself raises myriad complexities.[468] It requires careful contextual analysis to ascertain the scope and reach of armed conflict, to identify applicable norms, and to understand how they should apply in any given scenario.[469] The problems reflect the essential challenge of giving effect to evolving, overlapping norms of international law in changing factual contexts. These challenges may be compounded by co-applicability, but they are certainly not born of it.

It is, however, imperative to continue to clarify the undoubtedly complex issues that arise regarding interrelationship in particular situations. The role of adjudication, significant as it may be, is not an alternative (still less a threat) to

---

[467]　See, Iain Scobbie, 'Gaza', in Wilmshurst (ed.), *Classification of Conflicts* 2012 (n. 2), 280–316.
[468]　Section II.
[469]　As Section II makes clear, these range from when an armed conflict arises, be it from violence or cyber operations, to when the myriad, diverse groups engaged in violence globally might, when considered as a whole, be qualified as parties to such a conflict, the nature of the conflict(s) on the ground in places like Syria, the geographic scope of IHL, among many others.

myriad other processes through which law is developed. States have the key role, alongside other processes of international law and the role of bodies such as the ICRC, in clarifying principles governing the co-applicability of both bodies of law in theory and in practice.

An essential rule of law challenge is to marry up the approaches to applicable law by courts *ex post facto* and training on the law *ex ante*. There are two obvious dimensions to this. The first is more robust engagement with applicable law by international and national courts. The other is the duties of States to provide guidelines, training and support to those on the ground to clarify applicable law, including the interrelationship of IHL and IHRL in relation to particular norms and situations.

It is not, however, a solution to the complexity to apply IHRL or IHL in isolation, as if there were no other relevant applicable law, or to pretend that co-applicability is not now where the law stands. Such an approach was reflected for too long in the broad neglect of human rights norms in military manuals,[470] or the once myopic approach of human rights bodies to IHL.[471] Nor should controversies around the role of human rights bodies, and areas ripe for improvement, be manipulated by those motivated by effectively removing oversight in areas where it is most needed.[472]

This leaves us with little choice but to collectively 'lean in'. We need to grapple together with the normative and factual complexities of applicability of each area of law, and of co-applicability, in order to better understand, clarify and, as appropriate, develop the law. In an era of adjudication, we have reason to be cautiously optimistic about the potential for the law to be given greater effect, but realistic about the challenges.

---

[470] The *Practitioners' Guide* 2016 (n. 37), discussed in Sections III and V.
[471] Section III.
[472] Alice Donald and Philip Leach, 'A Wolf in Sheep's Clothing: Why the Draft Copenhagen Declaration Must be Rewritten', *EJIL:Talk!*, 21 February 2018, available at: www.ejiltalk.org /a-wolf-in-sheeps-clothing-why-the-draft-copenhagen-declaration-must-be-rewritten, noting the potential impact of proposals to create special 'separate mechanisms' to deal with cases arising from IAC to achieve a 'balanced caseload', divesting the Court of its current role in crucial litigation in conflict regions of Europe such as eastern Ukraine, Crimea, South Ossetia, Abkhazia, Nagorno-Karabakh and northern Cyprus.

2

Divisions over Distinctions in Wartime International Law

Ziv Bohrer[*]

In the movie *Stand by Me*, the following existential debate ensues: 'Mickey's a mouse, Donald's a duck, Pluto's a dog. What's Goofy?' 'Goofy's a dog. He's definitely a dog' 'He can't be a dog. He drives a car and wears a hat' 'Oh, God. That's weird. What the hell is Goofy?'[1]

In the legal classification of collective violence, cross-border fights between non-State and State forces (transnational conflicts) are Goofy, failing to neatly fit into any recognised category. It is important to classify them, however. Peacetime violence is regulated by 'general' international law, whereas armed conflict is regulated by radically different law: international humanitarian law (IHL). IHL is purportedly subdivided into two distinct corpora, setting apart the law governing international from that governing non-international armed conflicts.

Civil disturbances are peacetime violence; inter-State wars are international armed conflicts (IAC); civil wars are non-international armed conflicts (NIAC). What, then, are transnational conflicts? Unlike inter-State wars, but similar to civil wars and disturbances, organised non-State actors participate in them. Unlike civil wars and disturbances, but similar to inter-State wars, violence typically crosses borders. Unlike civil disturbances, but similar to inter-State and civil wars, violence is extensive, leading most to consider them 'armed conflicts'. What international law corpus, then, applies to

[*] Bar-Ilan University, Law Faculty. I wish to deeply thank the editors, Anne Peters and Christian Marxsen, my partners, Helen Duffy and Janina Dill, as well as Orna Ben-Naftali, Lena Bohrer, Adam H. J. Broza, Andrew Clapham, Emanuela-Chiara Gillard, Benji Grunbaum, Guy Keinan, Heike Krieger, David Landau, Gabriel Lanyi, Thilo Marauhn, Michael A. Newton, Jasmine Patihi-Goldofsky, Christian Tomuschat, Damion Young and the Max Planck Workshop participants.
[1] Bruce Evans and Raynold Gideon, *Stand by Me* (1985), Movie Script, available at: www.moviescriptsandscreenplays.com/johncusack/scripts/standbyme.txt.

transnational conflicts: peacetime general international law, IAC law, NIAC law or a new IHL altogether? Transnational conflicts' 'Goofiness' is commonly attributed to their novelty. But, nearly two decades have passed since 9/11 (which marked their rise) without reaching an accepted classification.

This classification dispute is not alone. Since the early 2000s, classification disagreements have intensified, notably with regard to: when and where does IHL apply (what constitutes 'war' and what constitutes 'peace')? When and where each of IHL's two sub-corpora apply and does IHL have a new (third) sub-corpus (what constitutes an IAC, what constitutes a NIAC and what legal corpus applies to transnational conflicts)? To whom do each of the two status-based sets of IHL rules apply (which individuals are 'combatants' and which are 'non-combatants')? Under what conditions, if any, does international human rights law (IHRL) apply alongside IHL? Such classification disputes are, presently, so strong that the legal materials that 'used to distinguish war and peace ... have become surprisingly fluid'.[2] This chapter addresses that classification crisis.

Some classification debates emerged even before transnational conflicts' 'rise', but all have subsequently intensified. Accordingly, transnational conflicts are considered a primary cause for the present classification crisis: wars of a new kind that erode IHL's long-standing distinctions.[3]

In the current classification debates, formalist attempts to 'objectively' determine the 'correct' interpretation of the relevant law have proven futile, leading only 'into a Wonderland of duelling dicta'.[4] To avoid similar fate, instead of focusing on the debated issues, this chapter critically examines the only generally accepted assumption: that transnational conflicts' rise is a main cause of the current crisis.

Such critical analysis of consensual legal issues is inspired by social discourse accounts of 'law'. According to such accounts, a legal system's community members 'inhabit ... a normative universe ... The rules and ... formal institutions ... are ... but a small part of the normative universe ... No set of legal institutions or prescriptions exists apart from the narratives that ... give it meaning.'[5] Unlike (hardline) formalist accounts, social

[2] David Kennedy, 'Lawfare and Warfare', in James Crawford and Martti Koskenniemi (eds.), *Cambridge Companion to International Law* (Cambridge University Press, 2012), 158–84 (165).

[3] E.g., Jed Odermatt, 'Between Law and Reality: "New Wars" and Internationalised Armed Conflict', *Amsterdam Law Forum* 5(3) (2013), 19–32 (19).

[4] David Luban, 'Human Rights Thinking and the Laws of War', in Jens David Ohlin (ed.), *Theoretical Boundaries of Armed Conflict and Human Rights* (Cambridge University Press, 2016), 45–77 (49).

[5] Robert Cover, 'Nomos and Narrative', *Harvard Law Review* 97 (1983/4), 4–68 (4–5). See also Hanoch Dagan, 'The Realist Conception of Law', *University of Toronto Law Journal* 57 (2007), 607–60; Hendrik Hartog, 'Pigs and Positivism', *Wisconsin Law Review* (1985), 899–935 (932);

discourse accounts recognise that law is not a wholly 'external, objective social fact'.[6] But, unlike (hardline) critical-legal studies (CLS) accounts, social discourse accounts acknowledge that law *does* tend to have a certain semi-objective social element that 'constrains the range of possible … juridical solutions';[7] a legal system's community members, including the powerful, often cannot simply claim that the law is whatever they wish it to be, even when the law has multiple interpretations.[8] Law's semi-objective element is the product of narratives that give the law meaning(s).[9] Narrative construction is a human tendency aimed at projecting order and causality onto a chaotic reality.[10] Due to reality's complexity, narratives cannot simply reflect reality; nevertheless, we often perceive narratives, especially widely accepted ones, not as opinions or stories, but rather 'as truth and reality'.[11] Because narratives are inevitably simplified accounts of reality, 'sharpen[ing] certain features and blur[ring] others',[12] critically examining widely accepted narratives enables us to see what was 'previously hidden'.[13]

This chapter begins by disproving the premise that the current crisis is due to novel wars. Section I reveals that transnational conflicts' attributes are not unprecedented. Section II uncovers that IHL regulation of conflicts with such attributes is not novel. Current uncertainty is, in part, chronic, stemming from the nature of 'law' and of 'war' which does not allow for a neat fit between war-related legal classifications and real wartime situations. This is not a crisis, but a fact of life. Moreover, the chapter gradually presents an IHL norm – *the adaptation approach* – that has long aided IHL in addressing such uncertainty. Section III reveals that the current classification crisis narrative is primarily the by-product of two competing attempts to take sole control over wartime international law: by hardline statists and by hardline IHRL advocates. These hardliners are also the main cause for the current *actual* legal crisis. In a legal system with a heterogeneous community, such as IHL, considerable

---

Pierre Bourdieu, 'The Force of Law: Toward a Sociology of the Juridical Field', *Hasting Law Journal* 38 (1987), 814–53 (816).

[6] Hartog, 'Pigs and Positivism' 1985 (n. 5), 932.

[7] Bourdieu, 'Force of Law' 1987 (n. 5), 816.

[8] *Ibid.*

[9] Cover, 'Nomos and Narrative' 1983/4 (n. 5), 17.

[10] Mark Currie, *Postmodern Narrative Theory* (New York: Palgrave Macmillan, 1998), 2.

[11] Richard Sherwin, 'The Narrative Construction of Legal Reality', *Journal of Assistant Legal Writing Directors* 6 (2009), 88–120 (91).

[12] Richard Ford, 'Law's Territory (A History of Jurisdiction)', *Michigan Law Review* 97 (1999), 843–930 (863).

[13] Martti Koskenniemi, 'Histories of International Law: Dealing with Eurocentrism', *Rechtsgeschichte* 19 (2011), 152–76 (176).

disagreements and uncertainty would inevitably result from the community's diversity. This condition should be accepted, if not celebrated, as it is
a mark of pluralism. Such uncertainties and disagreements amount to a crisis
only when they are expounded by attempts to eradicate pluralism;
a phenomenon herein called a *core jurisdictional struggle*. A core jurisdictional struggle begins when an influential faction within the legal system's
community rejects pluralism: attempting to take sole control over the shaping of the system's norms and narratives and dismissing competing norms
and narratives as non-obligatory and political. Once other community
members (understandably) resist, the core jurisdictional struggle erupts:
the different factions are no longer constrained by a shared normative
corpus, and each perceives its opponents' actions as political and responds
in kind. The system's law loses its independent (semi-objective) influence on
human behaviour, which places the system at a risk of dissolution. As Section
III shows, for two decades, a core jurisdictional struggle has been waging in
IHL, driven by the competing attempts of hardline statists and hardline
IHRL advocates to take sole control over its shaping. Current escalating
uncertainty and disagreements primarily stem from these attempts and from
the clash between them. The current classification crisis narrative, regarding
distinctions-eroding novel wars, has been propagated by both opposing
hardliners to justify and conceal their usurpation attempts. All this weakens
IHL and might eventually lead to its demise. Section III, thus, responds by
rebutting the fundamental premise of each hardline faction. It shows that
hardline statists' drive to loosen wartime legal constraints gravely underrates
existing IHL benefits and effectiveness. Likewise, the section shows that
hardline IHRL advocates mis-assume that extensive IHRL wartime application and a rights-oriented reading of IHL increase civilian protection;
counter-intuitively, doing so diminishes that protection, because of differences between obligations-oriented and rights-oriented systems that make
(obligations-oriented) existing IHL better suited to protect civilians in
wartime. This chapter as a whole is an attempt to quell the current core
jurisdictional struggle by embracing the adaptation approach, inevitable
indeterminacies and pluralism.

I. CLASSIFICATION CRISIS AND NOVEL WARS

Following 9/11, in a series of legal memos ('torture memos') the US administration reasoned that current IHL does not apply to transnational conflicts.
Existing IHL is subdivided into two distinct bodies: IAC law, which was created
to address inter-State wars; and NIAC law, which was created to address civil

wars; transnational conflicts do 'not fit into either category'.[14] Transnational conflicts, therefore, represent a new phenomenon that existing IHL was not designed to regulate; they are regulated, instead, by new IHL, consisting merely of the norms authorising States to kill, capture and detain enemy combatants.[15]

The US characterisation of transnational conflicts as novel has become quite accepted. The US conclusion, regarding the applicable law, has not. (1) Some jurists agree that transnational conflicts are regulated by a new wartime international law, but, unlike the torture memos, they hold that it is more constraining than existing IHL.[16] (2) Others hold that transnational conflicts are not wars and are, therefore, regulated by the existing general peacetime international law.[17] (3) Yet others claim that existing IHL can be adapted to regulate these new wars, but such jurists diverge on three main issues: (i) when do several violent situations constitute a single transnational conflict?; (ii) must the demanded adaptations ease or harden existing IHL?; (iii) what is the relevant existing IHL: IAC law or NIAC law (note that the United States modified its position and currently considers NIAC law the relevant IHL (subject to adaptations))?[18]

The difficulty in classifying transnational conflicts as either IAC or NIAC seems to support their characterisation as novel. Additional core legal classifications also become goofy in the context of transnational conflicts, which seems to further support the novelty characterisation.[19]

The following is the accepted account for the unsuitability of core IHL classifications to transnational conflicts. Traditional IHL was primarily designed to deal with inter-State conflicts, therefore, IHL generally depends

[14] Deputy Assistant US Attorney General John Yoo and Special Counsel Robert Delahunty, Memorandum for D.O.D. General Counsel William J. Haynes II: Application of Treaties and Laws to al Qaeda and Taliban Detainees, 9 January 2002, 12.

[15] See Naz Modirzadeh, 'Folk International Law: 9/11 Lawyering and the Transformation of the Law of Armed Conflict to Human Rights Policy and Human Rights Law to War Governance', *Harvard National Security Journal* 5 (2014), 225–304 (232–3) (summarising and citing the relevant memos).

[16] E.g., Daphne Visser, 'Conflicts, New Wars and Human Rights', Amnesty International Blog, 9 February 2017, available at: www.aisa.amnesty.nl/blog/142-9-february-2017-conflicts-new-wars-and-human-rights.

[17] E.g., Mary Ellen O'Connell, 'When is War Not a War? The Myth of the Global War on Terror', *ILSA Journal of International & Comparative Law* 12 (2005/6), 535–39 (535).

[18] ICRC, Report on the 31st International Conference of the Red Cross and Red Crescent, International Humanitarian Law and the Challenges of Contemporary Armed Conflicts, October 2011, 7–13, 48–53; Brian Egan, 'International Law, Legal Diplomacy, and the Counter-ISIL Campaign', 4 April 2016, available at: www.state.gov/s/l/releases/remarks/255493 .htm.

[19] Eyal Benvenisti, 'Rethinking the Divide between *Jus ad Bellum* and *Jus in Bello* in Warfare against Nonstate Actors', *Yale Journal of International Law* 34 (2009), 541–8 (541).

on 'reciprocity ... between ... roughly equal militar[ies]'.[20] Because in such symmetric (inter-State) conflicts battlefields tend to be compartmentalised, IHL premises that it is generally possible to distinguish areas of actual combat from elsewhere, setting various IHL norms to address only combat.[21] Since battlefield compartmentalisation, together with other State attributes, aids in distinguishing combatants from non-combatants, IHL further premises that such a distinction is generally possible; thus, IHL establishes different rules for each of these two categories of individual.[22] Admittedly, even in inter-State wars, IHL *does*, generally, apply outside the battlefield, but international law prohibits waging wars on territories of uninvolved States and States commonly follow this restriction, which creates considerable clarity regarding IHL's spatial application boundaries.[23] IHL's temporal application boundaries are, likewise, clear, because States' war aims tend to be limited, which helps to determine that a war was started and whether it was won or lost.[24] Due to these clear temporal and spatial boundaries, 'Traditional international law made a conceptually rigid distinction between peace and war.'[25] IHL also regulates civil wars, where temporal, spatial and status-based distinctions are less clear. Nevertheless, civil wars are commonly confined to a single State, and often belligerents are willing to adhere to IHL because legitimacy aspirations influence belligerents' relationship with the international community.[26] In contrast, in contemporary transnational conflicts all traditional distinctions vanish. Presumably, this is due to technological advancements (in weapons, transportation and communication) and unique attributes of transnational non-State forces (uncompromising ideology, open battle avoidance, non-confinement to territorial boundaries and disregard of IHL (especially of the principle of distinction)). Thus, in transnational conflicts victory is unclear as the temporal, spatial and combatant–civilian distinctions are fuzzy, and attacks can simply happen anywhere across the globe and at any time.[27]

[20]   Robert Sloane, 'Puzzles of Proportion and the "Reasonable Military Commander"', *Harvard National Security Journal* 6 (2015), 299–343 (334).

[21]   *Ibid.*

[22]   *Ibid.*

[23]   W. Michael Reisman, 'Assessing Claims to Revise the Laws of War', *American Journal of International Law* 97 (2003), 82–90 (83).

[24]   Sloane, 'Puzzles of Proportion' 2015 (n. 20), 339–40.

[25]   Lung-chu Chen, *Introduction to Contemporary International Law*, 3rd edn. (Oxford University Press, 2014), 392.

[26]   Toni Pfanner, 'Asymmetrical Warfare from the Perspective of Humanitarian Law and Humanitarian Action', *International Review of the Red Cross* 87 (2005), 149–74 (152).

[27]   *Ibid.*, 153–69; Sloane, 'Puzzles of Proportion' 2015 (n. 20), 336–9; Visser, 'Conflicts, New Wars and Human Rights' 2017 (n. 16); Jonathan White, *Terrorism and Homeland Security* (Belmont, CA: Wadsworth, 2011), 23.

Transnational wars have also blurred the application boundaries of the law of occupation (an IAC law sub-corpus) by muddling the distinction between occupied and unoccupied territories.[28] Given their novelty and prevalence since 9/11, transnational conflicts are considered to be a primary cause for the current legal crisis, challenging IHL's fundamental distinctions.[29]

A. Blurred Wartime–Peacetime Divide

Try to guess when the following statements were written:

(1) '[S]o great a change has occurred in modern times ... [that] there would seem to be an impalpable progress from a state of peace towards a state of war.'[30]

(2) A 'wide borderland of hostilities ... exists between peace and war'.[31]

(3) '[T]he old classification into war and peace ... is far too rigid ... [T]he traditional law as applied to war situations has become somewhat out of date if not irrelevant.'[32]

The dates are 1843, 1883 and 1977. There are also similar historical statements about NIAC's indeterminate beginning and end.[33] The 'consensus about a *recent* elision of the difference between war and peace is rooted in a deep historical misconception ... [That] distinction ... has *always* been blurred.'[34] Throughout this chapter, I bring past sources showcasing the rich antecedents of 'unprecedented' contemporary phenomena.

Legal sources addressing *current* inter-State or civil wars also describe indeterminacy regarding their temporal boundaries.[35] This further diminishes the actual uniqueness of transnational conflicts.

The blurring of the wartime–peacetime divide in current *inter-State* conflicts is considered a *recent* phenomenon resulting from the increasing rarity of

---

28   Pfanner, 'Asymmetrical Warfare' 2005 (n. 26), 169.

29   Benvenisti, 'Rethinking the Divide' 2009 (n. 19), 541.

30   John T. Graves, 'Lectures on International Law (Lecture I)', *Law Times* 1 (1843), 95–7 (96).

31   John F. Maurice, *Hostilities without Declaration of War* (London: HMSO, 1883), 8.

32   Leslie C. Green, 'The New Law of Armed Conflict', *Canadian Yearbook of International Law* 15 (1977), 3–41 (5).

33   E.g., Edward Creasy, *First Platform of International Law* (London: Van-Voorst, 1876), 108; Jean S. Pictet, *Humanitarian Law and the Protection of War Victims* (Geneva: Sijthoff, 1975), 61.

34   Mark Neocleous, 'War as Peace, Peace as Pacification', *Radical Philosophy* 159 (2010), 8–17 (9).

35   Vincent Bernard, 'Editorial: Delineating the Boundaries of Violence', *International Review of the Red Cross* 96 (2014), 5–11 (9).

formal war declarations and peace treaties.[36] But Maurice's 1883 survey showed that between 1700 and 1870, of 107 Western conflicts a declaration of war was issued in 'less than ten'.[37] Undeclared wars remained common even after the 1907 Hague Convention demanded otherwise.[38]

Indeterminacy regarding the end of inter-State wars was also, historically, common. US Secretary of State, William H. Seward, observed in 1868:[39]

> [P]eace may be restored by the long suspension of hostilities without a treaty ... History is full of such occurrences. What period of suspension of war is necessary to justify the presumption of the restoration of peace has never yet been settled ...

The blurring of the peacetime–wartime divide in current inter-State wars is also considered a side effect of a mid-twentieth-century legal reform. Earlier IHL treaties relied on the term 'war' and States wishing to avoid applying IHL argued 'that a situation not expressly recognised as a war did not constitute a war in the legal sense'.[40] To abolish this legal tactic, the 1949 Geneva Conventions (and subsequent treaties) primarily rely on the term 'armed conflict', because (presumably, unlike 'war') the determination that 'armed conflict' exists relies on objective-factual benchmarks.[41] But a side effect of this substitution has been reduced clarity regarding the temporal application boundaries of IHL, because it led to gradual 'abandonment of the traditional rigid distinction ... between ... peace and ... war'.[42] Oddly, the same terminological substitution is also depicted oppositely, as having enhanced clarity regarding IHL's temporal application boundaries by giving rise to a doctrine that applies IHL to inter-State conflicts starting from the first shot fired.[43]

---

[36] Marko Milanovic, 'The End of Application of International Humanitarian Law', *International Review of the Red Cross* 96 (2014), 163–88 (168).

[37] Maurice, *Hostilities without Declaration of War* 1883 (n. 31), 4.

[38] Article 1, Hague Convention (III) relative to the Opening of Hostilities (18 October 1907); Quincy Wright, 'When Does War Exist?', *American Journal of International Law* 26 (1932), 362–8 (363–5).

[39] 'Letter to Mr. Goni (22 July 1868)', in John B. Moore, *A Digest of International Law* (Washington, DC: US Government Printing Office, 1906), vol. VII, 336.

[40] Frits Kalshoven and Liesbeth Zegveld, *Constraints on the Waging of War*, 4th edn. (Geneva: ICRC, 2011), 31.

[41] *Ibid.*

[42] Jann Kleffner, 'Scope of Application of International Humanitarian Law', in Dieter Fleck (ed.), *The Handbook of International Humanitarian Law*, 3rd edn. (Oxford University Press, 2013), 43–78 (43–4).

[43] Bernard, 'Editorial' 2014 (n. 35), 9.

In truth, this terminological substitution neither increased nor decreased clarity.[44] Even cases like the ones that the substitution specifically sought to abolish, in which States deny IHL application by denying that their situation is an armed conflict, reappeared as early as the 1950s.[45] Admittedly, the first-shot doctrine reduces indeterminacy regarding the start of IHL application in inter-State conflicts. But the history of such an approach, deeming IHL application mandatory even in small-scale, undeclared conflicts, goes back at least two centuries, to the 'imperfect wars' era.[46]

Another indeterminacy commonly attributed to transnational conflicts' rise concerns the difficulty of clearly determining whether a conflict is an IAC or a NIAC.[47] However, this indeterminacy is, actually, quite old; as George G. Wilson observed in 1900:[48]

> [O]pportunities for legitimate differences of opinion as to the nature of hostilities ... are very great. From war in the full sense ... between States ... down to the unarmed struggle between individuals of the same State, there are many grades of conflict.

Even torture memo-like arguments are unoriginal. George Aldrich noted in 1973:[49]

> [T]he laws of war ... are ... in considerable part obsolete ... [T]heir applicability to more recent types of warfare [such as] ... mixed civil and international conflicts, and guerrilla warfare ... raise[s] problems ... Moreover, all too often nations refuse to apply the conventions in situations where they clearly should be applied. Attempts to justify such refusals are often based on differences between the conflicts presently encountered and those for which the conventions were supposedly adopted.

There is also nothing novel in asserting that 'the concept of "occupation" is juridically inoperative or disputed in practically all contemporary conflicts' (as this 1983 assertion demonstrates).[50] As early as 1876, it was observed that 'the definition of ... "occupied district" is very hard to realize'.[51]

---

44   Fred Green, 'United States: The Concept of "War" and the Concept of "Combatant"', *Military Law & Law of War Review* 10 (1971), 267–312 (283).
45   Kalshoven and Zegveld, *Constraints on the Waging of War* 2011 (n. 40), 31.
46   See John T. Graves, 'Lectures on International Law (Lecture III)', *Law Times* 1 (1843), 265–8 (267).
47   Bernard, 'Editorial' 2014 (n. 35), 5.
48   George G. Wilson, *Insurgency* (Washington, DC: US Government Printing Office, 1900), 3.
49   George Aldrich, 'Human Rights in Armed Conflict', *Department of State Bulletin* 68 (1973), 876–82 (876). See also, I. P. Trainin, 'Questions of Guerrilla Warfare in the Law of War', *American Journal of International Law* 40 (1946), 534–62 (550–1).
50   Michel Veuthey, *Guérilla et droit humanitaire* (Geneva: ICRC, 1983), 355.
51   Creasy, *First Platform of International War* 1876 (n. 33), 483.

Why do the terminological dichotomies – occupied versus unoccupied territories, IAC versus NIAC, and war/armed conflict versus peace – persistently suffer from indeterminacy? Why are such chronic problems always perceived as new?

First, as already observed by Plato and Aristotle, the actual world 'in its very essence, [is] a world of things that ... fall short of [their ideal model nature]'.[52] The jurisprudence that sprang from this Platonic and Aristotelian thinking would later prove to be significant in addressing the current classification crisis. For now, however, its aforesaid basic observation suffices. Platonic thinking considers this lack of sync between actual things and their ideal model form a result of the flawed nature of actual things. Alternatively, this lack of sync is because any attempt to define a category of things requires depicting a model form of those things that have only attributes generally shared among them; such generalising reasoning 'by its very nature involves simplification'.[53] That reasoning is dominant in law.[54] Law, in its ideal model form, provides certainty by setting clear rules, definitions and classifications. But in practice legal concepts are generalisations aimed at regulating numerous situations. Therefore, they unavoidably suffer from at least some measures of indeterminacy and over- and under-inclusiveness.[55] It is especially difficult to clearly define the application boundaries of a law that aims to regulate a category of exceptional cases, such as emergency situations, because each such case is unique and unpredictable.[56] War (armed conflict) and civil disturbances are categories of emergency situations; IAC and NIAC are sub-categories of war; and the distinction between occupied territories and unoccupied territories is between two wartime scenarios. Therefore, any attempt to enshrine in law *clear-cut* classifications (aimed at *accurately* defining the conditions under which each of these emergency scenarios exists), or *clear-cut* boundaries (aimed at *pinpointing* the *precise* transition point from one such scenario to another, or between any of them and peacetime scenarios) is bound to face 'the grey areas of ... emergency',[57] and, therefore, unable to attain its aspired clarity.[58]

[52] Christine Korsgaard, 'Prologue', in Christine Korsgaard and Onora O'Neill (eds.), *The Sources of Normativity* (Cambridge University Press, 1996), 1–5.
[53] Robert Flood and Ewart Carson, *Dealing with Complexity* (New York: Springer, 1993), 155.
[54] Frederick Schauer, 'The Generality of Law', *West Virginia Law Review* 107 (2005), 217–34.
[55] *Ibid.*
[56] Fionnuala Ni Aolain and Oren Gross, 'Emergency, War and International Law: Another Perspective', *Nordic Journal of International Law* 70 (2001), 29–63 (30–1).
[57] *Ibid.*, 60.
[58] *Ibid.*, 54.

Secondly, although legal terms inevitably suffer from some measure of indeterminacy, incorporating a term into a law often leads people to assume that it has a clear, objectively ascertainable definition.[59] This tendency is especially strong when the legal terms portray opposing categories, because 'thinking in antonymous pairs is natural to the manner we construct the world'[60] (even though binary classifications often 'do not [truly] produce coherent knowledge, only terminological mess').[61] Thus, a dissonance arises between the exaggerated clarity attributed to emergency-related legal terms and the chronic haziness of the situations these terms address.[62] The intuitive attribution of clarity ceases whenever reality demands that individuals determine whether, or not, a certain emergency-related, classifying legal term applies to a concrete situation; once our attention is focused on applying such law to actual emergencies, our illusion of a neat fit between it and reality bursts. Recall the statements quoted earlier: in each a jurist from a different period asserted that during his time war had changed in a manner that diminished the (presumably) long-standing, clear-cut distinction between war and peace. Such statements (found in abundance, throughout modern times) demonstrate the aforesaid illusion-bursting phenomenon, because comparing them reveals that in each period the fault for diminishing the 'traditional' 'clear-cut' war–peace dichotomy was attributed to the kind of conflict that caught the greatest contemporary public attention: in the nineteenth century it was attributed to 'imperfect wars';[63] in the early twentieth century, to the phenomenon of world wars;[64] post-Second World War, to the Cold War phenomenon;[65] and, subsequently, to conflicts with mixed international and non-international attributes (in the light of anti-colonial and Communist rebellions).[66]

Although attribution of exaggerated clarity to core IHL distinctions ceases whenever these distinctions are applied to a concrete conflict, such clarity

---

[59] Jessie Allen, 'A Theory of Adjudication: Law as Magic', *Suffolk University Law Review* 41 (2007/8), 773–831 (799).

[60] Orna Ben-Naftali, 'The Epistemology of the Closet of International Law and the Spirit of the Law', *Law, Society & Culture* 4 (2011), 527–42 (533–4) (in Hebrew).

[61] *Ibid.*

[62] Giorgio Balladore Pallieri, 'General Report: the Concept of "War" and the Concept of "Combatant" in Modern Conflicts', *Military Law & Law of War Review* 10 (1971), 313–51 (339–40).

[63] E.g., Graves, 'Lecture I' 1843 (n. 30), 96.

[64] E.g., Georg Schwarzenberger, 'Some Reflections on the Scope of the Functional Approach to International Law', *Transactions of the Grotius Society* 27 (1941), 1–29 (2–5).

[65] E.g., Philip Jessup, 'Should International Law Recognize an Intermediate Status between Peace and War?' *American Journal of International Law* 48 (1954), 98–103 (100–3).

[66] E.g., Green, 'New Law' 1977 (n. 32), 5.

attribution often retrospectively re-emerges in the collective memory of the conflict. Stated differently, the sense of stability projected by core IHL distinctions frames our recollection of past wars, marginalising attributes of these wars that do not fit the IHL distinctions. For example, the First World War is intuitively recalled as an inter-State war, despite the participation of various non-State forces (exiled government forces, rebels, partisans, tribes, national liberation forces, etc.).[67] The First World War is also recalled with a clear end date, even though that date was, for a long period, factually unclear and legally disputed.[68]

The exaggerated clarity attributed to legal terms often leads jurists to believe that indeterminacy would be eliminated if they could only agree on the exact phrasing (e.g., if we only replaced the term 'war' with 'armed conflict'). But phrasing has only limited influence on legal indeterminacy levels, especially when the law addresses emergencies.[69]

Despite the chronic nature of IHL distinctions' indeterminacy, this indeterminacy was not always considered a crisis, but rather an unavoidable, yet manageable, condition. Such a non-crisis attitude acknowledges that the 'difficult[y] to formulate clear and precise [legal] rules ... [to] define the character and the bearing of acts of war ... [is] inherent *in the very nature of things*';[70] and that all newly adopted IHL 'definitions [tend to] become obsolescent [almost] upon formulation',[71] because '[t]he *very nature of war* is such that it is impossible to anticipate every new development'.[72] Nevertheless, it asserts that despite being 'blurred and ... not always ... readily determinable, the established [IHL] concepts cannot be merely abandoned',[73] nor can the attempt to reduce the indeterminacy by means of adopting new treaty IHL,[74] because dismissiveness towards IHL 'opens the door to every kind of excess and suffering'.[75] We must, instead, be realistic regarding IHL's

---

[67]   *Wikipedia*, 'Allies of World War I', 30 December 2016, available at: en.wikipedia.org/wiki/Allies_of_World_War_I; *Wikipedia*, 'Central Powers', 30 December 2016, available at: https://en.wikipedia.org/wiki/Central_Powers.

[68]   Manley Hudson, 'The Duration of the War between the United States and Germany', *Harvard Law Review* 39 (1926), 1020–45 (1020); Robert Gerwarth, *The Vanquished: Why the First World War Failed to End, 1917–1923* (London: Penguin, 2016), 1–16.

[69]   Ziv Bohrer, 'Obedience to Orders and the Superior Orders Defense', PhD thesis, Tel-Aviv University, 2012, 73, 81–2, 413–15.

[70]   Prince Gortchacow, 'Observations on the Dispatch from Lord Derby to Lord A. Loftus (20 January 1875)', in *Correspondence Respecting the Conference at Brussels on the Rules of Military Warfare* (London: UK Parliament, 1875), 5–6 (emphasis added).

[71]   Green, 'United States' 1971 (n. 44), 284 (emphasis added).

[72]   *Ibid.*

[73]   *Ibid.*

[74]   E.g., Gortchacow, 'Observations' 1875 (n. 70), 5–6.

[75]   *Ibid.*, 6.

capabilities. Accordingly, *when making new treaty IHL* we should aim only to reduce '*as far as possible* ... th[e] uncertainties'.[76] Likewise, *when applying existing IHL*, the appropriate way to address the inevitable indeterminacy is to '*analogize, insofar as possible* ... [from the existing] law so as to preserve the intent thereof and thereby diminish the evils of war'.[77]

Past reliance on such a non-crisis 'adaptation' attitude indicates that the current crisis is not necessarily an unavoidable result of IHL distinctions becoming indeterminable due to changes in warfare. Those wishing to reform an existing law often propagate a crisis narrative that frames certain events as challenging that law; crisis narratives are used primarily by those who lack sufficient power, under the existing normative conditions, to shape the law.[78] Admittedly, not all factual circumstances can serve as a basis for a crisis narrative, and often those who support such a narrative honestly perceive a crisis. Nonetheless, most factual circumstances can be understood in various ways and different implications could be concluded from the same set of facts; our specific understanding of factual circumstances is shaped by the narratives we, consciously or unconsciously, construct.[79]

In international law, wars are often a basis for crisis narratives.[80] These crisis narratives have been mainly of two kinds: First, in various past conflicts States have claimed that changes in warfare and the indeterminacy of existing IHL have rendered that law obsolete and therefore inapplicable to their contemporary war.[81] Second, sometimes the crisis cry was subsequently also embraced by those wishing to increase the legal constraints on belligerents. They argued that the legal indeterminacy and warfare's changed, ghastlier nature prove that existing international law is inapt and contemporary conflicts necessitate new, more constraining laws.[82] Past successes of the second kind of crisis cries campaigns have shaped a prevailing narrative of IHL history, according to which

---

[76] *Ibid.* (emphasis added).

[77] Green, 'United States' 1971 (n. 44), 284 (emphasis added).

[78] Suzanne Katzenstein, 'In the Shadow of Crisis: the Creation of International Courts in the Twentieth Century', *Harvard International Law Journal* 55 (2014), 151–209 (153).

[79] Alasdair MacIntyre, *Whose Justice? Which Rationality?* (Notre Dame, IN: University of Notre Dame Press, 1988), 1–11.

[80] Katzenstein, 'In the Shadow of Crisis' 2014 (n. 78), 153.

[81] Aldrich, 'Human Rights in Armed Conflict' 1973 (n. 49), 886.

[82] Eleanor Davey, 'The Bombing of Kunduz and the Crisis of International Humanitarian Law', *Reluctant Internationalists Blog*, 21 January 2016, available at: www.bbk.ac.uk/reluctant internationalists/blog/the-bombing-of-kunduz-and-the-crisis-of-international-humanitarian-law; Katzenstein, 'In the Shadow of Crisis' 2014 (n. 78), 153.

advancing international law has, gradually, transformed quondam lawless wars into humane warfare.[83]

In truth, in some respects current IHL is more, and in others is less, constraining than past IHL. Both aforesaid kinds of crisis narratives, as well as non-crisis adaption attitudes, have influenced IHL development. The present prevalence of a crisis narrative merely attests to the increasing influence of factions that, in the existing normative setting, do not have sufficient power to shape IHL in accordance with their preferences.

B. *Blurred Principle of Distinction*

When do you think each of the following statements was made?

(1) Some view 'the new phenomena [of extensive civilian participation] ... as a general decadence of the art [of war]; and h[o]ld ... that in the evenly-balanced ... war game [i.e., battle warfare] the perfection of the art is realized.'[84]

(2) Who should 'be considered combatants according to the laws of war? ... [This] question ... continues to be the theme of much consideration'.[85]

(3) '[The recent] war has emphasized ... the archaic character of the [contemporary] Conventions. They speak the language ... of [the] nineteenth-century ... envis[ioning] war mainly as a trial of strength between opposing professional teams in which civilians would play the role of spectators. [Accordingly, these IHL conventions draw] ... [s]harp distinctions ... between the functions of the State and those of the individual ... Under modern conditions these distinctions have everywhere become blurred and often obliterated.'[86]

(4) Within two decades, a 'new form of warfare [widespread terrorism] has been born ... [It] differs fundamentally from the wars of the past in that victory is not expected from the [battlefield] clash of two armies'.[87] Unlike 'soldier[s] ... terrorist[s] ... [attack] without uniform ... far from a field of battle ... [and mainly] unarmed civilians'.[88]

---

[83] E.g., Daniel Thürer, *International Humanitarian Law* (The Hague: Martinus-Nijhoff, 2011), 44–6.

[84] Carl von Clausewitz, *On War*, trans. J. J. Graham (London: Trübner, 1873), 206 (*c.* 1816–30).

[85] Creasy, *First Platform of International War* 1876 (n. 33), 476.

[86] H. A. Smith, 'The Government of Occupied Territory', *British Yearbook of International Law* 21 (1944), 151–5 (151).

[87] Roger Trinquier, *Modern Warfare*, trans. Daniel Lee (Fort Leavenworth, KS: US Army 1985), 6 (*c.* 1961).

[88] *Ibid.*, 17–18.

The first statement is from Carl von Clausewitz's book *On War*, written follow-ing the French Revolution and Napoleonic Wars. Like the torture memos, Clausewitz argued that 'to introduce into the philosophy of war itself a principle of moderation would be an absurdity',[89] and dismissed existing wartime inter-national law as 'imperceptible'.[90] The second statement is from Edward Creasy's 1876 treatise, influenced by the failed 1874 Brussels Conference. The third statement is from a 1944 article, criticising the 1907 Hague Regulations in the light of the Second World War. The fourth source is a 1961 French analysis of *Modern Warfare*; inspired by Clausewitz, and like the torture memos, it dismisses IHL application to wars against terrorists.[91] These sources demonstrate that there is nothing novel in current claims that IHL is unable to deal with the supposedly recent blurring of the combatant–non-combatant distinction and the passing of battle warfare. This section addresses the former.

As Clausewitz's statement implies, irregular fighting has been on the rise since the late eighteenth century, beginning with a surge in civilian participa-tion in wars and the transition to conscripted national armies.[92] Since then, civilian participation in wars has often been influenced by views dismissive of IHL in popular revolutionary movements; as Winston Churchill exaggerat-edly noted, '[f]rom the moment Democracy … forced itself upon the battle-field, war ceased to be a gentleman's game'.[93] The nineteenth century was, therefore, not a period in which the principle of distinction was clear.

The inaccurate prevailing historical account is partly due to the previously discussed attributes of dichotomist emergency-related classifying legal terms. Because of these attributes, the blurring of the combatant–non-combatant distinction is somewhat unavoidable, as well as bound to be perpetually perceived as novel.

Due to this misguided perception, attention is primarily paid to the rather recent distinction-related reforms made in the 1949 Geneva Conventions and the 1977 Additional Protocols. Relative to earlier *treaties*, each of these reforms expanded: (a) POW status eligibility;[94] (b) the protections granted to 'unprivileged' (ineligible

---

[89] Clausewitz, *On War* 1816–30 (n. 84), 2.

[90] *Ibid.*, 1.

[91] Trinquier, *Modern Warfare* 1961 (n. 87), 22.

[92] Terry Gill, 'Chivalry: a Principle of the Law of Armed Conflict?', in Mariëlle Matthee, Brigit Toebes and Marcel M. T. A. Brus (eds.), *Armed Conflict and International Law* (The Hague: Springer, 2013), 33–51 (36–7); Carl Schmitt, 'The Theory of the Partisan (trans.) A. C. Goodson (c. 1962)', available at: www.obinfonet.ro/docs/tpnt/tpntres/cschmitt-theory-of-the-partisan.pdf.

[93] Winston Churchill, *A Roving Commission* (New York: Scribner, 1930), 64–5.

[94] Article 4 Convention (III) relative to the Treatment of Prisoners of War, Geneva, 12 August 1949, 75 UNTS 135 (unrecognised States' forces and exiled governments' forces); Arts. 1(4), 43–4, Protocol Additional to the Geneva Conventions of 12 August 1949, and relating

for POW status) enemy combatants (notably, until the 1949 adoption of Common Article 3, some still held that IHL authorised the extrajudicial execution of captured 'unprivileged' combatants).[95] But this focus on recent events neglects that the discourse dedicated to developing IHL since the 'nineteenth century, could not ignore questions relating to the [warfare] initiative of the people . . . in the form of hostile uprisings, guerrilla warfare, etc.'[96] Within this discourse two approaches often competed. One approach considered the blurring of the combatant–non-combatant distinction as a crisis likely to render IHL obsolete.[97] The second considered it an inevitable, manageable condition.[98]

The latter (non-crisis) approach is strongly expressed in a norm adopted long before 1949. At the 1874 Brussels Conference, a comprehensive proposal was advanced to resolve the combatant–non-combatant indeterminacy. But opposition was considerable, both because of political disagreements and because clarity is not in the nature of the thing. A compromise was therefore proposed, containing only two narrow distinction-related articles (other than those addressing regular State forces) setting the POW status eligibility conditions for: (a) certain irregular State forces (militia and volunteer corps), and (b) certain civilian fighters in unoccupied territories.[99] This compromise attempt failed, and only a non-binding declaration was adopted.[100] When States attempted again to codify IHL, in 1899, incorporating the above articles of the Brussels Declaration was suggested. Again, the proposal encountered strong opposition, which argued that (a) a clear-cut differentiation between those eligible and ineligible for POW status cannot be made because of the inherent blurriness of the principle of distinction, and (b) a clear determination of the existence of belligerent occupation is often impossible.[101] Eventually, a compromise was reached:[102] the articles were incorporated,

to the Protection of Victims of International Armed Conflicts (Protocol I), 8 June 1977, 1125 UNTS 3 (national liberation forces).

[95] Common Art. 3, 1949 Geneva Conventions; Protocol Additional to the Geneva Conventions of 12 August 1949 and relating to the protection of victims of non-international armed conflicts (Protocol II), 8 June 1977, 1125 UNTS 609; Aldrich, 'Human Rights in Armed Conflict' 1973 (n. 49), 879.

[96] Trainin, 'Questions of Guerrilla Warfare' 1946 (n. 49), 536.

[97] E.g., Schmitt, 'The Theory of the Partisan' 1962 (n. 92), 37.

[98] E.g., Percy Bordwell, *The Law of War Between Belligerents* (Chicago: Callaghan, 1908), 2–6.

[99] Articles 9–10, Project of an International Declaration concerning the Laws and Customs of War (Brussels, 27 August 1874).

[100] Bordwell, *Law of War between Belligerents* 1908 (n. 98), 100–13.

[101] Rotem Giladi, 'The Enactment of Irony: Reflections on the Origins of the Martens Clause', *European Journal of International Law* 25 (2014), 847–69.

[102] *Ibid.*

becoming Articles 1 and 2 of The Hague Regulations, but as a counter-balance the following statement was included in the preamble:[103]

> [The treaty] desire[s] to diminish the evils of war so far as military necessities permit . . . It has not, however, been possible to agree . . . on provisions embracing all . . . circumstances . . . [Nevertheless] the cases not provided for [in the treaty are not] . . . left to the arbitrary judgement of the military Commanders . . . [I]n [such] cases . . . populations and belligerents remain under the protection and empire of the principles of international law, as they result from the usages established between civilized nations, from the laws of humanity, and the requirements of the public conscience . . . [I]t is in this sense especially that Articles 1 and 2 of the Regulations adopted must be understood;

I suspect that upon realising that the current discussion concerns the 'Martens Clause', you (the reader) uncontrollably rolled your eyes. The general feeling among jurists is that the Martens Clause means anything one claims it to mean and therefore means nothing.[104] This dismissive attitude is partly due to the clause's vague terms. But to an even greater degree, it stems from later developments. In the last half a century, some jurists, in attempt to advance expansive interpretations of the clause, constructed a mythological account of its creation. Such interpretations treat the clause like constitutional law, or IHRL, using its vagueness to evermore expand civilian protection.[105] In response, Statist-positivist jurists criticised both the clause's vagueness and its expansive interpretations, arguing that it places no effective obligations on States.[106] The clause's authoritativeness has further diminished due to recent CLS-oriented historical research that refuted the mythology regarding its 'birth', stressing the politics behind its adoption.[107]

However, the CLS account of 'law as politics' tends to be inaccurate, because political influences on law formation often do not bar legal and moral factors from also having an influence.[108] As for the IHRL-like and Statist-positivist approaches, neither tells the whole jurisprudential-normative story of the clause's creation. At the time (even more than today), IHL was influenced by an additional jurisprudential approach (henceforth

---

[103] Preamble, The Hague Convention (II) with Respect to the Laws and Customs of War on Land (29 July 1899).

[104] Giladi, 'The Enactment of Irony' 2014 (n. 101), 847–50.

[105] See *ibid.*

[106] See *ibid.*

[107] E.g., *ibid.*

[108] Annette Freyberg-Inan, *What Moves Man* (Albany, NY: State University of New York Press, 2012), 111–12.

'nature-of-things jurisprudence'). Reading the clause through that jurisprudential lens can better our understanding of the clause. But, before such
a reading could be made, a (somewhat lengthy) presentation of the 'nature-
of-things jurisprudence' is required.

Nature-of-things jurisprudence, although it does assume the existence of
some universal rights and (even more so) obligations, considerably focuses on
profession/status-specific rights and (especially) obligations.[109] This focus stems
from its core jurisprudential premise that each kind of entity, including each
profession and legal status, has a distinct ideal nature from which distinct rights
and (especially) obligations derive.[110] State agents' obligations (e.g., those of
rulers, judges and soldiers), like those of private professionals (e.g., doctors), are,
accordingly, viewed as personal obligations deriving from the nature of their
profession.[111] By contrast, both Statist-positivist and IHRL-like approaches regard
State agents' obligations as derivatives of their State's obligations, based on
a vision of the State as a corporate entity and on conceptualised clear distinctions between public and private, and between sovereigns and individuals.[112]

Nature-of-things jurisprudence also offers a unique perspective on the relations
between positive and natural law, which, unlike Statist-positivism, does not
conceptualise sharp distinctions between international and domestic law, law
and policy, or morality and law. First, it expects positive law to reflect universal
natural law, and permits the punishment of individuals for violations of core
unwritten natural laws.[113] Secondly, it expects one's actions to be directed neither
by fear of punishment, nor by deference to positive law, but by an aspiration to
follow one's ideal nature; all the while, acknowledging that this aspiration could
never be fully attained (as evident in Platonic and Aristotelian thinking).[114]
Thirdly, this jurisprudence utilises both 'perfect' and 'imperfect' obligations.[115]

---

[109] Onora O'Neill, 'Rights, Obligations and World Hunger', in Thomas Pogge and Keith Horton
       (eds.), *Global Ethics: Seminal Essays* (Saint Paul, MN: Paragon House, 2008), 139–56 (150);
       Henry Sumner Maine, *Ancient Law* (London: Albemarle, 1908), 64–5; Christine Hayes,
       What's Divine about Divine Law? (Princeton University Press, 2015), 62–86.
[110] Maurice Keen, *The Laws of War in the Late Middle Ages* (London: Routledge, 1965), 15.
[111] *Ibid.*
[112] David Kennedy, 'International Law and the Nineteenth Century: History of an Illusion',
       Quinnipiac Law Review 17 (1998), 99–138 (131); David Kennedy, 'War and International Law:
       Distinguishing the Military and Humanitarian Professions', *International Law Studies* 82
       (2007), 3–33 (9).
[113] David Whetham, *Just Wars and Moral Victories* (Leiden: Brill, 2009), 74–5.
[114] Hayes, *What's Divine about Divine Law?* 2015 (n. 109), 62–86; Korsgaard, 'Prologue' 1996
       (n. 52), 2–3.
[115] Hilly Moodrick-Even-Khen, 'Obligations at the Border Line: On the Obligations of an
       Occupying State towards the Occupied State', *Mishpat v'Mimshal* 8 (2005), 471–519 (508)
       (in Hebrew).

These two obligation concepts have various definitions. A 'perfect obliga-tion' refers herein to a rather precise, non-discretionary normative duty that specifies its beneficiaries (a 'right' correlates to the duty).[116] An 'imperfect obligation' refers herein to a discretionary-aspirational normative duty, demanding its bearers be guided by a certain motivation, while according them extensive discretion: (a) regarding the (kind and amount of) resources they should invest into fulfilling the duty; and (b) towards whom to direct their efforts to fulfil that duty (no one has a correlating 'right').[117] This definition differs from imperfect obligations' popular definition as 'moral dut[ies] which cannot be enforced by law'.[118] Indeed, some prominent nature-of-things jur-isprudential views (such as those that greatly influenced IHL) *do* hold that blatant grave violations of imperfect obligations could give rise to legal sanc-tions, despite these obligations' open-endedness.[119] The aforesaid popular definition of imperfect obligations, like the prevailing rejection of unwritten (customary and natural law) crimes, reflects the prevailing understanding of the principle of legality, which gained prominence from the nineteenth century onward under the influence of both positivism and rights jurisprudence.[120] However, IHL and international criminal law (ICL), along with some domestic (common law) systems, still rely considerably on a different understanding of that principle (which reflects nature-of-things jurisprudence).[121] That understanding perceives normative prohibitions as having a non-legal (social-moral) penumbra and a legal (even criminal) core; despite the acknowledged murky border between the core and penum-bra, 'fair-warning' is assumed regarding perpetrators of blatant grave violations, based on the premise that a normative message to avoid that behaviour is already conveyed by the penumbra and that it amplifies as the breaching behaviour nears the prohibition's core.[122]

The aforesaid elements of the nature-of-things jurisprudence aid in addres-sing the limitations of law. Consider, for example, *in bello* proportionality law;

---

116   Graves, 'Lecture I' 1843 (n. 30), 95–6.
117   *Ibid.*; Moodrick-Even-Khen, 'Obligations at the Border Line' 2005 (n. 115), 508.
118   John Goldsworth, *Lexicon of Trust* (Saffron Walden: Mulberry House Press, 2016), 171.
119   E.g., *Britain v. Spain, Reports of International Arbitral Awards* 2 (1924), 645; Emer de-Vattel, *The Law of Nations* (London: Robinson, 1797), 369–70. See also Aaron X. Fellmeth, *Paradigms of International Human Rights Law* (Oxford University Press, 2016), 81.
120   M. Cherif Bassiouni, 'Universal Jurisdiction for International Crimes: Historical Perspectives and Contemporary Practice', *Virginia Journal of International Law* 42 (2001), 81–162 (99); Anne Peters, *Beyond Human Rights* (Cambridge University Press, 2016), 79–84.
121   See Peters, *Beyond Human Rights* 2016 (n. 120), 82–92.
122   See Andrew Ashworth, *Principles of Criminal Law* (Oxford University Press, 1999), 75–80.

that IHL instructs commanders not to cause incidental civilian harm that is excessive in relation to the concrete and direct military advantage anticipated from their attack.[123] This norm is undeniably vague and encourages 'judicial deference to the military commander's situational judgement'.[124] Furthermore, it is widely acknowledged that that norm cannot become clearer, due to the 'fog of war' and because the required comparison is 'between unlike quantities and values'.[125] Yet, despite this chronic vagueness, criminal responsibility still exists 'in cases where the excessiveness of the incidental damage was obvious',[126] because in such cases a wide consensus is deemed to exist regarding the commission of a violation.[127] It exists only in such cases due to 'fair-warning' concerns.[128] But, as Mark Osiel observes, the norm's influence extends beyond the extreme penal cases, attempting to instruct soldiers to embrace the 'belief that "internal morality" of professional soldiering constrains their use of force in ways far more demanding than [the enforceable] international law'.[129] This further constraining demand of martial virtue and honour is conceptualised as, considerably, 'deriv[ing] … from the fact that the weighty responsibilities demanded of [commanders] … cannot find full reflection within the law governing [them]';[130] similar normative settings exist 'wherever we expect … professionals … to behave in morally exigent ways that we cannot quite bring the law to require of them."[131] Furthermore, the extrajudicial 'forms and sources of inhibition on the measure of force employed in war have become integral to any acceptance of the proportionality rule'.[132] In short, *in bello* proportionality law is an imperfect obligation in the nature-of-things jurisprudence sense of that term.[133]

As evident in *ius in bello* proportionality's prominence, IHL has been strongly influenced by nature-of-things jurisprudence. That influence is further evident in the fact that 'humanity', 'necessity' and 'chivalry' – all

---

[123] ICTY, *Final Report to the Prosecutor by the Committee Established to Review the NATO Bombing Campaign Against the FRY*, PR/P.I.S./510-E, 13 June 2000, para. 48.

[124] Mark Osiel, 'Rights to Do Grave Wrongs', *Journal of Legal Analysis* 5 (2013), 107–219 (187).

[125] ICTY, *Final Report* (n. 123), para. 48.

[126] *Ibid.*, para. 21.

[127] *Ibid.*, paras. 48–51.

[128] Osiel, 'Rights to Do Grave Wrongs' 2013 (n. 124), 187.

[129] *Ibid.*, 191.

[130] *Ibid.*, 195.

[131] *Ibid.*

[132] *Ibid.*, 196.

[133] Above n. 117 and accompanying text.

imperfect obligations – have long been core IHL principles.[134] Humanity, as an imperfect obligation, constitutes a universal duty to act mercifully.[135] Necessity is an imperfect obligation of moderation, imposed on anyone committing legally authorised acts of violence.[136] The Martens Clause explicitly mentions both humanity and necessity. Chivalry (military honour) has long been regarded as an imperfect obligation imposed on professional warriors as part of their 'very essence ... [as guardians of the] fabric of international society',[137] holding that the 'soldier, be he friend or foe, is charged with the protection of the weak and unarmed ... [based on] the noblest of human traits – sacrifice'.[138] Chivalry conceptualises adherence to IHL as 'a personal rather than a state [obligation]'.[139] Accordingly, the Martens Clause is addressed not to the collective State entity, but rather to military commanders; thus, it is said that in the Martens Clause, '"Chivalry" find[s] ... [its modern] source'.[140]

The Martens Clause echoes the nature-of-things jurisprudence in additional ways. The non-positivist premise that wide discretion does not necessarily amount to the non-existence of obligatory norms is expressed in the assertion that cases unregulated by treaty are not 'left to the arbitrary judgement of the military commanders ... [but] remain under the protection and empire of the principles of international law'.[141] The interrelated perception of law, policy and morality is expressed in the definition of 'the principles of international law ... [as] result[ing] from the usages established between civilized nations, from the laws of humanity, and the requirements of the public conscience'.[142]

Given this history, the Martens Clause should, arguably, be viewed as a legally binding imperfect obligation to guide military commanders (and those reviewing commanders' decisions). At minimum (considering its

---

[134] Mark Antaki, *A Pre-History of Crimes against Humanity* (draft manuscript on file with author), 215–17.

[135] *Ibid.*

[136] Judith Gardam, *Necessity, Proportionality and the Use of Force by States* (Cambridge University Press, 2004), 32–8; Yishai Beer, 'Humanity Considerations Cannot Reduce War's Hazards Alone: Revitalizing the Concept of Military Necessity', *European Journal of International Law* 26 (2015), 801–28 (807–11).

[137] General Douglas MacArthur, 'Order Confirming the Death Sentence of General Tomoyuki Yamashita' (6 February 1946).

[138] *Ibid.*

[139] US Army, *International Law, vol. II: Laws of War* (PM-27-161-2, 1962), 15.

[140] Leslie C. Green, 'Enforcement of the Law in International and Non-International Conflicts: the Way Ahead', *Denver Journal of International Law and Policy* 24 (1995/6), 285–320 (300).

[141] Hague Convention 1899 (n. 103), preamble.

[142] *Ibid.*

explicit reference to Articles 1 and 2 of the Hague Regulations), the clause should be viewed as such when commanders need to address 'twilight' states between 'combatants' and 'non-combatants', or between 'occupation' and 'non-occupation'.[143]

Accordingly, for example, before the present classification frenzy, many held (and some still do) that:[144]

> [T]he rules which apply to occupied territory should also be observed as far as possible in areas through which troops are passing and even on the battlefield. All this is evidence of a more general tendency to think of the laws of war as a set of minimum rules to be observed in the widest possible range of situations, and not to worry excessively about the precise legal definition[s] …

C. The Demise of Battles

It is widely held that existing (aka 'traditional' or 'modern') IHL was designed primarily based on a conceptualisation of war as 'symmetric conflicts taking place between [equal] state armies',[145] on 'compartmentalize[d] … battlefield[s]'.[146] Therefore, many deem existing IHL to be unsuitable for transnational conflicts, as these wars do not fit that conceptualisation of war.[147]

But we have seen that for the past two centuries, similar forms of warfare – namely, irregular, civilian, indiscriminate, non-State and terrorist warfare – have been likewise described (in Carl von Clausewitz's words) as a 'new phenomenon [marking] … a general decadence of … the evenly-balanced … war game [of inter-sovereign battle-warfare]'.[148] How can it be that over the course of this long period similar forms of warfare have each been perceived, at one time or another, as a novel phenomenon that recently abolished battle warfare?

Originally, a 'battle' was a legal concept, referring to a specific form of fighting to which unique laws applied.[149] In late medieval times, *ius ad bellum* defined two categories of enemies: (a) illegitimate, including rebels and non-

---

[143] Trainin, 'Questions of Guerrilla Warfare' 1946 (n. 49), 541–51.
[144] Adam Roberts, 'What Is a Military Occupation?', *British Yearbook of International Law* 55 (1985), 249–305 (256). See also *infra*, n. 327.
[145] Robin Geiss, 'Asymmetric Conflict Structures', *International Review of the Red Cross* 88 (2006), 757–77 (760).
[146] Benvenisti, 'Rethinking the Divide' 2009 (n. 19), 543.
[147] *Ibid.*
[148] Clausewitz, *On War* 1816–30 (n. 84), 206.
[149] Whetham, *Just Wars* 2009 (n. 113), 103–14.

believers ('savages', 'infidels' and 'heretics'), against whom total war, without *ius in bello* restrictions, was prescribed; and (b) legitimate, against whom limited war must be fought, in which *ius in bello* applied.[150] Even in limited wars, non-combatant protections were slight: it was legal to execute most captured enemy combatants (only knights were eligible for POW status) and to harm most civilians (*ius in bello* prohibited harming only women, children, the elderly and select professionals).[151] Even limited wars were, usually, wars of attrition, conducted mainly through raids on the enemy's civilian population. Battles were a notable exception, conducted between opposing forces on a designated field, based on uniquely restrictive *ius in bello*.[152] Additionally, unlike victories attained otherwise, a battle victory was considered a binding legal ruling regarding the justness of the victor's cause; belligerents often avoided battles because of this decisive legal implication.[153]

In the sixteenth and seventeenth centuries, instances of total warfare increased because European conflicts were mainly rebellions and religious wars, and because knight-led forces were increasingly replaced by mercenaries.[154] But the ensuing trauma led to public pressure to humanise warfare, and mercenaries' indiscipline led to their replacement with professional, standing armies, whose officers, commonly, respected *ius in bello* because they saw themselves as the heirs of the knightly tradition.[155] Thus, 'chivalry' and 'humanity' inspired considerable legal reforms, including: (a) *all* regular soldiers, not only knights, wore uniforms and became eligible for POW status;[156] (b) contributions and requisitions, in return for protection, increasingly replaced raids against civilians;[157] (c) intentionally harming *any* non-combatant became illegal;[158] (d) 'use of [newer] more deadly weapon[s] . . . was [often perceived as] hostile to the law of war';[159] and (e) avoiding battles

---

[150]   Frederick Russell, *Just War in the Middle Ages* (Cambridge University Press, 1979), 7–19.

[151]   Keen, *Laws of War* 1965 (n. 110), 193; Geoffrey Parker, *Empire, War and Faith in Early Modern Europe* (London: Penguin, 2002), 146–60.

[152]   James Whitman, *The Verdict of Battle* (Cambridge, MA: Harvard University Press, 2012), 35–55.

[153]   *Ibid.*

[154]   Gill, 'Chivalry' 2013 (n. 92), 36.

[155]   *Ibid.*; Whitman, *The Verdict of Battle* 2012 (n. 152), 55–8.

[156]   Toni Pfanner, 'Military Uniforms and the Law of War', *International Review of the Red Cross* 84 (2004), 93–124 (98).

[157]   Whitman, *The Verdict of Battle* 2012 (n. 152), 55–8.

[158]   *Ibid.*; W. E. Hall, *A Treatise on International Law* (Oxford University Press, 1904), 397.

[159]   Francis Lieber, 'The Usages of War', *New York Times*, 19 January 1862, available at: www .nytimes.com/1862/01/19/news/usages-war-continuation-lectures-dr-lieber-columbia-college-admissibility.html.

became less acceptable.[160] This ushered in the era of limited or battle warfare. The decisive clash of opposing armies on a designated battlefield made it relatively easy to distinguish civilians from combatants and to identify IHL's spatial and temporal application boundaries. Because battles were perceived as collective jousts, and due to chivalry's strong influence, contemporary IHL was premised on a 'simple', tit-for-tat, fair-play conceptualisation of reciprocity.[161]

But that era should not be overly romanticised. Even at its eighteenth-century height, battles were still uncommon, merely more common than before.[162] Furthermore, the simplistic conceptualisation of reciprocity legit-imised harsh reprisal measures in response to IHL violations; especially so against civilians, because civilian participation in the fighting was regarded as a severe violation of the laws of the war 'game'.[163]

The demise of battle warfare began in the late eighteenth century with the beginning of the surge in civilian participation in warfare.[164] Weapons innovations and progress-oriented cultural changes eliminated the aver-sion to using new weapons and contributed to battle warfare's 'demise'.[165] But that 'demise' was protracted and non-linear. Commitment to battle warfare precepts weakened at the turn of the nineteenth century. Yet it recuperated by the mid-nineteenth century, creating *unmet* expectations that the American Civil War (1851–6) and the Franco-German War (1870–1) would be conducted accordingly. Widespread civilian parti-cipation, new weapons and harsh reprisal measures caused extensive suffering in these wars, leading many to realise that battle warfare was waning.[166]

Both early and late nineteenth century sources depict battle-warfare's 'demise' as recent. The non-linear, protracted nature of that 'demise' explains that incoherence regarding the time of that 'demise'. But, it fails to explain the continued depiction of battle-warfare's 'demise' as a recent phenomenon throughout the last century, because the battle-warfare era fully ended by

---

[160]   Whitman, *The Verdict of Battle* 2012 (n. 152), 55–9.
[161]   E.g., Evan Wallach, 'Pray Fire First Gentlemen of France: Has 21st Century Chivalry Been Subsumed by Humanitarian Law?', *Harvard National Security Journal* 3 (2012), 431–69 (431).
[162]   Whitman, *The Verdict of Battle* 2012 (n. 152), 59.
[163]   E.g., Antoine Henri de Jomini, *Histoire Critique et Militaire des Guerres de la Révolution* (Brussels: Librarie Militaire Petit, 1840), vol. II, 367.
[164]   Whitman, *The Verdict of Battle* 2012 (n. 152), 207–44.
[165]   *Ibid.*
[166]   *Ibid.*; Armand du Payrat, *Prisonnier de Guerre dans la Guerre Continentale* (Paris: Librairie Nouvelle de Droit et de Jurisprudence, 1910), 25–7; Allen Frantzen, *Bloody Good* (University of Chicago Press, 2004), 1–3.

WWI ('battle' ceased being a legal concept and compartmentalised battle-fields became much rarer).[167]

Note further that the conditions of the American Civil War and of the Franco-German War played a pivotal role in bringing about both the realisation that battle warfare was waning and an effective determination to codify and reform IHL.[168] In the course of that late nineteenth- and early twentieth-century reform, legal constraints were increasingly placed on recourse to reprisals, which strongly contributed to IHL's gradual shift from the tit-for-tat (battle warfare era) reciprocity notion towards the current more abstract, long-term reciprocity notion that aspires to facilitate postwar peaceful relations.[169] Given the nature of these (and later) legal reforms, the premise that existing IHL was chiefly designed for battle-warfare, and so for 'simple' reciprocity conditions, is clearly wrong.

How could the depiction of a recent 'demise' of battle warfare continue throughout the last century? Why is current IHL misperceived as having been designed for battle warfare? The best place to start explaining these anomalies is modern IHL's proclaimed beginning. '[A]s every student of the subject knows, modern IHL began when the Swiss businessman Henri Dunant visited the battlefield of Solferino ... [which led him to] found the Red Cross.'[170] As the story goes:[171]

> Dunant – a tourist as he described himself later – had walked across the [battle]field ... Shocked by the suffering of the wounded soldiers who lay abandoned on the field, he tried to organize nearby villagers ... to bring them relief. Shortly after, in 1862, Dunant gave the world his plan for protecting wounded and sick soldiers. Dunant's ... belief in the ability of the law to limit and control violence ... was in marked contrast to the attitude of the period ... The world has since caught up with him ...

Notice something odd with that historical account? It claims that the mid-nineteenth-century attitude, unlike that of today, did not believe in the legal regulation of warfare. But, if that is true, how come a similar, current battle-field visit feels much *more* (not less) dangerous than during Dunant's visit?

Dunant felt safer than we would, because Solferino was 'a classic single-day battle ... [which] resolved its war, producing a momentous historic verdict:

---

[167] *Ibid.*; US Army, *International Law* 1962 (n. 139), 11–19.

[168] *Ibid.*

[169] Patryk Labuda, 'The Lieber Code, Retaliation and the Origins of International Criminal Law', in Morten Bergsmo, Cheah Wui Ling, Song Tianying *et al.* (eds.), *Historical Origins of International Criminal Law* (Brussels: Torkel-Opsahl, 2015), vol. III, 299–341 (302, 322).

[170] Luban, 'Human Rights Thinking' 2016 (n. 4), 50 (acknowledging that this is a myth).

[171] Daniel Thürer, *International Humanitarian Law* (The Hague: Martinus Nijhoff, 2011), 44–6.

the unification of Italy'.[172] Dunant's self-depiction as a tourist was not a metaphor. The decisiveness (and compartmentalised nature) of battles led to 'a characteristic mid-nineteenth-century phenomenon':[173]

> [B]attle tourists ... appeared at every mid-nineteenth-century conflict ... They often arrived in fine dress, in coaches, with servants and picnic baskets ... Dunant ... started out as just such a battle tourist. He came to Solferino ... to witness history in the making.

These facts do not diminish Dunant's contribution. They do, however, reveal flaws in the humanitarian narrative that modern IHL was 'born' at Solferino. That narrative demonstrates a common tendency to examine the past not on its own merits, but, rather, in comparison with the present, which inevitably leads to exaggerated assumptions of similarity or difference between the past and the present.[174] The aforesaid narrative presumes exaggerated similarly between past and present by failing to realise that in the past the term 'battle' meant a legal (and not merely colloquial) concept that considerably constrained combat behaviour. The same is true for current sources that depict the demise of battle warfare as recent; the difference is that the aforesaid humanitarian narrative unreflectively attributes the disorderly qualities of recent battles to the compartmentalised ones of yore, while the forward-dating of battle warfare's 'demise' does the opposite. The aforesaid humanitarian narrative also presumes an exaggerated level of dissimilarly between past and present by assuming that in Dunant's time (unlike today) the prevailing attitude was dismissive of IHL. Dunant's actual experience reveals considerable adherence to IHL at Solferino. Contrary to that humanitarian narrative, a wide range of approaches influenced IHL's normative universe, then and now.

During the last two centuries, IHL has been shaped by three main types of approaches besides humanitarian ones: (a) 'warrior' approaches, usually held by military professionals; (b) Statist-positivist approaches that either deny IHL's effective existence or regard States as IHL's sole lawmakers; and (c) pacifist approaches, sceptical of IHL's combat influence. Each is responsible for a piece of the puzzle concerning the perpetual forward-dating of the 'demise' of battle warfare.[175]

---

[172] Whitman, *The Verdict of Battle* 2012 (n. 152), 4.

[173] *Ibid.*, 210.

[174] Randall Lesaffer, 'International Law and Its History: the Story of an Unrequited Love', in Matthew C. R. Craven (ed.), *Time, History and International Law* (The Hague: Martinus Nijhoff, 2007), 27–42 (34–8).

[175] Kennedy, 'Distinguishing the Military and Humanitarian Professions' 2007 (n. 112), 4–33.

(a) Many of the nineteenth-century military professionals who influenced IHL sought to adapt 'chivalry' to the changing warfare conditions. For them, symmetric battlefield clashes became desired ideals.[176] Nevertheless, warrior approaches tended to also acknowledge strong reasons against adopting 'the view that war is a sort of athletic contest, in which none but the authorized teams must play', because 'most wars are now contests of peoples rather than princes'.[177] Therefore, the influence of their aspirational battle-related ethos alone cannot explain the aforesaid persistent forward-dating.

(b) Statist-positivist approaches (fully crystalised in the late nineteenth century) hold that 'there was only one [form of] sovereignty ... the territorial State',[178] and posit sharp 'distinctions between public and private, law and politics, international and municipal, sovereigns and individuals'.[179] Based on such approaches:[180]

> [An] attempt ... [was] made to introduce another principle [to IHL] ... confining wars to governments themselves. Under this principle the state would become in effect a corporation with limited liability ... and war would become an athletic contest between two schools whose members ... must not participate except as members of the duly authorized teams.

(c) For opposite reasons, pacifist approaches also embraced the premise that '[t]he battlefield, the territory of belligerency, was legally demarcated':[181]

> The[ir] point was to shrink the domain of war through moral suasion, agitation, shaming, and proselytizing ... This conviction lent an ethical urgency to the emergence of a sharp legal distinction between war and peace ... [c]ombatants and non-combatants ...

Warfare did not reassume a compartmentalised battle form, and 'warriors' and 'humanitarians' have expressed much less faith than Statist-positivists and pacifists in sharp legal distinctions.[182] Nevertheless, this misleading narrative has caught on, and is likely the primary cause of the perpetual forward-dating of battle warfare's 'demise' and for the misconception of existing IHL as having been designed for battle warfare.

---

[176] Bordwell, *Law of War between Belligerents* 1908 (n. 98), 2–6.
[177] *Ibid.*, 3–4.
[178] Kennedy, 'History of an Illusion' 1998 (n. 112), 119.
[179] *Ibid.*, 131.
[180] Bordwell, *Law of War between Belligerents* 1908 (n. 98), 2.
[181] Kennedy, 'Distinguishing the Military and Humanitarian Professions' 2007 (n. 112), 9.
[182] *Ibid.*

The irony is that after their ideological forerunners created unrealistic expectations for sharp war-related legal distinctions, present-day peace-ordinated IHL sceptics (hardline IHRL advocates) and hardline Statists present IHL's failure to fulfil these unrealistic expectations as proof of its inability to regulate contemporary conflicts. Statists do so as part of their attempt to release States from existing IHL constraints. IHRL advocates do so to expend IHRL wartime application; after all, the 'once-sharp' distinction between peace (IHRL's original domain) and war has muddled.

D. Unprecedented Wars

When were the following statements made?

1. Because of technological developments, a 'war amongst the great powers is now necessarily a world war'.[183]
2. Technology changed warfare: 'Instead of a small number of well-trained professionals championing their country's cause with ancient weapons ... we now have entire populations, including even women and children, pitted against one another in brutish mutual extermination.'[184]
3. 'The war which we fight is an unprecedented war of global character ... because of the [current] age of modern technology and of world-wide interdependence.'[185]

The first source is from 1848, referring to naval innovations. Its use of the term 'world war' seems odd to us. Current reference to the war of 1914–18 as the First World War often makes us forget earlier multi-continent, multi-partisan wars (such as the Napoleonic Wars 1803–15). The second source is Winston Churchill's 1930 autobiography, deeming the demise of battle warfare 'the fault of Democracy and Science'.[186] The third source is an article from the Second World War. These sources, similarly to current ones, depict new technologies as revolutionising warfare by obliterating either the principle of distinction or wars' spatial confinements.

We tend to assume that our era is exceptional in its technological achievements. But empirical data indicates that the innovation rate peaked sometime

---

[183]   Hepworth Dixon, 'The American Republics: Part 1', *People's Journal* 4 (1848), 248–52 (250).
[184]   Churchill, *A Roving Commission* 1930 (n. 93), 64–5.
[185]   Hans Kohn, 'War Aims and Peace Patterns', *Saturday Review* (4 July 1942), 9–10 (9).
[186]   Churchill, *A Roving Commission* 1930 (n. 93), 64–5.

between 1873 and 1914, and has been decreasing since.[187] Nearly all significant weapons today debuted by the First World War: automatic rifles, machine guns, tanks, submarines, biological weapons, chemical weapons, rockets and (manned and unmanned) aircraft; the most notable exception, atomic weapons, debuted in the Second World War.[188] This is not to say that weapons ceased to develop, only that advances are occurring at a slower pace. This is also not to say that recent technological developments did not cause changes in warfare, only that we tend to exaggerate the significance of current changes *relative* to those of the past. This is an expression of a well-known phenomenon, 'temporocentrism', the 'largely unconscious . . . tendency . . . to place . . . an exaggerated emphasis upon our own period'.[189]

Temporocentrism goes beyond our attitude to contemporary innovations: 'We assume always . . . that the crisis of our age is somehow more critical than the crises of other ages.'[190] This may explain our perception of contemporary wars, because the overall picture is actually 'far more positive than many suppose . . . [S]tatistics suggests that there has been a sharp decline over recent decades in the number of deaths directly resulting from wars'.[191] The main reason behind the decline in casualties is the reduction in the incidence of inter-State conflicts, which (counter-intuitively) have tended to cause *more* casualties than NIAC.[192] Since the 1990s, NIACs have also been (non-linearly) declining.[193] Specifically regarding the fight between the United States and

---

[187] Jonathan Huebner, 'A Possible Declining Trend for Worldwide Innovation', *Technological Forecasting & Social Change* 72 (2005), 980–6; Robert Gordon, *The Rise and Fall of American Growth* (Princeton University Press, 2017), 1–23.

[188] Michael Marshall, 'Timeline: Weapons Technology', 7 July 2009, available at: www .newscientist.com/article/dn17423-timeline-weapons-technology; 'A Timeline of Weaponry!', 24 August 2014, available at: www.historyandheadlines.com/cracked-history-timeline-weaponry; Oren Gross, 'The New Way of War: Is There a Duty to Use Drones?', *Florida Law Review* 67 (2016), 1–72 (17).

[189] Harlan Cleveland, 'The Future of the Past', *Minnesota History* 47 (1981), 200.

[190] *Ibid.*

[191] Bruce Pilbeam, 'Reflecting on War and Peace', in Peter Hough, Shahin Malik, Andrew Moran *et al.* (eds.), *International Security Studies: Theory and Practice* (London: Routledge, 2015), 87–118 (95); Therese Pettersson and Kristine Eck, 'Organized Violence, 1989–2017', *Journal of Peace Research* 55 (2018), 535–47 (535).

[192] Pilbeam, 'Reflecting on War and Peace' 2015 (n. 191), 96; Bethany Lacina and Nils Petter Gleditsch, 'Monitoring Trends in Global Combat: a New Dataset of Battle Deaths', *European Journal of Population* 21 (2005), 145–66 (155–8).

[193] Pilbeam, 'Reflecting on War and Peace' 2015 (n. 191), 97; Kendra Dupuy Scott Gates, Håvard Mokleiv Nygård *et al.*, 'Trends in Armed Conflict, 1946–2016', Peace Research Institute Oslo, 2 (2017); Thomas S. Szayna, Stephen Watts, Angela O'Mahony *et al.*, 'What Are the Trends in Armed Conflicts, and What Do They Mean for U.S. Defense Policy?' (RAND Corporation, 2017), available at: www.rand.org/content/dam/rand/pubs/research_re ports/RR1900/RR1904/RAND_RR1904.pdf.

contemporary transnational terrorist groups: in 2016, US President Obama noted that US citizens are more likely to die from a fall in a bathtub than from a terrorist attack, suggesting that the perceived threat from such terrorism is inflated.[194]

Admittedly, NIAC's *percentage* among wars has increased. A popular account speaks of a ratio of two internal wars for every inter-State war prior to the Second World War, compared with a 4.7:1 ratio between 1945 and the 2000s.[195] Yet, the ratio change notwithstanding, inter-State wars remain a significant phenomenon (not to mention that another account speaks of a less drastic change, from a 3.2:1 ratio in 1816–1945, to a 4.4:1 ratio in 1945–2000s).[196] Likewise, even before 1945, internal wars were more common than inter-State wars; thus, clearly, a significant phenomenon. Statistical data indicates that during the last two centuries, even non-inter-State wars other than internal wars (e.g., colonialist wars and those against Al-Qaeda and ISIS), in and of themselves, have been 'much more common than inter-state wars, with 163 . . . [such] wars, compared with 95 inter-state wars'.[197]

Undeniably, each war has unique attributes, and current wars are not the same as they were several decades ago (change is, arguably, the only constant in history). But the characterisation of current transnational conflicts as wars of a new *kind* further assumes that they are *qualitatively* different than past wars.[198] Many scholars challenge this assumption, because:[199]

> [It] is based on an uncritical adoption of categories and labels grounded in a double mischaracterization. On the one hand, information about recent or ongoing wars is typically incomplete and biased; on the other hand, historical research on earlier wars tends to be disregarded.

This criticism has forced Mary Kaldor, the leading scholarly proponent of the new wars thesis, to qualify her position. Although still arguing that contemporary wars have new attributes, she adds:[200]

---

[194] Nicholas Kristof, 'Overreacting to Terrorism?', *New York Times*, 24 March 2016, available at: www.nytimes.com/2016/03/24/opinion/terrorists-bathtubs-and-snakes.html.

[195] E.g., Visser, 'Conflicts, New Wars and Human Rights' 2017 (n. 16).

[196] Jack Levy and William Thompson, *The Arc of War* (University of Chicago Press, 2011), 193–4, 206.

[197] Meredith Reid Sarkees and Frank Wayman, *Resort to War: 1816–2007* (Washington, DC: CQ Press, 2010), 333–5.

[198] Pilbeam, 'Reflecting on War and Peace' 2015 (n. 191), 95.

[199] Stathis Kalyvas, '"New" and "Old" Civil Wars: a Valid Distinction?', *World Politics* 54 (2001), 99–118 (99).

[200] Mary Kaldor, 'In Defence of New Wars', *Stability* 2(1) (2013), 1–16 (3).

The most common criticism of the 'new wars' argument is that new wars are not new ... Of course this is true. Many of the features of new wars can be found in earlier wars ... But there is an important reason, which is neglected by the preoccupation with empirical claims, for insisting on the adjective 'new' ... The term 'new' is a way to exclude 'old' assumptions about the nature of war ...

Even Al-Qaeda's and ISIS's attributes (the sources of the current archetypal transnational conflicts), though far from identical to those of their predecessors, are not as exceptional as commonly assumed. After 9/11, Paul Berman noted that this terror assault followed the warfare pattern exhibited by anti-liberal movements worldwide since the First World War.[201] These 'movements were never fully synonymous with national States'.[202] The Second World War, for example, 'was complicated by Nazism's ability to call on sympathizers and co-thinkers all over Europe'.[203] 'Communism was likewise an international affair.'[204] Berman concluded that since it is waged through terror attacks by an anti-liberal movement with transnational attributes, Al-Qaeda's war is 'a war of an old kind'.[205]

Berman's description of Nazism may sound odd to us, but this is because of the tendency to retrospectively marginalise past wars' non-State-like attributes. During the Second World War, this description was commonly held. After all, the Nazis: (a) maintained a party apparatus parallel to that of the German State; (b) aimed for global domination; (c) considered Nazism, at least to some degree, the German manifestation of a universal ideology (non-liberal nationalism); and (d) maintained ties with adherents of that ideology elsewhere. Justice Pal, of the Tokyo Tribunal, accordingly, doubted whether the Nazis could be called a State rather than a 'Shapeless force without recognised political character.'[206]

Pal's depiction reveals an inaccuracy in Berman's choice of the First World War as the starting point for the warfare pattern he describes. Pal quoted from the 1818 treaty concerning Napoleon's detention.[207] The treaty parties (the European Powers) considered Napoleon as waging war not as the ruler of

---

[201] Paul Berman, 'Terror and Liberalism', *The American Prospect* 12(8), 19 December 2001, available at: http://prospect.org/article/terror-and-liberalism.
[202] *Ibid.*
[203] *Ibid.*
[204] *Ibid.*
[205] *Ibid.*
[206] IMTFE, *Dissentient Judgment of Justice Pal* (Tokyo: Kokusho-Kankokai, 1999), 698 (c. 1948).
[207] Protocole Séparé Relatif à Bonaparte (21 November 1818).

France and as aiming for global domination; accordingly, the treaty deemed him 'the leader of a Shapeless force without recognized political character'.[208]

Napoleon was not the era's only feared transnational global enemy. At the same 1818 international congress, the European Powers also formed the European Concert (the UN's 'grandfather'), influenced by a belief 'that the French Revolution, and all subsequent [remotely resembling] political developments … were part of [a single] international … revolutionary threat',[209] because the *Comité Directeur*, a 'central but secret body[,] was coordinating rebellions throughout Europe'.[210] The *Comité Directeur* did not exist; but, throughout the nineteenth century, European Concert members 'truly feared it'.[211] The element of truth in this fear lay in the fact that since the late eighteenth century, both liberal and anti-liberal revolutionary movements often included elements that wished to globalise.[212] Berman's account, therefore, inaccurately depicts a clear-cut contrast between liberal and anti-liberal movements.

Berman's description of Communism has merits. Communism had global ideological aims, Communist States supported Communist revolutions worldwide, and Communist rebels employed irregular warfare. Westerners, thus, perceived Cold War era actual wars as 'a new kind of war',[213] in which 'victory [was] not measurable in territorial terms or human material loss'[214] and '[b]attlefronts seldom existed',[215] because the enemy 'preferred terrorist tactics',[216] 'rarely wore uniforms',[217] and consisted of globally connected forces, 'difficult to define',[218] a global 'network of … terrorists'.[219] This history brings into

---

[208] *Ibid.*

[209] Andrew Benedict-Nelson, 'Political Revolutionaries, International Conspiracies, and the Fearful, Frenzied Elites', *The Los Angeles Review of Books*, 10 February 2015, available at: https://lareviewofbooks.org/article/political-revolutionaries-international-conspiracies-fearful-frenzied-elites.

[210] *Ibid.*

[211] *Ibid.* See also, Adam Zamoyski, *Phantom Terror* (New York: Basic Books, 2015).

[212] Mary J. Maynes and Ann Waltner, 'Modern Political Revolutions: Connecting Grassroots Political Dissent and Global Historical Transformations', in Antoinette Burton and Tony Ballantyne (eds.), *World Histories from Below: Disruption and Dissent, 1750 to the Present* (London: Bloomsbury, 2016), 11–46.

[213] Howard Jones, 'The Truman Doctrine in Greece: America's Global Strategy and the "New Kind of War"', *Journal of Modern Hellenism* 5 (1988), 9–21 (9).

[214] *Ibid.*

[215] *Ibid.*

[216] *Ibid.*

[217] *Ibid.*

[218] *Ibid.*

[219] US President Ronald Reagan, 'Address to the Nation on Events in Lebanon and Grenada', 28 October 1983, New York Times, www.nytimes.com/1983/10/28/us/transcript-of-address-by-president-on-lebanon-and-grenada.html.

perspective claims, such as those of US presidents Bush (2006) and Obama (2016), concerning: 'an unprecedented war',[220] whereby 'terrorists ... defend no territory ... wear no uniform';[221] a 'new reality'[222] of 'terrorist networks'.[223]

If you still think temporocentrism is overrated, consider the following pronouncements:

1. A 'new kind of war' (1795, a French Convention Member, The French Revolution);[224]
2. The 'case was exceptional' (1818, treaty concerning Napoleon's detention);[225]
3. A 'somewhat novel kind of warfare' (1863, US Minister to the UK Adams, privateer attacks during the American Civil War);[226]
4. 'All the wars I can remember were "unprecedented"' (1916, Russian General Skugarevski, regarding the 1853–6 Crimean War, 1866 Austro-Prussian War, 1870–1 Franco-German War and the First World War);[227]
5. '[T]he most novel kind of warfare that history can record' (1900, British Colonel Brookfield, Second Boer War);[228]
6. An 'unprecedented war' (1916, President Wilson, the First World War);[229]
7. A 'moment unprecedented' (1941, President Roosevelt, the Second World War);[230]
8. A 'new kind of war' (1949, influential reporter, Anne O'Hare-McCormick, Greek Civil War);[231]

---

[220] US President George W. Bush, 'Speech on Terrorism', *New York Times*, 6 September 2006, available at: www.nytimes.com/2006/09/06/washington/06bush_transcript.html.

[221] *Ibid.*

[222] US President Barack Obama, '2016 State of the Union Address', *New York Times*, 12 January 2016, available at: www.nytimes.com/2016/01/13/us/politics/obama-2016-sotu-transcript.html.

[223] *Ibid.*

[224] Comte de Boissy d'Anglas, *Trial of Messrs. Pitt* (London: Citizen Lee, 1795), 8–9.

[225] Protocole Séparé Relatif à Bonaparte 1818 (n. 207).

[226] Charles F. Adams, 'Letter to US Secretary of State (27 March 1863)', *Foreign Relations of the US: Diplomatic Papers* 1 (1863), 159.

[227] A.P. Skugarevski, 'The Future of War', *Journal of the Military Service Institution of the United States* 59 (1916), 473–8 (474).

[228] 78 HC Deb., 202–3 (31 January 1900).

[229] US President Woodrow Wilson, 'Ultimatum to Germany's Foreign Minister', 18 April 1916, reproduced at: www.firstworldwar.com/source/uboat1916_usultimatum.htm.

[230] US President Franklin Delano Roosevelt, 'Four Freedoms Speech', 6 January 1941, reproduced at: www.presidency.ucsb.edu/ws/?pid=16092.

[231] As quoted in Jones, 'Truman Doctrine' 1988 (n. 213), 9.

9. 'The war in Vietnam is a new kind of war . . . not another Greece' (1965, US State Department);[232]

10. 'The world has changed' (1983, US President Reagan, the Beirut suicide attack and US intervention in Grenada).[233]

The similarity between these statements goes beyond contemporary temporocentrism. In all these sources, one or more of the following provoked the 'unprecedented war' cry: technological innovations; irregular fighting; transnational war aims; globalisation; atrocities; blurred peacetime–wartime divide.

II. NORMATIVE NOVELTY

Oddly, even some jurists who acknowledge that transnational conflicts are 'not historically new' still deem them to be 'new wars'.[234] Such jurists, just like those who believe that transnational conflicts are a new factual phenomenon, hold that normative novelty exists in IHL application to transnational wars, based on a premise that IHL was traditionally designed to regulate inter-State and, to a lesser degree, civil wars.[235]

That premise relies on a widely accepted historical account that traditional international law addressed only States. Only in response to twentieth-century horrors did international law gradually move away from its Statist model into areas that were traditionally left for States to regulate through domestic law. ICL, IHRL and NIAC law, each established in the mid-twentieth century, are the primary manifestations of this transition, as each penetrates the veil of State sovereignty and addresses entities other than States.[236] Many even believe that 'now for the first time in . . . half a millennium the State is on the way out'.[237]

Given the wide acceptance of this historical account, it is unsurprising that IHL application to transnational conflicts is widely deemed novel. More surprising is that each position with regard to the law that applies to

---

[232]   US State Department, 'Aggression from the North', 27 February 1965, reproduced at: source books.fordham.edu/mod/USStateDept-vietnamfeb1965.asp.

[233]   Reagan, 'Address to the Nation' 1983 (n. 219).

[234]   Nicolas Lamp, 'Conceptions of War and Paradigms of Compliance: the "New War" Challenge to International Humanitarian Law', *Journal of Conflict and Security Law* 16 (2011), 225–62 (226).

[235]   *Ibid.*; Sloane, 'Puzzles of Proportion' 2015 (n. 20), 334.

[236]   Antonio Cassese *et al.*, *International Criminal Law* (Oxford University Press, 2011), 8; Dill, in this volume, 237.

[237]   Frank Ankersmit, 'Political Representation and Political Experience', *Redescription* 11 (2007), 21–45 (36).

transnational conflicts is proclaimed by its proponents to derive from the accepted historical account.

First, some supporters of the position that a new, more constraining IHL applies to transnational conflicts, speculate regarding the larger normative implication of the (supposed) rise in these conflicts. Namely, they contemplate whether transnational conflicts signify not only that existing IHL ('devised for' 'wars between States') is 'becoming obsolete', but further that international law's traditional 'State-based model ... is ... losing its relevance'.[238]

Secondly, the torture memos also based their position on the accepted historical account, according to which NIAC law was created only in the mid-twentieth century, as traditional IHL was designed to regulate inter-State wars. Prior to the mid-twentieth century, internal wars were classified as either belligerencies or insurgencies. Belligerencies were conflicts in which the State-side made a discretionary decision to act as if it was fighting an inter-State war and apply IHL (granting its non-State rival 'belligerent status'). Insurgencies were all other internal conflicts, ungoverned by international law because States regarded them as falling under the sole jurisdiction of their domestic law. IHL began to shift away from its Statist phase with the development of the first customary NIAC laws, during the Spanish Civil War (1936–9) and with the adoption, a decade later, of Common Article 3 (the first NIAC multilateral treaty law). The torture memos relied on this accepted historical account and on Common Article 3's reference to NIAC 'occurring *in* the territory of *one* of the High Contracting Parties', to conclude that transnational wars 'could not have been within the contemplation of the drafters of [existing IHL]'.[239] The torture memos acknowledged that since the 1990s there have been efforts to move into a new phase, in which *all* conflicts would be extensively regulated by international law through attempts to expand the application of IHL to situations in which it did not originally apply, and of IHRL beyond peacetime into wartime situations. But the memos dismissed these efforts as illegitimate attempts to force upon States legal positions that disregard the phrasing and history of the relevant international law.[240]

Thirdly, as noted, in time, the United States moderated its position. It currently holds that NIAC law applies in transnational conflicts, because these conflicts are against non-State actors.[241] But the United States still holds

---

[238] Pfanner, 'Asymmetrical Warfare' 2005 (n. 26), 158.
[239] Yoo and Delahunty, 'Memo' 2002 (n. 14), 10.
[240] *Ibid.*, 9–11.
[241] Egan, 'International Law' 2016 (n. 18).

that existing NIAC law needs to be reinterpreted and even reformed, because it was not originally designed to address transnational conflicts.[242] Thus, disregarding the fact that it changed its legal position, the United States maintains that its *current* position derives from the accepted historical account.

Fourthly, unlike the United States, Israel classifies transnational conflicts as IAC, because they commonly cross borders. But Israeli motivation for legal reform is similar to that of the United States. The Israeli Supreme Court, in 2014, for example, called upon the international community to adopt a new, less restrictive IHL for transnational wars, holding that until such IHL is adopted, the existing relevant IHL (IAC law) must be interpreted less restrictively than before, because the traditional interpretations generally befit 'the old and known model of war between [State] armies'.[243]

Fifthly, in stark contrast to Israel and the United States, many jurists who argue that existing IHL, subject to adaptations, applies to transnational conflicts, find that the required adaptations must *increase* the restrictions on States, mainly by way of applying IHRL alongside IHL. Proponents' belief that this position derives from the accepted historical account is demonstrated by the minority opinion in the British *Serdar Mohammed* ruling.[244] The issue examined there was the international law applicable to the wartime detention of non-State fighters by British forces on Afghan soil. Unlike the United States, which considers the war in Afghanistan to be part of a larger transnational conflict, and unlike some jurists who consider it an IAC, the British courts classified it as a NIAC. Since IHL treaties do not address the authority to detain individuals in NIAC, the British judges looked for customary IHL for such authority, and were inclined to conclude that no such law exists.[245] The majority opinion, however, ruled that certain conflict-specific Security Council resolutions implicitly conferred detention authority to the British forces in the particular case.[246] The minority opinion disagreed and instead held that IHRL fills the gap in IHL; namely, they held that in NIAC no IHL constitutes a *lex specialis* that bars the IHRL pertaining to detention by State agents (that IHRL demands the *ex-ante* existence of a detention-sanctioning *domestic* law).[247] Their conclusion (shared by the majority) regarding the non-

[242] *Ibid.*

[243] E.g., HCJ, *HaMoked v. Minister of Defense*, Judgment of 31 December 2014, Decision of Justice Hayut, No. 8091/14, para. 2.

[244] UKSC, *Abd Ali Hameed Al-Waheed & Serdar Mohammed v. Ministry of Defence*, Judgment of 17 January 2017, UKSC 2014/0219.

[245] *Ibid.*, paras. 9–14, 158, 246.

[246] *Ibid.*, paras. 9–30, 68, 83, 94–8, 111–13, 134, 148, 158, 204–6, 224, 231, 235.

[247] *Ibid.*, paras. 233–75.

existence of relevant customary IHL in NIAC was derived from the premise
that '[t]raditionally, international humanitarian law, like other international
law, was concerned almost entirely with the reciprocal relationships between
states, and therefore with conflicts between states rather than internal
conflicts'.[248]

In response to positions expanding IHRL wartime application, the US
government asserted that: (a) in any war, IHL accords relevant States certain
authorities (to kill, capture and detain enemy combatants), and that IHL
constitutes a *lex specialis* that bars IHRL application; (b) IHRL is inapplicable
to extraterritorial wartime State actions, because each State is bound by IHRL
only regarding actions it commits within its 'jurisdiction', a term generally
referring only to its sovereign territory.[249]

Recently, the United States has slightly relaxed its position on these two
issues, illustrating the current diversity of legal positions.[250] Indeed, at this
point in the debate, the floodgates open to many disagreements, including: (a)
when does IHL constitute *lex specialis*?; (b) under what conditions and to what
extent does IHRL apply in wartime irrespective of IHL?; (c) is a State under
a duty to abide by IHRL only regarding actions it commits within its 'jurisdiction'?; (d) besides actions State agents commit within their State's sovereign
territory, what actions are regarded as committed within a State's
jurisdiction?[251]

Most of these disagreements began long ago and have implications far
beyond transnational conflicts. But all of them have drastically intensified
following the dispute over the law addressing transnational conflicts, increasingly transforming into 'weirdly metaphysical debates' over 'transcendental
nonsense' that mistakenly regard legal concept as 'magic solving words'.[252] The
discussion henceforth veers away from this transcendental nonsense by focusing on the more consensual issue: the history of international law.

As already discussed, consensual narratives are simplified accounts of reality,
and critically examining them can reveal issues that these narratives suppress.[253]
Accordingly, the discussion hereinafter critically examines the accepted historical narrative, exposing that past IHL was less Statist than assumed. Presently,
based on the accepted historical narrative, a consensus exists that a clear divide

---

[248] *Ibid.*, para. 246; see also paras. 9–14, 158 (majority judges' reliance on that account).
[249] Ryan Dowdy *et al.*, *Law of Armed Conflict Deskbook*, 5th edn. (Charlottesville, VA: US Army
       J.A.G., 2015), 8.
[250] *Ibid.*
[251] See Section III.
[252] Luban, 'Human Rights Thinking' 2016 (n. 4), 64.
[253] Above nn. 10–13.

between IAC law and NIAC law has long been enshrined in IHL. This divide creates uncertainty and disagreements with regard to which law addresses transnational conflicts. Refuting the accepted narrative reveals that the wide consensus regarding an IAC law/NIAC law divide is rather recent. Such a divide approach has always existed. However, an opposite ('adaptation') approach has also long existed, holding that only one IHL corpus exists: that corpus applies in inter-State wars as is, while in all other wars it applies subject to (truly necessary) adaptation. The misguided belief in the age-oldness of the IAC law/NIAC law divide is, actually (as explained later), proof that support for the 'adaptation approach' did not weaken following a defeat in a reasoned debate to the 'divide approach', but as a result of much slyer actions.

A. *Westphalia*

Returning to our period identification game:

1. Given the predictions that we are only now nearing the Statist model's demise, when do you think the following was written?[254]

   [T]he improvement of communication and … transport … with its consequent interdependence and solidarity of interest between groups situated in different nations … render[s] hostility based on the lines of political geography irrelevant … State lines do not follow the lines of the respective conflicts …

2. In the light of the accepted history of both ICL and NIAC law, identify the following conflict: (a) as a contemporaneous court noted, in a ruling that determined it was a 'war', the conflict was initiated by an ideological movement's 'armed forces dominated by the spirit of driving from th[eir] country or destroying all foreigners';[255] (b) that armed force also wished to exterminate compatriot members of a certain religion;[256] (c) a multilateral international declaration deemed these forces' 'murde[rs], tortur[es]', 'massacre[s] … desecrat[ions]', 'pillag[e] and destr[uction]' to be 'crimes against the law of nations, against the laws of humanity';[257] (d) the conflict was fought between the aforesaid non-State forces and a multinational allied force; (e) during the conflict, an international military tribunal

[254] Norman Angell, *The Foundations of International Polity* (London: William Heinemann, 1914), xxv–xxvi.

[255] C.C.D., *Hamilton v. McClaughry*, Judgment of 12 April 1905, No. 136 F, 445, 450.

[256] Ziming Wu, *Chinese Christianity* (Leiden: Brill, 2012), 49.

[257] The Allies' 'Joint Note' (1900), as reproduced in Paul Clements, *The Boxer Rebellion* (New York: Columbia University Press, 1915), 207–8.

tried some of the perpetrators of the atrocities;[258] (f) there was no state of war between the allies and the State in which the war was conducted, because that State officially considered movement members to be rebels.[259]

The source quoted above is from 1914, demonstrating that rumours about the demise of the Statist model have been (thus far) premature (together with prophecies about novel transnational conflicts being omens for that demise).[260] The aforementioned war is the Boxer War (1900–1). This conflict is rightly infamous for its Western atrocities and colonialist undertones. But it was also a multinational intervention aimed at stopping the massacre of 30,000 Chinese Christians and 200 foreigners. During the war, at Pao-Ting-Fu, an international military tribunal of British, German, Italian and French judges tried some of the perpetrators of the atrocities.[261]

The accepted history requires reassessment. Until a few decades ago, it was commonly held that traditional international law had formed, following the 'birth' of the modern State, at the 1648 Peace of Westphalia.[262] But historical research refuted the Westphalian myth, showing that the rise of States was a protracted process, having already begun in the late Middle Ages and culminating only in the late nineteenth century,[263] when the modern definition of the State was 'doctrinally consolidated'.[264] This modern 'European invocation [was then also] retrospectively backdated to the Peace of Westphalia and used to articulate an international order based on mutually recognized sovereign States'.[265] Positivist jurists, aiming to strengthen State sovereignty, contributed to the consolidation and back-dating.[266] The same aim also led them to embrace conceptual 'sharpening of distinctions … between international and … domestic law',[267] and between 'sovereigns and individuals'.[268] Today the Westphalian myth has been effectively debunked, but the full implications of its falsehood have yet to be internalised.[269]

---

[258] James Hevia, *English Lessons* (Durham, NC: Duke University Press, 2003), 224–9.

[259] C.C.D. Kan., *Hamilton v. McClaughry* (n. 255), 450.

[260] Quentin Skinner, 'A Genealogy of the Modern State', *Proceedings of the British Academy* 162 (2009), 325–70 (359).

[261] See nn. 255–9.

[262] Joseph Stromberg, 'Sovereignty, International Law and the Triumph of Anglo-American Cunning', *Journal of Libertarian Studies* 18 (2004), 29–93 (29–30).

[263] Andrew Phillips, *War, Religion and Empire* (Cambridge University Press, 2010), 136–7.

[264] Kennedy, 'History of an Illusion' 1998 (n. 112), 119.

[265] See Peter Wilson, *The Holy Roman Empire* (London: Allen Lane, 2016), 683.

[266] Kennedy, 'History of an Illusion' 1998 (n. 112), 100.

[267] *Ibid.*, 119.

[268] *Ibid.*, 131.

[269] Wilson, *Holy Roman Empire* 2016 (n. 265), 682.

One such implication concerns the application of international law to individuals. Historically, there was no sharp distinction between international and domestic law.[270] Not only piracy, but also war crimes and even felonies (murder, theft, arson, robbery, rape, etc.) were considered crimes against humanity and crimes against the law of nations, whose perpetrators were enemies of mankind; many European courts even applied universal jurisdiction to such crimes.[271] Only under the influence of nineteenth-century Statist-positivism did Western domestic civilian judicial systems abandon this universalist view. In contrast, Western military justice systems, having primary jurisdiction over war crimes and wartime felonies, continued to consider customary international law to be a legal basis for prosecuting such crimes.[272] Even a practice, dating back to medieval times, of occasionally creating joint military tribunals continued; namely, the Boxer Rebellion tribunal is far from the only pre-Nuremberg international military tribunal.[273] The 1900 Boxer Rebellion tribunal is not even the sole NIAC-*related* pre-Nuremberg international military tribunal (which indicates that not only ICL but also NIAC law has a longer history than assumed); such NIAC-related tribunals were created, for example, in 1839–46,[274] 1882,[275] 1912[276] and 1918.[277] Until the 1950s, alongside sources echoing the

---

[270] Mark Janis, *Introduction to International Law*, 2nd edn. (Boston, MA: Little, Brown, 1993), 228; Jeffrey L. Dunoff, Steven R. Ratner and David Wippman, *International Law: Norms, Actors, Process* (Aspen, CO: Aspen Publishers, 2006), 441.

[271] Ziv Bohrer, 'International Criminal Law's Millennium of Forgotten History', *Law and History Review* 34 (2016), 393–485 (422–30).

[272] *Ibid.*, 464–71.

[273] *Ibid.*, 480–3; Ziv Bohrer and Benedikt Pirker, 'Nuremberg Was Not the First International Criminal Tribunal – By a Long Shot' (draft paper, on file with author).

[274] Joint Prussian–Russian–Austrian tribunals tried Polish revolutionaries during the joint occupation of Cracow; Meir Ydit, *International Territories* (Leyden: Sythoff, 1961), 95–107.

[275] In an 1882 rebellion in Egypt, anti-Christian atrocities were committed, triggering (together with colonialist aims) a British military intervention. Eventually Britain assumed the role of belligerent occupier. But, initially, it treated the Egyptian government as a sovereign ally, and some perpetrators of atrocities were tried by a joint British–Egyptian military tribunal. Some of the charges were explicitly for violations of wartime international law; G. S. Baker, *Halleck's International Law* (London: Trübner, 1908), vol. II, 350–1; Evelyn Baring, *Modern Egypt* (New York: Macmillan, 1916), vol. I, 331–9.

[276] During the First Balkan War, when Strumnitsa was under joint Bulgarian–Serb occupation, sham proceedings were conducted by a joint military tribunal of Serb and Bulgarian officers, local leaders and Bulgarian insurgents; *Report of the International Commission to Inquire into the Causes and Conduct of the Balkan Wars* (Washington, DC: Carnegie Endowment, 1914), 73–4.

[277] During a military intervention by the First World War Allies in support of the White Russian forces, in a region jointly occupied by the White Russian and Allied forces, a 'special military court' was formed, consisting of four White Russian officers and a representative from each of

Westphalian narrative (depicting ICL as an innovation), other sources considered ICL a long-standing practice.[278] This narrative of continuity was forgotten during the Cold War, but norms originating from the aforesaid centuries-long practice are still part of ICL today.[279]

A second insufficiently internalised implication of the Westphalian falsehood concerns the application of international law to non-State entities. Originally, the (then) European system of international law was inapplicable to supposedly 'uncivilised' (i.e., non-Western) nations. According to the Westphalian myth, international law globalised gradually as evermore non-Western nations became States.[280] Presently, a competing narrative is gaining support, claiming that international law globalised rather abruptly at some time between the late nineteenth and mid-twentieth century, after Westerners abandoned their xenophobic 'standard of civilisation' for the application of international law.[281] The criterion adopted instead was statehood: a form of sovereignty that non-Western nations could attain.[282]

But history is less consistent and statehood-oriented than both narratives above assume. Throughout most of international law's history, various legal approaches existed concerning its application to non-Western nations.[283] The following are especially significant: (a) non-application approaches that authorised total war against 'uncivilised' nations based on the idea that international law did not apply there;[284] (b) punishment approaches that prescribed total war against 'uncivilised' nations as punishment for their supposed violation of international law;[285] (c) adaptation approaches that aimed to adapt the (then) Western international law to cross-cultural interactions (including

---

the three Allied armies; Leonid Strakhovsky, *Intervention at Archangel* (Princeton University Press, 1944), 46.

[278]   E.g., US Legal Memorandum, 'Trial of War Criminal by Mixed Inter-Allied Military Tribunals', 31 August 1944, 4, available at: www.legal-tools.org/doc/e5f070.

[279]   Bohrer, 'Forgotten History', 2016 (n. 271), 394–471.

[280]   Stromberg, 'Sovereignty' 2004 (n. 262), 29–30.

[281]   Cf. Carl Schmitt, *The Nomos of the Earth*, trans. G. L. Ulmen (New York: Telos, 2003), 226 (suggesting 1875–1919); Brett Bowden, 'The Colonial Origins of International Law', *Journal of the History of International Law* 7 (2005), 1–23 (21–2) (suggesting the Second World War); Martti Koskenniemi, *The Gentle Civilizer of Nations* (Cambridge University Press, 2001), 510–17 (suggesting the 1960s).

[282]   Gerrit Gong, *The Standard of 'Civilization' in International Society* (Oxford: Clarendon Press, 1984), 32–3.

[283]   Bohrer, 'Forgotten History' 2016 (n. 271), 409–18.

[284]   Elbridge Colby, 'How to Fight Savage Tribes', *American Journal of International Law* 21 (1927), 279–88 (285–7) (briefly contrasting non-application and punishment approaches).

[285]   *Ibid.*; Bohrer, 'Forgotten History' 2016 (n. 271), 410–11 (punishment approaches, unlike non-application approaches, authorised the prosecution of captured non-Western fighters for individual international law violations).

wars);[286] (d) minimalist-discretionary approaches that substituted the robust international law with an imperfect obligation to apply 'such rules of justice and humanity as recommend themselves in the particular circumstances of the case'.[287] Each approach was often considered by its supporters not only as *lex ferenda* (aspired law), but as *lex lata* (the actual existing law).

Historical evidence indicates that the likelihood that (some measure of) international law would be applied to wars against non-Westerners was influenced not only by case-specific, non-legal considerations, but also by the fluctuating support for competing legal approaches.[288] Support for adaptation approaches increased after the religious wars era (because that era's trauma increased aversion towards total war doctrines), culminating in the late eighteenth century.[289] Even later, that support remained considerable under the influence of a legal position that perceived both Western and non-Western communities as sovereign entities, simply of 'different sorts';[290] the latter supposedly formed based on 'race or nationality rather than territory'.[291] In the late nineteenth century, however, support for the applicability of international law to cross-cultural interactions drastically decreased under the influence, among other things, of rising support for the Statist-positivist position that the territorial State was the sole 'form of political [sovereign] authority'[292] and the sole 'subject [of] international law'.[293] The position considering international law as applicable only to Western sovereigns is not identical to the position considering it to be applicable only to States. But in an era in which very few non-Western sovereigns were considered by Westerners as having State attributes, the convergence between these two positions was considerable. Although these two positions enjoyed considerable support at the turn of the century, support for either was never unanimous, as demonstrated by the following two issues:

1. In some early twentieth-century interactions between Western States and non-Western, non-State entities, Westerners (or even both sides) considered as the applicable law one of the older approaches according

---

[286] Jennifer Pitts, 'Empire and Legal Universalisms in the Eighteenth Century', *American Historical Review* 117 (2012), 92–121.

[287] UK War Office, *Manual of Military Law* (London: HMSO, 1914), 235.

[288] Bohrer, 'Forgotten History' 2016 (n. 271), 409–18.

[289] Pitts, 'Empire and Legal Universalisms' 2012 (n. 286), 95; Parker, *Empire, War and Faith* 2002 (n. 151), 167–8.

[290] Kennedy, 'History of an Illusion' 1998 (n. 112), 127.

[291] Travers Twiss, *The Law of Nations*, 2nd edn. (Oxford: Clarendon Press, 1884), 444.

[292] Kennedy, 'History of an Illusion' 1998 (n. 112), 119.

[293] *Ibid.*, 127.

to which international law does address such interactions in some manner (i.e., minimalist-discretionary, adaptation or punishment approaches). One example is the Boxer War, as the joint military tribunal at Pao-Ting-Fu demonstrates.[294] Another example is the so-called 'Indian' wars; until about 1920, in some wars between the United States and Native American forces, the United States applied an adaptation approach and deemed much of IHL applicable, considering itself duty-bound to grant POW status to captured Native American combatants, and authorised to punish only those who committed *certain core* war crimes.[295]

2. Strong opposition to the Statist-positivist conceptualisation of the State and of international law appeared soon after the doctrinal consolidation of that conceptualisation. Rising support for State-sceptic positions was influenced by the creation of international legal organisations (notably, the 1899 and 1907 Hague Conferences, and the League of Nations in 1920) and by the contribution of hardline Statism to the outbreak of the First World War.[296] New international legal organisations (in which some non-Western sovereigns participated) and Western First World War barbarities also increased support for positions proclaiming international law's equal application to all nations, which helped some non-Western sovereigns attain Statehood.[297] However, not all non-Western entities attained statehood; regarding conflicts with such non-Western entities, the rising 'equal application' and 'State-sceptic' positions contributed to the eventual abolition of total warfare approaches and to the gradual merger of the minimalist-discretionary and adaptation approaches with similar legal approaches to internal conflicts.[298]

---

[294] The Allies differed on the approach they considered *lex lata*. The British applied a minimalist discretionary approach; UK, *Manual of Military Law* 1914 (n. 287), 235. The US approach placed greater IHL-related constraints on their forces than the British; A. S. Daggett, *America in the China Relief Expedition* (Kansas: Hudson-Kimberly, 1903), 57, 123, 128, 259–60. Germany applied a punishment-based total war approach, but kept it a secret to avoid opposition by its allies; Kaiser Wilhelm II, 'Hun Speech', 27 July 1900, available at: german historydocs.ghi-dc.org/sub_document.cfm?document_id=755.

[295] Jordan Paust, 'Nonstate Actor Participation in International Law and the Pretense of Exclusion', *Virginia Journal of International Law* 51 (2011), 977–1004 (979–83); G. H. Williams, 'The Modoc Indian Prisoners', *Opinions of US Attorney General* 14 (1875), 252–3.

[296] Kennedy, 'History of an Illusion' 1998 (n. 112), 131–8; Skinner, 'Genealogy of the Modern State' 2009 (n. 260), 359.

[297] Gong, *Standard of 'Civilization'* 1984 (n. 282), 28, 71, 124–8.

[298] E.g., Quincy Wright, 'Bombardment of Damascus', *American Journal of International Law* 20 (1926), 263–80 (265–72). See also, Colby, 'How to Fight Savage Tribes' 1927 (n. 284), 287. This gradual convergence began even earlier.

Jordan Paust noted:[299]

> [During] the last 250 years, international law has not been merely State-to-State. At best, claims to the contrary have been profoundly mistaken. At worst, they have been part of layered lies and attempts by malevolent myth-mongers to exclude and oppress others, to deny responsibility, or to support radical revisionist ambitions.

However, not only Statist-positivists propagated the myth of traditional international law being Statist (originally an element of the Westphalian myth). Many State-sceptics also concurred, though they thought that the Statist world order was about to expire.[300] Due to the propagation of that myth by both camps, we tend to overlook that the Statist-positivist position was never universally adopted and forget the long history of various contemporary international laws that originate in positions that competed against the Statist-positivist position, such as various ICL norms and the adaptation approach. Our recollection of the past remains 'the memory of an illusion'.[301]

B. NIAC Law

The accepted history of NIAC law is even less accurate than that of international law's application to non-Westerners. Admittedly, the rise of nineteenth-century Statist-positivism led to strong support for the position deeming international law to be inapplicable to internal wars, unless a State made a discretionary decision to apply it. But the belief that this was the *traditional* international law is simply untrue; the original basis for the authority to wage total war against rebels was the belief that rebellion was a criminal violation of international law.[302] Moreover, the horrors of the religious wars motivated subsequent attempts to restrain total warfare, yielding a doctrine where, under certain conditions in internal wars – mainly, intense fighting and high-level organisation – a ruler had a legal duty to recognise belligerency. Cases in which this duty approach was applied can be found from the seventeenth century through to the mid-twentieth century. This approach competed with the 'unlimited discretion' approach, with support for the perception of either approach as *lex lata* fluctuating over time.[303]

---

[299] Paust, 'Nonstate Actor Participation' 2011 (n. 295), 1002–3.
[300] Kennedy, 'History of an Illusion' 1998 (n. 112), 133–8.
[301] *Ibid.*, 138.
[302] Russell, *Just War* 1979 (n. 150), 7–19.
[303] George Mackenzie, *The Laws and Customs of Scotland in Matters Criminal* (Edinburgh: Anderson, 1699), 216; Graves, 'Lecture III' 1843 (n. 46), 266; Dov Levin, 'Why Following the Rules Matters: the Customs of War and the Case of the Texas War of Independence', *Journal*

Because historically there was no sharp distinction between international and domestic law, all situations meriting 'martial law' (aka 'state of siege'), including insurgencies, were regulated by the law of nature and nations, in the sense that the natural law principle of necessity applied.[304] Some understood this principle as allowing the ruler's forces to do as they pleased, but others regarded it as placing such forces under an imperfect obligation of moderation.[305] During the nineteenth and early twentieth centuries, Western States gradually shifted from international to domestic law for regulating emergencies short of war.[306] Yet, parallel to that shift, support increased for approaches that applied IHL, at least partially, in NIAC, even if the non-State side did not achieve belligerent status. By the late nineteenth–early twentieth century, the law pertaining to such NIAC had come to resemble the law pertaining to wars against non-State, non-Western entities. The following approaches competed for support: (a) an approach that authorised conducting internal wars as total war, on the basis of a Statist-positivist premise that international law did not apply to such wars, although in some cases still containing remnants of the idea that rebellions violate international law;[307] (b) a minimalist-discretionary approach, rooted in the imperfect obligations of necessity and humanity, which prohibited exceptionally cruel, clearly unnecessary measures (described by the *Institut de Droit International*, in 1900, as *lex lata*);[308] (c) an adaptation approach, according to which 'parties to . . . an insurrection shall observe, as far as possible, the rules of civilized warfare' (described by Wilson in his 1900 State practice survey, as *lex lata*).[309]

---

    of Military Ethics 7 (2008), 116–35 (116–26); Ti-Chiang Chen, *The International Law of Recognition* (New York: Praeger, 1951), 253–308; Pallieri, 'General Report' 1971 (n. 62), 345.

[304] H. W. Halleck, 'Military Tribunals and Their Jurisdiction', *American Journal of International Law* 5 (1911), 958–67 (958–60) (c. 1864); C. M. Clode, *The Military Forces of the Crown* (London: Murray, 1869), vol. II, 156–63, 500; T. E. Holland, *The Laws of War on Land* (Oxford: Clarendon Press, 1908), 14–17.

[305] Gaines Post, *Studies in Medieval Legal Thought* (Princeton University Press, 1964), 3–24; H. M. Bowman, 'Martial Law and the English Constitution', *Michigan Law Review* 15 (1916/17), 93–126 (118–19).

[306] Halleck, 'Military Tribunals' 1864 (n. 304), 960.

[307] See Wilhelm Grewe, *The Epochs of International Law*, trans. Michael Byers (Berlin: Walter de Gruyter, 2000), 499, 569–71.

[308] *Droits et devoirs des Puissances étrangères, au cas de mouvement insurrectionnel, envers les gouvernements établis et reconnus qui sont aux prises avec l'insurrection*, Institut de Droit International (Session de Neuchâtel, 1900), Arts. 3, 4(2); *Britain v. Spain* 1924 (n. 119), 645; Francis Lieber, *Guerrilla Parties* (New York: Van Nostrand, 1862), 21.

[309] Wilson, *Insurgency* 1900 (n. 48), 14. See also Wright, 'Bombardment of Damascus' 1926 (n. 298), 269–72.

Just as the NIAC-related minimalist-discretionary approach was a context-specific application of IHL's core principles, the NIAC-related adaptation approach was, likely, not aimed at creating a distinct IHL for internal wars, but rather a manifestation of the more general adaptation attitude discussed earlier. That general adaptation attitude, you may recall, is aimed at addressing the unavoidable absence of a neat fit between wartime reality and war-related legal classifications. Accordingly, the NIAC-related adaptation approach generally holds that in any non-inter-State conflict, 'regular' IHL must be applied *as far as possible* (namely, subject to the adaptations that are truly required by the particular attributes of the conflict); as James Garner noted in 1937: 'the statement . . . that the conduct of civil war is not governed by the same laws that apply to international war cannot be accepted – at least not without qualifications'.[310] This conceptualisation of IHL is quite different from that of the torture memos (and of many others today), which consider NIAC law and IAC law two distinct corpora.[311]

The attributes of the Spanish Civil War, designated by the torture memos as the birthplace of NIAC law, also weaken the memos' conclusions. Contemporaries considered that war to be part of a larger clash between global ideologies and it commonly crossed borders.[312] During that war, the prevailing view regarded the adaptation approach *lex lata*.[313]

The origins of NIAC law in the law pertaining to both internal wars and wars against non-Westerners, further weakens the torture memos' conclusions. Non-Westerners, such as Native American forces, were commonly perceived as belligerents that 'pay no regard to a mere imaginary [State] line'.[314] Moreover, as Geoffrey Corn noted (having nineteenth- and twentieth-century wars against non-Westerners in mind):[315]

> [T]he range of combat operations [that included such wars] . . . during this critical period of legal development is significant when assessing appropriate scope of application of the contemporary principles of the laws of war. This history supports the inference that regular armed forces historically viewed

---

[310] James Garner, 'Questions of International Law in the Spanish Civil War', *American Journal of International Law* 31 (1937), 66–73 (66).

[311] Yoo and Delahunty, 'Memo' 2002 (n. 14), 7–11.

[312] Philip Kunig and Johannes van Aggelen, 'Nyon Agreement', in Rüdiger Wolfrum (ed.), *Max Planck Encyclopedia of Public International Law* (online edn.), February 2015; Norman Padelford, 'The International Non-Intervention Agreement and the Spanish Civil War', *American Journal of International Law* 31 (1937), 578–603 (578).

[313] Garner, 'Spanish Civil War' 1937 (n. 310), 66.

[314] Lewis Cass (War Department), 'Letter to Major General Gains', Fort Jesup, Louisiana (4 May 1836) (supporting total war). See also Twiss, *Law of Nations* 1884 (n. 291), 444.

[315] Geoffrey S. Corn, 'Making the Case for Conflict Bifurcation in Afghanistan', *International Law Studies* 85 (2008), 181–218 (188).

combat operations – or armed conflict – as an *ipso facto* trigger for principles that regulated combatant conduct on the battlefield.

Common Article 3 of the 1949 Geneva Conventions clearly intends to abolish total war approaches. It contains elements of the minimalist-discretionary approach and of the adaptation approach by: (a) defining its prohibitions as duties that 'each Party to the conflict shall be bound to apply, *as a minimum*'; and (b) adding that '[t]he Parties to the conflict *should further* endeavour to bring into force, by means of special agreements, all or part of the other provisions of the present Convention'. The Article's history, however, does not indicate an intention to form two distinct IHL corpora.[316]

More important, even after 1949, the adaptation approach was applied in various cases, such as *Tsemel* in Israel (1983).[317] In 1981, the Israeli army invaded Lebanon as part of a conflict between Israel and non-State forces that were launching attacks from Lebanon. Members of these non-State forces petitioned the Israeli Supreme Court, claiming a lack of legal basis for their detention by the Israeli army. The Israeli government, similarly to the British government in *Serdar Mohammed*, responded that the petitioners' detention on Lebanese soil was sanctioned by customary IHL.[318] The petitioners argued that no IHL authority exists to detain civilians, except in occupied territories. The Court rejected this argument, holding that they were not peaceable civilians but unprivileged combatants, and that IHL has always provided State forces with authority to detain such combatants.[319]

In a succeeding case, *Al-Nawar* (1985), the Court similarly held that:[320]

> The incapability of the State from which the terrorists act ... [to] prevent the harming of its neighbour[-State], does not render the terrorists and their property immune from the measures that would have been taken against a regular enemy force. Whoever commits acts of hostility cannot wear the cloak of a private civilian whenever it sees fit. Namely, whoever maintains a complex organization that is engaged in terror and warfare cannot expect that when the military response arrives, it would enjoy the immunities and defences that the law of war provided to uninvolved civilian parties ... [Its combatants also] cannot enjoy the privileges ... of a POW ...

---

[316]   See George Schwarzenberger, *International Law* (London: Stevens, 1968), vol. II, 717–19.

[317]   HCJ, *Tsemel v. Minister of Defence*, Judgment of 13 July 1983, No. 102/82 (Isr.) (trans. Ziv Bohrer).

[318]   *Ibid.*, para. 3.

[319]   *Ibid.*, para. 5: '[T]he detention of weapon-carrying insurgents and those who aid them has always constituted an execution of a legal authority by the belligerent and it remains such.'

[320]   HCJ, *Al-Nawar v. Minister of Defence*, Judgment of 11 August 1985, No. 574/82, para. 21 (Isr.) (trans. Z. B.).

Statements like those made in *Tsemel* and *Al-Nawar* are currently made by those who hold that States have an inherent legal authority to detain captured enemy fighters until the conflict ends, irrespective of whether the captured enemy fighters are regular soldiers or unprivileged combatants, and irrespective of conflict classification (the only difference is that POWs have various privileges that detained unprivileged combatants do not).[321] But that was not *Tsemel's* ruling; it ruled that because the State did not grant these individuals POW status, nor did it prosecute them, only one legal basis remained providing authority to detain them: the IHL concerning detention of protected persons in occupied territories, as it applies, *subject to the necessary adaptations*, to non-occupation situations.[322] That law is quite constraining, demanding periodic review of each detainee's case and the release of anyone no longer *personally* posing a risk.[323]

Tsemel's ruling is preferable to the approach that IHL authorises States to detain unprivileged combatants (like enemy State soldiers) until hostilities end, but without POW privileges. The rationale behind detaining captured enemy combatants is to prevent them from serving the enemy. When States fight, they often find the end of active hostilities a congenial moment for the release of each other's detainees, because at that point neither side has strong fear of immediate threat from enemy soldiers. Occasionally, this mutual benefit could apply in cases where the State accords POW status to captured non-State enemy fighters, because some non-State forces can gain considerable political benefits from having their fighters treated as POWs, enabling States to incentivise such forces to adopt some State-like qualities.[324] However, in many conflicts, this is unlikely to become the case irrespective of whether the State accords POW status to the non-State fighters (which, also, means that States do not have an incentive to do so).[325] For various reasons, uncertainty regarding the end of a conflict is even greater in conflicts involving non-State forces than in inter-State wars. Hence, in conflicts involving non-State forces there is often no temporal benchmark to make prisoner release mutually beneficial. This means that authorising States to detain captured non-State fighters until hostilities end is likely to result in indefinite detention. Many captured non-State fighters would remain detained long after their *personal* risk of returning to serve the enemy abates.

Note that *Al-Nawar* ruled that IHL regarding an enemy State property, rather than private civilian property, applies to terrorist organisations'

---

[321] E.g., USSC, *Hamdi v. Rumsfeld*, Judgment of 28 June 2004, 517–24.
[322] HCJ, *Tsemel* 1983 (n. 317), paras. 5–8.
[323] *Ibid.*, para. 8.
[324] Aldrich, 'Human Rights in Armed Conflict' 1973 (n. 49), 880.
[325] *Ibid.*

property, *subject to the necessary adaptations*.[326] Nevertheless, *Tsemel* and *Al-Nawar* are not contradictory; both applied the adaptation approach. The *Tsemel* ruling, regarding the legal basis for the detention authority, relied on the following note from the contemporary British *Manual of Military Law*: 'Although the rules here discussed apply primarily in "occupied territory", they should nevertheless be observed, *as far as possible*, in areas through which troops are passing and even on the battlefield.'[327] Moreover, *Tsemel* considered its 'as far as possible' (adaptation) approach to be deriving from a more general 'trend . . . that has . . . found its expression in the modern law of war'.[328] *Al-Nawar* similarly described its (adaptation) approach as a legal trend – developed because too many cases lacked a neat fit between the wartime reality and its legal classifications – that demands the application of some or all of IHL to circumstances that do not constitute war *senso stricto*.[329]

The United States also adhered to the adaptation approach. Since the 1960s, the US Department of Defense, Law of War Program Directives (and similar military instructions) have stated:[330]

> The Armed Forces of the United States will comply with the law of war during the conduct of all military operations and related activities in armed conflict, however such conflicts are characterized.

The US adherence to the adaptation approach is demonstrated in this Vietnam era statement by American military lawyer, Fred Green:[331]

> [T]he terms 'war', 'armed conflict,' and 'combatants' … have become increasingly blurred with each new technological advance and change in military strategy and political intent … (for example … guerrilla type forces) … [Nevertheless] the established concepts cannot be merely abandoned. The American practice has been to analogize, insofar as possible, and attempt to apply the provisions of the Conventions and

---

[326] HCJ, *Al-Nawar* 1985 (n. 320), para. 21.

[327] HCJ, *Tsemel* 1983 (n. 317), para. 7 (quoting UK War Office, *Manual of Military Law* (London: HMSO, 1958), 141 n. 1; emphasis added).

[328] *Ibid.*, para. 5.

[329] HCJ, *Al-Nawar* 1985 (n. 320), para. 21.

[330] Section 4.1, Directive 2311.01E (9 May 2006; recertified 22 February 2011); Section 4.1, Directive 5100.77 (9 December 1998); Section E(1)(a), Directive 5100.77 (10 July 1979); Section V(a), Directive 5100.7 (5 November 1974); Para. 4a, US Chairman of the Joint Chiefs of Staff Instruction 5810.01 (12 August 1966).

[331] Green, 'United States' 1971 (n. 44), 283–4.

customary law so as to preserve the intent thereof and thereby diminish the evils of war . . .

The following Vietnam era statement by US Deputy Legal Advisor, George Aldrich, further reveals a significant element of the US understanding of that approach:[332]

> [T]he Geneva Prisoner of War Convention . . . accords to . . . guerrillas involved in international conflicts the right to be treated as prisoners of war . . . [only, if they] meet . . . five criteria . . . When viewed in the light of guerrilla war as we have known it in recent years, some of these criteria seem a bit quaint. In Viet-Nam, for example, thousands of the Viet Cong troops had no fixed sign, did not carry arms openly, and frequently did not abide by the laws of war. Nevertheless, except for terrorists, spies, and saboteurs, the United States and the Government of the Republic of Viet-Nam have treated them as prisoners of war . . . In addition, we treated other guerrillas as POW's whenever they were captured with weapons in battle.

As this statement demonstrates, unlike Israel, US reliance on the adaptation approach went as far as to grant POW status to combatants who did not meet the treaty conditions.[333] The United States applied a similar approach regarding POWs in nearly all conflicts between 1949 and 2000, including Korea, Vietnam, Panama, Somalia, Haiti and Bosnia.[334]

The application of this approach regarding POWs in each of the aforesaid conflicts was discussed in one of the torture memos (the Bybee Memo).[335] The memo dismissed it as merely the result of conflict-specific policy decisions, and not a legal precedent (exhibited through continuous State practice) preventing categorical denial of POW status to all Taliban and Al-Qaeda fighters.[336] At first glance, US Department of Defense directives since 1998 seem to support classifying the adaptation approach as a mere non-obligatory policy; these directives (like some,[337] but not all,[338] earlier directives) place the instruction, to comply with IHL irrespective of an operation's classification, under a 'Policy' heading.[339]

---

[332] Aldrich, 'Human Rights in Armed Conflict' 1973 (n. 49), 879–80.
[333] *Ibid.*
[334] Jay Bybee, 'Memorandum for Alberto Gonzales and William J. Haynes, Re: Application of Treaties and Laws to Al Qaeda and Taliban Detainees' (22 January 2002), 25–8.
[335] *Ibid.*, 25.
[336] *Ibid.*
[337] 1974 Directive (n. 330), Section V(a).
[338] 1979 Directive (n. 330), Section E(1)(a).
[339] 1998 Directive (n. 330), Section 4; 2006 Directive (n. 330), Section 4.

But it is wrong to dismiss past applications of the adaptation approach as mere non-legal, non-obligatory policy actions. The Israeli Supreme Court clearly considered the application of the adaptation approach a legal duty. The same holds true for the US pre-torture memos position. The torture memos devoutly applied the hardline Statist-positivist conceptualisation of law, policy and morality as distinct concepts; thus, the classification of the 'adaption approach' as 'policy', reflexively led the memos to deem that approach non-legal and non-obligatory. In contrast, 'warrior' positions (with roots in nature-of-things jurisprudence) regard imperfect obligations, like chivalry, as obligatory legal norms and maintain a less sharp distinction between law, policy and morality. For such positions, applying the adaption approach is both a policy action and a legal duty: *policy action*, in the sense that commanders are viewed as having considerable discretion in determining the manner and extent of IHL application in each non-inter-State conflict (after all, it is an imperfect obligation); *legal duty*, in the sense that commanders are considered to be legally duty-bound to apply the adaptation approach and in the sense that blatant grave violations of that obligation merit legal sanctions. Given the strong influence of the 'warrior' position and the chivalry principle on US military culture, it is doubtful that most US military professionals would have regarded the adaptation approach as mere non-legal policy. Indeed, within the Bush administration, Secretary of State Colin Powell, a former Chairman of the Joint Chiefs of Staff, most strongly opposed the Bybee Memo's categorical denial of POW status. Powell rejected the memo's presumption of a sharp distinction between law and policy, arguing that declaring the Geneva Conventions inapplicable would 'reverse over a century of US policy and *practice*',[340] and that 'while no one anticipated the precise situation that we face, the GPW [the Third Geneva Convention] was intended to cover all types of armed conflict and did not by its terms limit its application'.[341] Department of State Legal Advisor William H. Taft added: 'even in a new sort of conflict the United States bases its conduct on its international treaty obligations and the rule of law, not just its policy preferences.'[342]

---

[340] US Secretary of State Colin Powell, Memorandum to Council to President, Re: Draft Decision Memorandum to the President on the Applicability of the Geneva Convention to the Conflict in Afghanistan (25 January 2002), 2 (emphasis added).

[341] *Ibid.*, 5.

[342] Department of State Legal Advisor William H. Taft IV, Memorandum to Counsel to the President Alberto R. Gonzales, Comments on Your Paper on the Geneva Convention (2 February 2002), Insert A.

Powell's demand that the Bybee Memo be reconsidered only resulted in yet another torture memo:[343]

> [T]he war against terrorism is a new kind of war. It is not the traditional clash between nations adhering to the laws of war that formed the backdrop for GPW. The nature of the new war places a high premium on other factors, such as the ability to quickly obtain information from captured terrorists and their sponsors in order to avoid further atrocities against American civilians . . . [T]his new paradigm renders obsolete Geneva's strict limitations on the questioning of enemy prisoners and renders quaint some of its provisions . . .

Some consider the above paragraph to be the strongest demonstration of an element of truth in the post-9/11 call for a new, laxer IHL.[344] However, there is nothing new in its line of reasoning that (a) terrorism is a new kind of war that (b) obviates existing IHL, as evident from the fact that (c) torture, which existing IHL prohibits, must be used in such a war, (d) because IHL has become irrelevant in the context of that new war, it no longer applies and, therefore (e) torture is permitted when fighting terrorists. Such a line of reasoning was adopted by French forces in Algeria and advocated by some in the United States during the Vietnam War.[345] But the US government during Vietnam rejected it and considered torture illegal;[346] moreover, it stressed the need to liberalise treaty criteria for POW status eligibility because '[w]hen viewed in the light of [contemporary] guerrilla war . . . some of these criteria seem a bit quaint'.[347] The above paragraph, therefore, does not demonstrate an element of truth in the torture memos' reasoning, rather only the stark contrast between those memos and the earlier US allegiance to the adaptation approach. The issue is not the 'quaintness' of existing IHL (which, often actually stems from the nearly inevitable incomplete fit between wartime reality and war-related legal classifications), but one's response to it.

The Bybee Memo relegated more than just POW status eligibility to the entirely discretionary realm of policy decisions. For example, it asserted that:[348]

---

[343]   White House Counsel Alberto Gonzales, Memorandum to President Bush, Decision Re: The Application of the Geneva Convention on Prisoners of War to the Conflict with Al-Qaeda and the Taliban (25 January 2002), 2.

[344]   E.g., Michael Schmitt, '21st Century Conflict: Can the Law Survive?', *Melbourne Journal of International Law* 78 (2007), 443–76 (447, 472); Avihai Mandelblit, 'Lawfare and the State of Israel', PhD thesis, Bar-Ilan University, 2015, 48–50 (in Hebrew).

[345]   Pallieri, 'General Report' 1971 (n. 62), 349–50.

[346]   *Ibid.*

[347]   Aldrich, 'Human Rights in Armed Conflict' 1973 (n. 49), 879–80.

[348]   'Bybee Memo' 2002 (n. 334), 25.

[E]ven though Geneva Convention III may not apply, the United States may deem it a violation of the laws and usages of war for Taliban troops to torture any American prisoners ... [and] prosecute Taliban militiamen [that tortured] ... for war crimes ... [based on a] decision to apply the principles of the Geneva Conventions or of other laws of war as a matter of policy, not law ...

This 'policy basis' for war crime prosecution is incompatible with ICL's accepted normative justifications, and constitutes downright victor's justice, in the light of the torture memos' assertion that the 'new [war] paradigm renders obsolete Geneva's strict limitations on the questioning of enemy prisoners'.[349] More importantly, there is a contradiction between this legal reasoning and the one presented only three months earlier, in another memo, specifically addressing the legal basis for US authority in the war against Al-Qaeda and the Taliban 'to try and punish terrorists':[350]

The mere fact that the terrorists are non-state actors ... poses no bar to applying the laws of war here. American precedents [exist from] factual situation[s] ... more closely analogous to the current attacks ... [than] civil war ... Indian 'nations' were not independent, sovereign nations in the sense of classical international law ... Nevertheless, the Supreme Court has explained that the conflicts between Indians and the United States ... were properly under-stood as 'war' ... Similarly ... [an American] court concluded that the Boxer Rebellion in China was a 'war' ... [e]ven though the Boxers were not a government ... It is true that [unlike] many [past] situations involving application of the laws of war ... [t]he terrorist network now facing the United States ... operat[es] from the territory of several different nations ... [However,] the Indian Wars ... provide an apt analogy. Indian tribes did not fit into the Western-European understanding of nation-States ... But that posed no bar to applying the laws of war when the United States was engaged in armed conflict with them. Moreover, there is nothing in the logic of the laws of armed conflict that in any way restricts them from applying to a campaign of hostilities carried on by a non-State actor with a trans-national reach. To the contrary, the logic behind the laws suggests that they apply here. Generally speaking, the laws are intended to confine within certain limits the brutality of armed conflict, which might otherwise go wholly unchecked.

You (the reader) were probably somewhat baffled earlier by my insistence on discussing the bygone 'Indian' and Boxer wars. But I did so primarily because of

---

[349] 'Gonzales Memo' 2002 (n. 343), 2.
[350] US Deputy Assistant Attorney General Patrick Philbin, Memorandum Re: The Legality of the Use of Military Commissions to Try Terrorists (6 November 2001), 1, 23–6.

the above-quoted *recent* application of the adaptation approach (not my history fetish).

The torture memos did not persuade everyone to adopt their position regarding the law applicable to transnational wars, but they were successful in framing the legal discourse. This success is evident in the wide acceptance of the characterisation of transnational conflicts as novel, forcing international jurists to endlessly struggle 'against the claim that [wartime] international law was "quaint"'.[351] Success is further evident in the adaptation approach being somewhat forgotten, despite being a long-standing legal approach specifically developed to address the unavoidable absence of a neat fit between war-related situations and their legal classifications. The adaptation approach's long history and importance were not enough to prevent the torture memos from framing the discourse in a manner that buried the adaptation approach under a pile of misleading narratives (many of them pre-existing in IHL). As a result, excavating it required a journey into the distant past, even though it still enjoyed significant support as recently as the aftermath of 9/11 (as the above-quoted memo demonstrates).

Stated differently, I am not attempting to resurrect an archaic legal approach, rather to point attention to an approach that until quite recently enjoyed considerable support. Even today, this approach still enjoys some support[352] and cases still exist in which it is applied.[353] Yet, as such current sources demonstrate, the following important aspects of the adaptation approach were wholly forgotten: its long history; its pivotal role in IHL development; and its jurisprudential footing. Without recollection of these aspects (which this chapter aims to retrieve), support for the adaptation approach has declined, replaced by a classification obsession. That obsession is bound to increase uncertainty and disagreements, because it fails to acknowledge the inevitable absence of a neat fit between war-related situations and their legal classifications. That obsession, due to its rigidity, is also bound to hinder IHL development, opening the door to claims of increasing gaps in IHL. Therefore, re-embracing the (never fully abandoned) adaptation approach can reduce legal uncertainty and disagreements, while providing IHL with a normative tool, necessary for its development and adaptability to changes.

[351] Modirzadeh, 'Folk International Law' 2014 (n. 15), 227.
[352] E.g., Ryan Goodman, 'The Detention of Civilians in Armed Conflict', *American Journal of International Law* 103 (2009), 48–74.
[353] E.g., FCA, *Amnesty International v. Canada*, Judgment of 12 March 2008, No. T-324-07; HCJ, *Ahmed v. Israel*, Judgment of 27 January 2008, No. 9132/07.

C. Lotus

An alternative narrative is, gradually, superseding the Westphalian myth; it insists that 'traditional' international law only addressed States, but posits that that traditional law was 'born' in the nineteenth century (not 1648).[354] Wartime conduct used to be regulated by moral (non-legal) norms and force-specific (domestic) legislation and, only following IHL's nineteenth-century treaty codification did these non-legal and domestic 'rules of war' become laws of war'.[355] IHL's treaty codification, thus, marks a conceptual framework shift, transforming a customary regime of (status-based and universal) individual 'natural' obligations and (to a lesser degree) rights, into a regime of formal legal rules between States.[356] The *Lotus* ruling[357] is considered a primary manifestation of that Statist-positivist 'traditional international law',[358] by holding that States 'may act in any way they wish as long as they do not contravene an explicit prohibition'.[359]

The torture memos, proclaiming commitment to 'traditional' international law, asserted that because no IHL explicitly addresses transnational wars, States can do as they wish.[360] Even moderate Statists, based on that history, hold that IHL still 'does not confer rights or impose duties on individuals',[361] rather consists of 'obligations imposed on states'.[362] Therefore, IHRL and IHL have 'distinct . . . conceptual frameworks'.[363]

IHRL-oriented approaches agree that IHL traditionally had a Statist conceptual framework, but proclaim another shift: in the more recent IHL treaties, some articles are phrased as conferring individual rights, shifting IHL to an individual rights-based framework.[364] Presumably, IHRL's

---

[354] E.g., Luigi Nuzzo and Miloš Vec, 'The Birth of International Law as a Legal Discipline', in Luigi Nuzzo and Miloš Vec (eds.), *Constructing International Law* (Frankfurt am Main: Vittorio-Klostermann, 2012), ix–xvi (ix).

[355] Gary Solis, *The Law of Armed Conflict* (Cambridge University Press, 2010), 54.

[356] Grant Doty, 'The United States and the Development of the Laws of Land Warfare', *Military Law Review* 156 (1998), 224–55 (224).

[357] PCIJ, *Lotus* case (France v. Turkey), Judgment of 7 September 1927, Series A, No. 10.

[358] James Larry Taulbee, *Genocide, Mass Atrocity and War Crimes in Modern History* (Santa Barbara, CA: Praeger, 2017), 32.

[359] Mario Silva, *State Legitimacy and Failure in International Law* (The Hague: Martinus Nijhoff, 2014), 129.

[360] See Modirzadeh, 'Folk International Law' 2014 (n. 15), 232–3.

[361] Kate Parlett, *The Individual in the International Legal System* (Cambridge University Press, 2012), 180.

[362] *Ibid.*, 182.

[363] *Ibid.*

[364] Amanda Alexander, 'A Short History of International Humanitarian Law', *European Journal of International Law* 26 (2015), 109–38 (110). See also Peters, *Beyond Human Rights* 2016

modern rise also produced a parallel framework shift throughout international law.[365] IHRL's rise and said related framework shifts (along with the morality of rights) further demand interpreting additional IHL norms, not phrased as individual rights conferring, as conferring such rights.[366] IHRL's rise also diminished (if not abolished) *Lotus*, because universal IHRL applies to all issues previously ungoverned by international law.[367] Jurists, like my colleague, Helen Duffy, hold that this not only rebuffs torture memo-like positions, but also the adaptation approach, which addresses perceived gaps in IHL by analogising from related IHL. They assert that if IHRL universally applies, then a gap in IHL no longer means a gap in international law and, therefore, recourse to analogies is unjustified.[368]

But, as critics point out, even today there are only few individual rights-conferring IHL treaty articles.[369] Also, oddly, a framework shift is not similarly concluded from the even greater amount of individual obligations-imposing IHL treaty articles; such IHL (presumably) remains exceptional.[370] Both issues indicate that the claimed rights-oriented shift is less an impartial account of the law and more an attempt to bring about such a shift.[371]

The account of a nineteenth-century Statist conceptual framework shift is, likewise, inaccurate. Historically, force-specific legislation was not entirely domestic, because it was expected to reflect the unwritten, international laws of war.[372] These unwritten norms were not mere rules of ethics, but legal rules; violators of these unwritten laws of war were often punished, even in the absence of any formal legislation.[373]

Because jurisprudential diversity was always extensive: '[in] most eras ... practices and customary law constituted a more important source for the law of

---

(n. 120), 194–220 (which, based on a more nuanced analysis, reaches somewhat similar conclusions regarding existing IHL, and even more so regarding aspired IHL).

[365] E.g., Marco Odello and Sofia Cavandoli, 'Introduction', in Marco Odello and Sofia Cavandoli (eds.), *Emerging Areas of Human Rights in the 21st Century* (Abingdon: Routledge, 2011), 1. See also Peters, *Beyond Human Rights* 2016 (n. 120), 11–34, 526–55 (which, based on a more nuanced analysis, reaches somewhat similar conclusions regarding existing international law, and even more so regarding aspired international law).

[366] Peters, *Beyond Human Rights* 2016 (n. 120), 194–220.

[367] Duffy, in this volume, 88.

[368] *Ibid.*

[369] Parlett, *Individual in the International Legal System* 2012 (n. 361), 176–228.

[370] Peters, *Beyond Human Rights* 2016 (n. 120), 220–1. Peters considers the 'principle of legality' a primary reason for treating individualistic obligations as exaptational in IHL; *ibid.*, 76–85, 220–1. But much of that concern is resolved through the nature-of-things jurisprudential understanding of that principle; see above nn. 116–22.

[371] Luban, 'Human Rights Thinking' 2016 (n. 4), 50.

[372] Bohrer, 'Forgotten History' 2016 (n. 271), 430–1.

[373] *Ibid.*

nations';[374] especially for the laws of war.[375] Thus, between these past unwritten laws and current IHL, there is a 'remarkable continuity'.[376] 'Most of the actions today outlawed by the Geneva Conventions have been condemned in the West for at least four centuries.'[377]

The belief that international law (IHL included) was 'born' in the nineteenth century originated in that century. Some contemporary Statist-positivists asserted that international law, including the 'so-called laws of war[,] are mere practices ... [that] impose, at most, moral and not legal duties'.[378] More moderate Statist-positivists also rejected the legal obligation of customary international law, but considered treaty international law obligatory and supported treaty codifications.[379] Many further endorsed the Statist-positivist view of international law as only addressing States (not individuals), as evident in the Statist phrasing of most treaty IHL.[380]

But positivism was never the only jurisprudential influence on IHL, therefore, the transition to a Statist framework was never more than partial. Non-positivist influence is evident in the adoption (beginning with the Martens Clause) of treaty IHL that asserts the continued obligatory force of customary IHL and IHL principles.[381] It is, further, evident in ICL's survival (as seen through continued war crime prosecution of individuals based on the customary unwritten laws of war).[382] Accordingly, when defendants at Nuremberg claimed that they were not liable for violating the State-addressed Hague Regulations, the tribunal responded:[383]

> For many years past ... military tribunals have tried and punished individuals guilty of violating the rules of land warfare ... The law of war is to be found not only in treaties, but in the customs and practices of states which gradually obtained universal recognition, and from the general principles of justice applied by jurists and practiced by military courts.

---

[374] Lesaffer, 'Unrequited Love' 2007 (n. 174), 36.
[375] Parker, *Empire, War and Faith* 2002 (n. 151), 167–8.
[376] *Ibid.*
[377] *Ibid.*
[378] J. F. Stephen, *A History of the Criminal Law of England* (London: Macmillan, 1883), vol. II, 62–3.
[379] E.g., Gortchacow, 'Observations' 1875 (n. 70), 5.
[380] Bohrer, 'Forgotten History' 2016 (n. 271), 407.
[381] Jan Klabber, *International Law* (Cambridge University Press, 2017), 223–4.
[382] Bohrer, 'Forgotten History' 2016 (n. 271), 464–71.
[383] IMT, *Trial of the Major War Criminals*, vol. I (Nuremberg: International Military Tribunal Nuremberg, 1947), 220–1.

IHL's codifying treaties, therefore, did not abolish customary IHL rules and principles. Likewise, treaty IHL (primarily) Statist conceptual framework did not abolish, rather supplemented the longer-standing individual obligations-oriented framework; accordingly, the Nuremberg Tribunal asserted:[384]

> It was submitted that international law is concerned with the actions of sovereign States and provides no punishment for individuals … [This] must be rejected. That international law imposes duties and liabilities upon individuals as well as upon States has long been recognized.

Thus, IHL has remained '*Binding on States and Individuals*'.[385]

The persistent non-positivist influence on international law is further demonstrated by the following neglected fact: *Lotus* was 'ruled in six-six split with President Huber casting the deciding vote'.[386] Even at the height of the 'traditional' era, the core Statist-positivist '*Lotus*' precept was contested. The six other judges expressed a non-positivist perspective that a gap does not necessarily exist whenever no explicit rule applies, because international law consists not only of rules but also of principles, and often one should 'invoke [these] "soft" norms, or draw on analogous areas of the law to find that, in fact, there is no gap in the law'.[387] That non-positivist perspective is also expressed in the adaptation approach and in the Martens Clause.

Indeed, the Martens Clause is commonly considered IHL's rejection of the *Lotus* principle.[388] Based on the clause, even before treaty IHRL, jurists deemed illegal torture memo-like ('*Lotus-ian*') assertions of States being wholly unconstrained in issues '[un]anticipated by the Convention[s]'.[389]

The long-standing influence of such non-positivist perspectives also means that, with regard to certain issues, IHRL advocates wrongly assume a gap in non-IHRL international law. Despite the non-existence of clear-cut legal rules in such cases, a gap does not exist (and did not exist even before modern IHRL) because these issues have long been regulated by normative principles and analogising legal approaches. One such issue that has been discussed throughout this chapter is the *perceived* IHL gaps that result from the nearly inevitable incomplete fit between wartime situations and the legal concepts

---

[384] *Ibid.*, 222–3.
[385] US Army, *Law of Land Warfare* (FM-27-10, 1956), 4. See also Fellmeth, *Paradigms* 2016 (n. 119), 27.
[386] Hugh Handeyside, 'The Lotus Principle in ICJ Jurisprudence: Was the Ship Ever Afloat?', *Michigan Journal of International Law* 29 (2007), 71–94 (74).
[387] *Ibid.*, 77.
[388] Klabber, *International Law* 2017 (n. 381), 223.
[389] Trainin, 'Questions of Guerrilla Warfare' 1946 (n. 49), 550–1.

aimed at addressing them. These are merely perceived gaps and not actual gaps because a long-standing IHL norm exists to address such incomplete fits: the adaptation approach. That norm has long played a pivotal role in IHL development, leading to (among other things) the current considerable convergence between the IHL in IAC and in NIAC. Abandoning it would hinder that convergence trend. More generally, it would harm IHL's ability to adapt to change.

III. CORE JURISDICTION STRUGGLE: THE ACTUAL CRISIS

The discussion thus far seems to suggest that the current sense of crisis has resulted from 'semi-innocent' factors (unconscious tendencies, the nature of law and of emergencies, long-standing misleading narratives, etc.) and the nature of lawyers, who tend to proclaim as law the legal position that best serves their purposes. Even the crisis outcry seems attributable to 'semi-innocent' factors, such as temporocentrism, and to the nature of international lawyers (who love constructing war-related crisis narratives).

But there is true cause for concern. When certain conditions exist in a legal system's normative universe, then that system is at risk of dissolution. Such conditions tend to result from a phenomenon herein called: a *core jurisdictional struggle*. In recent decades, the normative universe of wartime international law has been nearing these conditions.

As mentioned earlier, there are two opposite extreme accounts of the role of law in the normative universe of a legal system.[390] Hardline formalist accounts depict legal norms as external, objective social facts that autonomously determine legal actions. Hardline CLS accounts depict legal norms as having no independent influence on actions; these accounts hold that actions and their legality are determined by non-legal factors (power and interests) and legal norms are (at best) merely means to cloak the interests of the powerful. But these opposing accounts equally fail to appropriately depict the actual role legal norms usually play in the normative universe of a functioning legal system.

In a functioning legal system's normative universe, legal actions commonly result from a mixture of legal and non-legal factors: contrary to hardline CLS accounts, legal factors (norms and narratives) do have an influence and contrary to hardline formalist accounts, legal factors only have partial influence (non-legal factors do also play a considerable role). Stated differently, in such systems, the 'normative reality' (i.e., legal actions' prevailing nature)

---

[390] Above nn. 5–9.

occupies the vast middle ground between the two extreme accounts of hard-line formalism and hardline CLS.[391] When the legal community is exceptionally homogeneous, the 'normative reality' resembles the formalist account.[392] But, usually, human diversity yields conflicting narratives in the normative universe, reducing the semi-objective element of the law.[393] Legal uncertainty and tense engagement between different factions are integral parts of a heterogeneous normative universe.[394] The normative reality can even come to match the hardline CLS account – namely, the legal system's norms cease to influence human behaviour – when members of a non-negligible faction within the legal community no longer feels obligated to defer to the legal system or share the normative universe with other factions;[395] although members of such factions tend to perceive themselves as followers of the law's 'true' meaning or of a 'superior' system.[396] The latter option echoes a related scenario, in which several legal systems (e.g., international law and a domestic legal system) simultaneously assert jurisdiction over the same group.[397] In practice, often the distinction between the inter- and intra-system scenarios is fuzzy and depends on opposing factions' narratives.[398]

Intra-system scenarios entail a clash between core jurisdictional narratives. *In its deepest sense,* 'jurisdiction' is concerned with the allocation of the power and authority to speak (*dictio*) in the name of the law (*juris*).[399] Within any legal system's normative universe, narratives exist that address this deep sense of jurisdiction.[400] These core jurisdictional narratives do not merely proclaim the basis for the system's, and its agents', authority, but establish, define and maintain the system itself, its community, agents and self-perceived boundaries.[401] These narratives determine the normative universe's core distinctions, setting apart: (a) the spatial, temporal and personal conditions under which the legal system exists;[402] (b) community members from non-

---

[391] *Ibid.*

[392] Cover, 'Nomos and Narrative' 1983/4 (n. 5), 14.

[393] *Ibid.,* 17.

[394] *Ibid.*

[395] *Ibid.,* 22–52.

[396] *Ibid.,* 22–8.

[397] Bohrer, 'Obedience to Orders' 2012 (n. 69), 108–9.

[398] Cover, 'Nomos and Narrative' 1983/4 (n. 5), 45–52.

[399] Shaunnagh Dorsett and Shaun McVeigh, 'Questions of Jurisdiction', in Shaun McVeigh (ed.), *Jurisprudence of Jurisdiction* (Abingdon: Routledge, 2007), 3–18 (3).

[400] *Ibid.*

[401] *Ibid.,* 3–5.

[402] *Ibid.,* 7.

members;[403] (c) authorised organs from those unauthorised to speak on behalf of the law;[404] (d) the legal from the political[405] and (more generally) from the non-legal.[406] The primary means used in core jurisdictional narratives to allocate legal authority is the 'categorization of persons, things, places and events'.[407]

When a core jurisdictional narrative is consensual, the legal community perceives its distinctions as 'organic' (clear-cut and nearly natural); the normative universe resembles the formalist account.[408] As diversity within the legal community increases, the organic conceptualisation of core jurisdictional narratives and their distinctions diminishes in several ways: (a) the placement of the boundaries defined by such narratives becomes disputed and less determinable;[409] (b) conflicting core jurisdictional narratives develop within the normative universe, each envisioning a different allocation of the power and authority to speak in the name of the law;[410] (c) because of the primary role of categorisations in allocating legal authority and power, contending factions propagate narratives that depict unfavourable distinctions and boundaries as 'synthetic' – that is, the products of policy or even of biased politics – which must be reformed. Note that the nature of a jurisdiction, distinction and boundary is usually neither organic nor synthetic in any objective sense; rather, its perception by community members determines it.[411]

In inter-system scenarios, the clash between conflicting core jurisdictional narratives is even more pronounced. To maintain their independence, normative systems must perceive themselves as superior to competitors. Therefore, the core jurisdictional narratives of contending legal systems clash, each one asserting superior or sole jurisdiction over the relevant people,[412] depicting its jurisdiction, with its related boundaries and classifications, as clear and organic, and that of its opponents as synthetic.[413] The shape of the jurisdictional wall, thus, 'differs depending upon which side of the wall our narratives place us'.[414]

---

[403] Costas Douzinas, 'The Metaphysics of Jurisdiction', in McVeigh (ed.), *Jurisprudence of Jurisdiction* 2007 (n. 399), 21–32 (23–4).

[404] *Ibid.*, 23–5.

[405] Lindsay Farmer, *Making the Modern Criminal Law* (Oxford University Press, 2016), 120.

[406] Douzinas, 'Metaphysics of Jurisdiction' 2007 (n. 403), 33.

[407] Dorsett and McVeigh, 'Questions of Jurisdiction' 2007 (n. 399), 5.

[408] Cover, 'Nomos and Narrative' 1983/4 (n. 5), 14.

[409] *Ibid.*, 31.

[410] *Ibid.*, 14–15.

[411] Ford, 'Law's Territory' 1999 (n. 12), 858.

[412] Bohrer, 'Obedience to Orders' 2012 (n. 69), 107–10.

[413] Ford, 'Law's Territory' 1999 (n. 12), 851; Douzinas, 'Metaphysics of Jurisdiction' 2007 (n. 403), 21–33.

[414] Cover, 'Nomos and Narrative' 1983/4 (n. 5), 31.

Diverging core jurisdictional narratives do not always lead to a CLS-like normative reality. Within a legal system's normative universe, such diverging narratives often exist because each faction, *ideally*, wishes to exclusively possess the legal power and authority to speak in the name of the system's law.[415] This narrative diversity unavoidably leads to some measures of legal uncertainty and tense cross-faction engagement.[416] But often, the different factions remain committed to sharing the normative universe. Narratives even develop that lead community members to accept unfavourable dominant narratives and norms because of second-order considerations (fairness, efficiency, pluralism, etc.).[417] Similarly, opposing legal systems often compromise, where each system accords primacy to some norms of the others.[418] Such compromises often include complementarity or *Solange* mechanisms: one system declares that it would grant primacy to *some* normative actions of the other even if they diverge from its preferred approach, as long as certain core principles are maintained.[419] Narratives, then, develop that enable people simultaneously addressed by both systems to accept the contradictions between the core jurisdictional narratives of the different systems. For example, various benefits are commonly presented in support of the coexistence of domestic and international law.[420]

In contrast, a *Core Jurisdictional Struggle* is likely, whenever factions attempt to fully realise their core jurisdictional narratives. Based on its core jurisdictional narratives, each faction dismissingly conceptualises its opponents' norms and narratives as non-legal (lacking the force of law) and even political (self-serving, unfair and biased).[421] The normative reality then matches the hardline CLS account: the factions are unconstrained by a shared normative corpus, and each perceives its opponents' actions as political and responds in kind. The law's semi-objective element vanishes: it no longer influences human behaviour. A core jurisdictional struggle, thus, places a legal system at a risk of dissolution.

There is an element of truth in the manner in which each side depicts its opponents. No legal system is perfect,[422] and no jurisprudential theory is

---

[415] *Ibid.*, 14–17.
[416] Orna Ben-Naftali and Rafi Reznik, 'The Astro-Nomos: On International Legal Paradigms and the Legal Status of the West Bank', *Washington University Global Studies Law Review* 14 (2015), 399–433 (409–10).
[417] Cover, 'Nomos and Narrative' 1983/4 (n. 5), 14–17.
[418] Bohrer, 'Obedience to Orders' 2012 (n. 69), 107–10.
[419] *Ibid.*
[420] See *ibid.*
[421] Ford, 'Law's Territory' 1999 (n. 12), 851; Douzinas, 'Metaphysics of Jurisdiction' 2007 (n. 403), 21–33.
[422] Asa Kasher, 'Refusals: Neglected Aspects', *Israel Law Review* 36 (2002), 171–80 (173).

consensual and flawless.[423] Therefore, any proclaimed basis for a legal system's authority can be 'shown to be of no value ... from a certain point of view'.[424] There is also an element of truth in how each side depicts itself, downplaying its own flaws and considering them insufficient to permit disobeying its law; a wide consensus exists among jurisprudential scholars (irrespective of their school of thought) that 'under the legal systems we are familiar with [despite their imperfections], in most cases and for most individuals there is a moral obligation to obey the law'.[425] Since there is an element of truth in the manner in which each side depicts both itself and its opponents, an objective determination of which system should be preferred is often impossible; these decisions are guided instead by the narratives one comes to perceive as true.[426]

A. US and International Law

Before 9/11, IHL discourse was rather formalist.[427] Also, the domestic US legal system ascribed considerable primacy and respect to IHL.[428] After 9/11 this changed because the United States, as expressed in the torture memos, began to claim that: (a) it 'is faced with a new war ... materially different from any [previous] war ... [requiring] either new law or no law';[429] (b) '[i]nternational law does not apply as law, but rather (at most [and if at all]) as a matter of policy'.[430] Thus, the United States embraced legal positions that either dismiss wartime international law (as non-existent or not having the obligatory force of law), or assert complete authority to speak in its name. Additionally, two months after 9/11, the term 'lawfare' was coined by a high-ranking American officer.[431] Although this term is sometimes treated a neutral reminder that legal argumentation and advocacy are necessary for attaining one's wartime aims, it is mainly used as an accusation for inappropriate political manipulation of international law and wartime events.[432] In some cases, lawfare

---

[423] MacIntyre, *Whose Justice?* 1988 (n. 79), 1–11.

[424] Blaise Pascal, *Thoughts*, trans. C. Kegan Paul (London: Bell, 1901), 65 (c. 1669).

[425] Ruth Gavison, 'Natural Law, Positivism and the Limits of Jurisprudence', *Yale Law Journal* 91 (1982), 1250–85 (1279).

[426] MacIntyre, *Whose Justice?* 1988 (n. 79), 333; Ben-Naftali, 'Epistemology of the Closet of International Law' 2011 (n. 60), 534.

[427] Modirzadeh, 'Folk International Law' 2014 (n. 15), 235.

[428] *Ibid.*

[429] *Ibid.*, 233.

[430] *Ibid.*, 232.

[431] Charles Dunlap, 'Law and Military Interventions: Preserving Humanitarian Values in 21st Century Conflicts', 29 November 2001, available at: people.duke.edu/~pfeaver/dunlap.pdf.

[432] *Ibid.*; Orde Kittrie, *Lawfare* (Oxford University Press, 2015), 1–40.

accusations have merit.[433] In others, such accusations are merely a symptom of the lawyerly tendency to confuse one's *lex ferenda* with the actual *lex lata* (especially when the latter is 'objectively' unclear) and, consequentially, suspect that anyone thinking otherwise is intentionally distorting the law. Many cases are somewhere in between the two possibilities and their classification to either is likely to be disputed. But the United States bluntly exaggerated with its lawfare accusations, calling anyone criticising its disregard of wartime international law politically biased.[434] The US Ambassador to the UN, for example, stated that 'the goal of those who think that international law really means anything ... [is] to constrict the United States'.[435] Even advancing international law-based justifications for US actions by the United States was merely considered 'a means of justifying [US] actions ... in the world of international politics'.[436] An embrace of such legal positions by the most powerful member of the international legal community had to have a destabilising effect and invite counter-actions by other members. A core jurisdictional struggle was inevitable.

As noted, a legal system's core legal classifications are main battlegrounds during core jurisdictional struggles. Indeed, since 9/11, legal strategies have increasingly depended 'on diluting the boundaries between various fields of international law and diminishing the clarity of binding rules and fields of legal application'.[437] Thus, the current indeterminacy crisis concerning wartime international law distinctions is largely a manifestation of a core jurisdictional struggle over the power and authority to speak in the name of wartime international law.

Core jurisdictional struggles have grave side-effects. During a struggle the normative universe is inflicted with extensive uncertainty and cross-faction clashes. Even if won by a certain faction, such a struggle often results in the alienation of other factions, reducing their readiness to defer to the legal system.[438] But this does not mean that a core jurisdictional struggle should never be initiated; for the right cause, the aforesaid side-effects are worthwhile.

---

[433] E.g., 'UK Human Rights Lawyer Struck Off for Iraq War Allegations', Jurist.org, 2 February 2017, available at: www.jurist.org/paperchase/2017/02/uhKhuman-rights-lawyer-struck-off-for-iraq-war-allegations.php.

[434] Michael Scharf, 'International Law and the Torture Memos', *Case Western Reserve Journal of International Law* 42 (2009), 321–58 (328–9).

[435] Samantha Power, 'Boltonism', *New Yorker*, 21 March 2005, available at: www.newyorker.com /magazine/2005/03/21/boltonism.

[436] 'Bybee Memo' 2002 (n. 334), 23.

[437] Modirzadeh, 'Folk International Law' 2014 (n. 15), 229 (see also, pp. 299–303).

[438] Bordwell, *Law of War between Belligerents* 1908 (n. 98), 112; Cover, 'Nomos and Narrative' 1983/4 (n. 5), 31, 39.

Therefore, the question must be asked: why should we not embrace torture memo-like, hardline Statist positions? Many believe that 'attempts to regulate warfare based on humanitarian principles [are] doomed ... and may exacerbate ... violence'.[439] If true, are we not foolish to commit ourselves to IHL?

'Scepticism about the value of the law of war is nothing new.'[440] Carl von Clausewitz similarly believed that contemporary IHL did not truly restrict warfare, and opposed adopting restrictive IHL, because, in war, 'mistakes which come from kindness are the very worst'.[441] German General von Moltke stated in 1880 that IHL plays a limited role in lessening the evils of war and might even be counter-productive, because 'the greatest [humanitarian] benefit in war is that it be [quickly] terminated'.[442] During the nineteenth and early twentieth century, such positions influenced IHL, giving rise to considerably supported doctrines that promoted unconstrained warfare.[443]

But as a 2011 US military manual observed, the influence of such positions facilitated horrors that mark 'a dark era for the rule of law'.[444] As for von Moltke's claim, empirically, 'nobody has demonstrated that the presence or absence of IHL norms ... causes or inhibits a speedy end to a war'.[445] Unconstrained warfare had in some past cases helped to achieve victory against non-State enemies; but in many others it backfired, only increasing popular support for the non-State enemy.[446] More generally, history demonstrates that often, once the commitment to IHL is abandoned, soldiers are swept up by the violence and commit horrific vengeful actions that are harmful to the war effort.[447]

Hardline Statist positions also undervalue IHL. A 2015 US military manual observed: 'Although critics of the regulation of warfare cite examples of violations of the law of armed conflict as proof of its ineffectiveness, a comprehensive view of history provides the greatest evidence of [its] overall validity.'[448] Past experience demonstrates that IHL moderates wartime actions more often than many assume.[449] The under-appreciation of many IHL

---

439   Gerald Steinberg, 'The UN, the ICJ and the Separation Barrier: War by Other Means', *Israel Law Review* 38 (2005), 331–47 (334).

440   Geoffrey Best, *Humanity in Warfare* (London: Weidenfeld & Nicolson, 1980), 10.

441   As quoted in Green, 'Enforcement of the Law' 1995/6 (n. 140), 286.

442   As quoted in Bordwell, *Law of War between Belligerents* 1908 (n. 98), 114–15.

443   Jeff A. Bovarnick *et al.*, *Law of War Deskbook* (Charlottesville, VA: US Army J.A.G., 2011), 14.

444   *Ibid.*, 14.

445   Steven Ratner, *The Thin Justice of International Law* (Oxford University Press, 2015), 388.

446   Molly Dunigan, *Victory for Hire* (Stanford University Press, 2011), 158.

447   Beer, 'Revitalizing the Concept of Military Necessity' 2015 (n. 136), 803–7.

448   Dowdy, *Deskbook* 2015 (n. 249), 8.

449   *Ibid.*; Best, *Humanity in Warfare* 1980 (n. 440), 9–11.

successes is probably the consequence of two related psychological biases: the 'availability heuristic' that leads individuals to overestimate the occurrence of vivid events (e.g., war crimes);[450] and the tendency to attribute insufficient importance to events that have not taken place ('non-events'), such as most cases in which IHL was not violated.[451] In sum, history illustrates that hardline Statist positions underestimate IHL's validity, overestimate the benefits of total warfare, and disregard the almost certain large-scale horrors of making no attempt to legally restrain warfare.

B. The Second Eye of the Storm: IHRL

As previously mentioned, popular history wrongly assumes that traditional international law did not address individuals. Its prevalence leads even most IHRL advocates to disregard pre-mid-twentieth-century influences of rights jurisprudence on IHL. The stronger influence of other jurisprudential narratives notwithstanding, over the centuries, various rights-oriented jurisprudential narratives influenced IHL.[452] But something has recently changed in that influence, because of the second instigator of the current core jurisdictional struggle: hardline IHRL advocacy rooted in a vision of IHRL as being at 'the heart of [all] international law'.[453] In IHL, this vision has found several expressions.

First, some IHRL advocates, like hardline Statists, reject the ability of international law to regulate combat behaviour. International law, they hold, should be as constraining as possible, because its only effective use is in politically denouncing and pressuring State agents to cease participating in wars. Extensively applying IHRL to wartime actions can enhance wartime international law as a denunciation means.[454] Although they would rarely admit it, *some* such IHRL advocates allow themselves to 'creatively' interpret legal norms and even the case-specific facts, so as to increase their ability to denounce State agents.[455] Such manipulations, which often accuse the relevant State agents of war crimes, have the potential to instigate a core jurisdictional struggle if used extensively, because

---

[450] See David Ahlstrom and Garry Bruton, *International Management* (Mason, OH: South-Western, 2010), 278–9.

[451] See James Parkin, *Judging Plans and Projects* (Ann Arbor, MI: Avery, 1993), 42.

[452] See Philip Alston, 'Book Review: Does the Past Matter? On the Origins of Human Rights', *Harvard Law Review* 126 (2013), 2043–81 (2068); Trainin, 'Questions of Guerrilla Warfare' 1946 (n. 49), 561; Maine, *Ancient Law* 1908 (n. 109), 105.

[453] Odello and Cavandoli, 'Introduction' 2011 (n. 365), 1.

[454] E.g., Samuel Moyn, 'From Aggression to Atrocity: Rethinking the History of International Criminal Law', in Markus D. Dubber and Tatjana Hörnle (eds.), *Oxford Handbook of International Criminal Law* (Oxford University Press, forthcoming).

[455] E.g., Jurist.org, 'Human Rights Lawyer Struck Off 2017 (n. 433).

even State agents are likely to push back when increasingly vilified. Additionally, such manipulations can turn their makers' disbelief in IHL's validity into a self-fulfilling prophecy. Research indicates that soldiers are more likely to abide by IHL when they believe that it contains moral laws originating in a *fair* system.[456] Denunciation-motivated political manipulation of the law and facts can diminish soldiers' perception of IHL as such. Because of such concerns, traditionally, humanitarian NGOs, such as the ICRC, have been reluctant to use IHL as a means of denunciation.[457] But, rights-oriented organisations began making such use of IHL in the 1960s–1970s; both the influence of these organisations and their denunciation-use of IHL increased in the 1990s, and has been further increasing since the 2000s.[458] To be clear, too many denunciations are justified and most IHRL advocates do not support political over-manipulation of wartime law and facts. However, such denunciation-motivated manipulations have increased and that has contributed greatly to the current crisis: weakening IHL's normative force and serving as an excuse for hardline Statists to respond in kind.

Secondly, many IHRL advocates *do* believe that international law can influence combat behaviour, though they too believe that IHL is insufficiently effective in diminishing wartime suffering. Hence, they hold that IHRL should replace IHL in regulating wartime conduct.[459] Such views also have the potential of instigating a core jurisdictional struggle if a strong attempt is made to implement them, because they try to generate 'not merely a shift in emphasis[,] but a regime change'.[460]

An ostensibly more moderate IHRL advocacy favours the co-application of IHL and IHRL.[461] Its mildest version 'only' (a) considers IHRL the primary normative guide to interpreting IHL,[462] and (b) interprets the *lex specialis* doctrine (where IHRL applies in wartime, unless barred by specific IHL) in a manner that rarely considers IHL as barring IHRL. This interpretation of the

---

[456] Ziv Bohrer, 'Is the Prosecution of War Crimes Just and Effective? Rethinking the Lessons from Sociology and Psychology', *Michigan Journal of International Law* 4 (2012), 749–819 (788–800).

[457] Kennedy, 'Distinguishing the Military and Humanitarian Professions' 2007 (n. 112), 12.

[458] Moyn, 'From Aggression to Atrocity' forthcoming (n. 454), 28–32.

[459] Aurel Sari, 'The Juridification of the British Armed Forces and the European Convention on Human Rights: "Because It's Judgment that Defeats Us"' (2014), 20 March 2014, available at: https://papers.ssrn.com/sol3/papers.cfm?abstract_id=2411070.

[460] Yoram Dinstein, 'Concluding Remarks: LOAC and Attempts to Abuse or Subvert It', *International Law Studies* 87 (2011), 483–94 (492).

[461] Robert Kolb, 'Human Rights and Humanitarian Law', in Rüdiger Wolfrum (ed.), *Max Planck Encyclopedia of Public International Law* (online edn.), March 2013, paras. 27–43.

[462] Ibid., paras. 35–7.

lex specialis doctrine gradually leads IHRL to become the primary normative source for addressing gaps in IHL, a role traditionally reserved for internal IHL norms (the Martens Clause principles, the adaptation approach, etc.).[463] Such actions are steadily changing the nature of IHL, making it increasingly rights-oriented. This 'righting' even increasingly leads IHRL advocates to hold that the correct way to conceptualise IHL is as 'IHRL in Times of Armed Conflicts'.[464] Or, as my colleague Helen Duffy phrased it:[465]

> The starting point for an assessment of the relationship between IHL and IHRL is what has been called the theory of complementarity, which ... 'means that human rights law and humanitarian law do not contradict each other but, being based on the same principles and values, can influence and reinforce each other mutually.'

But, as David Luban points out, this 'righted' conceptualisation of IHL attempts to change the nature of IHL by retroactively reinterpreting IHL in a manner that transforms IHRL into the primary jurisprudence shaping wartime international law, disregarding other, stronger long-standing jurisprudential influences.[466] Thus, it constitutes an IHRL-motivated attempt to obtain primary, if not sole, power and authority to speak in the name of wartime international law. Therefore, both co-application and substitution approaches have the potential to instigate a core jurisdictional struggle if attempts are made to apply them extensively.

Such attempts have been made since the 1960s, with a significant breakthrough in the mid-1990s when international judicial forums began expressing support for such views.[467] Their realisation has drastically intensified since the early 2000s.[468] One likely reason for this intensification is the increasing support for rights-based moral philosophy; namely, it is possible that IHL sceptic, IHRL advocates are more influential today than in the past.[469] But other reasons have led many jurists to support extensive co-application and substitution approaches. Although the rise of modern IHRL began after

---

[463]　*Ibid.*, paras. 33–4; Marko Milanovic, *Extraterritorial Application of Human Rights Treaties* (Oxford University Press, 2011), 249–60.

[464]　Kolb, 'Human Rights' 2013 (n. 461), para. 38.

[465]　Duffy, in this volume, 72 (quoting Droege).

[466]　Luban, 'Human Rights Thinking' 2016 (n. 4), 50.

[467]　Kolb, 'Human Rights' 2013 (n. 461), paras. 16–26.

[468]　Oona Hathaway *et al.*, 'Which Law Governs during Armed Conflict? The Relationship between International Humanitarian Law and Human Rights Law', *Minnesota Law Review* 96 (2012), 1883–1943 (1884–5).

[469]　See Dinstein, 'Concluding Remarks' 2011 (n. 460), 492.

the Second World War, until the 1990s the implications for a State being deemed an IHRL violator were much weaker than today.[470] IHL was also, arguably, weaker than today, nevertheless the stigma for violating IHL was non-negligible (following the trauma of the Second World War).[471] Therefore, States, wishing to evade legal scrutiny often employed a legal tactic of insisting that they were involved in violence that does not constitute an 'armed conflict', rather 'peace-time disturbance' (i.e., IHRL, but not IHL, applies).[472] Many of those wishing to counteract this evasion by States and to maximise legal scrutiny and civilian protection employed an opposite legal tactic of asserting that IHL, not IHRL, regulates borderline situations between 'armed conflict' and 'peacetime disturb-ance' – they preferred that tactic to expanding IHRL application because of 'the lack of a ... human rights ... operational body' (as ICRC Vice-President Pictet explained in 1975).[473] Ironically, after 9/11, the roles have, somewhat, switched. First, the influence of international judicial forums has been on the rise since the 1990s, and most international judicial forums to which those wishing to maximise legal scrutiny and civilian protection can, presently, turn to are regarded as having a subject-matter jurisdiction that is limited to IHRL. Secondly, the United States (and others) did not deny the existence of 'war' to evade legal constrains and judicial scrutiny; instead, they proclaimed engagement in a novel war that existing IHL is unfit to address. In the context of these two elements, many jurists have come to embrace extensive co-application and substitution approaches not out of a devout disbelief in IHL, rather out of fear that but for such an extensive IHRL-based framing of wartime actions, judicial scrutiny of these actions would be unavailable.[474] The fact that many have embraced such approaches for such reasons, means that they might embrace an alternative (non-IHRL) approach if it would bolster judicial scrutiny (and an attempt to present just such an alternative is made later herein). Yet, at present, the significant point is that, irrespective of the motivation behind one's support for extensive co-application and substitution approaches, the practical result is that international judicial forums increasingly scrutinise States' wartime actions and most of these forums are regarded as having a subject-matter jurisdiction that is limited to IHRL. As Rafi Reznik and Orna Ben-Naftali noted:[475]

---

[470] Niels Beisinghoff, *Corporations and Human Rights* (Frankfurt am Main: Peter Lang, 2009), 8–15.
[471] Pictet, *Humanitarian Law* 1975 (n. 33), 58.
[472] *Ibid.* Some States still employ such a legal tactic.
[473] *Ibid.*, 60.
[474] See Modirzadeh, 'Folk International Law' 2014 (n. 15), 299–303.
[475] Ben-Naftali and Reznik, 'Astro-Nomos' 2015 (n. 416), 409–10.

> Given that alternative visions ... exist and that the normative world [of a legal system] ... bridges ... vision and reality, any attempt to advance a revisionist interpretation requires an engagement with alternative visions and the meaning they invest in the normative world. Such engagement, as tense and wrought with conflicts as it surely is, is nevertheless a *sine qua non* condition for sharing a [normative universe].

As wartime international law is being evermore shaped in forums where the influence of non-IHRL visions of that law is very weak, a revisionist legal interpretation is being increasingly forced upon IHL's normative universe through institutional mechanisms that do not facilitate engagement with long-standing alternative (non-IHRL) visions. This development has been a primary cause for the current core jurisdictional struggle.

But what is wrong with granting an IHRL-oriented approach primary authority to speak in the name of wartime international law? Supporters of this move, such as my colleague Helen Duffy, believe that it would increase civilian protection.[476] Yet it actually diminishes that protection. As explained below, this counter-intuitive result stems from a core difference between IHL and IHRL: the former being obligations-based and the latter rights-based. Stated differently, like my colleague Janina Dill (though for different reasons), my analysis shows that, in wartime, compared with IHRL, 'IHL currently offers a better, but far from morally ideal, law'.[477]

1. IHL versus IHRL: Obligations versus Rights

According to the Hohfeldian theorem, for every right there is a corollary obligation.[478] This theorem leads some to unreflectively assume that rights and obligations orientations are interchangeable.[479] This is false, if only because of the incompatibility between rights-orientations and 'imperfect obligations' (in the previously explained sense of that term).[480] A core premise of rights-oriented legal regimes is that individuals' rights are the root of, any and all, obligations of others. In sharp contrast to that core premise, the benefits of imperfect obligations are not allocated to any specified recipients (no one has a correlating 'right' to such obligations). Therefore, rights-oriented

---

[476] Duffy, in this volume, Chapter 1, *passim*.
[477] Dill, in this volume, 201.
[478] Wesley Newcomb Hohfeld, *Fundamental Legal Conceptions* (New Haven, CT: Yale University Press, 1919), 38.
[479] Moodrick-Even-Khen, 'Obligations at the Border Line' 2005 (n. 115), 478.
[480] Above nn. 117–22.

legal regimes, unlike obligation-oriented regimes, simply cannot sustain imperfect obligations.[481]

There is also a less apparent reason that refutes even the narrower, more accepted assumption that rights and obligations orientations are interchangeable in relation to 'perfect obligations' and 'rights' (as they do correlate).[482] In practice, as Cover observed:[483]

> There are certain kinds of problems which a jurisprudence of [obligations] manages to solve rather naturally. There are others which present conceptual difficulties of the first order. Similarly, a jurisprudence of rights naturally solves certain problems while stumbling over others ... It is not ... that particular problems cannot be solved, in one system or the other – only that the solution entails a sort of rhetorical or philosophical strain.

The orientation of each legal system, rights or obligations, is related to certain fundamental jurisdictional narratives (the system's 'formative stories').[484] These narratives are so strongly embedded in the system's normative universe that community members tend to treat the jurisdictional landscape they create – rules, principles, institutions, distinctions, boundaries, etc. – as 'organic' (semi-natural and objective).[485] The problems that a legal system manages easily are those whose solution derives naturally from the landscape.[486] Solutions that do not derive naturally from the system's core narratives tend to be disputed and raise conceptual difficulties; the reasoning that could be presented for any potential solution involves rhetorical and philosophical strains.[487]

Rarely are formative stories fully coherent. Because they are the product of a continuous social discourse, they tend to incorporate elements of diverse jurisprudential origins. The conceptual difficulties and strains of some legal problems stem from such jurisprudential incoherence.[488] Incoherence can also be the result of communal diversity giving rise to diverging understandings of the fundamental jurisdictional narrative, and even to conflicting

---

[481] O'Neill, 'Rights, Obligations and World Hunger' 2008 (n. 109), 152.
[482] Hans Kelsen, *General Theory of Law and State* (Cambridge, MA: Harvard University Press, 1945), 77.
[483] Robert Cover, 'Obligation: A Jewish Jurisprudence of the Social Order', *Journal of Law and Religion* 5 (1987), 65–74 (70–1).
[484] *Ibid.*, 65; Cover, 'Nomos and Narrative' 1983/4 (n. 5), 54.
[485] Ford, 'Law's Territory' 1999 (n. 12), 850–1.
[486] *Ibid.*, 865.
[487] Cover, 'Obligation' 1987 (n. 483), 70–1; O'Neill, 'Rights, Obligations and World Hunger' 2008 (n. 109), 150.
[488] Maine, *Ancient Law* 1908 (n. 109), 19–38, 64–5.

narratives. Often a jurisdictional discourse has 'multiple, malleable and even contradictory [narrative effects]',[489] instead of 'straightforward ... "logical consequences"'.[490]

Cover observed that the original 'story behind the term "rights" is the story of social contract':[491]

> The jurisprudence of rights ... has gained ascendance in the Western world together with the rise of the national State with its almost unique mastery of violence over extensive territories ... [I]t has been essential to counterbalance the development of the State with a myth which ... establishes the State as legitimate only in so far as it can be derived from the autonomous creatures who trade in their rights for security ...

This brief account already reveals incoherence. First, rights jurisprudence embraces two potentially conflicting visions of rights: (a) rights existing in the 'state of nature'; and (b) rights stemming from the social contract (thus not universal). The conflict between the universalist and Statist visions is further evident in the wide range of positions about classification of different rights, with some jurisprudential versions going as far as to perceive the 'state of nature' as being practically devoid of rights.[492] In IHRL's normative universe, this issue manifests in a tension 'between the universal aspiration of human rights to apply to everyone in all situations, and the fact that human rights discourse is built upon the model of a relationship between an accountable state and its citizens'.[493] Secondly, rights jurisprudence includes three potentially conflicting visions of the benchmark for defining a legal system's jurisdiction. *Citizenship-based* jurisdiction derives naturally from social contract jurisprudence;[494] *universal* jurisdiction derives naturally from universalist rights jurisprudence;[495] yet, currently, a *territorial* jurisdictional benchmark has priority, and it owes much of its development to non-rights jurisprudences that also contributed to the rise of modern States (notably, Statist-positivism).[496] Despite all these elements of incoherence, there is still considerable

---

[489] Ford, 'Law's Territory' 1999 (n. 12), 864.
[490] *Ibid.*
[491] Cover, 'Obligation' 1987 (n. 483), 66–9.
[492] Luban, 'Human Rights Thinking' 2016 (n. 4), 50.
[493] Aeyal M. Gross, 'Human Proportions: Are Human Rights the Emperor's New Clothes of the International Law of Occupation?', *European Journal of International Law* 18 (2007), 1–35 (33).
[494] Lea Brilmayer, 'Consent, Contract and Territory', *Minnesota Law Review* 74 (1989), 1–35 (10–11).
[495] Milanovic, *Extraterritorial Application of Human Rights Treaties* 2011 (n. 463), 55.
[496] Richard Ford, 'Law and Borders', *Alabama Law Review* 64 (2012), 123–39 (134).

commonality between the different visions of rights and jurisdictions. Therefore, rights-based systems can solve various problems naturally.

What is IHL's formative story? (a) The humanitarian legend that 'modern IHL began when ... Dunant visited ... Solferino'?[497] (b) The Statist-positivist myth that modern IHL began once international law was acknowledged, 'through the Peace of Westphalia [treaties]',[498] as being based on the actual 'relations among States'?[499] (c) The credit-hogging knights' tale that IHL has been 'developed by warriors for warriors'?[500] (d) The 'righted' story about IHL becoming 'IHRL in Times of Armed Conflicts' (which 'drifts far from ... [IHL's actual] history')?[501] A normative universe encompasses 'various genres of narrative[s] [including] history [and] fiction'.[502] Therefore, it is not inaccuracy, but insufficient dominance that prevents each of these narratives from becoming *the* formative story of IHL.

But IHL is not bereft of a formative story. As David Luban points out, nearly 'everyone who participates in the project of furthering humanitarian law shares ... a commitment to eliminate unnecessary suffering and destruction'.[503] Military lawyers and commanders may consider it a matter of honour; IHRL advocates as a part of a larger human rights project; humanitarians also consider it a part of a human rights project or a distinct moral duty; and even cynics who do not think that individuals matter much may 'still favor regulating war to minimize suffering and destruction'.[504] IHL, thus, has a widely accepted, minimalist formative story, according to which a primary motivation for its formation has been a normative *obligation* to strive to reduce wartime suffering and destruction.

Another, less 'romantic', explanation also leads to the conclusion that IHL is primarily an obligations-based system. As discussed, IHL has its origins in the mainly obligations-oriented, medieval European status-based socio-legal structure, and because jurisprudential diversity has always been extensive, legal practices and customs constituted a more important source for IHL, leading IHL to exhibit remarkable continuity. Hence, to this day, IHL remains primarily obligations-oriented (and also, considerably, status-based).[505]

---

[497] Luban, 'Human Rights Thinking' 2016 (n. 4), 50.
[498] Dowdy, *Deskbook* 2015 (n. 249), 12.
[499] *Ibid.*
[500] Scott Morris, 'The Laws of War: Rules by Warriors for Warriors', *Army Lawyer* (1997), 4–13 (13).
[501] Luban, 'Human Rights Thinking' 2016 (n. 4), 50.
[502] Cover, 'Nomos and Narrative' 1983/4 (n. 5), 10.
[503] Luban, 'Human Rights Thinking' 2016 (n. 4), 50.
[504] *Ibid.*
[505] See *supra*, Section II.C.

2. Extraterritorial Action

As noted, the formative story of rights-based systems incorporates two potentially conflicting visions of rights and three potentially conflicting jurisdictional visions. When it comes to State actions committed within its sovereign territory and affecting its citizens, all the aforesaid visions generally concur that a State is duty-bound to secure the rights of those affected. In contrast, the different jurisdictional visions commonly differ on extraterritorial State actions, and when non-citizens are the ones affected the two visions of rights potentially diverge. Stated differently, in the context of extraterritorial State actions that affect non-citizens, tension arises between the core Statist and the core universalist elements of the normative universe.[506] Therefore, in a rights-oriented system, attempts to resolve problems that arise in such a context will likely exhibit conceptual difficulties, vagueness, disagreements and strained reasoning.

For example, international human rights courts ruled inconsistently on whether pilots (State agents) exercise, during extraterritorial aerial warfare, sufficient public authority and control for *State* jurisdiction to come into existence and give rise to a duty to safeguard the rights of affected non-citizens. If such a duty does not arise for a State party to the treaty creating the IHRL tribunal, that tribunal does not have subject-matter jurisdiction over the case. One international human rights court was more influenced by the Statist elements of rights jurisprudence and interpreted the concept of 'State jurisdiction' as primarily referring to the State's sovereign territory; it, therefore, considered that concept inapplicable to extraterritorial aerial warfare actions.[507] Another international human rights court was more influenced by the universalist elements of rights jurisprudence, and was therefore inclined to regard 'State jurisdiction' as determined by the extent of the influence State agents exert on the relevant individuals; consequently, it ruled that such jurisdiction exists in extraterritorial aerial warfare actions.[508] Attempts to create an intermediate approach differentiating between degrees of control and authority have proven difficult and 'dra[w] arbitrary distinctions'.[509]

Obligations-oriented systems are much less influenced by territorial boundaries, because obligations are attached to the obligation-bearers and, as such,

---

[506]   Milanovic, *Extraterritorial Application of Human Rights Treaties* 2011 (n. 463), 76–83.

[507]   ECtHR, *Banković v. Belgium*, Grand Chamber Judgment of 12 December 2001, No. 52207/99, paras. 59–73.

[508]   IACHR, *Alejandre v. Cuba*, Judgment of 29 September 1999, No. 86/99, para. 23.

[509]   EWCA, *Al-Saadoon & Ors v. Secretary of State for Defence*, Judgment of 17 March 2015, para. 102.

tend to follow them.[510] Consider, the Israeli Supreme Court position regarding judicial review of extraterritorial air bombings. In the light of the obligations-orientation of IHL, that court has long ruled that 'every Israeli soldier carries in his backpack ... the law of war' (i.e., Israeli soldiers are *obligated* by IHL wherever they go).[511] Additionally, that court has long regarded itself as having the constitutional 'role of safeguarding the rule of law ... [which] means ... that it must [always] ... ensure that the [Israeli] government acts in accordance with the law'.[512] Based on these two obligations-based precepts, the Israeli Supreme Court easily saw itself as authorised to review Israeli extraterritorial air bombings (after all, if (a) the court is obligated to review all (Israeli) State actions that are regulated by law, and (b) IHL is a law that regulates wartime actions of State agents (obligates them) wherever they go, then (c) the court is obligated to review the IHL adherence of State wartime actions, wherever they are performed).[513]

According to some, the proper way to solve the indeterminacy arising when IHRL is used to regulate extraterritorial State actions is to embrace a purely universalist approach that holds each State duty-bound by IHRL in relation to whomever it affects (or at least harms).[514] But opponents argue that purely universalist approaches impose unrealistic demands on States, especially during war,[515] and fail to grasp the nature of rights (which, according to such opponents, presupposes a unique relationship between the rights-bearers and those duty-bound to protect them).[516]

Irrespective of the above dispute, purely universalist approaches are unlikely to improve legal clarity because of the nature of the benchmarks upon which they rely. What kinds of relations (proximal, temporal, physical and, also, normative) need to exist in order for one's actions to be regarded as (a) having affected, or (b) being responsible for, another's condition? Try to answer and you will quickly find yourself facing a terminological and conceptual

---

[510] Naz Modirzadeh, 'The Dark Sides of Convergence: A Pro-Civilian Critique of the Extraterritorial Application of Human Rights Law in Armed Conflict', *International Law Studies* 86 (2010), 349–410 (352–5).

[511] HCJ, *Jamait-Askan v. IDF*, Judgment of 28 December 1983, No. 393/82, 810.

[512] HCJ, *Ressler v. Minister of Defence*, Judgment of 12 June 1988, No. 910/86, para. 23. See also, ibid.; and *infra*, 192–4.

[513] HCJ, *B'Tselem v. Military Advocated General*, Judgment of 21 August 2011, No. 9594/03. This petition was rejected on its merits; but only after the Court pressured the military to considerably change its policy.

[514] Milanovic, *Extraterritorial Application of Human Rights Treaties* 2011 (n. 463), 55.

[515] Michael Dennis, 'Non-Application of Civil and Political Rights Treaties Extraterritorially During Times of International Armed Conflict', *Israel Law Review* 40 (2007), 453–502 (473).

[516] Modirzadeh, 'Dark Sides of Convergence' 2010 (n. 510), 371–4.

maze. The theoretical disagreements regarding the proper basis for determining responsibility are extensive and so are those regarding the basis for determining causation; likewise, the practical difficulties in making such determinations in actual cases are often considerable. These issues are chronically fraught with indeterminacy.[517] This is not to say that a legal policy that demands the determination of responsibility or causation should never be adopted, only that such a policy should be expected to suffer from considerable indeterminacy.

Another problem with universalist approaches stems from their synthetic narratives of State jurisdiction, according to which international law can define and redefine that concept as it wishes.[518] Proponents of such synthetic narratives ignore the point that the formative stories of domestic legal systems conceptualise State jurisdiction as organic and primarily territorial.[519] As a result, most people are so 'accustomed to territorial jurisdiction . . . that it is hard [for them] to imagine that governments could be organized any other way'.[520] Thus, a strong attempt to implement the synthetic conceptualisation of State jurisdiction is likely to lead to a core jurisdictional struggle between IHRL and domestic legal systems.

Fully embracing a territory-oriented Statist vision of rights fares no better. According to this vision, the recognition of universal inalienable rights does not mean that agents of all States are under a duty to protect these rights. Each State is responsible only for securing the rights of individuals found in territories under its rule;[521] namely, its sovereign territory[522] and, according to many,[523] also territories it holds under belligerent occupation (as the occupier is the temporary ruler of the occupied territory).[524] The role of the IHRL regime is to ensure that no State shirks its territory-bound duty to protect human rights.[525] Supporters claim that reliance on such a territorial benchmark guarantees universal protection of rights and prevents indeterminacy about responsibility to secure the rights in each case, because it 'divide[s] between nations the space upon which human activities are employed, in

---

[517]   Antony Honoré, 'Causation in the Law', in Edward N. Zalta (ed.), *Stanford Encyclopedia of Philosophy* (online edn.), winter 2010.

[518]   Milanovic, *Extraterritorial Application of Human Rights Treaties* 2011 (n. 463), 23, 54.

[519]   Ford, 'Law's Territory' 1999 (n. 12), 843, 852.

[520]   *Ibid.*, 843.

[521]   See Vattel, *Law of Nations* 1797 (n. 119), 107.

[522]   Samantha Besson, 'The Extraterritoriality of the European Convention on Human Rights', *Leiden Journal of International Law* 25 (2012), 857–84 (859); ECtHR, *Banković v. Belgium* (n. 507), paras. 59–73.

[523]   But see, e.g., Modirzadeh, 'Dark Sides of Convergence' 2010 (n. 510), 363–7.

[524]   See sources cited in *Public Commission to Examine the Maritime Incident of 31 May 2010: Second Report* (Israel, 2013), 64, 67 ('Turkel Report').

[525]   Besson, 'Extraterritoriality of the European Convention' 2012 (n. 522), 863–4.

order to assure them at all points the minimum of protection of which international law is the guardian'.[526] But this claim is false. Various State actions negatively affect the human rights of non-citizens abroad, and there are strong moral reasons against leaving such non-citizens unprotected.

Given the flaws of both fully universalist and fully Statist approaches, many support a middle-ground approach that (a) regards 'State jurisdiction' as a conceptual constraint, but attempts to define it broadly, or (b) applies only some rights in only some extraterritorial wartime situations.[527] But such approaches have proven to be ambiguous and normatively incoherent.[528] Namely, the legal solutions they offer suffer from conceptual difficulties and involve jurisprudential strains; unsurprisingly so, given that these approaches attempt to balance conflicting visions of rights and of jurisdiction.

If I must choose, I would prefer some ambiguous middle-ground approach over either two polar extremes of fully and of never extraterritorially applying IHRL in wartime. But such a choice is unnecessary, because there is still another alternative: rely primarily on IHL, having properly interpreted and developed it. IHL's indifference to extraterritoriality is but one advantage.

3. Focusing on Obligation-Bearers

Because obligations-based systems focus on the obligation-bearer, they tend to be more attentive than rights-based systems to delineating the agent responsible for performing each legally prescribed act (i.e., the obligation-bearer).[529] Therefore, situations where the law has prescribed an act but the identity of the agent responsible for performing it is unclear are more likely in rights-based systems.[530]

The case of *Jaloud v. the Netherlands* illustrates this issue:[531]

---

[526] Permanent Court of Arbitration, *Island of Palmas* (Netherlands v. USA), Arbitral Award of 4 April 1928, *Reports of International Arbitral Awards* II, 839.

[527] E.g., ECtHR, *Al-Skeini v. United Kingdom*, Grand Chamber Judgment of 7 July 2011, Application No. 55721/07, paras. 130–50.

[528] Besson, 'Extraterritoriality of the European Convention' 2012 (n. 522), 858; Modirzadeh, 'Dark Sides of Convergence' 2010 (n. 510), 370–3.

[529] O'Neill, 'Rights, Obligations and World Hunger' 2008 (n. 109), 149.

[530] Cover, 'Obligation' 1987 (n. 483), 71–2. Note that both Raz and Peters argue that this non-specification makes 'rights' a more flexible paradigm than 'obligations', because it enables the 'dynamic' creation of new correlative obligations and of new obligation-bearers; Joseph Raz, *The Morality of Freedom* (Oxford: Clarendon Press, 1986), 170–1, 184; Peters, *Beyond Human Rights* 2016 (n. 120), 540–1. But, in practice, this non-specification leads to insufficient thought regarding who is obligated to fulfil the rights and in what manner; Cover, *ibid.*; Onora O'Neill, 'The Dark Side of Human Rights', *International Affairs* 81 (2005), 227–39.

[531] ECtHR, *Jaloud v. the Netherlands*, Grand Chamber Judgment of 20 November 2014, Application No. 47708/08, paras. 10–13.

On 21 April 2004, at around 2.12 a.m., an unknown car approached a vehicle checkpoint (VCP) [located in] south-eastern Iraq [and] fired at the personnel guarding the VCP, all of them members of the Iraqi Civil Defence Corps (ICDC). The ... car drove off and disappeared ... [A] patrol of six Netherlands soldiers led by Lieutenant A. arrived on the scene at around 2.30 a.m. ... fifteen minutes later a Mercedes car approached the VCP at speed. It hit one of several barrels ... form[ing] the checkpoint, but continued to advance. Shots were fired at the car: Lieutenant A. fired ... [and] shots may also have been fired by ... ICDC personnel ... At this point the driver stopped ... Jaloud, [a] passenger [inside] the car [was] hit [and] died.

Dutch authorities investigated the incident, determining that there was no misconduct. But the investigation was flawed: evidence, documents and witnesses were mishandled.[532] The right to life places a State under a duty to carry out an effective investigation when its agents use deadly force. The European Court of Human Rights (ECtHR) had already ruled in earlier cases that this duty may arise even during war.[533] The Netherlands was found to have violated Jaloud's right to life.[534]

In reaching the intuitively correct outcome of holding the Dutch accountable for mishandling the investigation, the ECtHR faced grave conceptual difficulties. According to the European Human Rights Convention, State 'Parties shall secure to everyone within their jurisdiction the rights and freedoms defined in ... th[e] Convention.'[535] The United States was the belligerent occupier of Iraq at large. Britain was the occupier of the relevant region, and Dutch forces were merely assisting them, receiving their day-to-day orders from the British (the Netherlands relinquished operational control over its forces). Furthermore, the Dutch forces did not regularly operate the checkpoint, arriving only 15 minutes earlier to aid Iraqi forces.[536] On what basis, then, could it be concluded that Jaloud was within *Dutch* jurisdiction?

Traditionally, the ECtHR definition of State jurisdiction was primarily territorial: the Court was reluctant to hold a State responsible unless actions were committed within its sovereign territory or a territory under its belligerent occupation. Over time, an exception was acknowledged for cases where State agents detained individuals extraterritorially, because it was held that in such

---

[532] *Ibid.*, paras. 39–48, 183–228.
[533] E.g., ECtHR, *Al-Skeini v. United Kingdom* (n. 527), paras. 163–7.
[534] ECtHR, *Jaloud v. the Netherlands* (n. 531), paras. 226–8.
[535] Article 1 [European] Convention for the Protection of Human Rights and Fundamental Freedoms, 4 November 1950, 213 UNTS 221. Similar articles exist in most IHRL treaties; Milanovic, *Extraterritorial Application of Human Rights Treaties* 2011 (n. 463), 11–17.
[536] ECtHR, *Jaloud v. the Netherlands* (n. 531), paras. 10, 44–5, 53–63.

cases the State, through its agents, exerts such power and control over the detainees that it brings them *personally* under the State's jurisdiction.[537]

In *Jaloud*, however, the ECtHR ruled that Dutch jurisdiction existed although the action did not fall within its territorial or personal jurisdiction, as these concepts were traditionally defined.[538] The Court determined that a State does not become divested of its jurisdiction merely by deferring operational control to another State, particularly in the case at hand, because the Dutch retained the power to determine the overall policy of their forces and because they assumed sole responsibility for the area. But these elements of control were insufficient for Dutch jurisdiction to exist. The determining factor, it seems, was that the checkpoint was manned by personnel under Dutch command. Namely, it was ruled that the public authority exercised over the small territory of the checkpoint was sufficient to deem those passing through to be under Dutch territorial jurisdiction.[539]

Presenting a legal basis for such a definition of State jurisdiction demanded conflating three distinct concepts of 'control': (a) effective State control over a *territory*: the IHL benchmark for determining belligerent occupation (a situation widely held to fall under the definition of the State's *territorial jurisdiction* for IHRL purposes); (b) effective (or overall, according to some) State control over an *organ*: a benchmark of general international law for determining State responsibility for international wrongs (determining that perpetrators are *de facto* State organs); (c) State control and authority over a *person*: the IHRL benchmark for determining that an individual is *personally* within a State's jurisdiction.[540] Because of this conflation, as even some of the judges in *Jaloud* partially admitted, 'the judgment setting out the relevant international law is ambiguous' and 'conceptually unsound'.[541]

The ambiguity in *Jaloud* is not isolated.[542] It is the result of another tension within IHRL's normative universe. As d'Aspremont explains, IHRL's successful expansion rests on the jurisprudential coexistence of two potentially opposing claims: (a) 'exceptionalist claims', conceptualising IHRL as distinct from, and even superior to, general international law; and (b) 'generalist claims',

---

[537]   See ECtHR, *Al-Skeini v. United Kingdom* (n. 527), paras. 130–50 (and sources cited there).
[538]   Deviation from the traditional definitions began earlier, see, e.g., *ibid.*, paras. 130–50.
[539]   ECtHR, *Jaloud v. the Netherlands* (n. 531), paras. 112–53 (the Court's ambiguous discussion may be open to other interpretations).
[540]   *Ibid.* The conflation began earlier; see Milanovic, *Extraterritorial Application of Human Rights Treaties* 2011 (n. 463), 21–53.
[541]   ECtHR, *Jaloud v. the Netherlands* (n. 531), Concurring Opinion of Judges Spielmann and Raimondi, paras. 5, 7.
[542]   Milanovic, *Extraterritorial Application of Human Rights Treaties* 2011 (n. 463), 41.

conceptualising IHRL as being part of general international law.[543] Whenever the rules of general international law place an obstacle before expanding IHRL application, giving primacy to a competing (non-IHRL) international law, the exceptionalist claims help to override these formal rules. The generalist claims help to expand IHRL influence, whenever the rules of general international law do give primacy to IHRL over a competing international law. IHRL reasoning switches between the two types of claims, without sufficient concern for the ensuing inconsistency. Legal concepts like 'control', '*lex specialis*' and 'jurisdiction' are defined, redefined, embraced and discarded almost on a case-by-case basis, because, in each case '[l]egal categories ... are consciously and carefully used in a way that inflates the size of IHRL'.[544]

But the ambiguity resulting from *Jaloud* goes further. The ruling makes it impossible to distinguish the Dutch case from that of the other States involved. This forced the ECtHR to accept the possibility that other States 'might have exercised concurrent jurisdiction'.[545] As noted, situations of indeterminacy regarding the identity of the agent responsible for performing the legally prescribed act are more likely to occur in rights-based systems. Often, in such situations, each potentially relevant agent tries 'to foist the responsibility off to someone else'.[546] The ECtHR's acceptance of the possibility that several States could be held responsible seemingly reduces this concern – but it does the opposite. Uncertainty regarding the conditions under which State jurisdiction materialises may tempt each State to assume that jurisdiction (i.e., a duty to investigate) has not materialised in its case. Moreover, simultaneous independent investigations of the same case are, usually, detrimental to truth-finding efforts; the aspiration to avoid such situations provides an excuse for each State not to start its own investigation.

In contrast, commanders' duty to enforce IHL is strongly embedded in IHL's normative universe,[547] as it was from its inception.[548] Historically, *ius in bello* was primarily under the jurisdiction of the military justice systems, and the original jurisprudential basis for creating these distinct systems was the convention that kings and commanders were not only domestic agents, but

---

[543] Jean d'Aspremont, 'Expansionism and the Sources of International Human Rights Law', *Israel Yearbook on Human Rights* 46 (2016), 223–42 (223).

[544] Ibid., 242.

[545] ECtHR, *Jaloud v. the Netherlands* (n. 531), para. 153.

[546] Cover, 'Obligation' 1987 (n. 483), 71–2.

[547] Turkel Report 2013 (n. 524), 73–82.

[548] Oded Mudrik, *Military Justice* (Tel Aviv: Bursi, 1993), 17–21 (in Hebrew).

also high-ranking members of the transnational professional warrior guild, duty-bound, as such, to enforce *ius in bello* and maintain the discipline of those under their command; the authority to create military judicial systems was aimed to enable them to fulfil that duty.[549] Once it was determined that the checkpoint was manned by personnel under Dutch command, the naturally derived conclusion was that the Dutch forces had the primary responsibility to conduct the investigation. Indeed, they assumed that responsibility (the botching of the subsequent investigation notwithstanding).[550] The natural inclination exhibited by the Dutch command is likely weakened under the influence of the rights-oriented ruling that fails to acknowledge any normative basis for it, constructing instead an indeterminate normative landscape of concurrent jurisdictions.

4. The Disempowered

As Cover observed, the formative story of rights-based systems posits active participation by the rights-bearers, based on 'a myth of coequal autonomous, voluntary act[ors]'.[551] This myth is of great moral significance, as it conveys the strong humanist message that one's basis for making normative claims is independent of others because it is inherent in human nature.[552] Due to this myth, rights-based systems tend to easily solve the problems of individuals who are able to demand that their rights be protected.[553] But the myth has a downside, often making it difficult for rights-based systems to manage problems concerning disempowered individuals who cannot be expected to demand the protection of their rights.[554] Obligations-based systems tend to better address such situations because of their focus on obligation-bearers.[555]

Cover demonstrates this issue by discussing how rights-based and obligations-based (domestic) systems ensure that convicts' and indigents' garbs would not unconsciously affect decisions of judges and juries. Rights-based systems often poorly address this problem, because courts are likely to rule that if the defendant appears in convict's garb 'in the absence of timely objection by counsel the right [to be dressed properly would be] deemed waived'.[556] While some rights-

---

549 *Ibid.*
550 ECtHR, *Jaloud v. the Netherlands* (n. 531), paras. 39–48.
551 Cover, 'Obligation' 1987 (n. 483), 73.
552 Moodrick-Even-Khen, 'Obligations at the Border Line' 2005 (n. 115), 476.
553 Cover, 'Obligation' 1987 (n. 483), 73.
554 O'Neill, 'Rights, Obligations and World Hunger' 2008 (n. 109), 150.
555 Moodrick-Even-Khen, 'Obligations at the Border Line' 2005 (n. 115), 475.
556 Cover, 'Obligation' 1987 (n. 483), 72.

based systems try to solve this problem, such solutions (as Cover demonstrated) unavoidably entail rhetorical and philosophical strains.[557] Obligations-based systems, generally, resolve this problem, because they conceptualise judges as duty-bound, by their responsibility to assure a fair trial, to ensure that defendants are properly dressed.[558]

The ECtHR *Hassan* ruling further demonstrates this issue.[559] On 23 April 2003, British forces in Iraq arrested Hassan, who was suspected of being a combatant, in his home and detained him in a joint UK–US camp. In September 2003, Hassan's body was found far away from both the camp and his home. According to British records, camp authorities released Hassan on 2 May 2003, after concluding that he was not a combatant. What happened between May and September remains a mystery.[560]

Deviating from earlier IHRL case law, the ECtHR ruled that during his detention Hassan was under British jurisdiction, despite the detention centre being jointly run by the United Kingdom and the United States.[561] Therefore, *Hassan* is celebrated for its expansive approach to extraterritorial IHRL application. But no human rights protection was extended in *Hassan*. Based on doctrines originating in general international law (*lex specialis* and interpretational harmony), the court ruled that although during hostilities IHRL generally applies alongside IHL, when an issue is addressed by a particular IHL norm, the test for what constitutes an IHRL violation is determined by IHL (IHRL does not add any protection, as it is violated only when the relevant IHL is violated). Because Hassan's detention was ostensibly in accordance with IHL, the Court ruled that Hassan's liberty was not violated.[562] The United Kingdom was also not found to have violated Hassan's right to life, because evidence indicated that he was killed long after having been released.[563]

IHL-based judicial review would have likely held the United Kingdom accountable. IHL demands that States take reasonable measures to ensure the

---

[557]   *Ibid.*

[558]   *Ibid.*

[559]   ECtHR, *Hassan v. United Kingdom*, Grand Chamber Judgment of 16 September 2014, Appeal No. 29750/09.

[560]   *Ibid.*, paras. 10–29.

[561]   Cf. *ibid.*, paras. 78–80 with ECtHR, *Hess v. United Kingdom*, Decision of 28 May 1975, Appeal No. 6231/73.

[562]   ECtHR, *Hassan v. United Kingdom* (n. 559), paras. 96–109.

[563]   *Ibid.*, paras. 62–3.

safe return of released wartime detainees.[564] Accordingly, the British military orders demanded the release of detainees close to their homes, 'in daylight hours'.[565] IHRL's focus on the rights-bearer and his right diverted the judges' attention from legal protections *Hassan* had not demanded and from the release moment, especially because Hassan was killed months later. An IHL-based judicial review, because of its obligations orientation which expects obligation-bearers to be proactive, would have likely taken greater notice of these issues. This would have led such a judicial review to recognise the unviability of the expectation (implicit in the ECtHR ruling) that Hassan (after being interrogated and detained) could have demanded daytime release upon discovering that he would be dropped off at night (according to British records he was dropped off in violation of the British military order at one minute after midnight).[566] Stated differently, an IHL-based judicial review would have, most likely, determined that the British forces violated their IHL obligation to reasonably ensure released detainees' safe return. British disregard of their own standards on the matter strongly indicates that the obligation was violated. Neither Hassan's consent to his night-time release nor the lack of direct link between the release manner and Hassan's death are relevant here.

Admittedly, certain rights-oriented courts would have scrutinised the British actions regarding Hassan's release and certain obligation orientation courts might not have. But narratives frame our thinking, pointing our attention to certain features and away from others.[567] Given this narrative effect, it is *likely* that, had the British forces been scrutinised based on IHL, they would have been more strongly reprimanded.

5. IHL's Status Basis

For centuries a battle was waged between rights and nature-of-things jurisprudence. Only in modern times did rights jurisprudence win, mainly because, unlike nature-of-things jurisprudence, it convincingly argues that all humans are equal.[568] But the focus on equality has its downside. It causes rights-based systems to face conceptual difficulties when attempting to justify agent-relative

---

[564]　ICRC, Customary IHL Rule 128, available at: https://ihl-databases.icrc.org/customary-ihl/e ng/docs/v1_rul_rule128#Fn_81_31ihl-databases.icrc.org/customary-ihl/eng/docs/ v1_rul_rule128.

[565]　ECtHR, *Hassan v. United Kingdom* (n. 559), para. 26.

[566]　*Ibid.*, para. 28.

[567]　See nn. 12–13.

[568]　O'Neill, 'Rights, Obligations and World Hunger' 2008 (n. 109), 145–9; Maine, *Ancient Law* 1908 (n. 109), 64–99.

duties, including those that moral intuition tends to support. Notably, regarding public servants, more demanding duties derive naturally from nature-of-
things rather than rights jurisprudence.[569] This is not to say that similar duties
cannot be constructed based on rights jurisprudence, only that doing so often
entails conceptual difficulties and jurisprudential strains; the result is also
likely to be legally disputed, despite the wide, intuition-based, support for
these duties. To avoid this downside, some legal systems, while adopting the
rights-oriented formative story, have maintained elements of the nature-of-
things jurisprudence in the construction of the formative ethos of certain
public professions (judges, police, soldiers, etc.), and have been using these
profession-specific formative stories to impose certain demanding ethical-legal
duties on such professionals.[570]

Over the last two centuries, even before the recent rise in IHRL influence,
'warrior' narratives' contribution to the shaping of IHL has decreased.[571]
Nonetheless, that contribution remained considerable, enabling using IHL
as a basis for imposing certain demanding ethical-legal soldierly duties.[572] But
IHRL's rising influence on IHL has exacerbated the decrease in the influence
of 'warrior' narratives', which diminishes the ability to use IHL to impose such
duties.[573] The imperfect obligation of 'necessity' – which has long 'impose[d]
residual constraints'[574] (i.e., such that go beyond those of 'humanity') – is now
becoming a 'hollow rule'.[575] 'Chivalry' (military honour) – soldiers' distinct
imperfect obligation – until only few decades ago was still considered a core
IHL principle that contained 'elements that go beyond humanity';[576]
currently, chivalry has been entirely abandoned outside military circles, and
even within these circles some have begun to consider it either anachronistic
or a mere non-legal virtue.[577]

This process comes at a price. Consider the following scenario:
a squad of soldiers approaches a house where enemy soldiers are using
a group of enemy State citizens as human shields. In attempting to take

---

[569] Mary Ann Glendon, *Rights Talk* (New York: Free Press, 1991), 76–108; Alexis de Tocqueville, *Democracy in America*, trans. Francis Brown (Cambridge: Sever & Francis, 1863), vol. II, 263–7.

[570] Glendon, *Rights Talk* 1991 (n. 569), 76–108; James Whitman, 'Enforcing Civility and Respect: Three Societies', *Yale Law Journal* 109 (1999/2000) 1279–1398.

[571] Bordwell, *Law of War between Belligerents* 1908 (n. 98), 112.

[572] Gill, 'Chivalry' 2013 (n. 92), 36.

[573] Antonio Cassese, *International Law* (Oxford University Press, 2005), 402.

[574] Beer, 'Revitalizing the Concept of Military Necessity' 2015 (n. 136), 807–8.

[575] *Ibid.*, 807.

[576] Wallach, 'Pray Fire First' 2012 (n. 161), 432 n. 4 (quoting Garraway).

[577] *Ibid.*, 431–44.

over the house, must the approaching soldiers offset risks posed to the civilians due to the fighting between them and the enemy soldiers by shouldering such risks themselves, and, if so, to what extent? This is only one example of the general combat-related issue of the allocation of combat risks between soldiers and civilians, often referred to as 'force protection'.

When IHRL advocates began propagating the self-evident truth that the right to life continues to apply in wartime, they did not have soldiers' lives in mind.[578] But, thereafter, others advanced the idea that soldiers are people too. According to the most extreme position of this type (the soldiers-first position), because compatriot soldiers are not only humans, with the right to life, but also part of the social compact, 'the State should favor the lives of its own soldiers over the lives of [foreign civilians] when it is operating in a territory that it does not effectively control'.[579] Currently, in rights-based discourse, a wide range of positions exist regarding 'force protection', ranging from soldiers-first to a position demanding that soldiers nearly sacrifice their lives to reduce any risk to civilians, irrespective of the civilians' nationality. Each position proclaims, with some merit, to be the correct IHRL interpretation of the matter.[580]

In contrast, the following is widely considered the customary IHL regulating force protection: 'In taking care to protect civilians, soldiers must accept some element of risk.'[581] This rule is undeniably vague, and a minority disputes that it is customary.[582] But neither this vagueness nor that disagreement lead to indeterminacy that is anywhere near that which arises when force protection is addressed based on IHRL.

The most straightforward normative basis for justifying this customary IHL is to conceptualise it as a legal-ethical professional obligation deriving from 'chivalry'[583] and 'necessity'.[584] Such a conceptualisation originates in the nature-of-things jurisprudence and is still echoed in current military sources,

---

[578] UKSC, *R (Smith) v. Secretary of State for Defence*, Judgment of 20 June 2010, paras. 145–6.

[579] Asa Kasher, 'Operation Cast Lead and Just War Theory', *Azure* 37 (2009), 43–75 (66).

[580] Ziv Bohrer, 'Protecting State Soldiers, Compatriot Civilians or Foreign Civilians: Proportionality's Meanings at the Tactical, Operational and Strategic Levels of War', *Israel Yearbook on Human Rights* 46 (2016), 171–222 (176).

[581] *Ibid.*, 204–6.

[582] *Ibid.*, 208–10.

[583] David Luban, 'Risk Taking and Force Protection', in Itzhak Benbaji and Naomi Sussman (eds.), *Reading Walzer* (Abingdon: Routledge, 2014), 277–301 (285).

[584] Beer, 'Revitalizing the Concept of Military Necessity' 2015 (n. 136), 806–7.

depicting '[t]his risk taking [a]s an essential part of the Warrior Ethos',[585] 'the essence of soldiering'.[586]

Regulating wartime actions solely based on IHL necessarily dismisses the soldiers-first position, whose practical implication is a drastic reduction of civilian protection, because that position violates the most fundamental, status-based IHL distinction: between civilians and combatants.[587] Indeed, the leading scholarly advocate of the soldiers-first position implicitly admitted that his aim is to reshape the IHL principle of distinction by conflating it with rights-oriented notions.[588]

Such conflation is not exceptional. IHRL proportionality analysis was originally designed to assess whether limitations imposed, due to public interests, on the rights of a member of that public, are proportional to the public interests at stake.[589] IHL 'proportionality analysis focuses on the effects of an attack against a legitimate target on surrounding people and objects to assess whether these effects are proportional to the objectives of military necessity at stake'.[590] As Gross demonstrated (through extensive critical examination of relevant case law), simultaneous application of IHL and IHRL leads to the conflation of these distinct proportionality analyses; public interests, other than military necessity, also come to be perceived as legitimate justifications for causing collateral harm: 'expanding the possibilities for limiting the humanitarian standards … beyond what is envisaged in IHL'.[591] Thus, the co-application of IHRL and IHL leads to the conflation of seemingly similar, but actually distinct concepts; the resulting hybrid norms 'provide more rather than less justifications for limiting rights'.[592]

One may respond that the *lex specialis* doctrine could be used to prevent co-application situations that lead to protection-reducing norm conflation. But such an argument ignores the flexible, inconsistent way the *lex specialis* doctrine has been used in IHRL reasoning, leaving it without an acceptable semi-objective meaning.[593] Such treatment stems from the tension inherent in

---

[585]   US Army–Marine Corps, *Counterinsurgency Field Manual* (University of Chicago Press, 2007), para. 7-21.
[586]   Luban, 'Risk' 2014 (n. 583), 285 (quoting an American officer).
[587]   Avery Plaw, 'Distinguishing Drones', in Bradley Jay Strawser (ed.), *Killing by Remote Control* (Oxford University Press, 2013), 62.
[588]   See Asa Kasher and Amos Yadlin, 'Military Ethics of Fighting Terror: An Israeli Perspective', *Journal of Military Ethics* 4 (2005), 3–32 (15); Amos Harel, 'Cast Lead Operation', *Haaretz*, 6 February 2009, available at: www.haaretz.co.il/news/politics/1.1244279 (in Hebrew) (interviewing Kasher).
[589]   Gross, 'New Clothes' 2007 (n. 493), 8.
[590]   *Ibid.*
[591]   *Ibid.*
[592]   *Ibid.*, 8; Aeyal Gross, 'The Righting of the Law of Occupation', in Nehal Bhuta (ed.), *The Frontiers of Human Rights* (Oxford University Press, 2016), 21–54 (23).
[593]   See Milanovic, *Extraterritorial Application of Human Rights Treaties* 2011 (n. 463), 249–60.

IHRL, between exceptionalist and generalist claims, which over time drains non-IHRL legal categories and benchmarks of determinable meaning.[594]

Furthermore, the attempt to cherry-pick IHL and IHRL norms disregards the larger picture. The benefits of massive wartime application of IHRL are overrated: 'experience teaches that introducing human rights analysis ... [does] not generate a jurisprudence granting better protection',[595] rather 'dilute[s] restrictions that are stronger in IHL'.[596] Beyond the dilution-conflation of any particular IHL norm, the massive wartime application of IHRL is 'righting' IHL, gradually causing IHL to cease being an obligations-oriented system. With the loss of that orientation, its benefits (discussed throughout this section) are also lost.

6. Enforcement

One additional argument could be raised for IHRL wartime application. Despite the potential harm from rights-oriented framing of wartime situations, such framing is necessary because otherwise international human rights courts would be unable to address these cases, and wartime actions would be insufficiently judicially scrutinised.[597]

Various domestic courts have dismissed petitions concerning IHL violations on the preliminary ground that IHL, supposedly, consists of State obligations that (as such) do not constitute a legal basis for individuals to raise claims against the violating State.[598] However, from such rulings one should not deduce that a rights-based conceptualisation of IHL is mandatory for juridical scrutiny. The scrutiny-barring element in such rulings stems not from their obligations-based conceptualisation of IHL, rather from their rights-based conceptualisation of the court's judicial review purview. This conceptualisation assumes that individuals have a legal basis to petition the court (aka 'standing') regarding a State's legal violation only when they can show that the violation harmed their rights. In contrast, obligations-based conceptualisation of the court's judicial review purview sees it as stemming from the judiciary's inherent role (and obligation) to maintain the 'rule of law'; as the Israeli Supreme Court held:[599]

---

594 d'Aspremont, 'Expansionism' 2016 (n. 543), 242.
595 Gross, 'New Clothes' 2007 (n. 493), 28.
596 *Ibid.*, 31.
597 See Modirzadeh, 'Dark Sides of Convergence' 2010 (n. 510), 390.
598 See Peters, *Beyond Human Rights* 2016 (n. 120), 218.
599 CA IsrSC, *Arpel-Aluminium v. Kalil*, Judgment of 15 July 1997, No. 733/95.

locking access to the court – either directly or indirectly – and even partially, undermines the judiciary's raison d'être . . . In the absence of judicial review the rule of law collapses . . . Denying access to the court makes judges extinct and in the absence of judges the law itself become extinct.

As the Court further explained, this obligations-based (rule of law) conceptualisation greatly extends standing compared with a rights-based conceptualisation.[600] Accordingly, that Court recognised public petitioners' standing even when they 'cannot claim to have been personally affected . . . [as] part of a broader view of th[e] Court . . . as responsible for the rule of law, even outside the context of resolving individual conflicts'.[601] Likewise, rulings from various countries reveal that when judges maintain this obligations-based (rule of law) conceptualisation of the basis of their judicial review purview – as opposed to a rights-based conceptualisation – they exhibit greater readiness to scrutinise extraterritorial State actions for international law violations (IHL included).[602]

Another more practical reason is usually found at the base of the concern that but for rights-based scrutiny by international human rights courts, wartime actions would not merit sufficient scrutiny. In wartime, domestic courts often assume (voluntarily or under governmental pressure) 'a highly deferential attitude when called upon to review governmental actions'.[603] But that is not necessarily the case, with some current domestic courts exhibiting impressive judicial review capabilities regarding wartime State actions.[604]

Additional domestic courts could be steered away from the deferential mode. This is where the IHRL regime can play a crucial function in IHL's normative universe. As noted, when legal systems settle a jurisdictional dispute, the compromise often includes complementarity or *Solange* mechanisms. An added benefit of such mechanisms is that they reduce the likelihood that the system that was given primacy would shirk its obligation to uphold

---

[600] HCJ, *Ressler* (n. 512), para. 19.
[601] HCJ, *Association for Civil Rights v. Elections Committee Chairman*, Judgment of 21 January 2003, No. 651/03, para. 7.
[602] Chimene Keitner, 'Rights Beyond Borders', *Yale Journal of International Law* 36 (2011) 55–114 (66–8); Galia Rivlin, 'Constitution Beyond Borders', *Boston University International Law Journal* 30 (2012), 135–227 (137–96).
[603] Oren Gross, 'Chaos and Rules: Should Responses to Violent Crises Always be Constitutional?', *Yale Law Journal* 112 (2003), 1011–134 (1034).
[604] For the Israeli example, see Guy Davidov and Amnon Reichman, 'Prolonged Armed Conflict and Diminished Deference to the Military: Lessons from Israel', *Law & Social Inquiry* 35 (2010), 919–56 (922–6). But see Gidi Weitz, 'The Supreme Court Model 2016', *Haaretz*, 28 January 2016, available at: www.haaretz.co.il/magazine/.premium-1.2832782 (in Hebrew).

these core principles. International human rights courts should adopt such a mechanism, declaring that they would not scrutinise a State's wartime actions based on IHRL if the State's domestic courts actively scrutinise those actions based on IHL. Such an approach is likely to increase domestic courts' proactivity and decrease the incentive of the State's political branches to interfere. Given recent practice in human rights courts, States are likely to take seriously these courts' threat to interfere if domestic scrutiny is lacking. Lastly, if these courts are compelled to scrutinise wartime actions, they should (as some of them did in the past) directly apply IHL, without co-applying IHRL, to avoid 'righting' IHL.[605]

7. Back to the Adaptation Approach

Rights-based systems tend to treat the obligation-bearers' obligations merely as means to secure the rights-bearers' rights. In contrast, obligations-based systems conceptualise the obligation-bearers' observance of their obligations as intrinsically valuable.[606] This conceptualisation is based on the premise that moral individuals aspire to act with the right intentions, but because they might be tempted by desires and other biases, an external normative obligation is necessary to ensure that their intentions will remain right.[607] Reliance on imperfect obligations is the most complete expression of this unique perspective.[608] More generally, rights-based systems are only able to maintain obligations that give rise to a corresponding right (perfect obligations); in contrast, obligations-based systems are able to also maintain 'imperfect obligations, which are not allocated to any specified recipients'.[609] In short, reliance on imperfect obligations is a core feature of obligations-based systems.[610]

As noted, IHL is rooted in the imperfect obligation to attempt to reduce wartime suffering as much as possible. Thus, manifestations of this imperfect obligation are expected to be integral to IHL. They should not be easily dismissed as mere (non-legal) policy considerations or as residual juridical tools (to be utilised only when IHRL is silent); especially because IHL has been strongly influenced by jurisprudential positions that regard imperfect obligations as obligatory legal norms.[611] Therefore, obligations-based systems'

---

[605] IACHR, *Abella v. Argentina*, Judgment of 18 November 1997, No. 11.137.
[606] Moodrick-Even-Khen, 'Obligations at the Border Line' 2005 (n. 115), 2–481.
[607] *Ibid.*
[608] *Ibid.*, 507.
[609] *Ibid.*, 508; O'Neill, 'Rights, Obligations and World Hunger' 2008 (n. 109), 152.
[610] Moodrick-Even-Khen, 'Obligations at the Border Line' 2005 (n. 115), 119–22.
[611] Above nn. 119–22.

nature (generally) and IHL's nature (specifically) support the conclusion that the adaptation approach is an integral element of IHL; it is neither a residual juridical tool (secondary to IHRL) nor an optional policy. That approach is a necessary derivative of the imperfect obligation to reduce wartime suffering, which brings about its realisation under the unavoidable indeterminacy that results from the imperfect fit between wartime reality and wartime legal norms.

Embracing the adaptation approach diminishes the proclaimed gap-filling benefits of massive IHRL wartime application. Furthermore, IHRL application requires flexible treatment of legal distinctions and benchmarks, which induces indeterminacy. In contrast, the adaptation approach enhances determinacy, taking advantage of the normative guidance provided by existing IHL, and adding to it an imperfect obligation to 'analogize, insofar as possible [from existing IHL] ... to preserve the intent ... [of] diminish[ing] the evils of war'.[612]

Lastly, is my position anachronistic? My colleague, Helen Duffy, asserts that current opposition to IHRL wartime application is negligible and diminishing, because, although in the past IHRL wartime application 'was seriously questioned, international authority and opinion now overwhelmingly confirms that IHRL continues to apply in times of armed conflict'.[613] I am less certain. History teaches us that IHL's normative universe commonly houses opposing legal positions and, over time, support for each position fluctuates. Do I want IHRL wartime application to be abandoned? If the alternative is normative 'black holes' where States do as they wish – clearly: NO. But if the alternative is the adaptation approach and increased IHL-based judicial scrutiny – unequivocally: YES.

IV. CONCLUSION

One of my teachers repeatedly told a fable about Napoleon. While besieging a town, Napoleon issued an ultimatum to the mayor: if the town wished to surrender, he must immediately sound the church bell, otherwise the French forces would storm the town and execute the mayor. The bell remained silent and Napoleon's forces conquered the town. Begging for his life, the mayor said: 'We wanted to ring the bell, but we couldn't for four reasons'. Napoleon cut him short: 'The truth demands a single explanation; only falsehoods demand plenty.' I always loathed this tale, a bloody version of Occam's

---

[612]   Green, 'United States' 1971 (n. 44), 284.
[613]   Duffy, in this volume, 39.

razor, because, as Immanuel Kant's anti-razor states: 'variety ... should not be rashly diminished'.[614] Reality is complex.

What are the causes for the current abundance of indeterminacies in wartime international law, or for its perception as indeterminate?: (a) the US post-9/11 attempt to remove any legal constraint that might impede the 'global war on terror'; (b) the attempt by hardline IHRL advocates to remove any constraint that might impede universal IHRL application; (c) the blurry nature of wartime activities; (d) the blurry nature of emergency laws; (e) temporocentrism; (f) lawyers conflating *lex lata* and *lex ferenda* in service of their goal; (g) international lawyers constructing war-related crisis narratives; (h) Westphalian Myth residuals; (i) the recent neglect of the adaptation approach. The most accurate answer is: all these reasons, and additional ones, combined.

In a legal paper, one should generally disregard Kant's anti-razor and avoid multi-factor accounts; simple explanations are easily conveyed. But, this time, I feel compelled to crusade for complexity. For two decades, a core jurisdictional struggle has been waging within IHL's normative universe, driven by faction mentality. Each faction's positions are increasingly held by faction members as irrefutable truths; all the while, the struggle diminishes any actual semi-objective element of the law (i.e., its potential ability to have an independent influence on human behaviour), to the point where it would eventually vanish. This chapter is an attempt to push the discourse in the opposite direction. It does so by advocating for the adaptation approach and for accepting inevitable legal, factual and social indeterminacies. More generally, the chapter does so by questioning misleading dominant narratives and by celebrating the complexity of our normative universe: its norms, narratives, processes and people. I have no illusions about universal consensus or about IHL becoming pristinely clear. Indeterminacy and tense engagements are inevitable in a normative universe as diverse as ours. But we have gone too far. A dose of complexity is, therefore, in order.

---

[614]   Immanuel Kant, *Critique of Pure Reason*, trans. Norman Kemp-Smith (London: Macmillan, 1929), 541 (c. 1781, in Latin).

3

Towards a Moral Division of Labour between IHL and IHRL during the Conduct of Hostilities

Janina Dill

I. INTRODUCTION

When should international humanitarian law (IHL) apply? When should it prevail over, and when should it give way to international human rights law (IHRL) in regulating the conduct of hostilities during international and non-international armed conflicts?[1] IHL and IHRL give diverging answers to the crucial question of when it is legally permissible to kill another person. Following the customary IHL principles of distinction, proportionality and necessity systematically leads to breaches of the legal provisions safeguarding the human right to life.[2] Some legal scholars, notably Helen Duffy in this volume, do not acknowledge this norm conflict, but aver that the two bodies of law can be reconciled through interpretation.[3] Those that reject a substantive convergence between IHL and IHRL tend to take one of three broad positions:

---

[1] This chapter focuses on the conduct of hostilities and specifically the rules concerning the permissibility of killing. I say very little about rules on such issues as humanitarian access, detention, internment or belligerent occupation.

[2] When referring to legal rights, I use the terms 'individual rights' and 'human rights' interchangeably. Even though these two categories are not congruent, it is uncontroversial that the right to life, which is at the centre of this investigation, is both an individual and a human legal right (see Joseph Raz, 'Human Rights Without Foundations', in Samantha Besson and John Tasioulas (eds.), *The Philosophy of International Law* (Oxford University Press, 2010), 321–38). When talking about moral rights, I will only use the term 'individual rights' and usually preface it with the designation 'moral' to avoid confusion.

[3] For instance, Louise Doswald-Beck, 'The Right to Life in Armed Conflict: Does International Humanitarian Law Provide all the Answers?', *International Review of the Red Cross* 88 (2006), 881–904; Alexander Orakhelashvili, 'The Interaction between Human Rights and Humanitarian Law: Fragmentation, Conflict, Parallelism or Convergence?', *European Journal of International Law* 19 (2008), 161–82. In a variation of this argument, Hakimi maintains that the two bodies of law can be applied simultaneously, but in instances in which their implications diverge, we should take a functional approach to reconciling them. Monica Hakimi, 'A Functional Approach to Targeting and Detention', *Michigan Law Review* 110 (2012), 1365–420.

many argue that the norm conflict can be resolved by reference to *lex specialis*;[4] others suggest that, in each instance, the rule should prevail that affords greater protection;[5] yet others cast the matter as depending on which rules States intended to apply in a given context.[6]

This chapter, in contrast, treats the question of when IHL should prevail over IHRL as a moral question. That means a moral standard, based on a general theory of the moral purpose of law explained in Section III.A, should determine the applicability scope of a body of law. Specifically, I will argue that when two bodies of law make diverging substantive demands – as IHRL and IHL do – that which better discharges the law's moral tasks should displace the other. The law's two moral tasks, according to this theory, are to guide its subjects' conduct, as often as possible, towards the course of action that conforms to their moral obligations (task one) and to secure the fullest feasible protection of rights in the outcome of conduct (task two). IHL and IHRL's scope of application should be determined by their respective ability to guide individuals towards the fulfilment of their moral obligations and to secure morally desirable outcomes in war.

Both, our moral obligations on the battlefield and the morally desirable outcomes of warfare, centre on fighting without violating the rights of the persons against whom we fight.[7] There are two scenarios in which it can be

---

[4] See, among others, Christopher Greenwood, 'Rights at the Frontier: Protecting the Individual in Time of War', in Barry Rider (ed.), *Law at the Centre: The Institute of Advanced Legal Studies at Fifty* (The Hague: Kluwer Law International, 1999), 277–93; Hans Joachim Heintze, 'On the Relationship between Human Rights Law Protection and International Humanitarian Law', *International Review of the Red Cross* 86 (2004), 789–814; Marco Sassòli, 'The Role of Human Rights and International Humanitarian Law in New Types of Armed Conflicts', in Orna Ben-Naftali (ed.), *International Humanitarian Law and International Human Rights Law* (Oxford University Press, 2011), 34–94.

[5] Cordula Droege, 'The Interplay between IHL and IHRL in Situations of Armed Conflict', *Israel Law Review* 40 (2007), 310–55. In a variation of this argument, Watkin holds that States should by default rely on IHRL when facing non-State belligerents, unless this is operationally infeasible (Kenneth Watkin, *Fighting at the Legal Boundaries* (Oxford University Press, 2016), 606). Ohlin argues that it should depend on whether a State acts in its capacity as sovereign or as belligerent whether IHRL or IHL prevails. Jens David Ohlin, 'Acting as a Sovereign versus Acting as a Belligerent', in Jens David Ohlin (ed.), *Theoretical Boundaries of Armed Conflict and Human Rights* (New York: Oxford University Press, 2016), 118–54 (129).

[6] For instance, Marco Milanovic, 'Norm Conflicts, International Humanitarian Law and Human Rights Law', *Journal of Conflict & Security Law* 14 (2009), 459–83; Daragh Murray, *Practitioners' Guide to Human Rights Law in Armed Conflict*, eds. Elizabeth Wilmshurst, Françoise Hampson, Charles Garraway, Noam Lubell and Dapo Akande (Oxford University Press, 2016), paras. 4.26, 4.31 and 4.37.

[7] A violation of a right is a morally unjustified failure to respect that right. As explained in this paragraph, infringing a right can be morally justified. Rights violations are hence a sub-set of rights infringements. See Judith Jarvis Thomson, 'Some Ruminations on Rights', in

morally justified to infringe an individual's right to life without violating it. First, if an individual A threatens an individual B with morally unjustified harm and B can only defend himself by harming A, then A has forfeited her moral right not to be intentionally harmed through non-performance of her duty not to harm B.[8] A has made herself morally liable to B's defensive harming. Individuals hence forfeit their moral right to life when they responsibly contribute to an unjustified threat and killing them is a necessary and proportionate defensive response. Secondly, besides killing individuals who have forfeited their right to life through their own conduct, it can sometimes be morally justified to override innocent bystanders' moral right to life in order to prevent a greater moral evil, namely, a greater number of unjustified rights violations.[9]

During the conduct of hostilities, law then has the following two moral tasks: its first moral task is to guide soldiers towards directing fire only against individuals who have forfeited their individual moral right to life.[10] If innocent bystanders are expected to be harmed in an attack, law must only permit the attack if overriding their moral right to life is a necessary and proportionate side-effect of the attack's contribution to achieving a morally just war aim.[11] The law's second moral task is to avoid and reduce as much as possible all morally unjustified infringements (i.e., violations) of individual rights in war. I will show that, if we compare IHL and IHRL, IHL's provisions governing the conduct of hostilities further diverge from the principles setting out when it can be morally justified to infringe individual rights.[12] IHL permits a wider

---

William Parent (ed.), *Rights, Restitution, and Risk* (Cambridge, MA: Harvard University Press, 1986), 49–65 (51).

[8] I am referring to forfeiture as a basis for liability to defensive harm rather than as a basis for liability to punishment. For the difference, see Massimo Renzo, 'Rights Forfeiture and Liability to Harm', *Journal of Political Philosophy* 25 (2017), 324–42.

[9] For detailed outlines of this account of the morality of defensive harming, see, among others, Cécile Fabre, *Cosmopolitan War* (Oxford University Press, 2012), 6; Jeff McMahan, 'The Ethics of Killing in War', *Ethics* 114 (2004), 693–732; Seth Lazar, 'The Morality and the Law of War', in Andrei Marmor (ed.), *The Routledge Companion to Philosophy of Law* (London: Routledge, 2012), 364–80.

[10] I use the term 'soldier' to refer to persons in two legal categories: (1) combatants, i.e., all members (other than medical and religious personnel) of armed forces, organised armed groups and units under a command responsible to a State party to a conflict; and (2) individuals with a continuous combat function in an organised armed group not connected to a State party to a conflict, whether in an international or non-international armed conflict. I sometimes refer to persons in the latter category as fighters or as members of non-State armed groups.

[11] As will be discussed further below, a war has a morally just aim if resorting to force is overall the lesser evil in terms of unjustified individual rights infringements.

[12] This divergence is well appreciated among just war theorists. See, among others, Jeff McMahan, 'The Morality of War and the Law of War', in David Rodin and

range of conduct that amounts to individual rights violations than IHRL. This makes IHRL the *prima facie* morally better law for governing hostilities.

However, even though IHRL more faithfully reflects fundamental moral principles, it is not necessarily better at discharging the law's two moral tasks during armed conflict. In situations in which the morally right course of action is systematically difficult to discern (epistemic barriers), a legal rule that diverges from moral prescriptions may be better than one that mirrors these prescriptions at guiding the individual towards what is typically the morally right course of action (task one). In such situations, a rule that does not simply repeat moral principles may also secure a better protection of individual rights in the outcome of conduct (task two). Epistemic barriers to discerning the morally right conduct affect a rule's ability to discharge both of law's moral tasks. In addition, if in certain situations individuals cannot be moved to fully conform to their moral obligations (incurable volitional defects), a legal rule that asks for conduct other than the morally right course of action may generate better moral outcomes (task two). Incurable volitional defects affect a rule's ability to discharge the law's second moral task.

Whether IHRL or IHL should prevail depends on the epistemic and volitional context of decision-making during the conduct of hostilities. In other words, the empirical reality of armed conflict shapes the morally ideal scope of application of IHL and IHRL. I raise the question of whether IHL or IHRL should govern the conduct of hostilities for six types of non-international and international armed conflicts (NIACs and IACs). One of two characteristics distinguishes them from confrontations that do not count as armed conflicts: either the intensity of hostilities or a State's (non-authorised) use of armed force outside its own territory. Armed confrontations count as law enforcement operations rather than armed conflicts if they are neither protracted, meaning hostilities remain below a threshold of intensity discussed in Section V.B, nor involve a State's use of unauthorised force outside its own territory.[13] If hostilities become protracted, but do not involve the unauthorised extraterritorial use of force by a State, they count as NIACs (types 1, 3 and 5a). If hostilities involve a State's armed forces crossing

Henry Shue (eds.), *Just and Unjust Warriors: The Moral and Legal Status of Soldiers* (Oxford University Press, 2010), 19–43; Adam Roberts, 'The Principle of Equal Applicability of the Laws of War', in Rodin and Shue (eds.), *Just and Unjust Warriors*, 226–54; Henry Shue, 'Do We Need a "Morality of War"?' in Rodin and Shue (eds.), *Just and Unjust Warriors*, 87–111.

13 In this chapter, I mostly bracket the question whether, from a moral point of view, IHRL should indeed govern those armed confrontations currently deemed to fall in the category of law enforcement operations rather than armed conflict. Given that IHRL is the morally *prima facie* better law for the regulation of permissible killing, I assume that the answer to this question is yes.

international borders without the authorisation of the territorial State, they currently count as IACs, whether they are protracted or not (types 2, 4, 5b and 6).

I will argue that when hostilities become protracted or cross international borders, IHRL needs to be applied 'symmetrically'. By this I mean that both sides should interpret their obligations under IHRL as if they faced unlawful threats and uses of violence from soldiers on the other side and as if they themselves had lawful aims, regardless of the legal status of their respective resorts to force. I will show in Section V.C that international law on the resort to force does not track moral principles. As a result, if we relied on general international law on the resort to force to determine the lawfulness of soldiers' aims during organised armed violence that crosses international borders, the *ius contra bellum* would often empower the side without a morally just war aim and hamstring the side fighting for a just cause. A State's armed forces crossing borders without the territorial State's consent does not otherwise affect 'symmetrical IHRL's' better ability to discharge the law's two moral tasks. An increase in the intensity of hostilities, in contrast, raises the epistemic barriers to identifying the morally right course of action and it renders more acute incurable volitional defects in soldiers' decision-making. Compared with IHL, 'symmetrical IHRL' nonetheless remains the better law for discharging the law's first moral task. Its ability to discharge the law's second moral task, however, declines as hostilities become protracted.

This analysis leads to the following proposal for a moral division of labour between IHRL and IHL: as the morally *prima facie* better law IHRL should govern the conduct of hostilities in law enforcement operations. In non-protracted IACs, 'symmetrical IHRL' should govern the permissibility of killing. Above the threshold of intensity at which hostilities count as protracted, hence during NIACs and protracted IACs we face a choice between affording individuals a guide towards what is typically the course of action that conforms to their moral obligations (task one) and reducing individual rights violations in the outcome of warfare (task two). 'Symmetrical IHRL' better discharges task one; IHL better discharges task two. It depends on the relative moral costs of prioritising one task over the other as to which body of law should prevail. I will argue that IHL currently offers a better, but far from morally ideal, law for governing the permissibility of killing during the conduct of hostilities, once these hostilities reach the crucial threshold of being protracted. IHL should therefore displace IHRL and govern, on its own, the conduct of hostilities during NIACs and protracted IACs.

An alternative way of thinking about the implications of this argument would be to assert that only protracted armed confrontations should count as armed conflicts in the first place. This would allow us to uphold the traditional under-standing that all armed conflicts should be governed by IHL and all law enforce-ment operations by IHRL, but it would mean redefining IACs as only confrontations among States that are protracted. Instead, I accept the dominant classification of armed confrontations as IACs if they involve the non-consensual crossing of borders by a State's armed forces even if hostilities are not protracted. The implication of the argument for a moral division of labour between IHL and IHRL is then that not all armed confrontations that count as IACs should be governed by IHL. Only those that are protracted should fall under its purview; non-protracted IACs should be governed by 'symmetrical IHRL'. In turn, IACs that are protracted and all NIACs (which *per definitionem* are protracted) should be governed only by IHL. This chapter hence presents a moral argument for the displacement of IHRL during certain types of armed confrontations, rejecting the intellectual coherence of a convergence between IHRL and IHL and the moral desirability of a parallel application of both bodies of law.

The argument proceeds as follows. Section II outlines the substantive conflict between the two bodies of law regarding the conditions of permissible killing. Section III defines the law's two moral tasks and thereby sets the moral standard that later determines which body of law should prevail. It then explores the extent to which IHRL and IHL, respectively, track moral principles about the permissibility of killing. Section IV offers a typology of armed conflicts, high-lighting what characterises six different types of confrontations as armed con-flicts. Section V systematises how these characteristics affect IHRL and IHL's respective ability to discharge the law's two moral tasks. Based on this, I propose a division of labour between the two bodies of law. The concluding section takes stock of the divergence between the current applicability scope of IHL and this morally better division of labour with IHRL.

II. THE HUMAN RIGHT TO LIFE AND THE PERMISSIBILITY OF KILLING ACCORDING TO IHL

A. *IHL and the Rights of Individuals in War*

As argued by Helen Duffy in this volume, it is largely uncontroversial now that IHRL does not simply cease to apply during armed conflict, even if the conflict extends beyond the territory of a State.[14] Indeed, the co-applicability of IHRL and IHL during armed conflict has become the

---

[14] For an affirmation of the extraterritorial applicability of IHRL, see UN Human Rights Committee, General Comment No. 31, Nature of the General Legal Obligation on States

'new orthodoxy'.[15] Co-applicability raises two logically distinct questions.[16] The first is whether the two bodies of law create a substantive conflict, in the sense that following one would systematically lead to or imply a breach of the other. Only if we answer this first question with yes, does the second question even arise: which body of law, or more specifically, which legal rule prevails?[17] One of the most frequently quoted authoritative statements on the relationship between IHL and IHRL conflates these two questions. The ICJ holds that '[i]n principle, the right not arbitrarily to be deprived of one's life applies also in hostilities. The test of what is an arbitrary deprivation of life, however, falls to be determined by the applicable *lex specialis*, namely the law applicable in armed conflict …'[18]

Parties to the Covenant, CCPR/C/21/Rev.1/Add.13 (2004), para. 10. For an affirmation of the applicability of IHRL during armed conflict, see, among others, ICJ, *Legal Consequences of the Construction of a Wall in the Occupied Palestinian Territory*, Advisory Opinion of 9 July 2004, ICJ Reports 2004, 136, para. 106. For a thorough discussion of the international jurisprudence supporting both claims, see Noam Lubell, 'Challenges in Applying Human Rights Law to Armed Conflict', *International Review of the Red Cross* 87 (2005), 737–54. For a dissenting voice against the extraterritorial application of the ICCPR, see Second and Third Periodic Report of the United States of America to the UN Committee on Human Rights Concerning the International Covenant on Civil and Political Rights, Annex I, Territorial Scope of Application of the ICCPR (21 October 2005). For the scholarly position against the applicability of IHRL in armed conflict, see Wolf Heintschel von Heinegg, 'The Rule of Law in Conflict and Post-Conflict Situations: Factors in War to Peace Transitions', *Harvard Journal of Law and Public Policy* 27 (2004), 868–964.

[15] Orna Ben-Naftali, 'Introduction: International Humanitarian Law and International Human Rights Law – Pas de Deux', in Orna Ben-Naftali (ed.), *International Humanitarian Law and International Human Rights Law* (Oxford University Press, 2011), 3–12 (5). For an extensive defence of this position, see also Helen Duffy in this volume, Chapter 1.

[16] The term co-applicability is used in a variety of ways. I will take it to imply merely that IHL and IHRL both apply during the conduct of hostilities in NIACs and IACs. It does not prejudge whether the two bodies of law have diverging implications for action or which prevails over the other.

[17] It is not the purpose of this section to provide another overview of the diverse positions in the legal literature on how IHL and IHRL formally relate to each other – several excellent discussions exist. See, among others, Droege, 'The Interplay between IHL and IHRL' 2007 (n. 5); Duffy in this volume, Chapter 1; Marco Milanovic, 'The Lost Origins of Lex Specialis: Rethinking the Relationship between HR and IHL', in Ohlin (ed.), *Theoretical Boundaries of Armed Conflict* 2016 (n. 5), 78–117; Christian Tomuschat, 'Human Rights and International Humanitarian Law', *European Journal of International Law* 21 (2010), 15–23.

[18] ICJ, *Legality of the Threat or Use of Nuclear Weapons*, Advisory Opinion of 8 July 1996, ICJ Reports 1996, 240, para. 25. For the position that IHL elucidates the meaning of IHRL in armed conflict, see also Magdalena Forowicz, *The Reception of International Law in the European Court of Human Rights* (Oxford University Press, 2010), 314; Tomuschat, 'Human Rights and International Humanitarian Law' 2010 (n. 17).

The ICJ's statement suggests that IHL elucidates the meaning of IHRL in times of war, which would imply that following IHL does not lead to conduct that amounts to a breach of IHRL. At the same time, the statement refers to IHL as *lex specialis*, a tool for resolving a conflict between laws.[19] In this section, I reject the ICJ's position that IHL elucidates what it means to protect human rights in war.[20] I argue instead that IHL and IHRL give diverging answers to the crucial question of when and whom it is permissible to kill during the conduct of hostilities. Complying with IHL, namely, with its customary principles of distinction, necessity and proportionality, leads to conduct that will often violate IHRL. Attacks that are lawful under IHL will regularly deprive individuals of the legal right to life that they hold under IHRL.

Before we compare the substance of the protections afforded to the individual under IHL and IHRL respectively, we need to address the formal question of whether, like IHRL, IHL bestows rights directly onto the individual at all. This remains controversial because IHL, unlike IHRL, does not afford individuals standing before an international court or tribunal tasked with adjudicating violations of IHL.[21] Crucially, the rise to prominence of international criminal law has largely settled any dispute over whether individuals

[19] A more charitable reading of the statement is that the ICJ, unlike much of legal doctrine, considers the rule of *lex specialis* a tool for the avoidance rather than the resolution of conflicts of laws. The ICJ reaffirmed its position in a later Advisory Opinion (ICJ, *Legal Consequences of the Wall* (n. 14), para. 106), but did not mention *lex specialis* in the case of *Congo v. Uganda*. ICJ, *Case Concerning Armed Activities on the Territory of the Congo* (Democratic Republic of the Congo v. Uganda), Judgment of 9 December 2005, ICJ Reports 2005, 168, para. 216.

[20] The most recent Human Rights Committee's Commentary on Art. 6 affirms the ICJ's assertion, stating that the use of 'lethal force authorised and regulated by and complying with international humanitarian law [is], in general, not arbitrary' (UN Human Rights Committee, General Comment No. 36, Art. 6 of the International Covenant on Civil and Political Rights, 'On the Right to Life', para. 64). At the same time, the Commentary suggests that all killing in an aggressive war amounts to a violation of Art. 6 (*ibid.*, para. 70), and it defines arbitrariness in such a way as to make it highly implausible that incidental civilian harm in conformity with IHL is not arbitrary. I return to this issue in the next sub-section.

[21] Of course, an inability to exercise a right is not itself a bar to bearing it. For the *obiter dictum* establishing this position as part of international law, see PCIJ, *The Peter Pázmány University* (Czechoslovakia v. Hungary), Appeal from a Judgment of the Hungaro/Czechoslovak Mixed Arbitral Tribunal, Merits, Judgment of 5 December 1933, PCIJ Series A/B 1933, 61, para. 231. For the view that individuals hold rights directly in virtue of IHL, see Christopher J. Greenwood, 'Historical Development and Legal Basis', in Dieter Fleck (ed.), *The Handbook of International Humanitarian Law*, 2nd edn. (Oxford University Press, 2009), 101–50 (134); Jean S. Pictet, *IV Geneva Convention: Commentary* (Geneva: International Committee of the Red Cross, 1958), 79; Theodor Meron, *The Humanization of International Law* (Oxford University Press, 2000), 240; Rüdiger Wolfrum, 'Enforcement of International Humanitarian Law', in Dieter Fleck (ed.), *The Handbook of International Humanitarian Law*, 2nd edn. (New York: Oxford University Press, 2009), paras. 1401–43 (para. 1434). For contestations of this position, see Françoise Hampson, 'Human Rights Law

incur duties directly by virtue of IHL. IHL imposes obligations on both the belligerent and the individual combatant.[22] A body of law that looks past the State long enough to bestow duties on the individual certainly recognises the latter as a subject for its purposes and by implication an agent capable, in principle, of bearing rights as well.

A textual interpretation of the Geneva Conventions supports the position that IHL indeed bestows some rights directly onto the individual. The four Geneva Conventions feature a common provision that prohibits special agreements among belligerents that would 'restrict the rights which [the Conventions] confer . . . upon' protected persons.[23] All Conventions enjoin protected persons from renouncing 'the rights secured to them'.[24] GCIII and GCIV, which are dedicated to the protection of prisoners and civilians, respectively, use the term 'right' pervasively and contain a long list of procedural[25] and substantive entitlements.[26] This leaves no room for doubt that, once in the power of an enemy belligerent, an individual, whether a civilian or combatant, bears legal rights. At the same time, it is arguably on the battlefield that individuals' fundamental legal rights are most directly threatened.

The First Additional Protocol, the most elaborate and recent legal regime for the conduct of hostilities, recognises a right of combatants to participate in hostilities.[27] However, this cannot be understood as a claim right in the

---

and Humanitarian Law: Two Coins or Two Sides of the Same Coin?', *Bulletin of Human Rights* 1 (1991), 46–54 (49); Kate Parlett, *The Individual in the International Legal System: Continuity and Change in International Law* (Cambridge University Press, 2011).

[22] Greenwood, 'Historical Development' 2009 (n. 21), para. 134.

[23] Articles 6 Convention (I) for the Amelioration of the Condition of the Wounded and Sick in Armed Forces in the Field, Geneva, 12 August 1949, 75 UNTS 31 (hereinafter: GCI); Convention (II) for the Amelioration of the Condition of Wounded, Sick and Shipwrecked Members of Armed Forces at Sea, Geneva, 12 August 1949, 75 UNTS 85 (hereinafter: GCII) and Convention (III) relative to the Treatment of Prisoners of War, Geneva, 12 August 1949, 75 UNTS 135 (hereinafter: GCIII), and Art. 7 Convention (IV) relative to the Protection of Civilian Persons in Time of War, Geneva, 12 August 1949, 75 UNTS 287 (hereinafter: GCIV).

[24] Arts. 7 GCI, GCII and GCIII, and Art. 8 GCIV.

[25] They include rights of defence (Arts. 84, 105 GCIII, Art. 72f GCIV), appeal or petition (Art. 106 GCIII), a fair and regular trial (Art. 174 GCIV), and the right to complain to a protecting power about the conditions under which an individual is being held (Arts. 50, 78 GCIII, Arts. 30, 52, 101 GCIV).

[26] For instance, Arts. 28, 57, 73 GCIII, Arts. 27, 35 GCIV. To the contrary, GCI and GCII, which are concerned with the protection of armed forces in the field and at sea, only mention the right of medical and religious personnel to 'wear the armlet' as a sign that they are immune from attack in Art. 40 GCI and Art. 42 GCIII, respectively.

[27] Article 43(2) Protocol Additional to the Geneva Conventions of 12 August 1949, and relating to the Protection of Victims of International Armed Conflicts (Protocol I), 8 June 1977, 1125 UNTS 3 (hereinafter: API).

Hohfeldian sense because no other subject – a combatant's own State, the enemy belligerent or other individuals – has a duty to not impede a combatant's participation in war. Most recently, Adil Haque has convincingly argued that this 'right' is therefore best thought of as being an immunity from being prosecuted for engaging in hostile actions.[28] Otherwise, the chapters concerned with battlefield conduct are silent on the matter of individual rights either with reference to combatants or civilians. Juxtaposed with several references to the rights of individuals who are under the control of an adverse party to the conflict in the Protocol,[29] this omission of individual claim rights in the chapters on the conduct of hostilities has an air of purposefulness.

Of course, many of IHL's restrictions on the conduct of hostilities evidently benefit individuals. If the substantive protections IHL affords soldiers and civilians were equivalent to those that individuals can claim as rights under IHRL, the formal question of whether or not IHL conceives of these protections as individual claim rights would be less important.[30] However, the observed disjuncture between provisions that regulate behaviour beyond the battlefield and the prescriptions concerned with the conduct of hostilities re-emerges when we inquire into the substance of IHL's principles. The Protocol reiterates many of the substantive protections that the Conventions confer on individuals who are in the hands of the enemy. In contrast, the next two subsections will show that, during hostilities, neither civilians nor soldiers enjoy protections by virtue of IHL that safeguard the human right to life that they hold under IHRL.

B. *IHL and Civilians' Human Right to Life during Hostilities*

During the conduct of hostilities civilians are generally immune from deliberate harming.[31] They are legitimate targets of intentional attack only for such time as they directly participate in hostilities.[32] This might suggest that civilians retain their right to life at least until they decide to directly contribute to

---

[28] Adil A. Haque, *Law and Morality at War* (New York: Oxford University Press, 2017), 28. Subsection D of this section argues that this right can also be considered an authorisation or liberty right in the Hohfeldian sense.

[29] Among others, Arts. 6(2)(a) and (e), 11(5), 32, 44(2), 45(2) and (3), 75(4), 85(4) API.

[30] If we deny that individual combatants or civilians hold rights during the conduct of hostilities, attackers' duties of protection which benefit civilians and, to a lesser extent, combatants could be anchored in rights held by the opposing belligerent. In contrast, some scholars maintain that IHL's duties are not mirrored in rights at all (see Bohrer in this volume, 59). The argument presented here does not hinge on which view is correct.

[31] Article 51(1) API.

[32] Article 51(3) API.

overcoming the enemy. However, according to the principle of proportionality, it is permissible under IHL to injure or kill civilians as a foreseeable side-effect of an attack against a military objective, if the expected 'incidental harm' is not excessive in relation to the military advantage that is anticipated to arise from the attack.[33] Can killing civilians in accordance with the principle of proportionality amount to an unlawful deprivation of the right to life that they hold under IHRL? The following paragraphs show that IHL-compliant proportionate incidental civilian harm is not systematically covered by any of the exceptions to the right to life that IHRL recognises.

One exception to the prohibition on depriving individuals of their human right to life, contained in Article 2(2)(c) ECHR, permits the killing of individuals who threaten others with 'unlawful violence' or who resist or flee from 'a lawful arrest'. The use of lethal force for the purposes of law enforcement is also widely recognised to give rise to an exception to Article 6 ICCPR. Depriving someone of their right to life is non-arbitrary, if it is necessary for the purposes of 'self-defence or the defence of others against the imminent threat of death or serious injury; to prevent a particularly serious crime involving grave threat to life; to arrest a person presenting such danger and resisting their authority; or to prevent his or her escape'.[34] Crucially, these exceptions permit killing individuals who through their own unlawful conduct pose a threat to others. Civilians in war cannot be assumed to have broken the law, whether it is IHL, IHRL or domestic law. These exceptions cannot therefore explain why IHL-compliant incidental civilian harm would systematically be permissible under IHRL.

That civilians have not necessarily broken any laws also means that capital punishment, another recognised exception to the prohibition on depriving individuals of their right to life, cannot explain why incidental civilian harm would comply with IHRL.[35] Of course, it would be ludicrous to bring killing in war in connection with capital punishment, but a closer look at this

---

[33]   Article 51(5)(b) API.

[34]   UN Economic and Social Council, United Nations Principles on the Effective Prevention and Investigation of Extra-legal, Arbitrary and Summary Executions, GA Res. 1989/65 of 24 May 1989, UN Doc. E/1989/89, 9, para. 52; similar Eighth United Nations Congress on the Prevention of Crime and the Treatment of Offenders, Basic Principles on the Use of Force and Firearms by Law Enforcement Officials, GA Res. 45/166 of 18 December 1990, para. 9; UN Human Rights Committee, 'On the Right to Life' 2017 (n. 20), para. 13.

[35]   See Art. 5 (sentence 2) Convention for the Protection of Human Rights and Fundamental Freedoms, Rome, 4 November 1950, 213 UNTS 221 (hereinafter: ECHR); Art. 6(2) International Covenant on Civil and Political Rights, adopted and opened for signature, ratification and accession by General Assembly Resolution 2200A (XXI) of 16 December 1966, 999 UNTS 171 (hereinafter: ICCPR).

exception is useful to elucidate what it means that a deprivation of the right to life is 'non-arbitrary' for the purposes of the ICCPR, in particular. The conditions that make a death sentence non-arbitrary are all oriented towards the goal of giving the defendant his or her individual legal due.[36] The Commentary to the ICCPR demands that 'the personal circumstances of the offender and the particular circumstances of the offence, including its specific attenuating elements must be considered'.[37] Incidental civilian harm in war, in contrast, is not individuated to the circumstances of the civilian that is killed.[38]

Killing civilians as a foreseen side-effect of an attack against a carefully selected and vetted military target may not seem arbitrary in the sense of being random, senseless or purposeless. Moreover, killing civilians in accordance with the principle of proportionality obviously has a basis in IHL and thus in law. However, the most recent UN Human Rights Committee's Commentary on Article 6 ICCPR emphasises that the lawfulness of a rights deprivation is not the sole determinant of whether it is arbitrary. Rather arbitrariness 'must be interpreted ... to include elements of inappropriateness, injustice, lack of predictability, and due process of law'.[39] Appropriateness is often in the eye of the beholder. The next section will argue in detail that IHL does not systematically take account of the moral status of civilians and thus of whether or not their incidental killing is morally justified. Here it warrants reiterating that vetting a target for compliance with IHL does not amount to a process aimed at giving the individual his or her legal due.

Indeed, what makes IHL-compliant incidental civilian harm irrevocably arbitrary for the purposes of IHRL is its unpredictability. Besides the intention of the attacker, the following factors account for the legality of a civilian being deprived of her or his life under IHL: his or her physical proximity to a military target; the military value that the target has at that moment in the attacker's campaign; the blast radius of the weapon the attacker happens to have at their disposal; and the absence of other civilians, who could render the expected incidental harm excessive. With the exception of the civilian's physical proximity to the target, these factors are entirely beyond his or her control.[40] From

---

[36]   See Art. 6(2)(4) and (5) ICCPR.

[37]   UN Human Rights Committee, 'On the Right to Life' 2017 (n. 20), para. 37.

[38]   Furthermore, the Commentary cautions that persons with 'limited moral culpability' must never be subjected to the death penalty (*ibid.*, para. 49). The next section will argue in detail that IHL does not take account of civilians' moral status when determining whether their harming is permissible.

[39]   *Ibid.*, para. 12.

[40]   Even a civilian's physical proximity to a military target does not affect her or his legal status. IHL does not impose on civilians an obligation to move away from military targets. I have made this argument in more detail with regard to the status of civilians who are deemed to

the point of view of the individual that is deprived of his or her life, IHL's permission to kill him or her incidentally is arbitrary in that the individual's legally sanctioned fate is entirely disconnected from – and it cannot be influenced by – his or her legally required conduct.

In addition to these exceptions to the human right to life that are rooted in the individual's own conduct, the ECHR also recognises an exceptional permission to kill individuals who are not themselves legally liable to harming, if this is 'absolutely necessary ... for the purpose of quelling a riot or insurrection'.[41] A legal permission to override rights that is unrelated to the conduct of the affected individual, but instead hinges on necessity is the most likely point of convergence between IHRL and IHL.[42] After all, the First Additional Protocol likewise stipulates that incidental civilian harm has to be necessary. Does the necessity to override an individual right to life in accordance with Article 2(2)(c) ECHR align with the necessity to kill civilians in order to pursue an anticipated military advantage under Article 57(2)(ii) API? No, two differences between necessity in IHL and necessity in IHRL account for why this exception to the human right to life does not systematically cover incidental civilian harm that complies with IHL.

The first difference between IHL and IHRL's necessity exceptions concerns the aim with regard to which necessity has to obtain. Under IHRL necessity confers an exceptional empowerment to override a human right in order to achieve a legitimate aim such as the protection of human life or the protection of public order.[43] In contrast, under IHL killing civilians has to be necessary

---

physically shield military objectives in Janina Dill, 'The DoD Law of War Manual and the False Appeal of Differentiating Types of Civilians', blog post on *Just Security*, December 2016 and Janina Dill, 'Israel's Use of Law and Warnings in Gaza', blog post on *Opinio Juris*, July 2014.

[41] Article 2(2)(c) ECHR. The ICCPR does not recognise an equivalent exception.

[42] Derogations in 'time[s] of public emergency which threatens the life of the nation' follow a similar logic of overriding individual rights in order to avoid what is recognised as a greater legal evil. However, neither the ICCPR nor the ECHR allow derogations from Art. 6 ICCPR and Art. 2 ECHR, respectively (see Art. 4(1) ICCPR and Art. 15 ECHR). Crucially, derogation would be a way to avoid rather than resolve a substantive conflict between IHRL and IHL. When Art. 15(2) ECHR allows deprivations of the right to life 'in respect of deaths resulting from lawful acts of war', it hence implies that IHL authorises deaths that do fall foul of Art. 2. Rather than bringing lawful deaths in war under one of the exceptions to the prohibition on depriving individuals of their right to life in Art. 2, the Convention refers to killing in war in accordance with IHL as a type of derogation from a State's obligations under the ECHR. The conflict between IHRL and IHL outlined here, as far as the ECHR is concerned, could be avoided by derogation. This is not the case for the conflict between the ICCPR and IHL.

[43] UN Human Rights Committee, 'On the Right to Life' 2017 (n. 20), paras. 10, 12; similar UN Human Rights Committee, General Comment No. 35, on Art. 9 of the International Covenant on Civil and Political Rights, 'Liberty and Security of Person', UN Doc. CCPR/

for the pursuit of a military advantage. This is not an emergency measure, but part and parcel of waging war. Notably, IHL does not require that a given military advantage is necessary to win a war. In turn, killing civilians under IHL does not have to be necessary for victory. Even if IHL did demand that incidental civilian harm was necessary also for victory, civilian harm would not automatically be necessary for the achievement of a legally recognised aim as required by the ECHR. To the contrary, at least on one side in each IAC, incidental civilian harm would be permissible because it was necessary for the furtherance of an aim that defies general international law.[44]

The second difference between the meaning of necessity in IHL and the ECHR concerns the epistemic threshold at which we may consider a course of action necessary. In situations in which a reasonable observer perceives an imminent threat to human life, both IHRL and IHL deem overriding a right 'necessary'. Where no such threat exists, the ECHR comes closer than IHL to still taking necessity literally to mean 'lastness'. Under the ECHR, the course of action that overrides an individual right to life has to be the only, in the sense of the mildest, available path to the achievement of the recognised aim.[45] Establishing necessity in this sense means taking steps to ascertain the infeasibility of milder measures and the absence of alternative courses of action.[46] Crucially, if these steps cannot with reasonable certainty determine that overriding individual rights is necessary, the State would not be permitted to proceed.[47] Necessity under the ECHR implies an absolute standard of

---

C/GC/35, 14 December 2014, para. 10. ECtHR, *McCann and Others v. United Kingdom*, Judgment of 27 September 1995, Application No. 18984/9, para. 194.

[44] Under IHL, expected incidental harm has to be not only necessary, but also proportionate/not excessive to the anticipated military advantage. At first glance, this principle of proportionality has no equivalent in IHRL treaty law. The ECtHR has held, however, that the use of lethal force must be proportionate to the aim of protecting human life (ECtHR, *Finogenov and Others v. Russia*, Judgment of 20 December 2011, Application Nos. 18299/03 and 27311/03, para. 210; ECtHR, *McCann and Others v. United Kingdom* (n. 43), para. 194). As in the case of necessity, the aim with regard to which proportionality has to obtain hence differs between IHRL (the protection of human life) and IHL (the pursuit of a military advantage).

[45] The UN Basic principles emphasise that the use of lethal force has to be 'strictly unavoidable' and 'less extreme means' have to be 'insufficient'. See Eighth United Nations Congress on the Prevention of Crime and the Treatment of Offenders, Basic Principles on Use of Force and Firearms by Law Enforcement Officials, GA Res. 45/166 of 18 December 1990, para. 9. See also, ECtHR, *Finogenov and Others v. Russia* (n. 44), para. 208.

[46] See ECtHR, *Isayeva, Yusupova and Bazayeva v. Russia*, Judgment of 24 February 2005, Application No. 57947/00, para. 189; ECtHR, *McCann and Others v. United Kingdom* (n. 43), paras. 148, 150. Any potential violation of the right to life, moreover, triggers a duty on the part of the State to investigate whether it was indeed necessary. *Ibid.*, para. 161.

[47] ECtHR, *Finogenov and Others v. Russia* (n. 44), para. 208.

minimum reasonable knowledge about the alternatives to and consequences of conduct that overrides human rights.

Under IHL, the epistemic threshold at which a commander may assert that an attack is without alternative is much lower. Article 57(3) API demands that '[w]hen a choice is possible between several military objectives for obtaining a similar military advantage' the attacker shall select the objective that can be attacked with the least expected incidental harm. This is not usually interpreted to mean that an attacker has to actively search as far and wide as reasonably possible for alternative targets with better expected incidental harm prognoses.[48] An attacker's required knowledge about the consequences of an attack hinges on the feasibility of acquiring this knowledge. An attacker has to 'take all feasible precautions in the choice of means and methods of attack with a view to avoiding, and in any event to minimizing, incidental loss of civilian life'.[49] That may often mean that an attacker explores the possibility of further reducing expected civilian casualties. However, equally as often, few or no measures to explore civilian harm mitigation may be feasible.

Crucially, an attacker is permitted to launch an attack even if all feasible verification measures were insufficient to establish with reasonable certainty that the expected incidental civilian harm could not have been further reduced while still achieving the military advantage at stake.[50] Although doing 'everything feasible' appears to be a demanding legal standard, it makes the level of knowledge required under IHL contingent on the circumstances of an attack.[51] It follows that complying with IHL does not vouchsafe that a reasonable observer (with reasonably sufficient knowledge about the

---

[48] Noam Neuman, 'Applying the Rule of Proportionality: Force Protection and Cumulative Assessment in International Law and Morality', *Yearbook of International Humanitarian Law* 7 (2004), 79–112 (98).

[49] Article 57(2)(ii) API.

[50] I have argued elsewhere in more detail that under IHL an attacker does not incur a robust duty of care to ensure that incidental civilian harm is truly necessary for the pursuit of a given military advantage. See Janina Dill, 'Do Attackers have a Legal Duty of Care? Limits to the "Individualization of War"', *International Theory* 11 (2019), 1–25.

[51] What the obligation to take precautions in attack requires in practice is subject to considerable controversy. The United Kingdom Law of War Manual acknowledges the legal uncertainty: 'The Law is not clear as to the degree of risk that the attacker must accept' (UK Ministry of Defence, *Manual of the Law of Armed Conflict* (Oxford University Press, 2004), 25, para. 2.7.1). For the range of views on this matter, see, among others, Eyal Benvenisti, 'Human Dignity in Combat: the Duty to Spare Enemy Civilians', *Israel Law Review* 39 (2006), 81–109; Yoram Dinstein, *The Conduct of Hostilities under the Law of International Armed Conflict* (Cambridge University Press, 2016), 168; Adil A. Haque, 'Killing in the Fog of War', *Southern California Law Review* 86 (2012), 63–116; David Luban, 'Risk Taking and Force Protection', in Yitzhak Benbaji and Naomi Sussman (eds.), *Reading Walzer* (London: Routledge (online edn.), 2011), 277–301 (277).

alternatives and consequences of an attack) deems the expected incidental civilian deaths the only possible path to the achievement of a given military advantage. This, however, is the connection between expected casualties and a military advantage that IHRL would require if achieving a military advantage was equivalent to a lawful aim recognised under IHRL.[52]

The jurisprudence of the European Court of Human Rights (ECtHR) corroborates the argument that incidental civilian harm permitted under IHL is not systematically covered by the ECHR's permission to exceptionally override an innocent bystander's right to life.[53] The Court has ostensibly drawn on IHL's requirement to take precautions in attack when elucidating the meaning of a necessary deprivation of the right to life in contexts of large-scale organised violence.[54] At the same time, the Court has mostly stayed faithful to the strict necessity standard of IHRL.[55] It has regularly enquired into the legitimacy of the aim behind the State's use of violence.[56] Moreover, judgments feature not only questions about the availability of milder means, but also about the care devoted to exploring the latter.[57] A close reading of Article 57 API leaves little room for doubt that the Court has thereby asked for

---

[52] I have argued above that these aims are not equivalent.

[53] For the general claim that necessity is stricter in IHRL than in IHL, see also Lawrence Hill-Cawthorne, 'The Role of Necessity in International Humanitarian and Human Rights Law', *Israel Law Review* 47 (2014), 225–51; Niels Melzer, *Targeted Killing in International Law* (Oxford University Press, 2008), 228; Jens David Ohlin, 'The Duty to Capture', *Minnesota Law Review* 97 (2013), 1268–315 (1298 *et seq.*); Jens David Ohlin and Larry May, *Necessity in International Law* (Oxford University Press, 2016), 273.

[54] Most notably in ECtHR, *Isayeva, Yusupova and Bazayeva v. Russia* (n. 46), paras. 168, 743. See also ECtHR, *Ergi v. Turkey*, Judgment of 28 July 2008, Application No. 23818/94, para. 79 *et seq.*; ECtHR, *Ozkan v. Turkey*, Judgment of 6 April 2004, Application No. 21689/93, paras. 305–6. Note that in *Isayeva* the Court explicitly casts the operation as a law enforcement operation 'outside of armed conflict'. *Ibid.*, *Isayeva, Yusupova and Bazayeva v. Russia* (n. 46), para. 191.

[55] For the argument that the standard of necessity that the Court employs across these cases is not uniform, but relaxed in situations of more intense hostilities to resemble an IHL standard, see Cordula Droege, 'Elective Affinities? Human Rights and Humanitarian Law', *International Review of the Red Cross* 90 (2008), 501 (532).

[56] ECtHR, *Isayeva, Yusupova and Bazayeva v. Russia* (n. 46), para. 200; ECtHR, *Finogenov and Others v. Russia* (n. 44), para. 219; ECtHR, *Case of Kerimova and Others v. Russia*, Judgment of 15 September 2011, Application Nos. 17170/04, 20792/04, 22448/04, para. 248. For the interesting point that this insistence on a legitimate aim is akin to regulating the resort to force by a State within its own territory, see Eliav Lieblich, '"Internal" Jus Ad Bellum', *Hastings Law Journal* 67 (2016), 687–748.

[57] For instance, ECtHR, *Isayeva, Yusupova and Bazayeva v. Russia* (n. 46), para. 200; ECtHR, *Kerimova and Others v. Russia* (n. 56), para. 253; similar David Kretzmer, 'Rethinking the Application of IHL in Non-International Armed Conflict', *Israel Law Review* 42 (2009), 23–31 (30); Noëlle Quénivet, 'The Right to Life in International Humanitarian Law and Human Rights Law', in Roberta Arnold and Noëlle Quénivet (eds.), *International Humanitarian Law*

more care towards persons not directly participating in hostilities than would be required under IHL.

C. IHL and Soldiers' Human Right to Life during Hostilities[58]

IHL permits intentional lethal attacks against combatants and members of organised armed groups who have a continuous combat function,[59] hence against persons who regularly participate in hostilities.[60] Could their participation in hostilities, even if it conformed to the principles of IHL, be considered unlawful so that their threat or use of violence might trigger an exception to their human right to life? Individuals fighting for an organised armed group against their own State are indeed likely in breach of their domestic legal obligations.[61] In an internal NIAC, when the State attacks enemy fighters, it thus deprives individuals of their right to life who engage in violence that is unlawful under domestic law. If an intervening State is authorised by the territorial State to use force against members of an organised armed group, it may also often be true that the latter's fighters have defied the territorial State's laws by taking up arms against a third State. We cannot assume this to be the case if an intervening State wages war against an

---

and Human Rights Law: Towards a New Merger (Leiden: Brill/Martinus Nijhoff, 2008), 331–53 (341). For an example of the application of this strict necessity standard outside the Court's case law, see First Public Commission to Examine the Maritime Incident of 31 May 2010, para. 232.

[58]   To recall, as discussed in Section I, the term 'soldiers' refers to combatants and to individuals with a continuous combat function who are members of organised armed groups not connected to a State party to a conflict.

[59]   An individual who is a member of an organised armed group assumes a 'continuous combat function' if his or her role 'involves the preparation, execution, or command of acts or operations amounting to direct participation in hostilities' (Niels Melzer, *Interpretive Guidance on the Notion of Direct Participation in Hostilities under IHL* (Geneva: International Committee of the Red Cross, 2010), 34). Even though the term was originally meant to designate individuals fighting for a non-State party in a NIAC, I use it to include individuals with similar roles in organised armed groups not belonging to any State party to an IAC.

[60]   I exclude from the discussion in this sub-section civilians who directly, but temporarily, participate in hostilities, including members of organised armed groups without a continuous combat function.

[61]   Similar Marco Sassòli, 'Jus ad Bellum and Jus in Bello – The Separation between the Legality of the Use of Force and Humanitarian Rules to be Respected in Warfare: Crucial or Outdated?', in Michael N. Schmitt and Jelena Pejic (eds.), *International Law and Armed Conflict: Exploring the Faultlines* (Leiden: Martinus Nijhoff, 2007), 242–64 (248). Members of organised armed groups, not recognised or associated with any State belligerent in an IAC, are likewise likely in breach of the domestic law of the State on whose territory they fight when they threaten or use violence.

organised armed group without the territorial State's consent.[62] Furthermore, we have no reason to believe that combatants fighting for a State party to a conflict have broken the domestic law applicable to them.

When it comes to the lawfulness of the use of force by combatants, rather than relying on domestic law, we could draw on general international law (namely, the *ius contra bellum*) to establish whether and when IHL-conforming participation in hostilities amounts to an unlawful threat or use of violence for the purposes of IHRL. Namely, we could argue that combatants who contribute to a State's use of force in contravention of Article 2(4) UN Charter and corresponding customary law are using violence unlawfully, even if it accords with IHL. In this reading, participation in a legal (defensive or mandated) IAC would *prima facie* leave intact combatants' right to life under IHRL. At the same time, none of the violence threatened or used by combatants on the side of the aggressor State would be lawful for the purposes of IHRL, even if it complied with the principles of IHL. Participation in hostilities on the side of an aggressor State would thus open a combatant to the permissible deprivation of their human right to life.

Of course, IHL permits attacks against combatants on all sides in an IAC, regardless of the status of a belligerent's resort to force. More importantly, it is highly problematic to suggest that general international law could trigger an exception to the prohibition on depriving individuals of their human right to life. This would amount to anchoring an individual's legal status under IHRL in the conduct of her or his State, over which she or he has likely little or no control.[63] Nonetheless, the United Nations Committee on Human Rights, in its recent commentary on Article 6, has endorsed a view that links the lawfulness of States' use of violence on the battlefield to the status of the resort to force under general international law. Though not addressing the implications of this stipulation for the status of individual combatants, the Committee has argued that '[s]tates parties engaged in acts of aggression as

---

[62] It is an unsatisfying legal situation that it may well depend on the political relationship between the territorial State and an organised armed group that threatens another State, whether or not the IHL-conforming attacks by the latter against members of the organised armed group violate these members' right to life under IHRL because the organised armed group is considered in violation of domestic law.

[63] It is noteworthy that IHL is agnostic as to whether individuals consent to assuming combatant status or whether they are conscripted, coerced or forced by circumstances. We might think that individuals who assume a continuous combat function in an organised armed group have made a free choice to do so. For the argument that this is not universally true either, see Center for Civilians in Conflict, *The People's Perspectives: Civilian Involvement in Armed Conflict* (New York: CIVIC, 2015), 50.

defined in international law [...] violate *ipso facto* Article 6 of the Covenant'.[64]

Even if a State's breach of the *ius contra bellum* could in principle trigger a permission to deprive an individual of his or her right to life under IHRL, even combatants whose IHL-compliant participation in hostilities contributed to waging an aggressive war would not necessarily have lost their human right to life. Depriving an individual who threatens another with unlawful violence of their right to life has to be necessary under IHRL.[65] Lethal attack has to be the last resort. IHL's permission to intentionally kill combatants at all times, except when they are *hors de combat*, on the other hand, is not tied to combatants' in fact using violence or posing a threat. The same is widely deemed to be true for members of organised armed groups with a continuous combat function.[66] Lethal attack against them can be the intended and planned first resort. Recent scholarly claims that IHL requires that killing soldiers is necessary[67] have been roundly rejected.[68]

IHRL's exceptional permission to override an individual's human right to life for the purposes of 'quelling an insurrection or emergency' or 'establishing public order' does not cover IHL's permission to intentionally kill soldiers either. IHRL again requires necessity, as discussed in the previous sub-section. Although combatants can through their conduct gain immunity from attack, namely, by surrendering,[69] no particular conduct on their part is required for

---

[64] Human Rights Committee, 'On the Right to Life' 2017 (n. 20), para. 70.

[65] Even though the principle of proportionality is not mentioned in the ECHR or the ICCPR, it is well established that in a law enforcement context, the use of force ought to be not only necessary, but also proportionate to the threat and the gravity of the offence (Lubell, 'Challenges in Applying Human Rights Law' 2005 (n. 14), 745). IHL, in contrast, does not recognise a proportionality restriction on the use of force against combatants or members of organised armed groups with a continuous combat function.

[66] For a critique of the continuous combat function as extending status-based targeting to individuals who are not combatants, see Philip Alston, Report of the Special Rapporteur on Extrajudicial, Summary or Arbitrary Executions, A/HRC/14/24/Add.6 (28 May 2010), para. 65.

[67] For this claim, see Melzer, *Interpretive Guidance* 2010 (n. 59), part I, recommendations VII and IX; Quénivet, 'The Right to Life' 2008 (n. 57), 340.

[68] Michael N. Schmitt, 'Military Necessity and Humanity in International Humanitarian Law: Preserving the Delicate Balance', *Virginia Journal of International Law* 50 (2010), 795–839; Michael N. Schmitt, 'The Interpretive Guidance on the Notion of Direct Participation in Hostilities: a Critical Analysis', *Harvard National Security Journal* 1 (2010), 5–44. For the argument that IHL *ought* to contain such a demand, see Gabriella Blum, 'The Dispensable Lives of Soldiers', *Journal of Legal Analysis* 2 (2010), 69–124; Janina Dill, 'Forcible Alternatives to War', in Ohlin (ed.), *Theoretical Boundaries of Armed Conflict* 2016 (n. 5), 289–314 (301).

[69] Individuals with a continuous combat function can more easily gain immunity from attack by opting out of this function or renouncing membership in the organised armed group.

IHL to endorse their killing in the first place.[70] IHL's provision that is most directly geared towards benefiting combatants who are not already *hors de combat* is the prohibition on employing 'weapons, projectiles and material and methods of warfare of a nature to cause superfluous injury or unnecessary suffering'.[71] This provision shines a glaring light on IHL's endorsement of virtually all intentional attacks against soldiers; its endorsement of conduct that will often amount to a deprivation of the soldiers' right to life in contravention of IHRL.

D. IHL's Authorisation of Conduct that Amounts to a Human Rights Violation

Some scholars argue that we can avoid the problematic conclusion that IHL authorises violations of IHRL by claiming that IHL is only 'prohibitory' and does not confer any authorisations at all. In this reading, the principle of proportionality is merely the absence of a prohibition on proportionate incidental civilian harm, not a legal liberty to cause foreseen non-excessive harm to civilians. Moreover, in this view, rather than a legally privileged course of action, killing combatants is conduct that IHL has simply omitted to outlaw. This interpretation is surprising because the Geneva Conventions as well as the Protocols contain a number of demands for positive causal interventions into the world, for instance, taking all feasible measures to minimise incidental harm or issuing a warning before an attack. Conduct meant to meet these requirements is surely, by logical implication, imbued with the authority of a legal permission. Nonetheless, this interpretation of the principles of distinction, proportionality and necessity as mere prohibitions is frequently stated rather than defended.[72] The two most convincing explanations ultimately both fall short.

---

[70] Even if an individual's prior consent could render his or her killing human rights-conforming, IHL would not vouchsafe that individuals who are permissible targets of intentional attack have forfeited their right to life. As adumbrated, IHL does not regulate the conditions under which States assign individuals the status of combatant. Predictably, IHL does not require that an attacker enquires into an individual's motives or potential consent in the course of establishing their continuous combat function either.

[71] Article 35(2) API.

[72] By way of explanation, many scholars do not point to the history, text, practice or structure of IHL, but to the observation that such an authorisation of force would challenge principles of justice, because IHL would authorise conduct that may well further an illegal or unjust aim. This is an interpretive path to the elucidation of what the law is that many of these scholars would otherwise eschew. For instance, John Westlake, *International Law: Part II War* (Cambridge University Press, 1907), 52.

Adil Haque maintains that IHL affords combatants immunity from prosecution for participation in hostilities. However, it cannot grant combatants an
authorisation to participate in hostilities because it does not 'authorize organized armed groups to kill State armed forces or to harm civilians'.[73] He holds
that this lack of authorisation for organised armed groups is evident because
members of organised armed groups are subject to domestic criminal prosecution for participation in hostilities. IHL cannot then authorise combatants
fighting for States, lest the principle of equal applicability is in jeopardy.[74]
This reasoning rests on four claims which are unlikely to be simultaneously
true: first, members of (non-State) organised armed groups are not authorised
to use force because they are not immune from prosecution for participation
in hostilities; secondly, combatants are not authorised to use force because
a divergence in formal authorisations between combatants and members of
non-State armed groups would challenge belligerent equality; thirdly, even
though they are not authorised to participate in hostilities, combatants are
immune from prosecution for participation in hostilities; fourthly, this divergence in immunities between combatants and members of non-State armed
groups does *not* challenge belligerent equality.

Let us assume that members of non-State organised armed groups are
indeed neither immune from prosecution nor authorised to use force (claim
one), but combatants are both. Only in NIACs would this asymmetry in
authorisations create an inequality among belligerents (claim two). In IACs,
claim two would not hold. IHL allows States to incorporate or recognise
paramilitaries or irregular armed groups.[75] This, in turn, confers the immunities and authorisations associated with combatant status on their members.[76]
Individuals who fight in an IAC as members of an organised armed group
without the backing of a State party share their lack of immunity from
prosecution, and, in Haque's view, the attending lack of authorisation to use
force, with civilians who temporarily directly participate in hostilities, spies
and mercenaries. As this fate befalls these groups of individuals on any side of
an IAC, it does not affect the equal applicability of IHL.[77]

---

[73]   Adil A. Haque, 'International Law in Armed Conflict', blog post on *Just Security*,
       23 November 2016.
[74]   *Ibid.*
[75]   Article 43 API.
[76]   Article 43(1) API.
[77]   Organised armed groups fighting in their own right in an IAC, without the backing of a State
       party to the conflict are a recent phenomenon. Nothing indicates that API would deem such
       an organised armed group a party to the conflict to which it seeks to extend the equal
       applicability of IHL enshrined in the preamble of the treaty.

In NIACs, on the other hand, if members of the State's armed forces were authorised to use force and a lack of immunity from prosecution meant that members of (non-State) organised armed groups were not authorised to use force, an inequality among belligerents would indeed follow. However, the equality IHL affords belligerents in wars that pit a State against a non-State actor has arguably always been, and necessarily remains, qualified.[78] This qualification is evidenced not least in the asymmetry in immunities that Haque affirms in claim three: he holds that IHL affords immunity for combatants' participation in hostilities (claim three), but his claim that IHL does not authorise participation in hostilities rests on the observation that IHL does not afford such immunity for participation to members of non-State organised armed groups. If in NIACs an asymmetry in immunities does not undermine belligerent equality (claim four), why should an asymmetry in formal authorisations to use force have this effect?

Even if we insisted on full belligerent equality also in NIACs, it would still not follow that IHL does not authorise killing in NIACs or indeed in IACs. In NIACs it is plausible to contest that IHL provides immunity from prosecution even for combatants fighting on behalf of the State. Article 6(5) APII urges the authorities in power at the end of hostilities to grant amnesty to persons who have participated in hostilities. Note that the provision refers to the 'authorities in power' at the end of hostilities, not the High Contracting Party. The Protocol evidently envisages the possibility that the regime challenger prevails and prosecutes soldiers who started out as combatants fighting on behalf of the State. The treaty hence acknowledges that in NIACs, IHL can afford immunity from prosecution to neither side. This is consistent with the absence in APII of a provision spelling out a 'right' of the State's combatants to participate in hostilities. If we think of lack of immunity from prosecution as indicative of a lack of authorisation to use force, we could hence conclude that APII indeed does not authorise either side to use violence. Alternatively, the Protocols' plea for immunity from prosecution under domestic law may simply not be indicative of whether IHL authorises participation in hostilities at all. In either case, nothing much follows for our interpretation of API and IHL's permissions in IACs. The difference between the two treaties – APII lacks most of the provisions on the conduct

---

[78]   For the argument that the principle of equality among belligerents does not apply in NIACs, see Doswald-Beck, 'The Right to Life in Armed Conflict' 2006 (n. 3), 881–904 (903). For the argument that belligerent equality is much weaker in NIACs, see Jonathan Somer, 'Jungle Justice: Passing Sentence on the Equality of Belligerents in Non-International Armed Conflict', *International Review of the Red Cross* 89 (2007), 655–90 (659 *et seq.*).

of hostilities that I argue authorise attacks – means that something that is true for APII does not by logical implication hold for API.[79]

Derek Jinks offers a different argument, unrelated to belligerents' power to prosecute individual soldiers, for why IHL does not authorise the attacks that do not defy it. He maintains that the Geneva Conventions cannot be 'read like domestic statutes' because they do not 'authorize states to engage in practices otherwise forbidden in law'.[80] It is not at all obvious, however, why international law should only be able to authorise conduct as an exception to its own prior prohibition. This evokes a bilateralist international system, in which States start out as utterly unfettered sovereigns whose actions are deemed acceptable unless expressly prohibited by international law. This view radically challenges dominant understandings of the contemporary international legal order.[81] Crucially, even if we subscribed to the view that all State conduct not prohibited by international law is permissible, we would not necessarily have to endorse the position that international law is *only* prohibitory. As a matter of logic, nothing would prevent international law from endowing with the legitimacy of a legal permission conduct that a State could otherwise have engaged in without either violating or actualising a legal rule.

Jinks' contention that IHL does not concern practices otherwise forbidden under international law is all the more astonishing because he is a proponent of the co-applicability of IHL and IHRL, but denies their convergence.[82] Jinks endorses the view that before conflicts of laws are resolved or a State derogates, during war, IHRL prohibits any and all deprivations of the right to life that do not meet any of its own recognised exceptions (for co-applicability). He also correctly deems 'perverse' the ICJ's view that IHL elucidates the meaning of such exceptions and that all killing in war permitted, or in his view not prohibited, by IHL does not violate IHRL (against convergence). Logically, IHL's principles for the conduct of hostilities then govern practices that are already heavily regulated by international law, namely, by IHRL. The conduct

---

[79]   The regimes for IACs and NIACs are now widely argued to converge as a matter of custom. This conclusion would therefore raise the question of whether the principles for the conduct of hostilities now deemed applicable in NIACs are indeed 'only prohibitory' there, even though they authorise the corresponding acts in IACs.

[80]   See Derek Jinks, 'International Human Rights Law in Time of Armed Conflict', in Andrew Clapham and Paola Gaeta (eds.), *Oxford Handbook of International Law in Armed Conflict* (Oxford University Press, 2014), 656–74 (666).

[81]   See, for instance, Jean Cohen, 'Sovereignty in the Context of Globalization: A Constitutional Pluralist Perspective', in Besson and Tasioulas (eds.), *The Philosophy of International Law* 2010 (n. 2), 261–82 (262).

[82]   Jinks, 'International Human Rights in Time of Armed Conflict' 2014 (n. 80), 688.

of hostilities is rife with 'prior prohibitions',[83] to which IHL could be deemed to afford exceptions.

Even if the argument that killing in compliance with IHL is not formally authorised by IHL were compelling, we would still face a legal situation in which IHRL prohibits conduct that IHL does not prohibit. A denial of IHL's authorisation of violence does not at all answer the question as to which body of law an individual on the battlefield ought to turn to for guidance. Moreover, regardless of whether IHL formally authorises the conduct that it does not prohibit, we have to grapple with the considerable expressive force of the uncontested legal situation that IHL does not prohibit intentional killings of soldiers and foreseen side-effect deaths of civilians.[84] The traditional reference to 'belligerent privilege' suggests that, scholarly debate notwithstanding, military practitioners widely assume that IHL endorses the attacks that do not defy it; attacks that will often breach IHRL, depriving civilians and sometimes soldiers of the right to life they enjoy under IHRL.

III. THE MORAL RIGHT TO LIFE AND THE LEGAL PERMISSIBILITY OF KILLING IN WAR

A. *The Law's Moral Tasks in War*

When two simultaneously applicable bodies of law make diverging demands, the morally better law should prevail. How do we decide which one is the morally better law? Largely side-stepping the extraordinarily complex question of how law conceptually relates to morality, I make two assumptions: first, the content of law can be determined without reference to morality. It is hence possible that law makes demands on its subjects that diverge from their moral duties. Secondly, individuals have a moral interest in the rule of law 'because human life goes better when subjected to governance by a (conscientious) authority'.[85] Legality therefore provides a moral reason for action. This reason

---

[83]   Even if we demanded that those prior prohibitions were anchored in IHL, in the case of the principle of proportionality, IHL creates what is in effect an exception to its own prohibition on targeting civilians intentionally. That this exception is likewise formulated as a prohibition on overstepping the limits of the exception does nothing to lessen the endorsement that, by logical implication, IHL affords conduct that does not fall foul of the prohibition.

[84]   For the concept of the law's expressive force and the argument that law does not only govern by means of formal authorisation and sanction, but also by 'shap[ing] individual preferences by changing one's taste for specific outcomes', see Elizabeth Anderson and Richard Pildes, 'Expressive Theories of Law: a General Restatement', *University of Pennsylvania Law Review* 148 (2000), 1503–75.

[85]   Joseph Raz, *Between Authority and Interpretation: On the Theory of Law and Practical Reason* (Oxford University Press, 2009), 173.

is not decisive. It may sometimes be morally impermissible to obey a wicked law. At the same time, a morally wrongful act can be less wrongful because it is required by law.[86] With these assumptions, I rely on Raz' conceptualisation of law as 'a kind of complex social practice [that] can be put to moral use, and that, where it exists ... has moral tasks to discharge'.[87]

What are the law's tasks through the performance of which it can morally improve human life? In Raz' view, a law exercises legitimate authority over its subjects if the latter better conform to the moral reasons that apply to them when they act according to the guidance of the law.[88] Law can provide a moral service to the individual by assisting him or her in adopting the morally right conduct. This is the law's first moral task. Crucially, this ability to guide the individual towards fulfilment of her or his moral obligations does not exhaust the law's ability to morally improve human life. Law can also serve the individual as a guarantor of her or his moral rights. Law can be of moral use to each individual by ensuring that the conduct of legal subjects overall better conforms to the moral goal of preserving individual rights. Guiding behaviour towards the fullest possible protection of individual rights is the law's second moral task.[89]

---

[86]   Buchanan speaks of a 'content-independent' reason to obey rules that emanate from legitimate institutions. This reason has to be considered alongside content-dependent reasons for or against compliance (Allen Buchanan, 'The Legitimacy of International Law', in Besson and Tasioulas (eds.), *The Philosophy of International Law* 2010 (n. 2), 79–98 (82)). Some scholars hold that the content-independent reason to obey legitimate rules is decisive (for instance, John Tasioulas, 'The Legitimacy of International Law', in Besson and Tasioulas (eds.), *The Philosophy of International Law* 2010 (n. 2), 97–118 (98)). Not least because the procedural legitimacy of international legal rules cannot universally be assumed, and I do not discuss it here, I maintain that the content-independent reason to obey a law is not decisive and can be defeated by stronger moral reasons.

[87]   Raz cautions that 'we cannot say that in its historical manifestations through the ages [law] has always, or generally, been a morally valuable institution, and we can certainly not say that it has necessarily been so'. Raz, *Between Authority and Interpretation* 2009 (n. 85), 179.

[88]   Joseph Raz, 'The Problem of Authority: Revisiting the Service Conception', *Minnesota Law Review* 90 (2006), 1003–44.

[89]   In his recent account of how IHL relates to the morality of war, Haque rejects the relevance of the second moral task for our moral assessment of IHL. He equates a Razian 'service view' of law with the task of guiding the individual towards the fulfilment of his or her moral duties in war and offers a detailed critique of IHL in the light of this moral goal (Haque, *Law and Morality at War* 2017 (n. 28)). Dill and Shue's account of the moral justification of IHL, in contrast, only focuses on IHL's second task of producing the best possible outcome for rights, i.e., a minimisation of unjustified infringements of individual rights in war overall (Janina Dill and Henry Shue, 'Limiting Killing in War: Necessity and the St. Petersburg Assumption', *Ethics and International Affairs* 26 (2012), 311–34). Building on both works, I show exactly how and where these two tasks make divergent demands on the rules of warfare. If we treat both tasks as *prima facie* equally important, the morally best possible rules for conduct in war offer a compromise, as discussed in the last section of this chapter.

When there is a conflict between simultaneously applicable legal rules, we should allow those rules to prevail that better accomplish these two moral tasks. The first step in determining whether IHL or IHRL ought to govern the conduct of hostilities is then to establish what moral obligations apply to the individual on the battlefield and what battlefield conduct leads to the best possible outcome in terms of protecting individual rights.[90] Ordinarily we forfeit our moral right to life only when we responsibly contribute to an unjustified threat against another person.[91] The defensive harm we make ourselves liable to by virtue of this conduct has to be proportionate and necessary to avert the unjustified threat. Moreover, it can sometimes be morally justified to override innocent bystanders' moral right to life in order to prevent a greater moral evil.[92] Crucially, the only moral evil that warrants overriding an innocent bystander's right to life is a great number of unjustified individual rights infringements.[93] Unintended, but foreseen harm against non-liable individuals has to be necessary for and proportionate to the moral aim of preventing a greater number of individual rights violations.

During the conduct of hostilities, law fulfils its first moral task if it guides soldiers towards directing fire against individuals who are morally liable to defensive harm or against targets that harm only individuals whose killing can be justified as a necessary and proportionate side-effect of the achievement of a morally just war aim. The law's second moral task is to reduce as much as possible unjustified infringements (i.e., violations) of individual rights in a war. Guiding agents towards the course of action that fulfils their moral

---

[90] Both conventional just war theory and the now dominant revisionist critique recognise the preservation of individual moral rights as the touchstone for justified conduct in war. For a comprehensive account of conventional just war theory, see Michael Walzer, *Just and Unjust Wars: a Moral Argument with Historical Illustrations* (London: Basic Books, 1977), 135, 137. For the most influential example of the revisionist critique, which challenges the conventional account on reductive individualist grounds, see Jeff McMahan, *Killing in War* (Oxford University Press, 2009); McMahan, 'The Ethics of Killing in War' 2004 (n. 9), 693–732.

[91] Fabre, *Cosmopolitan War* 2012 (n. 9), 6; Lazar, 'The Morality and the Law of War' 2012 (n. 9).

[92] This proposition is derived from the moral doctrine of double effect, which permits causing unintentional, but foreseeable harm (the bad effect) in pursuit of a good effect, if the latter is proportional to the former. It is widely credited to St. Thomas Aquinas. See Judith Lichtenberg, 'War, Innocence and the Doctrine of Double Effect', *Philosophical Studies* 74 (1994), 347–68.

[93] No other considerations, such as individual welfare or the rights of communities, 'count' towards the proportionality of the infringement of an individual right to life. The rule of law, as discussed below, is morally relevant also only to the extent that it serves the protection of fundamental individual rights.

duties and that thus avoids individual rights violations in each instance is normally the best way to avoid such violations overall. Both moral tasks therefore *prima facie* point towards the same morally ideal legal rules: international law that discharges its two moral tasks in war prohibits all killing that amounts to, or results in, morally unjustified infringements of the individual right to life.

Is the law that better discharges these moral tasks in war, then, the law that more closely restates these fundamental moral prescriptions about the permissibility of killing? No, if there are genuine epistemic barriers to establishing which course of action avoids unjustified infringements of individual rights on the battlefield, a law that simply mirrors the moral demand will fail to discharge the law's first moral task. By comparison, a law that accommodates systematic epistemic constraints on decision-making and that is clear, accessible and action-guiding in the context in which it actually addresses individuals is more effective in helping them conform to their moral obligations.[94] In general, a law that guides its addressees through the choice they typically encounter is better at discharging its first moral task than a law that addresses the individual as if he or she were omniscient. The epistemic context of decision-making on the battlefield is hence relevant to the question of whether IHL or IHRL better discharges the law's first moral task.

Epistemic constraints account for why even the best possible law for discharging its first moral task may not always point towards the morally right course of action. The harder it is to morally parse the situations in which a law typically addresses the individual – due to time pressure on action, moral complexity or uncertain consequences – the more we should expect the morally best law for discharging its first task to diverge from underlying moral principles.[95] The more we should also expect that law may have to stipulate what is *usually* the morally right course of action, but not necessarily the right course of action in all situations. Law discharges its first moral task if an individual guided by law *generally* better conforms to her or his moral obligations than an individual not guided by law. The closer and more often law-directed conduct fulfils the guided individuals' moral

---

[94] In order to fulfil the law's first moral task, a legal 'ought' should therefore presuppose 'can'. That is also a matter of fairness as law often claims the authority to impose a cost on those subjects that fail to meet its demands. In the context of the laws of war, this point is most forcefully articulated by Shue, 'Do We Need a "Morality of War"?' 2010 (n. 12).

[95] In contrast, the more straightforward it is how to follow one's moral obligations in any given situation, the more likely it is that the morally best law looks quite like the underlying moral principle.

obligations, the better the law is at discharging its first moral task. However, compliance with law may not vouchsafe that conduct in all situations is morally right.

That law is action-guiding and sensitive to the epistemic context in which its subjects actually operate is also crucial for law's ability to discharge its second moral task of securing the fullest feasible protection for individual moral rights. In addition, there is another reason why a law might better discharge its second moral task if it diverges from fundamental moral precepts: volitional defects, which are incentive structures, emotional or cognitive biases that account for why agents systematically fail to follow their moral obligations.[96] Law can cure some volitional defects by attaching sanctions to certain courses of action that subjects are tempted to take instead of the morally right course of action. Alternatively, law can counter some volitional defects by making detailed demands on how to act that 'would be unintelligible as elements in moral rules or principles'.[97] Both sanctions and detailed action guidance can improve a law's ability to secure a better moral outcome in terms of protecting individual rights in the face of volitional defects.

However, law cannot cure all volitional defects. Sometimes, outlawing morally wrongful actions creates incentives for further wrongdoing and thus morally worse results.[98] At other times, a law that prescribes the morally right conduct would be highly costly to obey, all while non-compliance is hard to sanction.[99] Such a law would likely be ignored and miss altogether the opportunity to morally improve the effects of conduct for the protection of individual rights.[100] By comparison, a law that accommodates the volitional defects that it cannot cure, by demanding less or other than the morally required course of action, may be able to secure better moral outcomes for rights. The volitional context of decision-making during armed conflict hence matters for the question of whether IHL or IHRL better discharges the law's second moral task.

---

[96] Tasioulas, 'The Legitimacy of International Law' 2010 (n. 86), 101.

[97] H. L. A. Hart, *The Concept of Law*, 2nd edn. (Oxford University Press, 1997), 237.

[98] For instance, enforcing a law against pre-natal behaviour that seriously harms the child would reflect the moral wrongfulness of such an action. At the same time, it would not only require a morally problematic interference into a women's physical autonomy, it would also create incentives to terminate pregnancies. This example is developed in McMahan, 'The Morality of War and the Law of War' 2010 (n. 12), 33.

[99] In this context, law might still serve its first moral task of affording the individual a guide towards meeting her moral obligations, even if the individual is likely to forgo this service.

[100] For instance, if a law demanded that soldiers accept so much risk that they are highly unlikely to survive, but this law could not be monitored or enforced, it would be unable to fulfil its second moral task as it would very likely be ignored.

Incurable volitional defects can create a tension between the morally better law for discharging the law's first task and the morally better law for discharging the law's second task. If law demanded conduct that typically points individuals towards the conduct that fulfils their moral obligations, considering epistemic uncertainty and the need for law to guide action across a range of situations (task one), but this demand would, due to incurable volitional defects, be ignored or create worse moral results, law would fall short in its second task. On the other hand, if law demanded less than the morally right conduct in order to accommodate an incurable volitional defect and thereby morally improve the results of conduct (task two), it would fall short in discharging its first moral task. Both moral tasks are equally important. When they imply divergent rules, what is the solution?

If the demands associated with discharging the law's two tasks diverge, a law that satisfices rather than maximises its ability to discharge either of its moral tasks may be morally preferable. Specifically, what such a law ought to look like depends on answers to two questions: first, how great a divergence from the morally right conduct would law have to prescribe in order to produce the fullest feasible protection of individual rights; and, secondly, how far from the morally best possible outcomes for the protection of individual rights would the results of conduct be, if law did not accommodate incurable volitional defects, but insisted on prescribing the typically morally right course of action? The law should strike the least morally costly compromise possible between its two tasks. In such a situation, the morally best possible law is then neither the law that, as often as possible, prescribes the typically morally right course of action (task one), nor the law that as much as possible protects rights in the outcome of conduct (task two).

There are two reasons then why even a law that discharges both its moral tasks (i.e., first, individuals guided by law, compared with those not guided by law, more often meet their moral obligations and, second, individual rights are better protected than in the absence of guidance by law) might permit or even ask for conduct that is morally wrongful in a particular situation: first, epistemic constraints mean law prescribes the course of action that is typically, but not always, the morally right course of action; and, second, law prescribes conduct other than the morally right course of action in order to accommodate incurable volitional defects. In situations in which law, as a result, demands conduct other than the morally right conduct, should an individual obey the law?

It can indeed be permissible or morally required to disobey a law that discharges its two moral tasks. However, such cases should be rare. As mentioned, law that discharges its moral tasks, but diverges from fundamental moral prescriptions, does so primarily because there are epistemic obstacles to determining the morally right course of action or volitional barriers to individuals' conforming to their obligations. Knowing this, individuals would need to have particularly compelling reasons to trust their own judgement over the law's guidance. Moreover, when deciding whether to obey a legal rule, besides the question of whether (non-)compliance would instantiate their moral obligations, individuals ought to consider how (non-)compliance would affect the rule of law. As alluded to above, that conduct is demanded by law adds a moral reason to the balance of reasons. This is not indefeasible, but it is a weighty reason, particularly if the law generally discharges its moral tasks of guiding individuals towards the fulfilment of their duties and of protecting their rights.

To recapitulate, when two bodies of law make diverging demands – as IHRL and IHL do regarding the permissibility of killing – that which better discharges the law's two moral tasks should prevail. The law's moral tasks are to guide individuals' actions as often as possible towards meeting their moral obligations of not violating individual rights (task one), and to secure the morally best possible outcomes for rights, meaning minimising unjustified infringements of individual rights overall (task two). Which rules better accomplish these two tasks depends on the epistemic and volitional context of decision-making on the battlefield.[101] If there is a tension between the demands of the law's two moral tasks due to incurable volitional defects, the morally better law strikes the morally less costly compromise between its two tasks. The next two sub-sections explore to what extent IHL and IHRL, respectively, diverge from fundamental moral prescriptions about the permissibility of killing. Sections IV and V then systematically map which body of law better performs the law's moral tasks in the epistemic and volitional context of real-world armed conflicts.

B. *IHRL and the Moral Right to Life*

Both moral justifications for infringing individuals' moral right to life, that is, forfeiture and avoidance of a greater evil, have echoes in IHRL. A person who threatens another with unlawful violence, and who may hence be deprived of their human right to life under Article 2(2)(a) ECHR, may also be morally liable to necessary and proportionate defensive harm due to the forfeiture of her or his moral right. If a person poses a threat by evading lawful detention or

---

[101] As we will see, it also depends on the legal rules that govern the resort to force because they manage the incentives and shape the epistemic context in which the law addresses soldiers.

arrest, just as they may have forfeited their legal right to life in accordance with Article 2(2)(b) ECHR, they may have forfeited their moral right to life. In addition, Article 2(2)(c) ECHR permits overriding individual rights with a view to allowing a State to avert an insurrection or riot, something that may well be a greater moral evil.[102]

Although these exceptions to the prohibition on depriving individuals of their legal right to life under IHRL have similar structures to moral justifications for killing, the scope of the moral and legal permissions does not necessarily always align. Not every evasion even of a lawful arrest or detention warrants a lethal attack from a moral point of view, even if such an attack is 'absolutely necessary' and proportionate to the threat as demanded by the ECHR.[103] After all, the threat posed by the fleeing individual may be morally justified.[104] By the same token, we cannot be sure that in every instance in which State agents kill individuals for the purpose of quelling a riot or insurrection in accordance with IHRL, individual rights are really sacrificed for the avoidance of a greater moral evil.[105] Whether an insurrection or riots amount to a greater moral evil depends on the harm to innocent bystanders that quashing the insurrection likely necessitates as well as on the likely implications of the insurrection for citizens' fundamental moral rights.[106]

By hinging its permissions on the lawfulness of the threat or the use of violence rather than on its moral justification, IHRL opens the door to a possible lack of congruence between morally and legally permissible killing.

---

[102]   Derogation clauses likewise echo the logic of a moral lesser evil justification. They grant an exceptional permission to override individual legal rights if this is unavoidable in the pursuit of safeguarding an important legally recognised aim.

[103]   Neither the ECHR nor the ICCPR actually mention proportionality as a condition for permissible killing. However, as discussed in the previous section, the UN Human Rights Committee suggests that the use of lethal force in law enforcement operations has to be proportionate to the gravity of the offence/threat.

[104]   Imagine a case in which the fleeing individual is evading arrest in order to save a great number of innocent bystanders and he or she poses a threat only to one innocent bystander. Infringing that person's right to life may be proportionate to the threat she or he poses to the one individual, but if the latter is justified on lesser evil grounds, then killing her or him may not be morally justified.

[105]   Neither is it universally true from a moral point of view that in any given public emergency, a State should always be permitted to derogate from some of its legal obligations and override individual moral rights in the process.

[106]   On the other hand, there may well be contexts in which it could be exceptionally morally justified for the State to override individual rights for the protection of an even greater number of individual rights, but such conduct would not be condoned by IHRL because it would not fit the recognised context of an insurrection, riot or organised violence, for instance, the use of force to prevent the spread of a deadly disease or to prevent an environmental catastrophe.

At the same time, the more legitimate the authority of a State is and the more a State's laws in general fulfil their moral tasks, the more likely it is that there will nonetheless often be an alignment between legally permissible human rights deprivations and morally justified killing. The reason is that overriding individual rights for the sake of establishing public order is more likely to be morally justified if the State institutions are morally legitimate, protecting individual rights in the first place. In turn, a riot or insurrection is more likely to be morally unjustified if the State exercises legitimate authority. Similarly, the morally better a State's laws are at discharging their two moral tasks, in general, the more likely it is that an unlawful threat of violence or the evasion of a lawful arrest is also morally unjustified.

Moreover, as IHRL hinges the permissibility of individual rights infringements on the lawfulness of the arrest, the unlawfulness of the threatened violence and the preservation of the State's legal authority, it generally permits the deprivation of individual rights in furtherance of the rule of law. As mentioned above, the latter is itself a morally important goal in as much as law performs its dual service to the individual of guiding him or her towards his or her moral duties and protecting a person's moral rights. Some infringements of individual rights that IHRL authorises, which would on the balance of reasons be morally unjustified, might end up being morally permissible, or at least less morally wrongful, if we account for the moral importance of upholding the rule of law. Nonetheless IHRL's focus on unlawful rather than on unjustified threats means that divergences between legally and morally permissible killing cannot be ruled out.

This very focus on unlawful rather than on unjustified threats, however, may improve IHRL's ability to discharge its first moral task. When making what is potentially a split-second decision about whether it is necessary to shoot a fleeing individual, a law-enforcement officer may have neither the requisite information nor the cognitive capacity to make a judgement about whether the fugitive's threat is morally justified. That lawfulness, not moral justification, is the reference point for the legal permissibility of rights deprivations according to IHRL is one way in which this law lightens the individual agent's 'burden of judgement'.[107] Similarly, by replacing 'avoiding a greater moral evil in terms of individual rights violations' with the morally potentially over- and under-inclusive, but much more concrete goal of 'establishing public order in an emergency', the ECHR better discharges its moral task of guiding action towards what is, in a State that exercises legitimate authority,

---

[107]   John Rawls, *Political Liberalism* (New York: Columbia University Press, 1996), 54.

typically the course of action that conforms to an individual's moral obligations.

Of course, not all divergences between moral principles and IHRL's rules on the protection of the individual right to life will necessarily serve the law's ability to discharge its first moral task and guide its subjects towards the morally right course of action all while accommodating epistemic constraints. After all, drafting a treaty, such as the ICCPR or the ECHR, is a political process, which gives expression to the interests of the drafters. IHRL, for instance, allows deprivations of the right to life in the execution of a lawful death sentence. A convicted criminal in custody rarely poses an imminent threat. Whether killing a person because of their past culpable wrongdoing, hence for reasons of retribution and possibly in the uncertain hope of deterrence, can ever be morally justified is much more contestable than the justifiability of necessary lethal harm to avoid a future wrong.[108] Nonetheless, both mentioned treaties permit it.[109]

At the same time, the permissibility of capital punishment may serve the law's ability to discharge its second moral task. As mentioned above, considering the incentive structure of its addressees is one condition for law's ability to morally improve the outcome of conduct. This not only means managing volitional defects of the individual whose conduct law seeks to guide, for instance, law-enforcement officers or soldiers. International law, unlike most domestic laws, also needs to accommodate the incentives of the agents who decide whether a treaty is ratified. It bears noting, however, that a treaty's divergence from underlying moral prescriptions that are necessary to ensure ratification ultimately only helps law discharge its second moral task if, the pragmatic divergence from moral precepts notwithstanding, guidance of law still results in morally better outcomes for the protection of individual rights than conduct not guided by law.

From a moral point of view there is a limit then to how far international law should accommodate incurable volitional defects in order to secure treaty ratification and hence the law's applicability. If law prescribes conduct that is not the morally right conduct in order to avoid being ignored, this has costs in terms of the law's ability to discharge its first moral task. If the course of conduct that law prescribes in order to be deemed applicable also leads to

---

[108]   Reviewing the insufficiency of moral reasons for capital punishment is beyond the scope of this chapter. For a succinct overview of moral arguments for and against capital punishment, see Theodore L. Dorpat, *Crime of Punishment: America's Culture of Violence* (New York: Algora, 2007), ch. 9.

[109]   The ICCPR only reluctantly permits the death penalty, calling for its abolition in the same provision.

outcomes that are overall morally worse or no better than those of conduct unguided by law, then accommodating incurable volitional defects also undermines law's discharging of its second moral task. In this case, law should prioritise its first moral task and risk being ignored or not ratified, thereby failing to discharge its second task.

C. IHL and the Moral Right to Life

Both moral justifications for infringing the individual moral right to life, forfeiture and avoidance of a greater evil, have echoes also in IHL. IHL's rules governing the conduct of hostilities, however, diverge significantly further than IHRL's from the moral principles that determine the moral permissibility of killing. The general lack of congruence between IHL's rules and moral principles centred on the protection of individual rights is well appreciated among just war theorists.[110] This section briefly discusses the three main features of IHL that account for this further divergence: first, the legal permission to intentionally kill all soldiers, regardless of necessity and proportionality; secondly, IHL's failure to demand actual necessity when permitting the deaths of innocent bystanders/civilians; and, thirdly, IHL's equal empowerment of all parties to a war, regardless of the moral or legal status of their aims.

First, according to IHL, all combatants are always legally permissible targets of attack; civilians are *prima facie* immune from intentional harm. There may be a systematic coincidence between having combatant status and having the skills and intention to pose a threat to the enemy.[111] Ultimately, however, being a combatant is an assigned status, which first and foremost results from membership in a belligerent State's organised armed forces. Military cooks, mechanics and logistics personnel are all permissible targets of lethal attack.[112] In fact, neither the ability nor the inclination to inflict harm on the enemy is a condition for combatant status under IHL. Even combatants actually trained for combat may lack the skills, courage or motivation to pose a threat. Finally,

---

[110]   In their influential exchange on this issue, McMahan and Shue agree that the laws of war diverge from fundamental moral principles on the permissibility of killing and that moral reasons account for some of this divergence. However, they disagree on the question of whether IHL should therefore be considered morally less than ideal. McMahan, 'The Morality of War and the Law of War' 2010 (n. 12); Shue, 'Do We Need a "Morality of War"?' 2010 (n. 12). See also Lazar, 'The Morality and the Law of War' 2012 (n. 9).

[111]   For an exploration of factors that make soldiers more likely to be morally liable to attack than civilians, see Seth Lazar, 'The Responsibility Dilemma for Killing in War: a Review Essay', *Philosophy and Public Affairs* 38 (2010), 180–213.

[112]   Only religious and medical personnel are exempt.

combatants retain their status as legal targets of intentional attack when their location or occupation makes them decidedly non-threatening. The latter is also true for members of non-State armed groups with a continuous combat function. They remain permissible targets of intentional attack regardless of their actual conduct, intention or location until they opt out of their combat function.

Moreover, even if all soldiers indeed posed a threat to the enemy, they would not all be *morally* liable to being killed. To be morally responsible for a threat they pose, individuals either have to be aware or reasonably should be aware of the moral status of this threat. In reality, soldiers often systematically lack the information necessary to make the determination of whether their aim in war is just.[113] Moreover, some soldiers may have been coerced into fighting either by a State, an organised armed group or by circumstances. Soldiers who are coerced or who act in the reasonable, but mistaken, belief that their use of violence is justified may therefore be excused, in which case their moral liability to defensive harm is in question.[114] Finally, even soldiers who are fully morally responsible for an unjustified threat they pose, are not necessarily morally liable to lethal attack if it is possible to avert the threat they pose by milder means.[115] Just as many soldiers, who are permissible targets of lethal attack under IHL, retain their legal right to life under IHRL, many will not have forfeited their moral right to life.[116]

It is not hard to find reasons for why IHL *should* not attempt to restate the conditions of moral liability to harm in lieu of the principle of distinction. If it did, rather than a blanket permission to kill all soldiers and an obligation to spare all civilians, IHL would have to dictate that attackers direct harm towards individuals who responsibly contribute to the threat posed by a belligerent, but only if lethal attack is a necessary and proportionate response to that contribution. Such a law might fail in its first moral task of guiding soldiers who generally lack the information necessary to determine the moral status of the person they face on the battlefield.[117] Indeed, such a law might fail

---

[113] On this account a war has a just aim if resorting to force is the lesser moral evil in terms of unjustified rights infringements, as outlined in detail in Section V.C.

[114] For a discussion of potential excuses for participating in an unjust war and their moral implications, see Judith Lichtenberg, 'How to Judge Soldiers Whose Cause is Unjust', in Rodin and Shue (eds.), *Just and Unjust Warriors* 2010 (n. 12), 112–31 (118).

[115] IHL does not only permit unnecessary attacks against soldiers, it also allows disproportionate harm against them. From a moral point of view, in contrast, intentional defensive harm has to be proportionate to the gravity of an unjustified threat.

[116] In turn, IHL likely shields some civilians from attack who are morally liable to harm in virtue of a significant, but indirect, contribution to an unjust war.

[117] This argument is elaborated further in Dill and Shue, 'Limiting Killing in War' 2012 (n. 89). For the view that a more fine-grained differentiation among individuals than IHL demands

to fulfil its second moral task as well. In the supremely stressful environment of battle, combatants who are subject to dehumanising narratives about and physical threats from the enemy may well perceive any individual 'on the other side' as morally liable to harm. A law that explicitly endorsed killing individuals based on their moral status, might exacerbate rather than cure this volitional defect, leading to more rather than less unjustified killing.

The second divergence of IHL's prescriptions from moral principles concerns unintentional but foreseeable harm to innocent bystanders. When moral principles demand that such incidental harm has to be necessary, much like IHRL, that means harm ought to be the only and the mildest available course of action for the achievement of an aim. As outlined in the previous section, IHL in contrast only requires that an attacker does not eschew a target with a more favourable 'collateral damage' prognosis 'when a choice is possible' between similar targets. IHL further demands that the attacker takes all 'feasible' steps to reduce expected incidental civilian harm. Even if an attacker caused incidental civilian harm in order to achieve a morally just aim, IHL's epistemic standard for when an attacker may deem necessary an attack that kills civilians is too low to vouchsafe that killing civilians is morally permissible.[118]

Thirdly, as already indicated, both moral permissions – intentionally killing an individual in defence against a threat and foreseeably killing an innocent bystander on grounds of necessity – depend on the attacker's pursuing a morally just aim. In war that means that even if all soldiers responsibly contributed to the threat posed by their belligerent State, from a moral point of view only those on the unjust side would *prima facie* be liable to defensive harm. In contrast, the equal applicability of IHL, specifically the 'right to participate in hostilities' of combatants on both sides in an IAC without regard to 'the causes espoused by ... or attributed to the parties to the conflict',[119] means that IHL also endorses killing in defence against a morally justified threat. It is also due to the equal applicability of IHL that IHL's principle of proportionality regularly permits killing civilians, hence potentially innocent bystanders, in pursuit of an aim that is morally unjust.[120]

would be possible, see Bradley Jay Strawser, 'Revisionist Just War Theory and the Real World: a Cautiously Optimistic Proposal', in Fritz Allhoff, Adam Henschke and Nick Evans (eds.), *Routledge Handbook of Ethics and War: Just War in the Twenty-First Century* (London: Routledge, 2013), 76–90. Section IV.B returns to this issue in more detail.

[118] See Section II.B for a detailed analysis of the epistemic threshold at which IHL permits deeming civilian harm necessary.

[119] Preamble to API.

[120] For a similar critique, see Thomas Hurka, 'Proportionality in the Morality of War', *Philosophy & Public Affairs* 33 (2005), 34–66.

Again, it is not difficult to find epistemic constraints that account for why IHL needs to bracket the moral status of the resort to force when prescribing conduct in war if it is to fulfil its first moral task. Determining whether or not a belligerent's resort to force is morally justified, and hence whether an attack contributes to the pursuit of a morally just aim, is a complex, future-oriented judgement. It involves estimating whether waging war is the lesser moral evil in terms of unjustified individual rights infringements compared with not resorting to force. I have argued elsewhere in detail that this question in reality regularly amounts to an 'epistemically cloaked forced choice'.[121] Even if we could overcome the inherent difficulty of judging whether the resort to force will be a moral lesser evil, this judgement is unlikely to be sound without precise information about what is at stake when a State resorts to force and how a war is meant to unfold from a military point of view. This is information that States typically do not share with their soldiers.[122]

Tying the permissibility of conduct in war to the moral status of a war's aim, would not only mean that compliance with law would require that combatants answer a question to which they almost certainly do not know the answer, undermining the law's ability to discharge its first moral task. A law that tied the legal permissibility of killing to whether or not an attack was launched in pursuit of a just aim would also be undermined in the fulfilment of its second moral task of reducing individual rights violations as much as possible. In an international system of sovereign and formally equal States, who would hold to account a State that resorted to force for an unjust aim, but allowed combatants to avail themselves of the legal empowerments that IHL reserves for just combatants? An alternative IHL which differentiated between belligerents depending on the justice of their aim would, at best, secure both sides' compliance with the law for the just side. Worse even, such an 'asymmetrical IHL' might simply miss the opportunity to better protect individual rights on at least one side in each war.

If we compare all three codes of conduct – IHRL's prescriptions, IHL's demands and moral obligations – side by side, it becomes evident that IHL diverges further from moral precepts than IHRL along the three lines mentioned: first, individuals are morally liable to lethal attack only if they pose or

---

[121] Janina Dill, 'Should International Law Ensure the Moral Acceptability of War?', *Leiden Journal of International Law* 26 (2012), 253–70.

[122] Judging the moral permissibility of a resort to force is in principle equally difficult if the belligerent is a non-State organised armed group rather than a State. Whether in reality fighters in non-State organised armed groups have more or less information than combatants in States' armed forces about the true aims and likely consequences of a resort to force may vary depending on the hierarchy and organisation of an armed group.

contribute to an unjustified threat for which they are responsible, and the threat means a lethal attack is necessary and proportionate. IHRL demands that intentional lethal attacks are directed against individuals who use or threaten un*law*ful violence which makes the use of defensive lethal force necessary and proportionate. In opposition, IHL permits targeting soldiers based on their status as combatants or because they assume a continuous combat function, regardless of the necessity or proportionality of the attack.

Secondly, it may be morally permissible to unintentionally kill an innocent bystander if this is necessary for and proportionate to preventing a greater number of individual rights violations. IHRL likewise demands that unintentional killing of innocent bystanders is strictly necessary for and proportionate to the achievement of a *legally* recognised aim, generally involving the protection of human life. In contrast, IHL only demands that attackers do everything feasible to minimise expected incidental civilian harm. And if two attacks are expected to yield the same military advantage and a choice is possible, they should attack the target that is expected to cause less incidental civilian harm. Civilian harm needs to be proportionate only to the achievement of a military advantage, not the achievement of a war's aim.

Thirdly, from a moral point of view, individuals only forfeit their right to life if they contribute to an *unjust* threat. Similarly, it is only ever morally permissible to kill innocent bystanders in pursuit of a just aim – only then can their deaths potentially be justified as the lesser moral evil. Under IHRL, law enforcement officials may use violence only during a *lawful* arrest and in defence against unlawful violence. By the same token, the State needs a legally recognised aim to override the right to life of innocent bystanders, for instance, quelling an insurrection or averting 'danger to life or limb'.[123] IHL, in contrast, is symmetrical. That means IHL affords the same permissions to both sides in a war, regardless of the legal or moral status of the resort to force or the aims that belligerents pursue in a war.

The first section of this chapter established that IHRL and IHL give diverging answers to the question of when it is permissible to use lethal force. This section showed that IHL's answer diverges further than IHRL's from the answer that moral principles give to the question of whether and when it is permissible to kill a person. This makes IHRL *prima facie* better suited to discharging the law's two moral tasks. However, whether IHRL is actually better at guiding the individual soldier towards the course of action on the battlefield that typically conforms to her or his moral obligations (task one)

---

[123] ECtHR, *Nachova and Others v. Bulgaria*, Judgment of 6 July 2005, Application Nos. 43577/98 and 43579/98, para. 107.

and whether it really is better at securing the protection of individual rights in war (task two) depends on the epistemic constraints and the volitional defects of decision-making during the actual conduct of hostilities. The next section will delineate the empirical phenomenon IHL is meant to govern, identifying the characteristics of armed conflicts that could affect epistemic barriers to and volitional defects in soldiers' decision-making.

IV. SIX TYPES OF ARMED CONFLICT

A. *When is a Violent Confrontation an Armed Conflict?*

The preceding section showed that IHRL more closely than IHL tracks moral principles regarding the permissibility of killing. Although this makes IHRL the *prima facie* morally better law, which body of law should prevail in a given context depends on which law better discharges the law's moral tasks in that context. Traditionally, we think of the division of labour between IHRL and IHL as the former governing the use of force during law enforcement operations and the latter governing armed conflicts.[124] This section brackets the question of whether IHRL should indeed govern law enforcement operations. Given its status as the *prima facie* morally better law for governing permissible killing, I assume the answer to this question is yes. Instead, I seek to establish whether IHL should govern the conduct of hostilities during violent confrontations that are currently deemed to constitute armed conflicts.[125] In order to establish this, we need to analyse what characterises an armed conflict. Or, put differently, what distinguishes a confrontation that counts as an armed conflict from one that does not?

Historically wars were declared. In order for a confrontation to be considered a war, it had to be recognised as such by the warring States. This recognition, in turn, triggered the applicability of IHL.[126] The Hague and

---

[124] An alternative approach distinguishes between 'active hostilities', guided by IHL, and 'security operations', guided primarily by IHRL. The latter include the use of force in the context of an IAC, but without nexus to the conflict and 'low-intensity military operations' against a non-State belligerent in a NIAC. See Murray, *Practitioners' Guide to Human Rights Law in Armed Conflict* 2016 (n. 6), paras. 5.05, 5.08.

[125] As mentioned, the general claim that, for moral reasons, IHL has to diverge from underlying moral principles is widely accepted among analytical just war theorists. Some international lawyers similarly argue that IHRL is ill-suited for governing the conduct of hostilities, even though it may be relevant for the regulation of armed conflict more generally. These claims are, however, rarely rooted in a systematic analysis of the features of armed conflict that account for these intuitions.

[126] ICRC, 'Article 2: Application of the Convention', *Commentary on the First Geneva Convention: Convention (I) for the Amelioration of the Condition of the Wounded and Sick*

the Geneva Conventions of 1929, as a result, did not define war or armed conflict. The Geneva Conventions of 1949 radically break with this understanding of war as depending on recognition. According to Common Article 2, the Geneva Conventions shall 'apply to all cases of declared war or of any other armed conflict which may arise between two or more of the High Contracting Parties'.[127] The Commentary stresses that 'the determination of the existence of an armed conflict … must be based solely on the prevailing facts demonstrating the de facto existence of hostilities between the belligerents'.[128] But what are those prevailing facts?[129] What we can infer from the wording of the provision is no more and no less than that an armed conflict is any situation that involves the use of force between States.[130]

Are any and all uses of force by States against States armed conflicts? In 1949, State-on-State violence not governed by IHL would have been beyond the purview of international law. Drafters therefore deemed it appropriate to conceive of the applicability of the Geneva Conventions in the widest possible terms. The Commentary describes it as 'in conformity with the humanitarian purpose of the Conventions that there be no requirement of a specific level of intensity of violence to trigger an international armed conflict'.[131] Scholarly opinion is in almost total agreement that '[i]t makes no difference how long the conflict lasts, how much slaughter takes place, or how numerous are the participating forces'.[132] Neither is the existence of an armed conflict between States contingent on the purpose for

---

Armed Forces in the Field of 12 August 1949 (Geneva: International Committee of the Red Cross, 2016), para. 192.

[127] Common Art. 2 GCI–GCIV.

[128] ICRC, 'Article 2: Application of the Convention' 2016 (n. 126), paras. 209, 211. This understanding of war as a matter of fact has been reaffirmed in the case law of international criminal tribunals. See, among others, ICTY, *Prosecutor v. Boškoski and Tarčulovski*, Case No. IT-04-82-T, Trial Chamber Judgment of 10 July 2008, para. 174; ICTR, *Prosecutor v. Akayesu*, Case No. ICTR-96-4-T, Trial Chamber Judgment of 2 October 1998, para. 603.

[129] The prohibition on the use of force at roughly the same time as the adoption of the Geneva Conventions accounts for this change. As war morphed from a legitimate expression of sovereign statecraft into a deviation from the recognised rules of inter-State relations, it became unlikely that States would declare war and acknowledge a presumptive breach of international law.

[130] Similar ICRC, 'How is the Term "Armed Conflict" Defined in International Humanitarian Law?' *Opinion Paper of 17 March 2008*, 1.

[131] ICRC, 'Article 2: Application of the Convention' 2016 (n. 126), para. 243.

[132] Pictet, *IV Geneva Convention: Commentary* 1958 (n. 21), 20–1; similar Dapo Akande, 'Classification of Armed Conflicts: Relevant Legal Concepts', in Elizabeth Wilmshurst (ed.), *International Law and the Classification of Conflicts* (Oxford University Press, 2015), 32–79 (41); Richard Baxter, 'The Duties of Combatants and the Conduct of Hostilities (Law of The Hague)', in *International Dimensions of Humanitarian Law* (Henry Dunant Institute/UNESCO, 1988), 98; Christopher J. Greenwood, 'Scope of Application of International Humanitarian Law', in Fleck (ed.), *Handbook of International Humanitarian Law* 2009 (n. 21), 46, paras. 201–63 (para. 202); Jean Pictet, *Commentary on the Geneva Conventions of*

which they use force.[133] The phenomenon that IHL is meant to govern then includes *all* situations in which one State uses armed force against another.

The identification of armed conflicts between a State and a non-State actor is by comparison more complicated. Even in 1949, the use of force by a State on its own territory would have been regulated by domestic law. An intensity threshold for the applicability of IHL to internal armed conflicts did therefore not create a legal black hole.[134] NIACs, first mentioned in Common Article 3 of the Geneva Conventions, are correspondingly widely deemed to be defined by a threshold of minimum intensity.[135] For the Second Additional Protocol of 1977 to apply to an armed confrontation the organised armed group has to be 'under responsible command, exercise such control over a part of its territory as to enable them to carry out sustained and concerted military operations and to implement this Protocol'. Crucially, these criteria trigger the applicability of the treaty. They are not constitutive of an armed conflict because Common Article 3 is applicable to 'armed conflict[s] not of an international character', but it makes no such demands.

Where then is the threshold of minimum intensity for a NIAC more generally? One of the most widely reproduced concretisations of the required threshold of minimum intensity was articulated by the Appeals Chamber of the ICTY. It defines a NIAC as 'protracted armed violence between governmental authorities and organised armed groups or between such groups within a State'.[136] Though widely accepted, this definition does not necessarily

---

12 *August 1949*, vol. III (Geneva, 1960), para. 23; Sylvain Vité, 'Typology of Armed Conflicts in International Humanitarian Law: Legal Concepts and Actual Situations', *International Review of the Red Cross* 69 (2009), 69–94 (72). For the minority view that there is a threshold of intensity for the applicability of IHL in IACs, see International Law Association, Committee on the Use of Force, *Final Report on the Meaning of Armed Conflict in International Law* (The Hague Conference, 2010), 32–3.

[133] The First Additional Protocol demands that it 'must be fully applied in all circumstances . . . without any adverse distinction based on the . . . causes espoused by or attributed to the Parties to the conflict' (preamble of the First Additional Protocol). See also ICTY, *Prosecutor v. Duško Tadić*, Case No. IT-94-1-A, 66, Decision on the Defence Motion for Interlocutory Appeal on Jurisdiction of 2 October 1995, para. 218.

[134] Akande, 'Classification of Armed Conflicts' 2015 (n. 132), 42.

[135] The Commentary to Common Art. 3 argues that an 'armed conflict not of an international character' is a situation 'in which organised Parties confront one another with violence of a certain degree of intensity.' ICRC, 'Article 3: Conflicts not of an International Character', *Commentary on the First Geneva Convention: Convention (I) for the Amelioration of the Condition of the Wounded and Sick Armed Forces in the Field of 12 August 1949* (Geneva: International Committee of the Red Cross, 2016), para. 387.

[136] ICTY, *Tadić*, Decision on Jurisdiction (n. 133), para. 70. It is noteworthy that this definition dispenses with State participation as a necessary element of an armed conflict and extends the applicability of IHL to the use of armed force solely by and against non-State actors. The

provide a definitive and incontestable test for each empirical case. Specifically, what criteria make armed violence 'protracted' is far from obvious.[137] Indicators drawn on in international jurisprudence include the frequency of hostile confrontations, the type and range of weapons and the calibre of munitions used, the number of persons participating in combat, wounded or killed as a result of hostilities, the severity and extent of the physical destruction and the number of displaced persons.[138]

Assuming we can tell when these indicators of intensity point towards the existence of an armed conflict, is killing in all such situations really meant to be governed by IHL's principles of distinction, proportionality and necessity? Common Article 3 does not itself concern the conduct of hostilities and not all NIACs also trigger the applicability of APII. The most recent authoritative commentary to Common Article 3, however, states that 'when common Article 3 is applicable, other rules, especially those on the conduct of hostilities, with different restraints on the way force may be used compared to peacetime law, may also apply'.[139] This statement does not rule out that IHRL is simultaneously applicable during NIACs, but the contrast to 'peacetime law' is a gesture towards the traditional view that IHL's rules for the conduct of hostilities displace otherwise applicable more stringent rules when armed violence meets the threshold of a NIAC.[140]

In sum, IHL's principles for the conduct of hostilities are meant to govern the permissibility of killing in *all* situations of armed force used between States and in all situations of '*protracted* armed violence between governmental

---

threshold of minimum intensity is thus crucial also for the differentiation of armed conflicts from private violence. The ICC Statute further excludes 'situations of internal disturbances and tensions, such as riots, isolated and sporadic acts of violence or other acts of a similar nature' as falling below this threshold. Art. 8(2)(d) and 8(2)(f) ICC Statute, following Art. 1 APII; similar ICRC, 'Article 3: Conflicts not of an International Character' 2016 (n. 135), para. 386.

[137] Although the term clearly suggests that there is a minimum length of hostilities, the *Abella* case affords a counter-example of an armed conflict taking the guise of one intense, but discrete and relatively short attack. Inter-American Commission on Human Rights, *Juan Carlos Abella v. Argentina*, Case No. 11.137, Report No. 55/97 of 18 November 1997, OEA/Ser L/V/II.98.

[138] For an overview, see Akande, 'Classification of Armed Conflicts' 2015 (n. 132), 53, referencing, ICTY, *Prosecutor v. Haradinaj et al.*, Case No. IT-04-84-T, Trial Chamber Judgment of 3 April 2008, para. 49; similar Watkin, *Fighting at the Legal Boundaries* 2016 (n. 5), 583.

[139] ICRC, 'Article 3: Conflicts not of an International Character' 2016 (n. 135), para. 386.

[140] The ICRC Customary Law study identified 148 out of 161 rules applicable in IACs as also applicable in NIACs, without differentiating between NIACs under the purview of APII and those only under the purview of Common Art. 3. Jean-Marie Henckaerts and Louise Doswald-Beck (eds.), *Customary International Humanitarian Law, Vol. I: Rules* (Geneva: International Committee of the Red Cross, 2005).

authorities and organised armed groups or between such groups within a State'.[141] It is, hence, either a particular configuration of belligerents, namely States on both sides, or the intensity of a confrontation between a State and non-State challenger on the former's territory that defines the real-world armed confrontations that count as armed conflicts under the purview of IHL. The former characterises and differentiates an IAC, the latter a NIAC from armed confrontations presumed to be governed by IHRL.

B. When does Intensity Matter?

In recent years instances of armed violence that seem to fit neither the definition of IACs as violence purely between States, nor that of NIACs as protracted violence on the territory of one High Contracting Party have become more frequent. Instead, these conflicts cross international borders while also involving non-State organised armed groups. As we have already established the applicability of the rules for the conduct of hostilities to all NIACs and IACs, we might be tempted to bracket the contested question of how to classify armed confrontations that appear to have elements of both types. However, to delineate the universe of real-world confrontations that IHL is meant to govern, and to understand the epistemic and volitional context of decision-making in these situations, we have to know whether we need to enquire into the intensity of a particular armed confrontation to assert the applicability of IHL (NIAC) or not (IAC).

Beyond classic NIACs (1) and IACs (2), we can distinguish four types of armed confrontation that cross international borders while also involving non-State organised armed groups:[142] (3) internal confrontations in which the territorial State is supported by a third State; (4) internal confrontations in which the non-State actor is supported by a third State; (5) internal confrontations that involve only one State, but spill over onto the territory of a neighbouring State; and (6) transnational confrontations between a State and a non-State actor entirely conducted on a third State's territory, but without the consent of that territorial State. Which of these four types of armed confrontations are NIACs and which IACs? Or, put differently, which of these confrontations only fall under the purview of IHL if hostilities are 'protracted'?

---

[141]   ICTY, *Tadić*, Decision on Jurisdiction (n. 133), para. 70 (emphasis added).
[142]   For a slightly different typology, see Jelena Pejic, 'Conflict Classification and the Law Applicable to Detention and the Use of Force', in Wilmshurst (ed.), *Classification of Conflicts* 2015 (n. 132), 80–116 (84).

When another State or coalition of States intervenes in an internal confrontation on the side of the territorial State, we have an 'internationally-supported internal confrontation' (3). While the intervention lends the confrontation an international element, hostilities remain confined to one territory and there is no violence of one State *against* another, so that such internationally supported internal confrontations should be deemed NIACs. They fall under the purview of IHL only if they cross the threshold of being protracted.[143] The outside intervention on the side of the territorial State will often intensify hostilities that were previously below that threshold. Outside intervention can thus turn a situation from a law enforcement operation into a NIAC by intensifying hostilities, but this is not automatically the case and has to be separately established.

In contrast, if a State or coalition of States intervenes on the side of the non-State actor in an internal confrontation (4), the use of force between States ensues. Such an 'internationalised internal confrontation' is hence an IAC.[144] Even an internal confrontation that did not rise to the intensity of a NIAC before the intervention becomes an IAC once internationalised. Internationalised internal confrontations are therefore not subject to a requirement of minimum intensity in order to come under the purview of IHL. The difference between an 'internationally supported internal confrontation' and an 'internationalised internal confrontation' shows that it is not the involvement of more than one State in an armed confrontation per se that constitutes it as an IAC, but the crossing of borders by a State's armed forces into another State's territory without the latter's consent or authorisation.

What about the use of force by a State on another State's territory without the latter's consent, but against a non-State actor rather than against the territorial State? Both 'spill-over internal confrontations' (5) and 'transnational confrontations' (6) raise this question. Dapo Akande has convincingly argued that in such situations, two armed conflicts exist in parallel: a NIAC between the State and the non-State actor; and an IAC between the intervening and the territorial State.[145] He

---

[143] For the view that intervention with the consent of or on behalf of the territorial State does not turn a conflict into an IAC, see also Dieter Fleck, 'The Law of Non-International Armed Conflict', in Dieter Fleck (ed.), *The Handbook of International Humanitarian Law*, 3rd edn. (New York: Oxford University Press, 2013), 589–610 (605); ICC, *Prosecutor v. Jean-Pierre Bemba Gombo*, Case No. ICC-01/05-01/08, Confirmation of Charges Decision (Pre-Trial Chamber), 15 June 2009, para. 246.

[144] Watkin, *Fighting at the Legal Boundaries* 2016 (n. 5), 336.

[145] Akande, 'Classification of Armed Conflicts' 2015 (n. 132), 73.

has further stressed that it is practically impossible to establish whether an attack by the intervening State, meant to weaken the non-State actor but carried out on the territory of another State, is part of the NIAC or the IAC. Whether or not their intensity means that they meet the threshold of a NIAC, all attacks by a State against a non-State actor on another State's territory are hence also part of an IAC.[146]

In the case of a transnational confrontation (6), the cross-border scope of hostilities in effect moots the intensity requirement for the applicability of IHL. In the case of spill-over internal confrontations (5), attacks outside the State's territory are likewise inevitably part of an IAC. However, this is not true for attacks carried out on the State's own territory. We will have to separately establish that these internal hostilities cross the required threshold of intensity of being protracted to count as a NIAC. Spill-over internal confrontations might hence present the odd situation in which hostilities between the State and the organised armed group on the State's own territory remain below the threshold of a NIAC, but their hostilities on another State's territory are inextricably intertwined with and therefore part of an IAC, even if they are no more intense.[147]

In sum, IHL is meant to govern the permissibility of killing in purely internal confrontations or classic NIACs with the involvement of no more than one State on that same State's territory (1), internationally supported internal confrontations (3), and the internal part of a spill-over confrontation (5a), but only if hostilities cross a threshold of minimum intensity at which they count as 'protracted'. In addition, IHL is meant to govern any armed force used by a State on the territory of another State, without the consent and not on behalf of the territorial State, regardless of its intensity. This category includes classic State-on-State IACs (2), internationalised internal confrontations (4), the part of an internal confrontation that spills-over into another State's territory (5b), and transnational confrontations (6). It is thus one of two features that distinguish an armed confrontation that counts as an armed conflict under the purview of IHL from a law enforcement operation governed by IHRL: either the intensity of hostilities, that is, their protracted nature, or a State's (non-authorised) use of armed force outside its own territory.

---

[146] Similar Human Rights Council, 'Report of the Commission of Inquiry on Lebanon Pursuant to Human Rights Council Resolution S-2/1', A/HRC/3/2 (23 November 2006), paras. 50–62.

[147] To recall, '[t]he requirement for a degree of intensity indicates that the threshold of violence that is required for the application of international humanitarian law in non-international armed conflicts is higher than in the case of international armed conflicts'. Akande, 'Classification of Armed Conflicts' 2015 (n. 132), 53–4.

V. DISCHARGING THE LAW'S MORAL TASKS
IN ARMED CONFLICTS

Section III showed that IHRL is *prima facie* better than IHL at guiding soldiers towards the conduct that conforms to their moral obligations (task one) and better at securing the protection of individual rights in the outcome of conduct (task two). However, epistemic constraints and volitional defects might make a law that further diverges from underlying moral principles, such as IHL, better at discharging one or both of the law's moral tasks. Section IV suggested that an armed confrontation qualifies as an IAC that comes under the purview of IHL when a State is using force outside its own borders on the territory of another State without the territorial State's authorisation or consent, regardless of the intensity of hostilities.[148] Moreover, armed confrontations count as NIACs that are governed by IHL when they do not involve a State's using unauthorised force outside its own borders, but hostilities reach a threshold of intensity at which they count as 'protracted'. In this section, we seek to answer the question as to whether either of these two features *should* trigger the applicability of IHL because they create epistemic barriers or volitional defects that undercut IHRL's ability to better discharge the law's two moral tasks.

Section A will show that the use of force beyond a State's own territory does not per se create epistemic barriers that could affect IHRL's ability to guide soldiers towards the fulfilment of their moral obligations (task one). Section B asserts that hostilities becoming more intense, in contrast, does create such epistemic barriers. Still, IHRL remains the better law for discharging its first moral task compared with IHL. Section C shows that it is not only the reality of armed conflict, but also the legal context that structures the epistemic environment in which law addresses the soldier on the battlefield. Due to the open-endedness of the *ius contra bellum* and its divergence from moral principles, IHRL only retains its ability to better discharge the law's first moral task as hostilities become protracted or cross international borders if it is applied 'symmetrically', meaning as if both parties to an armed confrontation had a lawful aim. Finally, Section D turns towards the law's second moral task and the implications of extraterritoriality and the intensity of hostilities for the volitional context of decision-making on the battlefield. It again finds that extraterritoriality does not per se create volitional defects. When hostilities

---

[148] This does not mean that there is currently scholarly consensus that the conduct of hostilities in such a situation is exclusively governed by IHL. Watkin, for instance, argues that a State should be guided by IHRL when facing a non-State opponent – so in IAC types (4), (5b) and (6) – for as long as this is 'operationally feasible'. Watkin, *Fighting at the Legal Boundaries* 2016 (n. 5), 550.

reach the threshold of becoming protracted, however, IHL is better than 'symmetrical IHRL' at discharging the law's second moral task.

A. *The Use of Force across International Borders and the Law's First Moral Task*

Does the unauthorised use of force by a State outside its own borders create epistemic constraints that could interfere with IHRL's ability to discharge the law's first moral task? Let us imagine an internal confrontation between State A and an organised armed group, which spills-over into neighbouring State B's territory (type 5). In A's territory hostilities are not protracted and therefore governed by IHRL alone. However, on B's territory, hostilities are part of an IAC and thus under the purview of IHL. It is important to stress that the question at hand is not whether State A would be able to guarantee the full panoply of human rights just as easily on State B's territory as it would be able to do so on its own territory. Instead, the question is whether soldiers on the battlefield are less able to discern the implications of the more complex demands of IHRL regarding the permissibility of killing when they operate in neighbouring State B compared with when they use armed force on their own territory. Traditionally, State A would have been less familiar with the terrain across the border, which could reduce the situational awareness of its soldiers operating in B's territory compared to those fighting at home. In the twenty-first century, however, satellite imagery mostly makes up for any such shortfall.

In other than spill-over confrontations, a State may face a less familiar enemy when fighting beyond its own borders. For instance, a State opposing a non-State armed group in a transnational IAC (type 6) or another State in a traditional IAC (type 2), might have less insight into the opponent's organisation and conduct, compared with a State fighting an organised armed group that operates on its territory. However, ultimately the level of intelligence that belligerent C has about belligerent D has much more to do with the sophistication and length of C's intelligence-gathering than with where D operates. Moreover, in internationalised internal confrontations (type 4), which involve the use of extraterritorial unauthorised force, just like in internationally supported internal confrontations (type 3), which do not, the intervening State can benefit from the intelligence of the belligerent it supports about the belligerent it opposes. These examples suggest that a State's unauthorised crossing of international borders does not *necessarily* change the epistemic context of battlefield decision-making, though sometimes it can.

Familiarity with the terrain and with the enemy, which are contingently linked to where a belligerent is conducting hostilities, may speak to what human rights jurisprudence conceives of as a State's 'effective control'. Although the ECHR and the ICCPR both define their jurisdictional reach primarily with reference to a State's own territory,[149] domestic as well as international case law has over the last decades converged on the interpretation that IHRL applies extraterritorially if a State exercises effective control.[150] Effective control, like familiarity with an enemy and terrain, is systematically linked to, but not necessarily only a function of whether the State operates on its own territory. The ECtHR and the Human Rights Committee indicate that just as a State does not necessarily lack control outside its borders, it does not always have control over all individuals on its own territory. Organised armed violence on a State's territory is one possible reason for why a State might lack internal control.[151] At the same time, a State can have *extra*-territorial control 'as a consequence of ... military action'.[152] It follows that crossing international borders normally reverses the presumption from a State having effective control to a State not having effective control. On a State's own territory, armed violence may signal the absence of control. Beyond a State's territories it may be an indicator of the opposite.

Does IHRL require that a State has effective control in order to discharge the law's first moral task? Or, put differently, is the loss of effective control associated with the emergence of epistemic barriers to discerning the morally right course of

---

[149] Article 2(1) ICCPR. See also Sarah Joseph and Melissa Castan, *The International Covenant on Civil and Political Rights Cases, Materials, and Commentary* (Oxford University Press, 2013), para. 4.11. For a discussion of the jurisdictional reach of the ECHR, see ECtHR, *Banković and Others v. Belgium and Others*, Decision of 12 December 2001, Application No. 52207/99, para. 59; ECtHR, *Khan v. United Kingdom*, Decision of 28 January 2014, Application No. 11987/11, para. 25.

[150] For a review of the relevant jurisprudence, see Oona Hathaway, Philip Levitz, Elizabeth Nielsen, Aileen Nowlan, William Perdue, Chelsea Purvis, Sara Solow and Julia Spiegel, 'Human Rights Abroad: When Do Human Rights Treaty Obligations Apply Extraterritorially?', *Arizona State Law Journal* 43 (2011), 1–38.

[151] For limits on the intra-territorial applicability of the ICCPR, see Joseph and Castan, *The International Covenant* 2013 (n. 149), para. 4.21. ECtHR case law suggests that such limits can be due to a secessionist party's operating on a State's territory (ECtHR, *Ilaşcu and Others v. Moldova and Russia*, Grand Chamber Judgment of 8 July 2004, Application No. 48787/99, para. 312) or because the State hosts an international court or tribunal. ECtHR, *Djokaba Lambi Longa v. the Netherlands*, Decision of 9 October 2012, Application No. 33917/12, para. 80; ECtHR, *Galić v. the Netherlands*, Decision of 9 June 2009, Application No. 22617/07, para. 44; ECtHR, *Blagojević v. the Netherlands*, Decision of 9 June 2009, Application No. 49032/07, para. 44.

[152] The Court has concluded that the ECHR applies 'when, as a consequence of lawful or unlawful military action, a Contracting State exercises effective control'. ECtHR, *Al-Skeini v. United Kingdom*, Decision of 7 July 2011, Application Nos. 55721/07 and 27021/08, para. 138. See also ECtHR, *Loizidou*, Decision of 8 December 1996, Application No. 15318/89, para. 62.

action which would undercut IHRL's ability to guide soldiers' actions? If this were true, then the morally right point for IHL to displace IHRL would be the (now widely accepted) *de iure* limit of IHRL's extraterritorial applicability: where the State lacks effective control. This raises the question of what it looks like when a State exercises extraterritorial effective control in the context of the use of force. The ECtHR's jurisprudence asserts that a belligerent can exercise 'temporarily, effective overall control of a particular portion' of another State's territory,[153] in which case IHL's rules for occupation, enshrined in GCIV, will likely apply. Alternatively, a belligerent State can exercise authority and control over persons without controlling territory.[154] Although this latter type of extraterritorial control over a person has mostly been found to obtain in the context of detention,[155] the Court has also asserted that a State can have control over an individual passing through a checkpoint[156] and even one affected by the use of force.[157]

When it comes to defining the factual indicators of such extraterritorial effective control over persons during the conduct of hostilities, the literature unfortunately often verges on tautology. Murray, for instance, mentions 'factors such as, troop density, effective command and control, control of the skies, control of the sea lines of communication, a robust intelligence picture, suitable military hardware, control of cyberspace, or control of infrastructure and logistic support'.[158] The case law meanwhile overwhelmingly focuses on the parameters of a State exercising effective control over individuals in detention.[159] 'What is decisive in such cases is the exercise of physical power

---

[153] ECtHR, *Issa and Others v. Turkey*, Judgment of 16 November 2004, Application No. 31821/96, para. 74.

[154] As indicated, once a belligerent State has effective control over an enemy State's territory, IHL's rules on occupation rather than those governing hostilities may apply. In the following, in order to elucidate the epistemic implications of a State having effective control during the conduct of hostilities, I therefore focus on the parameters of effective control over persons rather than the parameters of effective control over territory.

[155] For an overview of the case law, see Sarah H. Cleveland, 'Embedded International Law and the Constitution Abroad', *Columbia Law Review* 110 (2010), 225–51.

[156] ECtHR, *Jaloud v. the Netherlands*, Judgment of 20 November 2014, Application No. 47708/08, para. 125.

[157] See, for instance, ECtHR, *Pad and Others v. Turkey*, Judgment of 28 June 2007, Application No. 60167/00, para. 54.

[158] Murray, *Practitioners' Guide to Human Rights Law in Armed Conflict* 2016 (n. 6), para. 3.4. The commentary lists 'the extent to which the military, economic, and political support for the local subordinate administration provides it with influence and control over the region'. William Schabas, *The European Convention on Human Rights: a Commentary* (Oxford University Press, 2015), 103.

[159] The ECtHR uses 'effective control' in three different ways: first, to designate the attributability of an agent's conduct to a State; second, to refer to a State's legal competence to exercise public powers; and, third, as a description of the factual conditions that mean a State

and control over the person in question'.[160] This leaves unclear what it looks like when a State has effective control over persons affected by the use of force, that is, during the conduct of hostilities. Actual physical control, the literal power to handle a person's body and command them to be in one place rather than another, is a feature of detention. The use of force against a person during the conduct of hostilities, however, will often signal the absence of this power.

Indeed, if we home in on the ordinary meaning of the word 'control' as 'the power to influence or direct people's behaviour or the course of events',[161] it becomes evident that the use of violence is either itself an exercise of such control or it is a sign of its absence. If an attacker subdues a challenger through the use of armed force, this is an expression and indeed conclusive evidence of their effective control over the challenger. Exchanges of armed force that go on, in contrast, suggest that neither side has the power to subdue, that is, to control, the other. During an ongoing violent confrontation neither side then has effective control. It follows that it is the intensity of hostilities, particularly their quality of being 'protracted' that determines whether a party to an armed confrontation has effective control and whether IHRL can discharge the law's first moral task. We can thus conclude that crossing international borders does not itself undercut the ability of IHRL to discharge the law's first moral task. In peacetime, extraterritoriality may reverse the presumption of a State's effective control, but whether the use of force is an exercise of effective control or the expression of its absence, depends on the intensity of hostilities not on where the confrontation takes place.

B. The Intensity of Hostilities and the Law's First Moral Task

How does an increase in the intensity of hostilities affect IHRL's ability to guide soldiers towards fulfilling their moral obligations? The more intense hostilities are, the more difficult it is to determine whether, at any given moment, IHRL indeed exceptionally permits the use of intentional lethal force. If IHRL governed hostilities, it would address the soldier on the battle-field with the prescription to kill combatants or enemy fighters only if they in

---

is presumed to be able to discharge its obligations under the ECHR (for this point, see Marco Milanovic, 'From Compromise to Principle: Clarifying the Concept of State Jurisdiction in Human Rights Treaties', *Human Rights Law Review* 8 (2008), 411–49 (423)). It is only this third use of the term effective control that is relevant for the moral question of whether or not IHRL or IHL are the better law for guiding an individual towards the fulfilment of his or her moral obligations.

[160] ECtHR, *Al-Skeini v. United Kingdom* (n. 152), para. 137.

[161] 'Control', see Oxford English Dictionary, available at: https://en.oxforddictionaries.com/definition/control.

fact used or threatened violence, and a lethal attack was necessary to defend themselves or a third party against this threat.[162] Soldiers would not be allowed to plan on using force as a first resort against enemy fighters as soon as they present themselves. Capture would have to be impossible.[163] Implementation of this provision requires a judgement about an individual's likely conduct and about their intention. Two recognised indicators for the intensity of hostilities, in particular, diminish the attacker's capacity to divine a potentially hostile individual's state of mind and predict their behaviour: the type of weapons, namely, their range, and the number of persons involved in hostilities. The latter accounts for how many different individuals' conduct and state of mind a soldier likely has to evaluate at the same time, potentially straining her or his cognitive capacity beyond the humanly possible.

An intensification in hostilities similarly increases the epistemic barriers to discerning when IHRL exceptionally permits overriding an innocent bystander's right to life on grounds of necessity. IHRL either requires an immediate threat to human life or it imposes on the attacker a duty of care. A duty of care means an attacker is only authorised to launch the attack if a reasonable observer would with reasonable certainty affirm that this attack was the last and mildest means of achieving the aim which is legally recognised to unlock this exception. It may not be possible to establish true 'lastness' even in an environment in which the attacker has relatively solid knowledge about how reality will likely unfold in the near future. As the adversary gets a vote in the consequences of an attack, and success in war partly depends on not being predictable to the enemy, achieving reasonable certainty about the consequences of one's conduct during an armed confrontation is likely rare. The more numerous, complex and fast-paced exchanges of violence are, the rarer will be moments in which the attacker can fulfil a duty of care towards innocent bystanders.[164]

That it becomes harder to discern when IHRL exceptionally permits an attack on the battlefield does not mean IHRL ceases to have implications for action. Both Conventions discussed in Section II start out with a blanket prohibition on deprivations of the right to life. The use of lethal force is an

---

[162]   We assume for now that the use of violence 'on the other side' is unlawful. I return below to the implications of IHRL demanding a lawful aim for the deprivation of the right to life to be permissible.

[163]   Intentionally killing civilians would be equally permissible, subject to the same conditions.

[164]   Whereas an intensification of hostilities reduces instances in which an attacker can fulfil a duty of care, it may increase the number of instances in which soldiers have to counter an obvious and immediate danger to their own life or that of civilians. Under IHRL, soldiers would be permitted to defend themselves or third parties in such situations by using lethal force if necessary.

exceptional empowerment. If the conditions of an exception cannot be established with reasonable certainty, the obligation not to deprive individuals of
their human right to life remains intact. In the midst of hostilities, if it is
impossible to establish who is threatening human life by using the kind of
unlawful violence that can only be neutralised through lethal attack, then not
carrying out a lethal attack is the reaction IHRL demands. Similarly, if it is
impossible to establish with reasonable certainty the necessity of overriding
a bystander's right to life, IHRL does not grant such a permission.

As hostilities intensify, IHL's rules of distinction, proportionality and necessity do not become harder to apply in the same measure as do IHRL's rules.
Neither does IHL revert to a default of no permission to use lethal force as does
IHRL. Combatants do not necessarily become harder to distinguish from the
civilian population in all-out war. Members of organised armed groups with
a continuous combat function may even be easier to tell apart from the general
population the less sporadic and more protracted hostilities are. Moreover, the
implications of IHL's principles of proportionality and necessity depend on an
attacker's expectations. The care in formulating these expectations that is
owed to civilians under Article 57 API diminishes with intensifying hostilities,
as the range of verification measures that are 'feasible' shrinks. As hostilities
intensify it may also be less often true that 'a choice is possible' among several
targets, which are anticipated to yield the same military advantage.[165] As its
permissions do not hinge on an absolute threshold of minimum knowledge
about the status of a target or the consequences of an attack, IHL is no less
likely to permit attacks as intensifying hostilities decrease the knowability of an
attack's alternatives and consequences.[166]

Which body of law then guides the soldier towards what is typically the
morally right course of action as hostilities intensify? Moral principles, like
IHRL, start with a presumption against killing and only allow infringing or
overriding an individual's moral right to life in exceptional circumstances. If
these circumstances cannot be established with reasonable certainty, the
morally right course of action is typically *not* to kill another person or launch
an attack that is expected to kill an innocent bystander. Past a certain point of

---

[165]   I bracket the substantive implications of IHL's principle of proportionality here because it
       fails to be action-guiding regardless of the care invested in formulating expectations about the
       consequences of an attack. It is hence not only the degree of action guidance, but also the
       substantive implications for action of the principle that remain unaffected by an intensifica-
       tion of hostilities. For this argument, see Dill, 'Do Attackers have a Legal Duty of
       Care?' (n. 50).
[166]   The exception is that an intensification in hostilities may make attacks against persons less
       likely to be permissible. This is due to Art. 50(1) API, which stipulates that 'in case of doubt
       whether a person is a civilian, they shall be considered to be a civilian'.

doubt, I would not be permitted to defend myself by killing an individual that may or may not threaten me. Similarly, past a certain point of doubt, rescuing innocent bystanders by killing an individual who I thought was attacking them would not be the morally right course of action. Inaction, as demanded by IHRL, is *prima facie* the morally appropriate reaction to uncertainty. That IHRL, on epistemic grounds, permits fewer attacks as hostilities intensify hence means it continues to guide the individual towards what is typically the course of action that conforms to his or her moral obligations.

One may reasonably interject here that compliance with IHRL would surely hamstring a belligerent in prosecuting a war. Not winning or not even fighting a war, in turn, can carry a moral cost if the war has a just aim, such as repelling a brutal aggressor or preventing a genocide and thereby protecting individual rights overall. Here we need to note what we have so far bracketed: IHRL requires a lawful aim for the exceptional deprivation of an individual right to life. Of course, moral principles also only permit the use of lethal force in pursuit of a just aim and in defence against an unjustified threat. If having a lawful aim for the purposes of IHRL was the same as having a morally just aim, IHRL would guide soldiers on both sides of an armed conflict towards what is typically the morally right course of action in their respective situations: inaction on the side in want of a lawful/just aim and exceptional permissions to infringe individual rights on the side pursuing a lawful/just aim. This would make the belligerent with the just/lawful aim likely to win, the constraining effect of IHRL notwithstanding.

We can conclude that intensifying hostilities change the epistemic context of decision-making on the battlefield, making it more difficult to discern the implications of IHRL's demands and reducing the instances in which IHRL affords an exceptional permission to deprive an individual of their right to life. In contrast, it does not become more difficult to follow the prescriptions of IHL as hostilities become protracted. IHRL nonetheless continues to be a better guide to soldiers meeting their moral obligations on the battlefield. An intensification of hostilities does not undermine its better ability to discharge the law's first moral task.

C. The Legal Context and the Law's First Moral Task

The above assertion that IHRL better discharges the law's first moral task even in the context of protracted armed hostilities and when States cross borders to use unauthorised force on other States' territory rests on the assumption that having a lawful aim for the purposes of IHRL coincides with having a morally just aim. If this were not the case, IHRL would risk guiding soldiers with an unjust aim towards the perpetration of individual rights violations. It would also systematically prohibit soldiers with a morally just aim from committing infringements of individual rights that are necessary and justified in order achieve this aim. The above assertion further rests on the second assumption that soldiers are generally able to determine whether they have a lawful aim. Otherwise they would not be able to establish the implications of IHRL for their actions and IHRL would in fact fail to guide them towards meeting their moral obligations. Let us focus on the first assumption for now: is it systematically the case that in each armed conflict, the side that uses force lawfully also has a morally just aim and the side that has broken the law uses morally unjustified violence?

Section II.C touched on the difficult question of what it means to use or threaten unlawful violence for the purposes of IHRL during an organised armed confrontation that counts either as a NIAC or an IAC. For armed conflicts that pit non-State organised armed groups against State belligerents, we can sometimes rely on domestic law to establish that members of the organised armed group, specifically if they challenge their territorial State, use force unlawfully.[167] For conflicts among States, we could draw on general international law, namely, the *ius contra bellum*, to determine which side has a lawful aim.[168] We need to establish then whether the domestic law-based differentiation between State and non-State belligerents and the *ius contra bellum* track the moral principles that determine when it is morally justified to resort to armed force.

According to the moral standard outlined in Section III.A, the sole locus of moral value is the individual and resorting to force is justified only in defence of individual rights. States' and other political communities' rights are derivative of the rights of the individuals that constitute them. A community's moral right to resort to force in self-defence is contingent on its being a vehicle for the protection of individual rights.[169] Crucially, this justification for resorting to force is the same for non-State organised armed groups as it is for States. There is no reason to assume that a non-State actor that challenges the territorial State has necessarily resorted to force unjustifiably and that the territorial State

---

[167] Section III.C also emphasised the legal uncertainty surrounding the resort to force by and against non-State actors across international borders. Relying on domestic law does not, for instance, afford a definitive answer to the question of which side uses force unlawfully during a transnational armed confrontation (type 6).

[168] Section III.C also highlighted that it would be highly problematic to tie individuals' loss of their human right to life to the conduct of their State over which they likely have little control.

[169] These rights may include individually held political rights to collective self-determination alongside the basic moral right to life.

is always morally justified in fighting back. In contrast, as mentioned above, if we rely on domestic law to determine the lawfulness of a soldier's use of violence during a NIAC, we will often find that the belligerent State's soldiers have a lawful aim, whereas members of non-State organised armed groups threaten and use unlawful violence. This domestic law-based differentiation between State and non-State belligerents' use of force does not track moral principles.

Having a morally just war aim means fighting to preserve individual rights or to prevent their violation. Past a certain level of intensity, armed confrontations inevitably involve the killing of innocent bystanders. As warfare thus always leads to infringements of individual rights, establishing a just cause means determining whether a resort to force is the lesser moral evil. When facing an outside aggressor or when deciding whether to intervene to halt a genocide, the State or non-State actor resorting to force has to ask: what is the lesser evil in terms of morally unjustified infringements of individual rights, resorting to war or refraining from using force? If the individual rights infringements that a resort to force will inevitably cause are the lesser evil, are they also proportionate to the aim of avoiding the greater number of rights violations?[170] If, but only if, the answers to both questions are yes, is a resort to force morally justified?[171]

Calculating whether a resort to force would entail fewer or more unjustified infringements of individual rights than would not responding militarily to an aggression or a humanitarian catastrophe, is an extraordinarily difficult, future-oriented judgement. It not merely requires divining the intended and unintended consequences of one's own actions. The extent to which a defensive war jeopardises individual rights – which rights, for how many individuals and how severely – also depends on the reactions of the adversary.[172] From a moral point of view, the decision as to whether or not

[170]   I assume that lesser evil and proportionality calculations require a consideration of both the likelihood and the gravity/number of necessary individual rights infringements compared to the individual rights violations to be prevented. It follows that the resort to force is not subject to a separate criterion of 'reasonable chance of success'.

[171]   Whether the individual rights infringements inflicted to avoid a greater evil are proportionate to the rights violations prevented is an even more difficult question to answer than whether a war will be a lesser evil, in the first place. I mostly bracket the proportionality question in the following discussion.

[172]   Whether the agent resorting to force for a morally just aim bears any moral responsibility for the individual rights violations the other side commits in reaction to their resort to force is subject to contestation. For a discussion of this issue, see Henry Shue, 'Last Resort and Proportionality', in Seth Lazar and Helen Frowe (eds.), *The Oxford Handbook of Ethics of War* (Oxford University Press, 2018), 260–76.

to resort to armed force therefore often takes the form of what I have termed an 'epistemically cloaked forced choice'[173] between allowing individual rights violations to occur and committing potentially unjustified individual rights infringements by resorting to force. Given this high epistemic barrier to determining whether and when resort to armed force is morally justified, it is not surprising that general international law diverges from moral principles. Just restating that a resort to armed force is lawful if it is a lesser evil in terms of individual rights infringements would be rather unhelpful. At the same time, if general international law on the resort to force discharges the law's first moral task, it will *typically* both permit morally justified resorts to force and prohibit those that are not. Does it?

The resort to force is prohibited according to Article 2(4) of the UN Charter and under customary international law.[174] Article 51 of the UN Charter recognises individual and collective self-defence as an exception to this pro-hibition. It is the only such exception where the unilateral resort to force by States is concerned. The continued lack of a legal permission to resort to force for the purposes of humanitarian intervention means that a class of cases of potentially morally justified resort to force – necessary intervention to rescue individuals from their own State's egregious individual rights violations – does not qualify as lawful.[175] There may be good moral reasons for the continued legal prohibition on humanitarian intervention,[176] but the absence of a clearly delineated international legal empowerment to use force as a means of rescue is one source of a likely divergence between a morally justified and a legally permissible resort to armed force.

International law empowers the Security Council to authorise the use of force. However, Article 39 UNC does not ask the Security Council to author-ise specifically measures that are necessary to protect individual rights or even

---

[173] Dill, 'Should International Law Ensure the Moral Acceptability of War?' 2012 (n. 121).

[174] Olivier Corten, *The Law Against War: the Prohibition on the Use of Force in Contemporary International Law* (Oxford: Hart, 2010), 200; Yoram Dinstein, *War, Aggression, and Self-Defence*, 5th edn. (Cambridge University Press, 2012), 86–98; Jochen A. Frowein, 'Jus Cogens', in Rüdiger Wolfrum (ed.), *Max Planck Encyclopedia of Public International Law* (online edn.), March 2013.

[175] For the continued contestability of a right to unilateral humanitarian intervention, see, among others, Sir Nigel Rodley, 'Humanitarian Intervention', in Marc Weller (ed.), *The Oxford Handbook of the Use of Force in International Law* (Oxford University Press, 2015), 775–96.

[176] For moral critiques of humanitarian intervention, see Beate Jahn, 'Humanitarian Intervention: What's in a Name?', *International Politics* 49 (2012), 36–58; Jennifer Welsh, 'Taking Consequences Seriously: Objections to Humanitarian Intervention', in Jennifer Walsh (ed.), *Humanitarian Intervention and International Relations* (Oxford University Press, 2004), 52–70.

measures that are necessary to defend a State's right to territorial integrity, which could be a vehicle for protecting individual rights. Rather, it empowers the Security Council to authorise measures that are necessary 'to maintain or restore international peace and security'. Some scholars argue that the Security Council's mandate of maintaining peace and security coincides with the broader goal of enforcing international law.[177] Individual rights are protected under international law, but is the protection of individual rights therefore co-extensive with the preservation of international peace and security? That may sometimes be the case. However, that a resort to force can be in defence of both international peace and security and individual rights does not mean that these goals never conflict and that measures necessary for the achievement of the former are also necessary (or sufficient) for securing the latter. Whether or not Security Council-mandated resorts to force have a morally just cause is therefore entirely contingent.

Does Article 51 UNC at least permit, more often than not, resorts to force that are also morally justified while excluding those that are not? The right to use force in self-defence is triggered 'if an armed attack occurs against a Member of the United Nations'. Scholarly opinion broadly coalesces around the understanding that not just any use of force on another State's territory amounts to an armed attack,[178] and that a mere threat of force is not enough to warrant forcible self-defence.[179] A State that is subject to the use of force below

---

[177]   Daniel Joyner, *International Law and the Proliferation of Weapons of Mass Destruction* (Oxford University Press, 2009), 178; Louis Cavaré, 'Les sanctions dans le cadre de l'ONU', *Recueil des Cours de l'académie de droit international* (1951), 191–291 (221); Jean Combacau, *Le pouvoir de sanction de l'ONU. Étude théorique de la coercition non militaire* (Paris: Pedone, 1974), 9–16; Marco Roscini, 'The United Nations Security Council and the Enforcement of International Humanitarian Law', *Israel Law Review* 43 (2010), 330–59 (334).

[178]   Corten, *The Law Against War* 2010 (n. 174), 403; Dinstein, *War, Aggression and Self-Defence* 2012 (n. 174), 174; Eritrea–Ethiopia Claims Commission, Partial Award of 19 December 2005, *Jus Ad Bellum Ethiopia's Claims 1-8*, para. 11; ICJ, *Case Concerning the Military and Paramilitary Activities in and Against Nicaragua* (Nicaragua v. United States of America), Merits, Judgment of 27 June 1986, ICJ Reports 1986, 14, para. 195; ICJ, *Oil Platforms case* (Iran v. United States of America), Merits, Judgment of 6 November 2003, ICJ Reports 2003, 161, para. 51. For the minority position that an armed attack does not have to cross a particular threshold of gravity, but includes all cross-border uses of force by States, see Chatham House, 'The Chatham House Principles of International Law on the Use of Force in Self-Defence', *International and Comparative Law Quarterly* 55 (2006), 963–72 (966); Adam Sofaer, 'Terrorism, the Law, and the National Defense', *Military Law Review* 126 (1989), 83–93 (89).

[179]   Michael Bothe, 'Terrorism and the Legality of Pre-emptive Force', *European Journal of International Law* 14 (2003), 227–40 (230); Michael Bothe, 'Das Gewaltverbot im Allgemeinen', in Wilfried Schaumann (ed.), *Völkerrechtliches Gewaltverbot und*

the threshold of an armed attack 'is bound, if not exactly to endure the violation, at least to respond only by means falling short of the use of cross-border force'.[180] Any threat or use of force clearly jeopardises the State's right to territorial integrity, but from a moral point of view, this is not a sufficient just cause for war. If a 'bloodless invasion' only violated individuals' political rights, but an armed response would also endanger their right to life, not resorting to war in self-defence could be the lesser moral evil.

For us to understand whether armed attacks in the meaning of international law usually create a cause for morally justified resort to force, we need to know whether a use of force that rises to this threshold typically threatens individual rights, while a use of force below this threshold typically does not. The first obstacle to answering this question is the contestability of the minimum threshold that the use of force has to meet in order to fall in the category of an armed attack.[181] As the ICJ in the *Nicaragua* case assumed there was a 'general agreement on the nature of the acts which can be treated as constituting armed attacks',[182] the Court expended little ink on discussing the minimum intensity or scale of violence required to meet the threshold.[183] Every time the Court has returned to the concept of an armed attack, its application has been highly context-specific. Scholars have

---

Friedenssicherung (Baden-Baden: Nomos, 1971), 11–30 (16 *et seq.*); Mary Ellen O'Connell, 'The Myth of Pre-emptive Self-Defence', *American Society of International Law Task Force on Terrorism* (2002), 8; Corten, *The Law Against War* 2010 (n. 174), 403; Dinstein, *War, Aggression, and Self-Defence* 2012 (n. 174), 184, 207; Christine Gray, *International Law and the Use of Force*, 3rd edn. (Oxford University Press, 2008), 118; Malcom N. Shaw, *International Law*, 6th edn. (Cambridge University Press, 2008), 1133.

[180] Georg Nolte and Albrecht Randelzhofer, 'Ch. VII Action with Respect to Threats to the Peace, Breaches of the Peace and Acts of Aggression, Article 51', in Bruno Simma, Daniel-Erasmus Khan, Georg Nolte, Andreas Paulus and Nikolai Wessendorf (eds.), *The Charter of the United Nations: a Commentary*, 3rd edn. (Oxford University Press, 2012), 1397–428 (para. 6). For the minority view that customary law permits forcible self-defence against military violence below the threshold of an armed attack, see Shaw, *International Law* 2008 (n. 179), 1131; ICJ, *Military and Paramilitary Activities* (n. 178), para. 12.

[181] Dapo Akande and Thomas Liefländer, 'Clarifying Necessity, Imminence, and Proportionality in the Law of Self-Defense', *American Journal of International Law* 107 (2013), 563–70 (569); Daniel Bethlehem, 'Self-Defense Against an Imminent or Actual Armed Attack by Nonstate Actors', *American Journal of International Law* 106 (2012), 769–77 (774); David Kretzmer, 'The Inherent Right to Self-Defence and Proportionality in Jus ad Bellum', *European Journal of International Law* 24 (2013), 235–82 (235).

[182] ICJ, *Military and Paramilitary Activities* (n. 178), para. 195.

[183] I bracket a discussion of the legal necessity and proportionality of the resort to force in self-defence. Akande and Liefländer argue convincingly that, at the 'ad bellum level', these criteria are mostly deemed fulfilled when the initial use of force reaches the threshold of an armed attack. Akande and Liefländer, 'Clarifying Necessity, Imminence, and Proportionality' 2013 (n. 181).

correspondingly found the concept 'too vague to be useful'[184] in adjudicating real-world cases.

An alternative way of gauging whether the kind of war that responds to an armed attack is typically a morally justified resort to force is to delineate the goals that Article 51 UNC envisages as a lawful purpose of self-defence. However, like the minimum threshold of intensity that defines an armed attack, the horizon towards which defensive force has to be directed is subject to uncertainty.[185] Some scholars argue that it is 'halting and repelling' the armed attack.[186] Other scholars maintain 'that the legitimate ends of using force in self-defence may differ, depending, *inter alia*, on the nature and scale of the armed attack, the identity of those who carried it out, and the preceding relationship between the aggressors and the victim state'.[187] Crucially, even scholars who agree on the interpretation that a State must seek to halt and repel the attack admit that what that means is controvertible. Many argue that it must be more than an empowerment to end an ongoing aggression.[188] As it is not clear what counts as a lawful aim for the resort to force in self-defence, there is no reason to assume that it is necessarily a morally just aim.

In sum, we can*not* assume that soldiers using unlawful violence for the purposes of IHRL necessarily lack a just aim while those who use lawful violence fight in pursuit of a morally just aim. International law does not regulate the resort to force by non-State armed groups. If we rely on domestic law, a non-State actor that rises up against the territorial State in order to prevent the latter's individual rights violations, likely uses violence unlawfully

---

[184]   Dinstein, *War, Aggression and Self-Defence* 2012 (n. 174), 195; Abdulqawi A. Yusuf, 'The Notion of "Armed Attack" in the Nicaragua Judgment and its Influence on Subsequent Case Law', *Leiden Journal of International Law* 25 (2012), 461–70 (463).

[185]   Nolte and Randelzhofer, 'Ch. VII Action with Respect to Threats to the Peace' 2012 (n. 180).

[186]   Roberto Ago, Special Rapporteur to the International Law Commission, 'Eighth Report on State Responsibility', *International Law Commission Yearbook I* (1980), UN Doc. A/CN.4/318/ ADD.5-7121, 13, para. 120.

[187]   Kretzmer, 'The Inherent Right to Self-Defence' 2013 (n. 181), 240. Christian Tams has noted that defensive operations often follow purposes of deterrence, prevention and even retaliation. Christian Tams, 'The Use of Force against Terrorists', *European Journal of International Law* 20 (2009), 359–97 (391).

[188]   See, among others, Christopher Greenwood, 'Self-Defence', in Rüdiger Wolfrum (ed.), *Max Planck Encyclopedia of Public International Law* (online edn.), April 2011, para. 28; Judith Gardam, *Necessity, Proportionality and the Use of Force by States* (Cambridge University Press, 2004), 160 *et seq.*; Tarcisio Gazzini, *The Changing Rules on the Use of Force in International Law* (Manchester University Press, 2005), 148; Gray, *International Law and the Use of Force* 2008 (n. 179), 150; Rosalyn Higgins, *Problems and Process* (Oxford: Clarendon Press, 1994), 232; Georg Nolte, 'Multipurpose Self-Defence, Proportionality Disoriented: a Response to David Kretzmer', *European Journal of International Law* 24 (2013), 283–90 (286) (more references).

even if it is in pursuit of a morally just aim. In addition, we uncovered three major sources of divergence between moral principles and the *ius contra bellum*. First, the absence of a humanitarian intervention exception accounts for why international law may prohibit morally justified resorts to force. Second, the Security Council's focus on international peace and security rather than on individual rights means mandated resorts to force may or may not be morally justified.[189] Third, it is very likely that international law systematically authorises the use of force by States in self-defence when this is not morally justified in cases in which the territorial integrity of a State is threatened by an armed attack, but resorting to force would be a greater evil in terms of individual rights infringements.

Moreover, the *ius contra bellum* does not afford a straightforward guide for soldiers according to which they can easily determine the lawfulness of their cause. Specifically, the threshold for and permissible aims of self-defence are contestable. Our second assumption made above – soldiers on the battlefield are generally able to determine the lawfulness of their aims – is therefore not warranted either. The combination of a significant substantive divergence from moral principles and a high degree of contestability means that general international law on the resort to force poorly discharges its first moral task. As it partly determines what individuals on the battlefield know about the lawfulness of their aims, its limitations affect the epistemic context of soldiers' decision-making. The law that determines the permissibility of resort to armed force, when force is protracted or crosses international borders, thereby undermines IHRL's ability to discharge its first moral task during hostilities. Even if individuals knew whether their aims were (un)lawful, and they acted accordingly, IHRL might fail to guide them towards the course of action that fulfils their moral obligations because the *ius contra bellum* sometimes empowers and hamstrings the wrong sides, respectively.

Given these limitations of general international law on the resort to force, IHRL may better discharge the law's first moral task if it is applied 'symmetrically', meaning as if both sides in a war had a lawful aim and as if the threats and uses of violence that soldiers on both sides encountered from their opponents on the other side were unlawful. As mentioned, IHRL will regularly empower what is from a moral point of view 'the wrong side' and undermine the pursuit of a just aim on 'the right side'. 'Symmetrical IHRL' would still empower rights violations on the part of soldiers who lack a morally just war aim. It would, however, avoid undercutting soldiers' pursuit of morally just war aims not recognised as lawful under international law. Whereas regular

---

[189]   Furthermore, the Security Council is, of course, a political, rather than an adjudicative body.

IHRL might vouchsafe that the side with the morally unjust aim secures victory, 'symmetrical IHRL' would merely fail to prejudge which side prevails.

Would IHRL that is applied as if both sides had a lawful aim still better discharge the law's first moral task than IHL? The answer is certainly yes. If soldiers on both sides in a war ended up applying IHRL as if their war aim was lawful and the violence they encountered from soldiers on the other side amounted to a threat or use of unlawful violence, IHRL would still guide soldiers on the just side towards the typically morally right course of action. IHL, in contrast, would not. Its status-based distinction and laxer standard of care towards civilians would license additional unnecessary (and therefore unjustified) infringements of individual rights. On the unjust side, even if soldiers were permitted to act as if their aim was lawful, IHRL would guide soldiers towards courses of action that are less morally wrongful than IHL. A 'symmetrical IHRL', one in which soldiers on both sides act as if the threat or use of violence on the other side was unlawful, still better discharges the law's first moral task than IHL.

In sum, given that the *ius contra bellum* diverges from moral principles, lacks determinacy and leaves questions unanswered where non-State actors are concerned, 'symmetrical IHRL' will more often guide individuals towards the conduct that conforms to their moral obligation than asymmetrical, that is, regular IHRL. 'Symmetrical IHRL' will typically guide soldiers fighting for a just aim towards the course of action that conforms to their moral obligations, and soldiers fighting for an unjust aim towards conduct that is less morally wrongful than the conduct allowed by IHL, given the latter's greater divergence from moral principles. Before the next section turns to the moral implications of compliance with law for the protection of individual rights (task two); it is worth emphasising that, if general international law on the resort to force were clarified or changed, if it were to systematically regulate the resort to force by and against non-State actors across international borders, we would have to revisit the question of whether IHRL should be symmetrical or not with a view to fulfilling the law's first moral task.

D. *The Use of Force across International Borders, the Intensity of Hostilities and the Law's Second Moral Task*

We have assumed that in typical law enforcement contexts, in which hostilities are neither protracted nor do they cross international borders, IHRL discharges both of the law's moral tasks better than IHL. The analysis in the preceding sections then revealed that neither a state using unauthorised force beyond its own borders nor an increase in the intensity of hostilities undercuts

IHRL's better ability to discharge the law's first moral task. However, given the shortcomings of the international legal regulation of the resort to force, 'symmetrical IHRL' discharges the law's first moral task better than regular IHRL when hostilities cross borders or become protracted. A law that better discharges the law's first moral task also *prima facie* better discharges its second moral task of securing the fullest feasible protection of individual rights. That is unless incurable volitional defects mean that a law that reminds soldiers of their moral obligations and guides them towards the course of action that typically fulfils these obligations fails to attract compliance or leads to morally worse outcomes.

In this final sub-section, we turn to the law's second moral task. We have to answer two questions. First, does a State's use of unauthorised force beyond its own territory create volitional defects that would undermine 'symmetrical IHRL's' ability to discharge its second moral task in IACs that are not protracted?[190] Secondly, does an increase in the intensity of hostilities mark the emergence of such defects in NIACs and protracted IACs? I will discuss these two questions in turn.

Our assumption that in regular law enforcement contexts IHRL better than IHL fulfils both of the law's moral tasks implies that States and their law enforcement officials are by and large willing to obey IHRL in such situations. Again, a spill-over armed confrontation (type 5) that remains below the threshold of being protracted in a neighbouring State's territory proves instructive in showing that extraterritoriality does not on its own undercut this ability of IHRL to attract compliance. If hostilities are not protracted, the State has the capacity to subdue a non-State challenger. There is no reason then why soldiers should be less willing to follow the guidance of IHRL simply because they operate in a neighbouring State's territory. But what if the opponent is not a non-State actor on another State's territory, but really another State, such as in a classic IAC (type 2) or an internationalised internal confrontation (type 4)? If hostilities are not protracted, a State has effective control as a result of the extraterritorial use of force and is, by logical implication, able to subdue the opposing State's soldiers. In other words, if the use of force is itself an exercise of control rather than a struggle signalling the absence of such control, the volitional context is conducive to compliance with IHRL.[191] Extraterritoriality alone does not create volitional defects.

---

[190] Armed confrontations that according to their belligerent configurations would count as NIACs (i.e., types 1, 3, and 5a), but which are not protracted, count as law enforcement operations under the purview of IHRL for the purposes of this discussion.

[191] What happens when the opposing State's soldiers put up enough resistance to render hostilities protracted is addressed below.

Here it becomes obvious that, when States use force beyond their own borders, IHRL needs to be applied as if both sides had a lawful aim not only for the purpose of discharging its first moral task, as discussed above, but also in order to fulfil its second moral task. Let us again imagine a non-protracted classic IAC (type 2). It is highly unlikely that combatants on the side that lacks a lawful aim would comply with regular IHRL. Assuming that State A's combatants knew their State's resort to force violated the *ius contra bellum*, the only guidance IHRL would have to offer them would be to hold still, to cease threatening or using violence like a criminal in a domestic law enforcement context. Section III.C has already highlighted that this could violate the spirit of IHRL if A's combatants were conscripted or had little choice but to participate in hostilities. Even if A's combatants fought voluntarily in a war which they knew to lack a lawful aim, it would not necessarily be reasonable to expect them to hold still while according the authority to enforce international law to State B's combatants. Even if this were a reasonable expectation, the international legal order, in which soldiers are primarily and much more directly subject to the authority of their own State rather than any international institution, provides soldiers with few incentives to follow the demand of IHRL to hold still over their State's command to participate in hostilities. Regular IHRL would likely miss the chance to guide the actions of soldiers on one side in each war, forgoing the opportunity to morally improve the outcome of warfare and to discharge the law's second moral task.

If 'symmetrical IHRL' is meant to attract compliance from both sides in non-protracted IACs, is there not a more fundamental challenge to its discharging its second moral task? Contrary to IHL, IHRL does not bind non-State armed groups.[192] IHRL is addressed to the State; it concerns the State's obligations vis-à-vis its subjects. The horizontal implications of IHRL are traditionally fairly weak.[193] However, three out of the four types of IACs discussed here involve non-State actors (all except type 2). How can a body of law hope to better secure the protection of individual rights in the outcome of warfare if it does not even address all belligerents in each of these confrontations? For an analysis that sought to establish *lex lata*, this would be a crucial limitation. However, this section provides an answer to the question

---

[192] ICTY, *Prosecutor v. Kunarac et al.*, Case No. IT-96-23-T&1-T, Trial Chamber Judgment of 22 February 2001, para. 470.

[193] Pejic, 'Conflict Classification' 2015 (n. 142), 6. For the argument that IHRL is increasingly deemed applicable and applied horizontally, see Phillip Alston (ed.), *Human Rights and Non-State Actors* (New York: Oxford University Press, 2005); Andrew Clapham, *Human Rights in the Private Sphere* (Oxford University Press, 1993); Andrew Clapham, *Human Rights Obligations of Non-State Actors* (Oxford University Press, 2006).

of when and to whom IHRL *should* apply from a moral point of view. Nothing prevents us from stipulating that in instances of organised armed violence in which 'symmetrical IHRL' ought to govern the permissibility of killing by a State, that is, in non-protracted IACs (types 2, 4, 5b and 6), it ought to also govern the permissibility of killing by a non-State organised armed group. After all, the applicability of IHL to non-State actors is also stipulative. Non-State armed groups are not parties to the pertinent IHL treaties. 'Symmetrical IHRL' is hence no less procedurally legitimate than IHL as a framework for non-State actors' conduct, nor is 'symmetrical IHRL' less likely than IHL to in fact attract compliance by non-State armed groups.[194]

What about armed confrontations that are protracted, either NIACs or protracted IACs? Does crossing this threshold of intensity create volitional defects that could undermine the ability of 'symmetrical IHRL' to secure the protection of individual rights in the outcome of warfare? Could IHL potentially better discharge the law's second moral task? Volitional defects are in the first instance created by compliance costs, that is, incentives to ignore the demands of moral principles. Moral principles that demand that soldiers fight wars without violating the rights of the individuals against whom they fight have two major compliance costs: first, diminished military effectiveness, that is, a reduced likelihood of prevailing in the armed confrontation; and, secondly, diminished survival chances, that is, a reduced likelihood of escaping the confrontation unharmed and alive. These compliance costs increase radically as hostilities become more intense and they account for why individuals left to their own devices often fail to meet their moral obligations in protracted armed confrontations.

Compliance with IHL and 'symmetrical IHRL' likewise bears a cost of reduced military effectiveness. Crucially, 'symmetrical IHRL's' compliance costs rise much faster than IHL's as hostilities intensify. As previously noted, under IHRL, during protracted hostilities, a soldier will often have to forgo attacks because it is unclear whether the targeted individual really does present a threat that makes force necessary. Under IHL, in contrast, an attacker may kill opposing soldiers to further military progress, even if it is not strictly necessary. The duty of care towards innocent bystanders, imposed by IHRL, likewise means that an attacker who cannot establish with reasonable certainty the consequences of their attack on a military objective – and the strict

---

[194]   Unfortunately, we can be confident about this because IHL attracts very little compliance among non-State armed groups. For a discussion of measures that could be taken to assist non-State armed groups in applying IHRL during the conduct of hostilities, see Sandesh Sivakumaran, 'Re-envisaging the International Law of Internal Armed Conflict', *European Journal of International Law* 22 (2011), 219–64.

necessity of the expected incidental deaths – would be enjoined not to attack. IHL's verification demands, in opposition, shrink with the increasing intensity of hostilities, as described above.

The other type of compliance costs, diminished survival chances, likewise expand more quickly for 'symmetrical IHRL' than for IHL as hostilities intensify. The faster-paced, more numerous and more violent confrontations are, the more likely it is that any additional effort devoted to establishing that killing a *prima facie* hostile person is indeed strictly necessary, reduces the attacker's own chances of survival. IHRL would not demand that a soldier sacrifice him- or herself on the battlefield, but if he or she was averse to taking the increased risk involved in establishing the strict necessity of infringing the human rights of innocent bystanders, this would diminish the soldier's ability to launch attacks. Resisting the rise in one type of IHRL's compliance costs (diminished survival chances) could thus further accelerate the rise in the other type of compliance costs (diminished military effectiveness). Under IHL, in contrast, a soldier may attack all other soldiers even before they pose a threat to him or her. Although contestation persists about exactly what makes a verification measure 'infeasible' for the purpose of Article 57 API, many militaries limit the extent to which they put their own forces at risk in order to verify the necessity of expected incidental civilian harm.[195]

Compliance costs incentivise non-compliance, a volitional defect that law would normally cure by making non-compliance costly. This can be achieved by making visible unreasonable interpretations or outright violations of law, by opening them up to social opprobrium, or by attaching sanctions to compliance failures. However, there is a general lack of oversight over the conduct of hostilities that may allow soldiers to obscure an unreasonable prioritisation of the attacker's safety over that of civilians. Although lack of oversight is a challenge in all armed confrontations, it is exacerbated as the fog of war thickens during more protracted hostilities. Indeed, the more intense hostilities are, the less likely it becomes that an investigation and assessment after the fact would even uncover intentional attacks against non-threatening individuals or incidental harm that was not strictly speaking necessary. As hostilities become protracted, law cannot easily cure the volitional defects associated with IHRL's higher compliance costs. These compliance costs hence create the kind of volitional defect that means law risks being ignored.

A different type of volitional defect – affective and cognitive bias – risks that law is systematically misinterpreted leading to morally worse rather than better

---

[195] Thomas W. Smith, 'Protection of Civilians or Soldiers? Humanitarian Law and the Economy of Risk in Iraq', *International Studies Perspectives* 9 (2008), 144–64.

outcomes. In an armed confrontation in which one side is strong enough to subdue the other before hostilities become protracted, we may be able to count on soldiers' being no more biased than most of us are in our day-to-day lives. That means soldiers likely have an affective preference for their compatriots and fellow soldiers over members of the 'outgroup'. And they likely display varying degrees of outgroup hostility.[196] In all-out war, in contrast, the exhaustion of battle, the stress of being under lethal threat and seeing comrades die likely amplify these biases against individuals 'on the other side'.[197] Protracted hostilities breed bias which, in turn, creates biased interpretations of the law.

The more uncertain a law's implications are in the situation in which it typically addresses the individual, the more room there is for the individual's bias to distort these implications. As previously indicated, the implications for actions of 'symmetrical IHRL' become harder to discern the more intense hostilities become. Under an IHRL paradigm, all individuals 'on the other side', including civilians, are potentially lawful targets of intentional attack, depending on their conduct. For a soldier during protracted hostilities, every person 'on the other side', whether they wear a uniform or not, may appear threatening. Neutralising that threat may appear of paramount necessity the more often a soldier has seen a comrade die or the further out of reach military victory appears. If a soldier in that situation draws on 'symmetrical IHRL', the law risks empowering morally unjustified individual rights infringements that the soldier would not have committed if they had been left to their own devices. 'Symmetrical IHRL' might not merely miss the opportunity to secure a better protection of individual rights in the outcome of warfare, it might make these outcomes worse compared with soldiers' following their own judgement.

Bias against individuals on the other side, like high compliance costs, creates volitional defects during protracted hostilities that law cannot easily cure. IHL, however, accommodates these volitional defects. It forestalls, as much as possible, the effect of bias against individuals 'on the other side' by reducing the individual soldier's burden of moral judgement. Indeed, IHL demands that soldiers suspend their moral judgement: civilians are immune from attack and combatants are legitimate targets of lethal attack regardless of

---

[196] Joshua D. Kertzer, Kathleen E. Powers, Brian C. Rathbun and Ravi Iyer, 'Moral Support: How Moral Values Shape Foreign Policy Attitudes', *Journal of Politics* 76 (2014), 825–40.

[197] If an outgroup is 'morality based', as enemies in war tend to be, outgroup hatred often intensifies. See Ori Weisel and Robert Boehm, '"Ingroup Love" and "Outgroup Hate" in Intergroup Conflict between Natural Groups', *Journal of Experimental Social Psychology* 60 (2015), 110–20.

necessity, regardless of their conduct,[198] their mental state or their cause, hence irrespective of any parameter that requires a moral judgement or that is open to biased interpretation. IHL severs the rules for the conduct of war as much as possible from moral judgements. In circumstances in which bias is pervasive, this means IHL can secure better outcomes for individual rights. Of course, it is exactly this disconnect from underlying moral principles that enhances IHL's ability to discharge the law's second moral task that also makes IHL so bad at guiding soldiers towards the fulfilment of their moral duties.

If we focus on the law's second moral task of securing the fullest feasible protection of individual rights in the outcome of warfare – that is, minimise as much as possible unjustified infringements of individual rights – IHL's principles for the conduct of hostilities perform better than IHRL even if IHRL is applied as if both sides had lawful aims. IHL accommodates the volitional defects that it cannot cure; volitional defects that stem from higher costs of compliance and soldiers' more acute bias during protracted hostilities. That does not mean IHL is the morally ideal law for the performance of law's second moral task during the conduct of protracted hostilities. It may well be possible that law could demand the necessity of lethal attacks against enemy soldiers and still attract reciprocal and good faith compliance even during highly intense hostilities. Such a law would reduce the number of unjustified infringements of individual moral rights compared with IHL as it currently stands. However, if the choice is between IHL as it stands and 'symmetrical IHRL', then from the point of view of the law's second moral task, IHL should govern the conduct of hostilities above the threshold of intensity at which the discussed incurable volitional defects kick in, meaning when hostilities become protracted.

VI. CONCLUSION

When should IHL apply? When should it prevail over, when give way to IHRL in regulating the conduct of hostilities during IACs and NIACs? The argument presented in this chapter leads to the following proposal for a moral division of labour between IHL and IHRL. IHRL better discharges both of the law's moral tasks during law enforcement operations, when organised armed violence neither involves the use of unauthorised force by a State beyond its own borders nor rises to the threshold of being protracted. When a State uses unauthorised extraterritorial violence, IHRL needs to be applied as if both

---

[198] The exception for civilians is direct participation in hostilities and for combatants surrender.

sides were facing unlawful threats and uses of violence from the other side. Applying IHRL 'symmetrically' is necessary due to the failure of general international law to discharge its first moral task. It also helps IHRL attract compliance from soldiers on both sides of a non-protracted IAC. As long as hostilities do not become protracted, 'symmetrical IHRL' discharges the law's two moral tasks better than IHL. A moral division of labour between IHRL and IHL, then clearly requires that non-protracted hostilities during armed conflicts are governed by 'symmetrical IHRL' rather than by IHL.

Among the six types of armed conflicts we distinguished, currently only NIACs – that is, purely internal NIACs (type 1), internationally supported NIACs (type 3) and the internal part of spill-over confrontations (type 5a) – are subject to an intensity requirement. That means that if conflicts with these belligerent configurations are not protracted, they do not count as armed conflicts at all and they are governed by regular IHRL. Classic IACs (type 1), internationalised internal conflicts (type 4), the extraterritorial part of a spill-over confrontation (type 5b) and transnational confrontations (type 6), in contrast, fall under the purview of IHL regardless of their intensity. From a moral point of view, if conflict types 1, 4, 5b and 6 are not protracted, they should instead be governed by 'symmetrical IHRL'. Conflicts with States on both sides may not seem amenable to governance by IHRL. However, this intuition is likely rooted in the association of these conflicts with intense hostilities. In reality, extraterritorial spill-over conflicts and transnational conflicts, in particular, are often characterised by sporadic rather than protracted hostilities.[199] 'Symmetrical IHRL' should prevail over IHL during such non-protracted IACs.

Above the threshold of intensity at which hostilities count as protracted, meaning during protracted IACs and during NIACs, 'symmetrical IHRL' remains the better law for guiding individuals towards conformity with the moral reasons that apply to their conduct (task one). However, IHL generates morally better outcomes for individual rights (task two). Insisting that 'symmetrical IHRL' should prevail over IHL would have moral costs. 'Symmetrical IHRL' has compliance costs that are almost as high as those of moral principles. It thus risks being ignored. Moreover, due to the acute bias associated with intense hostilities, those soldiers who do recur to the guidance

---

[199]   The guidelines for targeted killings outside areas of active hostilities of the previous US administration come indeed somewhat closer to a human rights standard in terms of the threat that the target has to pose and the requirement of zero expected incidental harm. Executive Order, Procedures for Approving Direct Action Against Terrorist Targets Located Outside the United States and Areas of Active Hostilities of 22 May 2013, available at: https://fas.org/irp/offdocs/ppd/ppg-procedures.pdf.

of 'symmetrical IHRL' might mistakenly feel empowered to commit more individual rights violations than if they had been left to their own judgement. Allowing IHL to displace 'symmetrical IHRL' during protracted hostilities would, however, also have moral costs. IHL operates as if soldiers on the battlefield inevitably ceased to be active centres of moral intelligence. It effectively asks soldiers to suspend their moral judgement. In reality, soldiers might be better served by law reminding them of the morally right course of action even if taking this course of action is costly and recognising it requires that soldiers transcend their bias against the enemy.

This chapter nonetheless makes a moral case for the displacement of 'symmetrical IHRL' and for IHL alone to govern the conduct of hostilities during protracted IACs and during NIACs. This is not because securing individual rights in the outcome of war (task two) is more important than guiding the individual towards the typically morally right course of action (task one). Both of the law's moral tasks are equally important. Rather, it is because IHL falls short of discharging the law's first task by a metre, whereas IHRL falls short of discharging its second moral task by a mile. IHL still guides soldiers towards a course of action that is less morally wrongful than the course of action they would likely take if left to their own devices. IHRL, even if applied symmetrically, in contrast, either fails to improve outcomes altogether or risks making them worse. As a result, the moral costs of 'symmetrical IHRL's' failing to fulfil task two are higher than the moral costs of IHL's not fully discharging task one. Put differently, allowing IHL to prevail for the sake of securing individual rights in the outcome of warfare is less morally costly than risking that protracted hostilities are unguided by law. The staggering moral catastrophe presented by armed conflicts waged beyond the international community's gaze and thus seemingly out of reach of international law serve as a reminder of how important it is for international law to stand a chance at attracting the good faith compliance of individuals on the battlefield.

It warrants restating though that allowing IHL to prevail in governing the conduct of protracted hostilities during NIACs and intense IACs means failing the soldier as a moral agent. We have a legitimate expectation that law, at least to some extent, helps us to meet our moral obligations. That IHL fails in this crucial task makes the ICJ's claim that compliance with IHL actualises what it means to uphold human rights in war not only false as a matter of legal exegesis, but morally problematic. The least societies can do when sending soldiers into protracted battle with the demand that they obey IHL, is not pretend that this is the be-all and end-all of a moral conversation about battlefield conduct.

Conclusions: Productive Divisions

Christian Marxsen and Anne Peters

Which law applies to armed conflict situations? The contributions to this Trialogue have tackled and answered this question from different angles. Helen Duffy studied the current practice of co-application of IHL and IHRL with a particular focus on litigation before international human rights courts and developed a framework for the co-applicability of both regimes. Ziv Bohrer espoused a historical perspective to challenge recent crisis narratives which assert that IHL is unfit to respond to the latest developments in warfare. He made the case that IHL is the better suited system to regulate armed conflict situations. Janina Dill approached the interplay between IHL and IHRL as a moral question and proposed a moral division of work between both regimes which caters for the moral goals of guiding soldiers' behaviour and protecting victims. Which overall conclusions can we draw? Where do the chapters converge in substance, where do they disagree? Our concluding reflections aim to pull the strings of the Trialogue together and seek to identify common positions and fault lines.

I. CLASSIFYING ARMED CONFLICTS

A first concern was the crux of applying IHL to today's armed conflicts. Both Helen Duffy and Ziv Bohrer highlight the difficulties in classifying armed conflicts.[1] Bohrer speaks of a felt 'classification crisis'; Duffy diagnoses a 'classification conundrum' epitomised by the recent armed conflict(s) in Syria. Classification becomes a challenge because the realities of contemporary armed conflict do not neatly fit with IHL's traditional categories, above all not with the bifurcation of IACs and NIACs that we find in existing treaty law. Different layers of conflict exist at the same time for which the law provides

---

[1] Duffy in this volume, 28; Bohrer in this volume, 109.

different normative guidance, partly depending on random circumstances. Some scholars have therefore suggested abandoning altogether the established classification between IAC and NIAC.[2] Ziv Bohrer explicitly argues along that line. He points out that the importance attached to the distinction between IAC and NIAC is a rather recent phenomenon and that the customary rules of IHL are identical in IACs and NIACs, so that a distinction is without merit here.[3] Helen Duffy sympathises with the proposal to overcome the division between IACs and NIACs without actually advocating it.[4] She emphasises that, in any event, the law's evolution has diminished the significance of the bifurcation between IAC and NIAC. In contrast, Janina Dill suggests even further and nuanced differentiations among diverse types of IACs and NIACs to grasp the full spectrum of conflicts that we actually observe in the twenty-first century.[5]

All three authors confirm that these classification challenges do not constitute a severe crisis. Ziv Bohrer argues that the history of IHL could be viewed as one continuing classification crisis. New developments in warfare have always drawn the established legal framework into question and required the adaptation of existing rules. Accordingly, Bohrer regards the current confusion about the applicability of IHL as the normal state: 'Current uncertainty is, in part, chronic, stemming from the nature of "law" and of "war" which does not allow for a neat fit between war-related legal classifications and real wartime situations. This is not a crisis, but a fact of life.'[6]

Duffy and Bohrer's approach to classification exhibit similarities – both acknowledge the complexities of classification that emerge under the *lex lata* and advocate case- and context-sensitive solutions. Moreover, both argue that legal solutions must be found through interpretative adaptations of existing law. Helen Duffy and Ziv Bohrer differ, however, on the reservoirs for the solution. Bohrer suggests finding the answers within IHL itself. According to him, the ostensible gaps in IHL are, in fact, merely 'perceived gaps', because there is a long-standing IHL technique for addressing such situations. According to the adaptation principle, existing norms of IHL can and must be used in order to adapt IHL to new situations so as to provide normative

---

[2] James G. Stewart, 'Towards a Single Definition of Armed Conflict in International Humanitarian Law: a Critique of Internationalized Armed Conflict', *International Review of the Red Cross* 85 (2003), 313–50 (349); Emily Crawford, 'Unequal before the Law: the Case for the Elimination of the Distinction between International and Non-International Armed Conflicts', *Leiden Journal of International Law* 20 (2007), 441–65 (441).

[3] Bohrer in this volume, 163–4.
[4] Duffy in this volume, 32.
[5] Dill in this volume, 235 *et seq.*
[6] Bohrer in this volume, 108.

guidance in line with what is already established.[7] According to Bohrer, it is inevitable that there is an 'incomplete fit between wartime situations and the legal concepts aimed at addressing them'.[8] Helen Duffy has a different point of departure. She starts from the view, generally accepted in legal scholarship, that IHL and IHRL are in principle applicable, and she is therefore open to finding legal solutions by resorting both to IHL and IHRL – a difference between both authors we will turn to shortly.

To sum up, a conclusion of the Trialogue is that the mere fact of difficulties in applying established IHL categories to contemporary wartime situations should not be regarded as a crisis of law applicable to armed conflict. Such law has always struggled to adjust to new situations and related challenges. The resulting uncertainty cannot be avoided, but must be addressed by continuous efforts to transpose existing rules to new situations in order to find adequate solutions. Controversies persist when it comes to determining where and how the line between war and peace, between IHL and IHRL, should be drawn and how activities that seem to fall into a grey zone shall be addressed.

II. NORM CONFLICT BETWEEN IHL AND IHRL

Most legal problems tackled throughout this book are linked to the question of how the two bodies of law relevant in situations of armed conflict can and should be coordinated. An undertone of the general academic debate appears to be that IHL and IHRL can generally operate more or less in harmony with each other. It is asserted that both regimes converge[9] and stressed that they are 'complementary'.[10] The notions of 'interoperability'[11] and – as spelled out by

---

[7] Bohrer in this volume, 160 *et seq.*

[8] *Ibid.*, 163–4.

[9] Jean-Marie Henckaerts and Ellen Nohle, 'Concurrent Application of International Humanitarian Law and International Human Rights Law Revisited', *Human Rights and International Legal Discourse* 12 (2018), 23–43 (36): 'There are, in fact, not many examples where rules of humanitarian law and human rights law are in a relationship of conflict.'

[10] UN Human Rights Committee, General Comment No. 36 (2018), Art. 6 of the International Covenant on Civil and Political Rights, on the right to life, 30 October 2018, UN Doc. CCPR/C/GC/36, para. 64: 'While rules of international humanitarian law may be relevant for the interpretation and application of article 6 when the situation calls for their application, both spheres of law are complementary, not mutually exclusive.' See also Laura Olson, 'Practical Challenges of Implementing the Complementarity between International Humanitarian and Human Rights Law: Demonstrated by the Procedural Regulation of Internment in Non-International Armed Conflict', *Case Western Reserve Journal of International Law* 40 (2009), 437–61 (437).

[11] Sarah McCosker, 'The Limitations of Legal Reasoning: Negotiating the Relationships between International Humanitarian Law and Human Rights Law in Detention Situations', in Gregory Rose and Bruce Oswald (eds.), *Detention of Non-State Actors Engaged in Hostilities* (Leiden: Brill, 2016), 23–64 (58).

Helen Duffy – 'co-applicability' also point towards the possibility of harmonious coexistence of both regimes.[12] Many have stressed that some sub-fields, such as the different regimes on detention,[13] may be irreconcilable. However, the prevailing overall perception is that 'contemporary IHL has become increasingly similar to international human rights law'.[14]

Whether the general relationship of IHL and IHRL can, in fact, be reconciled so as to be seen as harmonious or whether it has to be seen as one of conflict remains a subject of dispute among the authors. Ziv Bohrer argues that there is a regime conflict between IHL and IHRL which he regards as the 'actual crisis'.[15] Two normative systems, supported by different factions, propagate competing regulatory paradigms and struggle 'over the power and authority to speak in the name of wartime international law'.[16] This regime conflict has a hegemonic character in that two particular systems purport to represent the generally preferable approach.[17] Such hegemonic struggles are mainly about definitional power.[18] Definitional power is crucial because the legal vocabulary in which we describe a situation introduces normative background assumptions. For example, speaking of 'combatants' or of 'terrorists' has completely different normative overtones.

Ziv Bohrer depicts this clash of regimes as the result of a confrontation between two opposing camps, reflecting a deeply entrenched 'faction mentality'.[19] On the one side, he places supporters of 'hardline IHRL advocacy rooted in a vision of IHRL as being at "the heart of [all] international law"'.[20] On the other side,

---

[12] Helen Duffy, 'Harmony or Conflict? The Interplay between Human Rights and Humanitarian Law in the Fight against Terrorism', in Larissa van den Herik and Nico Schrijver (eds.), *Counter-Terrorism Strategies in a Fragmented International Legal Order: Meeting the Challenges* (Cambridge University Press, 2013), 482–526 (523); Duffy in this volume, 79 *et seq.*

[13] Marko Milanovic, *Extraterritorial Application of Human Rights Treaties: Law, Principles, and Policy* (Oxford University Press, 2011), 232–5; Henckaerts and Nohle, 'Concurrent Application' 2018 (n. 9), 36.

[14] Derek Jinks, 'International Human Rights Law in Time of Armed Conflict', in Andrew Clapham and Paola Gaeta (eds.), *Oxford Handbook of International Law in Armed Conflict* (Oxford University Press, 2014), 656–74 (673).

[15] Bohrer in this volume, 164.

[16] *Ibid.*, 169.

[17] Martti Koskenniemi, 'Hegemonic Regimes', in Margaret A. Young (ed.), *Regime Interaction in International Law: Facing Fragmentation* (Cambridge University Press, 2012), 305–24 (311–12).

[18] Martti Koskenniemi speaks of 'a politics of re-definition, that is to say, the strategic definition of a situation or a problem by reference to a technical idiom so as to open the door for applying the expertise related to that idiom, together with the attendant structural bias.' Martti Koskenniemi, 'The Politics of International Law: 20 Years Later', *European Journal of International Law* 20 (2009), 7–19 (11).

[19] Bohrer in this volume, 196.

[20] *Ibid.*, 171.

'hardline Statists'[21] strongly oppose human rights application to armed conflict situations, accusing – as Marko Milanovic puts it – 'the enthusiasts of being a utopian, dovish bunch of fluffy, mushy-wushy do-gooders, who know nothing about the realities on the ground in wartime'.[22]

Helen Duffy, by contrast, rejects the notion of a regime-wide normative conflict between IHL and IHRL. Her conception of a co-application of IHL and IHRL aims to reconcile both regimes and thus to move beyond the two camps dichotomy.

Janina Dill, like Ziv Bohrer, also diagnoses a substantive norm conflict between IHL and IHRL, but does not focus on the sociology or politics of the actors propagating either IHL or IHRL. She seeks to resolve the conflict on a theoretical level by establishing a moral division of labour between IHL and IHRL.

The authors' assessments vary significantly, and they situate the potential normative conflicts between IHL and IHRL differently. Ziv Bohrer sees a generalised regime conflict, Helen Duffy perceives a norm- and context-specific conflict, and Janina Dill addresses the moral conflicts that come with the competing demands of IHL and IHRL.

III. LEGAL MECHANISMS OF COORDINATION

These potential conflicts raise the question of how the (partly) competing demands of IHL and IHRL can be reconciled. To a significant extent, this is a technical legal question which raises methodological issues of regime coordination.

The authors of this Trialogue present quite diverging accounts of how IHL and IHRL can, from a legal perspective, be coordinated. Helen Duffy provides a comprehensive analysis of the practice as well as of the academic debate on such legal mechanisms of coordination. She shows that the co-application of IHL and IHRL to armed conflict situations has emerged as the new normal. Some even consider that the 'momentum behind the complementarity is too powerful to reverse'.[23] The initial step of such coordinating attempts is the

---

[21]   Bohrer in this volume, 171.

[22]   Marko Milanovic, 'The Lost Origins of *Lex Specialis*: Rethinking the Relationship between Human Rights and International Humanitarian Law', in Jens David Ohlin (ed.), *Theoretical Boundaries of Armed Conflict and Human Rights* (Cambridge University Press, 2016), 79–117 (79).

[23]   Geoffrey S. Corn, 'Mixing Apples and Hand Grenades: the Logical Limit of Applying Human Rights Norms to Armed Conflict', *Journal of International Humanitarian Legal Studies* 1 (2010) 52–94 (56).

quest to avoid regime conflicts by means of 'harmonious interpretation'.[24] Where such conflict avoidance is not possible, another approach is the application of the *lex specialis* principle to which the ICJ referred in two decisions.[25] However, the usefulness of the *lex specialis* approach has been widely questioned, because it seems too sweeping.[26] Even the ICJ has avoided referencing the *lex specialis* concept in a later decision.[27]

Duffy suggests that the current debate and legal practice have become more nuanced. It is widely accepted that the prevalence of one or the other set of rules is not *regime dependent*, but rather *rule specific*. That means that we cannot decide on the applicability of IHL to a given situation in general and then apply all of its rules, regardless of further specificities of the concrete situation at hand. Rather – and this is the core of Helen Duffy's approach – we must take a look at the concrete provisions that are at stake and at their interaction.[28]

Moreover, Duffy shows that situations cannot easily be placed into either the IHL or the IHRL realm. It is not sufficient, for example, to circumscribe in broad geographical terms whether a situation takes place within an armed conflict. Rather, a much more fine-tuned approach is warranted.[29] 'It's contextual and it's complicated',[30] as Andrew Clapham points out.

Helen Duffy suggests a framework of co-applicability that relies on a norm by norm and context by context analysis.[31] First, she identifies the potentially

---

[24] Duffy in this volume, 79.

[25] ICJ, *Legality of the Threat or Use of Nuclear Weapons*, Advisory Opinion, ICJ Reports 1996, 226, 240 (para. 25); ICJ, *Legal Consequences of the Construction of a Wall in the Occupied Palestinian Territory*, Advisory Opinion, ICJ Reports 2004, 136, 178 (para. 106).

[26] Duffy in this volume, 74–7; Paul Eden and Matthew Happold, 'Symposium: the Relationship between International Humanitarian Law and International Human Rights Law', *Journal of Conflict and Security Law* 14 (2010), 441–66 (441–2); Jinks, 'International Human Rights Law in Time of Armed Conflict' 2014 (n. 14), 673.

[27] ICJ, *Armed Activities on the Territory of the Congo* (Democratic Republic of the Congo v. Uganda), Judgment, ICJ Reports 2005, 168, 242–3 (para. 216).

[28] Duffy in this volume, 80. This approach also finds support in the current academic debate. See, for example, Alexander Orakhelashvili, 'The Interaction between Human Rights and Humanitarian Law: Fragmentation, Conflict, Parallelism, or Convergence?', *European Journal of International Law* 19 (2008), 161–82 (182); Eden and Happold, 'Symposium: the Relationship between International Humanitarian Law and International Human Rights Law' 2010 (n. 26), 446; Milanovic, *Extraterritorial Application of Human Rights Treaties* 2011 (n. 13), 232–5.

[29] Andrew Clapham, 'Human Rights in Armed Conflict: Metaphors, Maxims, and the Move to Interoperability', *Human Rights and International Legal Discourse* 12 (2018), 9–22 (19).

[30] Andrew Clapham, 'The Complex Relationship between the Geneva Conventions and International Human Rights Law', in Andrew Clapham, Paola Gaeta and Marco Sassòli (eds.), *The 1949 Geneva Conventions: a Commentary* (Oxford University Press, 2015), 701–35 (735).

[31] Duffy in this volume, 79–81.

relevant rules for guiding a specific conduct. Secondly, she asks for the particular context in which these rules shall be applied. Thirdly, she determines which rule provides the more specific regulation for a concrete situation and which should, therefore, be the priority rule to provide normative guidance in the concrete situation. Fourthly, Duffy points out that even though one rule has been identified as having priority, this does not mean that the secondary rule becomes irrelevant. Rather, there is 'an ongoing dynamic interrelationship' so that the background rule remains relevant for informing the interpretation of the other rule that enjoys priority.[32]

Thus, Helen Duffy shows that sufficient legal, interpretative techniques do exist to bring IHL and IHRL together and to coordinate them in a legally sound manner. According to her, a coordination of IHL and IHRL no longer takes place at the level of overall regimes. Such coordination has become more nuanced and has permeated from the macroscopic level of overall regime interaction to the microscopic level of rule selection and rule application in concrete cases.

In the Trialogue, Helen Duffy's approach does not go unchallenged. Her approach of co-application is rejected by the other two authors. Against her rule- and context-based method of coordination, Ziv Bohrer and Janina Dill defend approaches that entirely displace the other regime, under specific circumstances. Ziv Bohrer, based on analysis of State practice that, as he contends, was dominant until around 9/11 (2001), argues for an IHL-specific adaptation approach. He suggests that normative guidance in armed conflict situations should be sought primarily in the rules of IHL. In this sense, IHRL should be displaced in armed conflict.

Janina Dill draws the line differently. In contrast to Bohrer, she does not suggest a general displacement of IHRL in favour of IHL, but proposes nuanced criteria for choosing the proper legal regime. Based on a moral analysis, to which we will turn in more detail shortly, her claim is that IHRL *prima facie* is the better law to provide normative guidance to soldiers in armed conflicts because it is more in conformity with moral demands. However, Dill points out that where the intensity of conflicts increases, IHRL turns out to be deficient. IHL therefore becomes the preferable legal regime where armed conflicts become 'protracted'.[33]

For Helen Duffy and Janina Dill, intensity plays a significant role. But while for Duffy the intensity of conflicts is but one criterion for determining which

---

[32] Duffy in this volume, 83.

[33] See for the concept of a 'protracted', i.e., more intense and complex conflict, *infra* n. 52.

rule gets priority in particular contexts, it is the crucial criterion for Dill for choosing the application of the entire regime of either IHL or IHRL.

All three approaches make different claims as to whether their position represents the *lex lata*. Helen Duffy alleges that her account of co-applicability reflects the current state of positive law. Bohrer acknowledges that Duffy's account reflects a mainstream sentiment that IHL and IHRL must be co-applied, but he asserts that his competing conception of an adaptation approach which requires us to apply IHL, not IHRL to armed conflict situations, was – at least until recently – the prevailing understanding. According to Bohrer, this view continues to linger and is therefore the correct understanding of the law. Janina Dill, by contrast, does not make any claims as to whether her position reflects established law, because – as a moral philosopher – she is concerned with the underlying theoretical principles.

IV. NORMATIVE PERSPECTIVES

It has been observed that '"regime interaction" cannot be meaningfully reduced to technical coordination'.[34] Rather, coordination and interpretative choices depend on underlying normative convictions that are usually not openly brought to the fore. Such normative choices are crucial for all three approaches presented in this Trialogue. Janina Dill undertakes an analysis and assessment from a moral point of view – normative arguments are centre stage for her. This is similar for Ziv Bohrer, whose main argument is that IHL furnishes the better protection of individuals. Normative choices also matter for Helen Duffy's account of co-application. Although Duffy highlights that a harmonious co-application of IHL and IHRL is in principle often possible, there is no dispute that potential conflicts between both regimes may emerge. These conflicts are then carried out at the level of the interpretation and application of specific rules. The process of 'prioritisation' is in itself an interpretative endeavour which is necessarily creative.[35] Moreover, both legal regimes continue to follow quite different logics, which – despite a general trend towards convergence – may lead to significantly different results. Above all, IHL allows the curtailment and, in the end, even the annihilation of individual rights of civilians because of the military advantage this may provide. Such a balancing of innocent lives against other political values is, of course, alien to human rights law. It is therefore a significant difference whether, for example, a drone strike against a leading terrorist falls

---

[34] Koskenniemi, 'Hegemonic Regimes' 2012 (n. 17), 308.
[35] Cf. Christian Marxsen and Anne Peters, 'Introduction' to this volume, 11.

under the IHL or under IHRL paradigm. In the former paradigm a strike might, depending on the circumstances, be justified; under the latter most certainly not. In the drone strike example, the assessment of the military benefit and the outcome of the balancing would depend on the weight one assigns to human rights considerations vis-à-vis a specific military advantage – assuming that human rights come into play at all. As this example shows, the legal techniques for coordinating IHL and IHRL are important, but they do not provide answers to the question of which paradigm – IHL or IHRL – should prevail in concrete cases.

It seems as if ultimately the underlying paradigm will forge the interpretation of the law and therefore determine the outcome as much as the simultaneous formal choice of the applicable provisions. What is required, therefore, are choices which States, policymakers, and also scholars have to make.[36] These choices hinge on the normative considerations which run through the chapters of this Trialogue as a red line.

The three Trialogue authors have espoused different normative visions. Helen Duffy's context- and norm-sensitive framework for co-applicability does not prefigure the balance to be struck between both regimes. She rejects any hardline approach that would categorically deny the application of one or the other regime to armed conflict situations. Beyond that, Duffy's framework allows priority to be given either to IHL or to IHRL, depending on the concrete legal norms and their interpretation, on the assessment of their salience and adequacy for concrete situations, and on the evaluation of the particular context. In substance, however, Helen Duffy places more emphasis on human rights, albeit often in situations where no clear rules of IHL exist: 'If there is no norm specifically directed to the situation, there is no *lex*, and presumably no *lex specialis*, and no norm to take priority over another.'[37] Her conclusion on procedural safeguards governing detention in NIACs, for example, is that they must be governed by a flexible interpretation of IHRL, because this body of law contains detailed requirements whereas IHL does not.[38] In her reading, thus, IHRL should play a very prominent role (albeit handled flexibly in the light of principles of the interpretation of human rights law).

Ziv Bohrer opposes this approach. Although he does not completely reject the application of IHRL to armed conflict situations, he advocates an IHL-

---

[36] Matthew Happold, 'International Humanitarian Law and Human Rights Law', in Christian Henderson and Nigel White (eds.), *Research Handbook on International Conflict and Security Law* (Cheltenham: Edward Elgar, 2013), 444–66 (465).

[37] Duffy in this volume, 82.

[38] *Ibid.*, 84–90.

oriented approach. If asked to choose he 'would prefer some ambiguous middle-ground approach over either two polar extremes of fully and of never extraterritorially applying IHRL in wartime. But such a choice is unnecessary, because there is still another alternative: rely primarily on IHL, having properly interpreted and developed it.'[39] Thus, Bohrer has more faith in the regulatory and protective potential of IHL. According to his view, the gaps in IHL shall be filled by adapting existing rules of IHL to new situations, but not by filling those gaps with human rights.

Bohrer opposes the 'righting' of IHL, by which he understands 'the massive wartime application of IHRL'. This practice, he finds, 'gradually caus[es] IHL to cease being an obligations-oriented system'.[40] Bohrer rejects the view that a rights-based approach would increase the protection of civilians, and rather claims that this approach 'diminishes that protection'.[41] In fact, Bohrer argues for a broader applicability of IHL not out of concern for military effectiveness (as is often done in the academic debate), but rather because he regards IHL as providing better protection to the individual. Bohrer enumerates several benefits of an obligation-based system. First, it can easily be applied extraterritorially because 'obligations are attached to the obligation-bearers and, as such, tend to follow them'.[42] Secondly, the focus on obligation-bearers should make it more likely that the acting commanders actually implement the legally prescribed measures. Rights-based systems, by contrast, refer to the rights of third persons, and are therefore more prone to being disregarded. Thirdly, Bohrer finds obligation-based systems more adequate for protecting the disempowered, those who are incapable of 'demand[ing] the protection of their rights'.[43] Fourthly, Bohrer points out that the traditional chivalry narrative, reflected in the status orientation of IHL, has been the 'basis for imposing certain demanding ethical-legal soldierly duties'.[44] By contrast, the rights orientation effaces that aspect and even incites soldiers to place their individual rights first, as reflected in the debates on 'force protection'. Overall, according to Bohrer, IHL is the better law to guide armed conflict situations and should – from a normative point of view – be preferred to human rights law.

Janina Dill proposes a division of labour between IHL and IHRL that runs counter to both Duffy and Bohrer's accounts. She suggests that both IHL and

[39] Bohrer in this volume, 182.
[40] *Ibid.*, 192.
[41] *Ibid.*, 175.
[42] *Ibid.*, 179–80.
[43] *Ibid.*, 186.
[44] *Ibid.*, 189.

IHRL should be applied to armed conflict, but each under specific circumstances. She proposes – from a moral perspective – a moral division of work between both legal regimes. Here she determines the optimum reach for both regimes so that their respective benefits can unfold while avoiding that their limitations yield negative effects. Dill's first finding is that IHRL generally ranks better at directing soldiers towards a course of action that conforms to their moral obligations. Therefore, IHRL is the *prima facie* morally better law for guiding actions in armed conflicts. Once armed confrontations cross international borders, however, human rights law can unfold its benefits only if it is applied 'symmetrically'. By 'symmetrical application', Janina Dill means IHRL should come into play as if 'both parties to an armed confrontation had a lawful aim'.[45] This is important because under human rights law, curtailments of rights always require a lawful aim. Thus, an unlawful aim – for example a military intervention in violation of the *ius contra bellum* – would inevitably affect the legal assessment of concrete military actions under IHRL and would normally render such actions illegal, too.[46] As a result, human rights law could not unfold any normative power – Dill speaks of 'law discharging its moral tasks' – and guide the behaviour of all parties to an armed conflict, because it would simply not allow any military action by the party acting in violation of the *ius contra bellum*.

The moral superiority of IHRL, even if it is applied symmetrically, however, is limited to situations where armed conflicts remain of limited intensity.[47] Any increase in intensity of an armed conflict will affect soldiers' decision-making both in epistemic terms (what they can know) and in volitional terms (what they want). First, intensity of hostilities 'raises the epistemic barriers to identifying the morally right course of action'.[48] As discussed in the Introduction to this book, IHRL's focus on the rights of individuals is likely to cognitively overburden the individual charged with applying the law in complex combat situations.[49] Secondly, Dill points out that the intensification of armed conflict 'renders more acute incurable volitional defects in soldiers' decision-making'.[50] Soldiers

---

45   Dill in this volume, 242. This understanding of 'symmetry' (of human rights law) has nothing to do with the concept of an 'asymmetrical conflict' which, rather, relates to the size, tactics and military capacities of parties to a conflict, notably a State's armed forces versus guerrilla groups.

46   Dill does not distinguish between the broad objectives of an armed conflict and the micro-objectives of concrete actions which interfere with rights, such as rendering an enemy combatant harmless.

47   As opposed to 'protracted conflicts' (see *infra* n. 52).

48   Dill in this volume, 201.

49   Christian Marxsen and Anne Peters, Introduction to this volume, 9

50   Dill in this volume, 201.

will be under pressure to mitigate risk to themselves and to prioritise military effectiveness. Put simply, by requiring a complex analysis and balancing of rights, the human rights perspective risks compromising military effectiveness which would put the life of the acting soldier at greater jeopardy. This creates an incentive structure detrimental to the protection of individual rights.[51]

Janina Dill's central argument is that human rights law is not always inadequate to govern armed conflict situations. Rather, it becomes inadequate only at a certain point, which Dill identifies as the point where conflicts become 'protracted'.[52] In this situation, IHRL might still – in theory – guide fighters towards the morally better course of action, but in practice, this body of law tends not to be complied with by the fighters due to their knowledge deficits and incentive structures. Therefore, human rights law, although in theory the better law, will tend to remain a dead letter in 'protracted' combat situations.

In such situations, and taking into account not only the law in the books but the law in action, IHL becomes the morally better law because it establishes principles that can guide action towards morally better outcomes. In that sense IHL makes concessions, but it does so in order to provide effective legal regulation also for complex combat situations instead of leaving such situations in fact lawless. While IHL's regulatory approach is less fine-grained and therefore more readily authorises the infringement of individual rights, it fares better in 'the fog of war' because it lends itself more to compliance.[53] Therefore, it is, according to Dill, the morally preferable law where conflicts have risen above a certain intensity threshold.

The substantive divergence of these three approaches shows that there is – maybe unsurprisingly – no common normative position among the authors on which rules *should* govern situations of armed conflict. However, the three authors have comprehensively surveyed the legal terrain in which the complex norm- and context-dependent decision on the application of IHL or IHRL must be taken. It would be presumptuous to conclude this book with arguments in favour of one or the other option. The legal questions are too difficult for easy answers.

---

[51] Dill in this volume, 224.

[52] Dill uses the term 'protracted' in the meaning given by the ICTY, *Prosecutor v. Duško Tadić*, Case No. IT-94-1, Decision on the defence motion for interlocutory appeal on jurisdiction, 2 October 1995, para. 72, to denote not only or mainly a temporal extension but a degree of complexity.

[53] It is, we might add, independently of Janina Dill's different argument, an open question as to whether less violence occurs in fact, or whether better compliance is merely the result of a lower threshold of illegality. In other words, are modest standards that have a chance of being complied with preferable to more demanding standards that are for factual reasons hardly respected?

V. CONCLUDING REFLECTIONS

The Trialogue about law applicable to armed conflict sought to build on and take advantage of multi-perspectivism. The trialogical setting was supposed to increase our awareness of how some arguments might be viewed differently from a different perspective, and to stimulate engagement with those diverging perspectives. It is hoped that notably value-laden decisions at stake have emerged clearly.

Helen Duffy rigorously analyses the legal evolution over the course of the last two decades, and examines the law as it stands today (according to the prevailing reading). An important contribution of Duffy's chapter lies in the development of a framework for the co-application of IHL and IHRL. Moreover, Duffy convincingly predicts a trajectory of legal evolution towards further interlocking of both legal regimes.

Ziv Bohrer enriches the debate on the law applicable to armed conflict with three provocative thoughts. First, he refutes the received historical account that the current (perceived) crisis results from a new kind of war. Bohrer shows that the attributes of current conflicts are much less new than usually assumed. Secondly, Bohrer refutes the generally recognised (overly) statist historical account of IHL, showing that the application of IHL to NIACs, including transnational wars, is much older than widely thought. Thirdly, he argues that, counter-intuitively, the co-application of IHRL and IHL diminishes (and does not increase) civilian protection and thus invites us to radically question the role human rights law should play in armed conflict situations.

Janina Dill provides a creative and innovative moral analysis of the IHL versus IHRL debate. Dill forces us to question our most basic moral assumptions on the likely effects of each of these bodies of law. Moreover, she reaches surprising conclusions that run counter to the premises of many protagonists in the IHL versus IHRL debate. On the one hand, she concludes that IHL is the body of law that reaches morally preferable results where armed conflicts have become protracted. On the other hand, she maintains that the currently accepted scope of the applicability of IHL is too broad and that IHRL should be the dominant body of law in many cases which are currently governed by IHL.

This Trialogue has been a conscious attempt to pluralise the relevant interpretive communities around the concrete question of which law to apply in armed conflict. We submit that the direct confrontation of three different approaches in the Trialogue teased out some committed arguments and truly manifested engaged scholarship as opposed to armchair international law. We suggest that – despite the differences summarised above – the

Trialogue did reveal the existence of an 'overlapping consensus' across disciplines and diverging theoretical approaches, for example, on the law's ultimate objective to protect individuals. The Trialogue thereby strove for a modest contribution, in a discursive process, to universalising some legal ideas surrounding the *ius in bello*. At the same time, it meant to celebrate intellectual stylistic diversity and ultimately sought to defy an intellectual monoculture.[54] It is for the readers to judge whether this has worked.

---

[54] See on the trialogical method Anne Peters, 'Trialogical International Law: Introduction to the Series', in Mary-Ellen O'Connell, Christian Tams and Dire Tladi, *Self-Defence against Non-State Actors: Max Planck Trialogues on the Law of Peace and War Vol. I*, Anne Peters and Christian Marxsen, series editors (Cambridge University Press, 2019).

Index

accountability, investigation and, 95–9

ACHPR. *See* African Commission on Human and Peoples' Rights

acquisition of territory. *See* occupation of territory

Additional Protocols to Geneva Conventions (1977)
combatant/non-combatant distinction, 120
human rights and, 5
IACs and, 2
NIACs and, 3

African Commission on Human and Peoples' Rights (ACHPR)
co-applicability of IHL and IHRL, 64–5
geographical applicability (*ratione loci*) of IHRL, 50, 52

Akande, Dapo, 240

Aldrich, George, 114, 155

Al-Qaeda. *See* terrorism

applicable law. *See* co-applicability of IHL and IHRL; human rights; international humanitarian law (IHL); peacetime violence; transnational conflicts

Aristotle, 115

armed conflict. *See also* classification of conflicts; international armed conflicts; non-international armed conflicts; transnational conflicts; use of force
applicability of law of, 1
armed attacks, definition of, 254
battle as legal concept, 127
boundaries of, 4
causes of indeterminacies in law of, 196
civilian participation, 120, 129
classification of conflicts. *See* classification of conflicts

combatant/non-combatant distinction, 119–27
complexity of, 17–18
crisis narratives, 118
determination of existence of, 235
distinctiveness of current conflicts, 135
existence of, 22–4
historical development of law of war, 127
irregular fighting, rise of, 120, 127–33
legal controversies, 10
moral approach to. *See* morality
normative approach to, 11
'overlapping consensus' on law of, 278
protracted armed confrontations as, 201
reduction in casualties, 134
technological developments, 133–9
total warfare, 128
traditional warfare, reduction of, 127–33
Trialogue approach to, 10–14, 266

battle as legal concept, 127

Baxter, Richard, 15

bearers
duty-bearers, 22–39
rights-bearers, 43–4

Ben-Naftali, Orna, 173

Berman, Paul, 136

Brussels Declaration (1874), combatant/non-combatant distinction, 120

Bush, George W., 137

Charter of the UN. *See* United Nations

chivalry as obligation, 125

Churchill, Winston, 120, 133

civil disturbances. *See* peacetime violence

BOOKS IN THE SERIES